THE NATIONAL UNDERWRITER COMPANY

Critical Issues in CGL, 3rd Edition

Michael F. Aylward, Esq., Shaun McParland Baldwin, Esq., Gregory G. Deimling, CPCU, and Carol P. Keough, Esq.

For years, the CGL policy has held its place as one of the broadest coverage forms in the industry. Predictably, this widespread use has given rise to a number of conflicts. Even today, its application continues to be hotly debated in agent, insurer, and risk manager offices, as well as in the courts.

You hold in your hands the third, fully revised and completely updated edition, of *Critical Issues in CGL*, the resource that insurance professionals, business advisors and attorneys have come to rely on as the "go-to" guide in this complex area. This latest edition makes it possible to confidently handle the commercial general liability coverage form topics that consistently create the most conflict.

In short, *Critical Issues in CGL, 3rd Edition*, delivers the information and provides what is needed to successfully apply and defend this broad coverage form.

This logically organized, professional reference gives you everything you need in four easily accessible chapters:

- Additional Insureds and Contractual Liability

- The Business Risk Exclusions

- Occurrence Issues

- And the all-new Cyber Liability

Critical Issues in CGL, 3rd Edition, illuminates the trends in cyber-related crimes. It also provides a practical, historical perspective that delivers the most informed understanding of the CGL's treatment of cyber-related crimes and anticipates how the courts will continue to interpret the CGL for cyber losses in light of the most recent court decisions.

All of this enables professionals to tackle cyber risks and prevention in a lucid and practical way, even as technology continues to evolve.

The CGL is the linchpin of all business insurance programs. Whether large or small, companies simply cannot afford to operate without general liability insurance.

Critical Issues in CGL, 3rd Edition, gives you everything you need to guide your clients and confidently manage the issues that can arise in connection with the CGL.

For customer service questions or to place additional orders, please call 1-800-543-0874.

Coverage Guides Also Available:

- Businessowners Policy

- Business Interruption

- Condominium Insurance

- Commercial Auto Program

- Commercial General Liability

- Commercial Property

- Directors and Officers Liability

- Employment Practices Liability

- Guide to Captives and Alternative Risk Financing

- Homeowners

- Personal Auto

- Personal Umbrella

- Workers Compensation

3rd Edition

Commercial General Liability
Critical Issues in CGL

Commercial Lines Series

Michael F. Aylward, Esq.
Shaun McParland Baldwin, Esq.
Gregory G. Deimling, CPCU
Carol P. Keough, Esq.

The National Underwriter Company

ABOUT SUMMIT PROFESSIONAL NETWORKS

Summit Professional Networks supports the growth and vitality of the insurance, financial services and legal communities by providing professionals with the knowledge and education they need to succeed at every stage of their careers. We provide face-to-face and digital events, websites, mobile sites and apps, online information services, and magazines giving professionals multi-platform access to our critical resources, including Professional Development; Education & Certification; Prospecting & Data Tools; Industry News & Analysis; Reference Tools and Services; and Community Networking Opportunities.

Using all of our resources across each community we serve, we deliver measurable ROI for our sponsors through a range of turnkey services, including Research, Content Development, Integrated Media, Creative & Design, and Lead Generation.

For more information, go to http://www.SummitProfessionalNetworks.com.

ABOUT THE NATIONAL UNDERWRITER COMPANY

For over 110 years, The National Underwriter Company has been the first in line with the targeted tax, insurance, and financial planning information you need to make critical business decisions. Boasting nearly a century of expert experience, our reputable Editors are dedicated to putting accurate and relevant information right at your fingertips. With *Tax Facts, Tools & Techniques, National Underwriter Advanced Markets, Field Guide, FC&S®, FC&S Legal* and other resources available in print, eBook, CD, and online, you can be assured that as the industry evolves National Underwriter will be at the forefront with the thorough and easy-to-use resources you rely on for success.

The National Underwriter Company
Update Service Notification

This National Underwriter Company publication is regularly updated to include coverage of developments and changes that affect the content. If you did not purchase this publication directly from The National Underwriter Company and you want to receive these important updates sent on a 30-day review basis and billed separately, please contact us at (800) 543-0874. Or you can mail your request with your name, company, address, and the title of the book to:

The National Underwriter Company
4157 Olympic Boulevard
Suite 225
Erlanger, KY 41018

If you purchased this publication from The National Underwriter Company directly, you have already been registered for the update service.

National Underwriter Company
Contact Information

To order any National Underwriter Company title, please

- call 1-800-543-0874, 8-6 ET Monday – Thursday and 8 to 5 ET Friday

- online bookstore at www.nationalunderwriter.com, or

- mail to The National Underwriter Company, Orders Department, 4157 Olympic Blvd., Suite 225, Erlanger, KY 41018

Preface

The commercial general liability policy is the linchpin of business insurance programs. Virtually all companies carry liability insurance, under businessowners (BOP), commercial package, or monoline forms. Whether mom-and-pop operations or multinational corporations, they cannot afford to operate without general liability insurance.

In the 1970s the form was called the *comprehensive* general liability policy, but that title seemed to imply that all third-party liability risks were insured. And so it was changed to *commercial general liability coverage form* with the 1986 Insurance Services Office (ISO) edition.

The CGL policy remains one of the broadest coverage forms in the industry. It promises to pay "those sums that the insured becomes legally obligated to pay as damages because of 'bodily injury' or 'property damage' to which this insurance applies." It also pledges to defend suits against the insured as long as the coverage may apply to the allegations.

Despite the breadth and depth of this coverage and its long history, the application of coverage continues to be debated in agent, insurer, and risk manager offices—as well as in the courtroom. The editors of the *FC&S Bulletins* field their share of questions about how various types of coverage could be interpreted. Many of those questions involve the CGL form.

Related Publications

Both the *FC&S Bulletins* and the National Underwriter Company's *Commercial General Liability (CGL)* coverage guide (Malecki 2014) dedicate hundreds of pages to the CGL coverage form. The CGL coverage guide, currently in its Tenth Edition, is one of the most consistently used CGL reference sources in the industry. This *Critical Issues in CGL* book was developed as a logical progression from the best-selling CGL coverage guide. This newest CGL offering from the National Underwriter Company will equip professionals with the information and wherewithal they need to confidently apply and defend this broad and complex coverage form.

In addition, the cumulative experience of the *FC&S* staff in dealing with CGL coverage problems was called upon in designing this book. Four areas that stood out as particular problems are discussed. They are:

- the business risk exclusions,

- additional insureds and their interrelationship with contractual liability coverage,

- the occurrence trigger's impact on coverage, and

- cyber liability.

The third edition provides a distinguished cast of authors to tackle some of the toughest situations faced in commercial general liability. They are experienced litigators in their fields and are well-versed presenters and authors. Their combined expertise will equip the reader with the knowledge to identify their unique vulnerabilities under the CGL and prepare the reader to best manage loss thereunder.

Additional Insureds/Contractual Liability

Any business that has entered into a contract with a vendor, subcontractor, or other business owner has been asked to provide both contractual liability coverage and additional insured status for one or more of its contracting partners. This is so much a regular part of the business landscape that risk managers and insurance agents seldom blink an eye when asked to provide the coverage. In fact, questions from underwriters about the contractual relationship and need to provide the coverage often are seen as needless efforts to prevent business from being conducted.

In reality, many risk managers, business owners, and insurance practitioners are unaware of how the interplay of these contractual requirements may impact the named insured—the party that should be most concerned about its exposures and how they are being managed. The section written by Carol P. Keough, Esq., outlines and explains many of the intricacies of this interplay.

Business Risk Exclusions

Five exclusions provide some of the hottest fodder for debate for businesspeople and insurance practitioners. They are exclusions j., Damage to Property; k., Damage to Your Product; l., Damage to Your Work; m., Damage to Impaired Property or Property Not Physically Injured; and n., Recall of Products, Work, or Impaired Property. Collectively referred to as the *business risk exclusions,* they provide a road map of the difference between the uninsurable cost of doing business and insurable business liabilities.

Despite the long-standing history of these or similar exclusions, they remain some of the most controversial in their application. Shaun McParland Baldwin, Esq., explains how these exclusions define the coverage that is available to commercial insurance clients.

What Is an Occurrence?

One of the first premises drilled into insurance novices is that bodily injury and property damage coverage must be triggered by an occurrence: an accidental happening that results in injury to a third party. Although the concept seems simple enough, the way in which occurrences are *counted* can have profound effects on insureds and insurers alike.

This subject can affect how many self-insured retentions or deductibles an insured must exhaust before tapping into the insurer's limits, as well as how soon excess coverage will be pierced. It can have profound effects on how much an insurance company must pay and an insured may collect. Michael F. Aylward, Esq., explains these concepts in detail with substantial case law references.

Cyber Liability

A majority of Directors and Officers recently surveyed identified cyber risks as their biggest concern to profitability. However, less than a third of companies currently hold cyber liability insurance policies.

By illuminating factual trends in cyber-related crimes, while taking a historical approach to the CGL's treatment of cyber-related claims, Gregory G. Deimling offers advice as to how to use the CGL and cyber policies to build a comprehensive loss prevention scheme.

Forms and Endorsements

The 2013 ISO CGL form is reproduced, along with many of the most often used endorsements for valued reference sake.

About the Authors

Michael Aylward is a senior partner in the Boston office of Morrison Mahoney, LLP where he chairs the Complex Insurance Claims Resolution group. For over thirty years, Mr. Aylward has specialized in insurance coverage disputes involving the availability of liability insurance for complex claims involving CGL policies. He has tried large, multi-party coverage cases and has argued numerous landmark appeals. He regularly lectures on insurance, ethics and bad faith claims and is a contributing editor of the IADC's flagship publication, Defense Counsel Journal. Mr. Aylward has taken a leadership role in numerous legal organizations, including the national Board of Directors of the Defense Research Institute (2000-2003), Insurance Law Committee (2000-2002), and the Reinsurance, Excess and Surplus Line Insurance Committee of the International Association of Defense Counsel. He is also a founding member of the DRI Blue Ribbon Committee on issues confronting the tripartite relationship. Mr. Aylward is a graduate of Dartmouth College and received his Juris Doctor from the Boston College Law School.

Shaun McParland Baldwin is a partner based in the Chicago office of Tressler LLP, concentrating in the areas of insurance coverage, bad faith, and other insurance-related services. She also has an active appellate practice and has briefed and argued over 40 appeals in states and federal courts of appeal. Ms. Baldwin is an avid lecturer on insurance coverage law and has authored numerous articles. She has taken a leadership role in numerous legal organizations, including DRI, Member, Vice Chair, 2014 Insurance Roundtable; Chair, Excess, Umbrella and Surplus Sub-Committee of Insurance Law Committee; former Chair - Insurance Law Committee, Illinois Appellate Lawyers Association, Member and Past Director, Illinois Association of Defense Trial Counsel, Member and Past Director; former Chair – Amicus Committee, International Association of Defense Counsel, Member, former Chair – Casualty Insurance Committee, The Foundation of the International Association of Defense Counsel, Past Director, and Professional Liability Underwriting Society, Member. Ms. Baldwin was named to the "Top 5 Women Illinois Super Lawyers" for the tenth consecutive year, has been elected as a fellow of the American Bar Foundation, honored as a "Corporate Partner Woman of Achievement" by the National Association of Women Business Owners, and has achieved an AV Preeminent rating from Martindale-Hubbell. She is a graduate of Northern Illinois University and received her Juris Doctor from The John Marshall School of Law, where she graduated with distinction.

Gregory Deimling is a principal in Malecki Deimling Nielander and Associates, LLC in Erlanger, Kentucky. He has been in the insurance and risk management industry as an agent, instructor and consultant for over 40 years. Mr. Deimling provides Risk Management and General Management services to a diverse group of both public and private firms and individuals covering a wide range of subject matter and assignments. He provides litigation support and assistance as an expert witness regarding insurance coverage interpretation, policy formation, technical analysis of insurance contracts, and agent, broker and insurer standards of conduct. Mr. Deimling is a principal in Globe Insurance Agency, Inc., a family owned independent insurance agency located in Cincinnati, OH. Mr. Deimling received his CPCU, Chartered Property and Casualty Underwriter designation in 1976. A member and past president of the Society's Cincinnati Chapter, and a member of the CLEW Consultants, Legal, and Expert Witness Section, he has also served nationally as Secretary-Treasurer, regional vice president, East Central Region, national governor, member of the Strategic Planning Committee, and chairman of the Interest Sections Governing Committee and Budget and Finance Committee. In addition to earning the CPCU designation, Deimling also holds the AMIM Associate in Marine Management and ARM Associate in Risk Management designations from the Insurance Institute of America and other industry designations. Mr. Deimling is a graduate of the University of Cincinnati with an undergraduate degree in Business Administration with insurance major. He received his Masters of Business Administration, majoring in Finance from Xavier University in 1980. Additional professional affiliations include the national and Ohio Association of IIABA, the American Association of Insurance Management Consultants, Cincinnati Insurance Board, and ACORD. Mr. Deimling has been a featured speaker and an accredited CE instructor at various insurance venues for personal lines and commercial property, flood insurance, general liability, risk management, general management consulting, litigation management, mock trials, the MCS 90 coverage, condominium insurance, and general property and casualty insurance topics.

Carol Keough is the Managing Attorney at Barita & Keough Law Firm, PLLC in Houston, Texas. Ms. Keough's practice provides legal defense and consultation to Business Owners and HR Directors on employment law policies, as well as complex litigation including insurance coverage, bad faith and extra-contractual, property damage and commercial business law. Prior to forming Barita & Keough, she was a Director with the law firm of Coats, Rose, Yale, Ryman & Lee. Ms. Keough is a member of the Texas State and Federal Bar, the American Bar Association in the Tort and Insurance Law and the Labor and Employment sections, the Houston Bar Association Litigation and Labor and Employment sections, the Texas Women's Lawyers, Association of Woman Attorneys, the Society for Human Resource Management and DRI. She is regularly lectures and writes in the areas of insurance coverage and extra-contractual liability. Before attending law school, Ms. Keough worked as a special education teacher. She holds a BA in psychology from the College of New Rochelle in New York, and M.S. in education from the State University of New York at New Paltz, and received her Juris Doctor from the South Texas College of Law.

About the Publisher

Richard H. Kravitz is Vice President and Managing Director of the Professional Publishing Division of The National Underwriter Company. He is a CPA, MBA, and Fellow of the American College of Forensic Examiners and a member of the AICPA, the New York State Society of CPAs, and the American Society of Pension Professionals and Actuaries.

Prior to joining The National Underwriter he was Senior Vice President and Group Publisher of International Law and Business at Aspen/Wolters Kluwer and former Accounting and Tax Publisher at Thomson Reuters.

About the Editors

David D. Thamann, J.D., CPCU, ARM, is Managing Editor of the *FC&S Bulletins®*, with specialties in Commercial Auto, Commercial General Liability, Personal Auto, and Workers Compensation.

His thirty-eight years of industry experience include working as claims manager and senior underwriter for companies TransAmerica, Safeco, and CNA. Mr. Thamann also wrote *The Business Auto Coverage Guide* and coauthored *The Workers Compensation Coverage Guide*, and the *Commercial Auto Program Coverage* Guide published by the National Underwriter Company. Mr. Thamann also writes articles on insurance issues for *Claims* magazine.

Katherine Caudill, J.D., is a Staff Writer for *FC&S®*. Her focuses include Commercial General Liability, Personal Auto, and Cyber Liability.

Ms. Caudill is a graduate of Georgetown College where, as a student-athlete, she received a Bachelor of Arts degree in Political Science and double-minored in National Security Studies and History. While in college, Ms. Caudill worked for the United States Attorney's Office for the Eastern District of Kentucky in its Criminal Unit and served as a Legislative Intern for Kentucky General Assembly Senate Majority Leader, Senator Damon Thayer.

Ms. Caudill earned her Juris Doctorate from the Northern Kentucky University Salmon P. Chase College of Law. During law school she clerked for Legal Aid of the Bluegrass, the Kentucky Department of Public Advocacy, the National Underwriter Company, and for the Honorable Joseph Hood, Senior Judge of the United States District Court for the Eastern District of Kentucky.

Managing Editor – Professional Publishing Division

Christine G. Barlow, CPCU, is Managing Editor of the Professional Publishing Division, a division of Summit Professional Networks. Christine has fifteen years' experience in the insurance industry, beginning as a claims adjuster then working as an underwriter and underwriting supervisor handling personal lines. Before joining *FC&S®*, Christine worked as an Underwriting Supervisor for Maryland Auto Insurance Fund, and as Senior Underwriter/Underwriter for companies Montgomery Mutual, Old American, Charter Group, and Nationwide.

Editorial Services

Connie L. Jump, Supervisor, Editorial Services

Karen L. Combs, Editorial Assistant

Table of Contents

Section I: The Business Risk Doctrine and the Business Risk Exclusions 1
Introduction 1
The Business Risk Doctrine 2
The Insuring Agreement 4
Was the Property Damage Caused by an "Occurrence"? 9
The Business Risk Exclusions. 13
Exclusion j.—Damage to Property 15
Exclusion k.—Damage to "Your Product" 27
Exclusion l.—Damage to "Your Work" 31
Exclusion m.—Damage to Impaired Property or
    Property Not Physically Insured 35
Exclusion n.—Recall of Products, Work or Impaired Property 38
Conclusion. 42

Section II: Additional Insureds and Contractual Liability 43
Risk Shifting—A Critical Part of Commercial Business 43
The Scope of Additonal Insured Endorsements 44
Contractual Risk–Shifting Common 45
Typical Additional Insured Endorsements 46
Difference between Additional Insured and
    Contractual Liability Coverage 49
Courts Broadly Interpret "Arising out of" Wording 50
"Arising out of" Equates to Broad Coverage
    in Many Jurisdictions. 51
Broad Coverage for An Additional Insured, but Not Unlimited. 53
Underwriter Evaluations of Risk. 53
New Trend to Restrict Additional Insured Coverage 55
The Policy and The Contract – Are They Separate and Independent?. 56
Different Types of Additional Insured Status 57
Coverage Limits in Primary Policies Need
    More Careful Examination. 58
Analysis of the Coverage Needed Must Include Many Factors 59
Potential Agent E&O Problem 60
Level of Care. 61
Contractual Liability Issues. 62
Insured Contracts. 62
Contractual Indemnity Wording 64
Hold Harmless Wording and Defense Costs. 64

Assume the Tort Liability for Another 66
Potential Conflict. 66
Fair Notice. 67
Additional Insureds and Defense Costs 68
Who Pays First?. 68
Primary and Noncontributory Coverage—CG 20 01 04 13 69
Careful Reading of The Contract: What Is Agreed?. 69
Insurance Company Review of Contracts. 70
Failing to Add an Additional Insured 71
Certificate of Insurance Issues 71
Problems with Certificates of Insurance and
    Additional Insured Status. 72
Best Practices for Getting the Right Insurance for the
    Insured and the Additional Insured 74
Conclusion. 75

Section III: One Occurrence, Two Occurrences **77**
The Role of Occurrence Wordings 78
Limiting Coverage. 78
Trigger of Coverage Distinguished. 78
Policy Wordings and Occurrences Determinations. 80
Indemnity Limits. 80
Definition of Occurrence. 81
Aggregates. 83
Completed Operations and Products Hazards. 83
Occupational Disease 84
Premium Bases: Remuneration and Otherwise. 84
Earlier Aggregate Wordings 85
Stacking and Anti-Stacking Clauses 86
Stacking. 86
Anti-Stacking Terms: Noncumulation and Deemer Clauses. 87
Batch Clauses 90
Annualization: Multi-Year Policies. 92
Combined Single Limits 93
Cases in Which Disputes Arise 94
Multiple Plaintiffs 94
Multiple Insureds. 95
Widespread Injuries. 95
Parties to Occurrence Disputes 95
Insured versus Insurer 95
Insurer versus Insurer 96
Insurer versus Reinsurer 96

Legal Tests for Counting Occurrences 96
Cause Meanings. 97
Immediate Physical Cause of Injuries (Proximate Cause) 97
Event Giving Rise to Insured's Liability (Legal Cause). 98
Burden of Proof Issues 100
External Factors Impacting Occurrence Determinations 100
Role of Insured 100
Physical Proximity/Continuity of Damage 102
Insured's Coverage Profile 102
Small Claims/Large Retentions. 103
Deductibles and Self-Insured Retentions (SIRs). 104
Low Indemnity Limits. 108
Insurer Insolvency 109
Case Law Survey. 109
Premises Liability Claims 109
Food Poisoning Claims 112
Construction Defect and Building Claims 112
Discrimination Claims: Housing and Employment 115
Environmental Liability Claims 118
Sources of Contamination at a Site. 118
What Is the Cause of Pollution Liabilities? 118
Case Law Examples 119
Molestation and Sexual Assault Claims 127
One Occurrence: Failure to Prevent Abuse 127
One Occurrence per Policy Year 128
Multiple Locations or Perpetrators as Separate Occurrences 129
Each Child a New Occurrence 129
Impact of Aggregating Provisions. 130
Nursing Home Claims. 130
Shooting and Criminal Assault Claims 131
Products Liability Claims 134
Single versus Multiple Occurrences 134
Single Occurrence Products Cases 138
Multiple Occurrence Products Cases 139
Toxic Tort Litigation 140
Asbestos Claims 142
Conclusion. 153

Section IV: Cyber Liability **155**
The Epidemic of Cybercrime 155
Types of Cybercrimes 155
Computer-Targeted Crimes 156

Financial Crimes 156
Exploitation Crimes 156
Opportunity Costs 157
Employment 157
Cybercrime in the United States 157
Correlation of U.S. Cybersecurity Expenditure to
    Detected Events 160
Cyber Liability 166
Applicability of the CGL Policy to Cyber Risk Exposures 166
In the Beginning–Y2K 167
Covered Territory 167
Tangible Property 168
Electronic Data 171
Recording and Distribution of Material or
    Information in Violation of Law 172
Distribution of Material in Violation of Statutes 172
Absolute Exclusion 173
Endorsement CG 21 06 05 14 173
Endorsement CG 21 07 05 14 175
Complex Underwriting 176
The Coverage Availability 177
New Optional Coverage 178
Third-Party Outsourcing 181
A Risk Management Approach to Cyber 182
Conclusions and Trends 184

Appendix A: ISO Forms 187

**Appendix B: The Status of Data Breach Notification Laws
in the United States** 267

Index 271

Case Index 277

Section I

The Business Risk Doctrine and the Business Risk Exclusions

By: Shaun McParland Baldwin, Esq.

Introduction

Commercial general liability ("CGL") policies provide coverage for the risk that the insured's work or product may cause "property damage" to a third person's property. The scope of that coverage, however, is not unlimited. As stated by the court in *American States Insurance Co. v. Mathis*, 974 S.W.2d 647, 649 (Mo.App. 1998):

> The intent of such policies is to protect against the unpredictable and potentially unlimited liability that can result from accidentally causing injury to other persons or their property... A commercial general liability policy is not intended to protect business owners against every risk of operating a business....

Id. at 649. This concept was also addressed in James T. Hendrick & James P. Wiezel, The New Commercial General Liability Forms an Introduction and Critique, 36 Fed'n Ins. & Corp. Couns. Q. 319, 322 (Summer 1986), where the authors stated:

> It is not the function of the CGL policy to guarantee the technical competence and integrity of business management. The CGL policy does not serve as a performance bond, nor does it serve as a warranty of goods or services. It does not ordinarily contemplate coverage for losses which are a normal, frequent or predictable consequence of the business operations. Nor does it contemplate ordinary business expense, or injury and damage to others which results by intent or indifference.

The insuring agreement in the CGL policy itself imposes limitations on the coverage. The policy applies only to damages payable because of "property damage," a defined term under the policy. In addition, the "property damage" must be caused by an "occurrence" or accident. The "property damage" must take place during the policy period and not be known by the insured to have occurred, in whole or in part, prior to the inception of the policy. Once those threshold requirements are met, the policy exclusions further limit the risks covered by the CGL policy.

Some of the most litigated exclusions in the CGL policy are the "business risk" exclusions. These exclusions apply solely to property damage claims. The business risk exclusions are designed to make certain that the insured's responsibility for the performance and quality of its own work or products is not passed off to its liability insurer. A secondary purpose is to prevent policyholders from obtaining first-party type protections from their liability insurance. The CGL exclusions that fall into the category of "business risk exclusions" and that are discussed below are: 1) Exclusion j.–Damage to property, 2) Exclusion k.–Damage to "your product," 3) Exclusion l.–Damage to "your work," 4) Exclusion m.–Damage to "impaired property," and 5) Exclusion n.–Recall or sistership exclusion.

The business risk exclusions are an expression of the "business risk doctrine." That doctrine permeates all aspects of the property damage liability coverage.

The purpose of this section is to provide a general overview of the business risk exclusions contained in coverage part A of the 2013 CGL coverage form drafted by the Insurance Services Office as well as the prior versions of the CGL policy form. This section relies upon this standard form because that policy form is used by insurers throughout the United States without any significant variation. The section will first address the business risk doctrine that underlies the business risk exclusions and other limitations in the property damage liability coverage. It will then explain the limitations of the property damage liability insuring agreement. Finally, each of the business risk exclusions are addressed in greater detail.

The Business Risk Doctrine

Business risks have been defined as the "normal, frequent, or predictable consequences of doing business and which business management can and should control and manage." *Columbia Mut. Ins. Co. v. Schauf*, 967 S.W.2d 74, 77 (Mo. banc 1998). Excluding these risks lowers insurance rates and provides incentives for the insured to perform business effectively. As noted by the Minnesota Court of Appeals in *Thommes v. Milwaukee Mutual Ins. Co.*, 622 N.W.2d 155, 159-60 (Minn. App. 2001), *aff'd*, 641 N.W.2d 877 (2002):

> The business risk doctrine is the expression of a public policy
> applied to the insurance coverage provided under commercial

> general liability policies…. Reduced to its simplest terms, the risk that an insured's product will not meet contractual standards is a business risk not covered by a general liability policy…. To ensure predictable and affordable insurance rates, the business risk doctrine limits an insurer's assumption of risk to those risks that are beyond the "effective control" of the insured.

(Citations omitted).

In its simplest terms, business risks are those risks that management can and should control because of the nature of the business operations, for example, the risks that relate to the repair or replacement of faulty work or products. These risks are a normal, foreseeable and expected incident of doing business and should be reflected in the price of the product or service rather than as a cost of insurance to be shared by others. *See Sphere Drake Ins. Co. v. Tremco, Inc.*, 513 N.W.2d 473, 477 (Minn. App. 1994) *review denied* (Minn. Apr. 28, 1994).

Since the quality of the insured's work is a "business risk" that is solely within an insured's own control, liability insurance generally does not provide coverage for claims arising out of the failure of the insured's product or work to meet the quality or specifications for which the insured may be liable as a matter of contract.

This doctrine prevents "the opportunity or incentive for the insured general contractor to be less than optimally diligent in … the performance of his contractual obligations to complete a project in a good workmanlike manner." *Wanzek Constr., Inc. v. Employers Ins. of Wausau*, 679 N.W.2d 322, 326 (Minn. 2004). In short, the business risk doctrine prevents a contractor who performed unsatisfactory work and received compensation for that work, from being paid a second time by its insurer in order to fix the unsatisfactory work. Thus, while an insured may have a contractual obligation to make good on its products or work, or to replace or rebuild deficient products or work, that is a not a risk covered under the CGL policy.

The seminal case on this subject is *Weedo v. Stone-E-Brick, Inc.*, 405 A.2d 788 (1979). There, the Supreme Court of New Jersey summarized the policy underlying the business risk doctrine, as follows:

> The risk intended to be insured is the possibility that the goods, products or work of the insured, once relinquished or completed, will cause bodily injury or damage to property other than to the product or completed work itself, and for which the insured may be found liable. The insured may be liable as a matter of contract

> law to make good on products or work which is defective. This may even extend to an obligation to completely replace or rebuild the deficient product or work. This liability, however, is not what the coverages in question are designed to protect against. The coverage is for tort liability for physical damages to others and not for economic loss because the product or completed work is not that for which the damaged person bargained."

Id., 405 A.2d at 791 (*quoting Henderson, supra*, note 13 at 441).

The court in *Centex Homes Corp v. Pre-Stressed Systems*, 444 So.2d 66, 67 (1984), likewise explained:

> If insurance proceeds could be used to pay for the repairing and/ or replacing of poorly constructed products, a contractor or sub-contractor could receive initial payment for its work and receive subsequent payment from the insurance company to repair or replace it. Equally repugnant on policy grounds is the notion that the presence of insurance obviates the obligation to perform the job initially in a workmanlike manner.

The public policy inspiring the business risk doctrine has largely been incorporated into the language of the standard CGL policy. Some courts cite to the "business risk doctrine" to justify enforcement of their interpretation of whether the claim involves "property damage" caused by an "occurrence" in the first instance, as well as support for application of the business risk exclusions. However, today, most courts only view the business risk doctrine as merely the public policy concern behind the language in CGL policies. Even in Minnesota, a strong proponent of the business risk doctrine, the courts have recognized that it is the policy language itself that should govern the rights and obligations of the parties. As the Supreme Court in *Thommes v. Milwaukee Mutual Ins. Co.*, 641 N.W.2d at 882 (2002), observed:

> If parties to an insurance contract demonstrate their intent, using clear and unambiguous language, then there is no need to look to business risk principles to ascertain whether the policy was intended to cover such risks.

The Insuring Agreement

Before considering the "business risk" exclusions, it is important to determine whether the claim falls within the insuring agreement in the first instance. The insuring agreement states that the insurer will pay "those sums that the insured becomes legally obligated to pay as damages because of 'property damage' to which this insurance applies." In addition, the "property damage" must be caused by an "occurrence," take place during the policy period and not be known to have occurred, in whole or in part, by the insured prior to the policy period. Both "property damage" and "occurrence" are defined terms in the CGL policy. These definitions also contain important limitations to the scope of coverage provided by the CGL policy.

A.   Is there a claim for "Property Damage"?

The term "property damage" has been defined in the CGL policy as:

a.   Physical injury to tangible property, including all resulting loss of use of that property. All such loss of use shall be deemed to occur at the time of the physical injury that caused it; or

b.   Loss of use of tangible property that is not physically injured. All such loss of use shall be deemed to occur at the time of the "occurrence" that caused it.

In 2001, the following language was added to the definition:

For the purposes of this insurance, electronic data is not tangible property.

As used in this definition, electronic data means information, facts or programs stored as or on, created or used on, or transmitted to or from computer software, including systems and applications software, hard or floppy disks, CD-ROMS, taps, drives, cells, data processing devices or any other media which are used with electronically controlled equipment.

More significant than the clarification regarding electronic data was the change in another aspect of the definition between the 1966 CGL form and all subsequent forms. In the 1966 form, the definition of "property damage" did not require "*physical* injury to tangible property." It merely required "injury to tangible property." Thus, policies containing the earlier form of the definition were often required to respond to claims for economic loss and diminution of value. *See, e.g., Bowman Steel Corp. v. Lumbermens Mut. Cas. Co.*, 364 F.2d 246 (3d Cir. 1966) (diminution in value to claimant's building resulting from the attachment of the insured's defective siding qualified as "injury to tangible property" under the 1966 CGL coverage form).

The significance of the requirement of "*physical* injury to tangible property" was addressed in *Tobi Engineering, Inc. v. Nationwide Mutual Ins. Co.*, 214 Ill.App.3d 692, 574 N.E.2d 160 (1st Dist. 1991). In that case, the insured was sued for failure to timely deliver non-defective bearing pads. It sought a defense from its insurer under the "property damage" coverage. The court concluded that since the underlying claims sought only the return of the purchase price and reimbursement of delay damages, the claims were only for "intangible," purely "economic" losses. Thus, the claims did not involve "property damage" that required "physical injury to tangible property."

The Illinois Supreme Court discussed in detail the significance of the change in the policy definition of "property damage" in *Travelers Ins. Co. v. Eljer Mfg, Inc.*, 197 Ill.2d 278 (2001). In *Eljer*, thousands of products liability claims were filed against the policyholder by persons who owned homes in which the Qest plumbing system had been installed. Many of these claims involved homes in which the Qest plumbing system had leaked. However, some of the claims involved buildings that had not experienced leaks, but the homeowners removed the Qest plumbing system as a preventative measure. Those homeowners sought reimbursement from the insured for the costs of removing and replacing the plumbing system.

The insured argued that all of the claims involved "property damage" and that the "property damage" occurred at the time that the allegedly defective Qest plumbing system was installed in the home. The Illinois Supreme Court disagreed. It held that the mere propensity of the Qest system to leak prematurely, without actual leaking, did not qualify as "physical injury to tangible property." Thus, those complaints that sought reimbursement for removal and replacement of the allegedly defective pipes did not seek damages *because of* "property damage." The court explained:

> Although a claimant may understandably be concerned by reports that an estimated five percent of the Qest systems have experienced failures, the damage caused to a home by the removal of a functional system prior to a leak does not constitute "physical injury to tangible property" arising from a covered occurrence under the policies. The "injury" caused by the Qest system under these facts flows from the claimant's disappointed commercial expectations in the performance of the Qest system and is not an injury which is "physical" in nature. As stated, the post-1981 policies do not provide coverage for economic loss claims against the policyholders. Consistent with the policy language agreed upon by the parties to the insurance contract, the insurers did not consent to become guarantors of the product quality or the performance of the Qest systems. We therefore agree with the insurers in their cross-appeal that the appellate court erred in finding that coverage under the post-1981 policies may be triggered prior to the occurrence of an actual leak if, in the course of

replacing the Qest system, actual physical damage is caused to the home itself.

Id. at 308.

Numerous other courts have similarly noted the significance of the requirement in the "property damage" definition that the claim involve "physical" injury to tangible property. *See, e.g., Aetna Casualty & Sur. Co. v. McIbs, Inc.*, 684 F. Supp. 246, 248 (Nev. 1988) (the inclusion of the word "physical" in this policy was designed to preclude recovery for consequential or intangible damages such as a diminution or depreciation in value); *Dewitt Constr. Inc. v. Charter Oak Fire Ins. Co.*, 307 F.3d 1127, 1134 n.4 (9th Cir. 2002) (proof of diminished value would not be sufficient to establish property damage because the policy requires physical injury as opposed to injury); *Utica Mut. Ins. Co. v. Weathermark Investments, Inc.*, 292 F.3d 77, 82 (1st Cir. 2002) (diminution in the fair market value of property is not within scope of coverage; the definition of "property damage" plainly does not encompass this type of intangible economic loss); *Aetna Life & Cas. v. Patrick Indus., Inc.*, 645 N.E.2d 656 (Ind. Ct. App. 1995) (diminution in value arising out of the insured's defective particle board was not "property damage" within the 1973 definition); *Neth. Ins. Co. v. Main St. Ingredients, LLC*, 2014 U.S. App. LEXIS 5018 (8th Cir. Minn. Mar. 18, 2014) (instant oatmeal was not physically injured when dried milk used in the product that was recalled).

In *Esicorp, Inc. v. Liberty Mutual Ins. Co.*, 266 F.3d 859, 863 (8th Cir. 2001), the court also considered whether claims for the cost of removal and repair of the insured's defective product qualified as damages because of "property damage." The insured argued that the cost should be covered as "property damage" because the removal of its product, defective shop welds, required the invasion of pipe sections already integrated into the pipe system in the construction project. The court rejected the policyholder's argument that the mere incorporation of the defectively welded pipe sections into the pipe system was covered "property damage." The court held that there is no "property damage" "unless and until the incorporation of a defective product or component results in 'physical injury to tangible property' in at least some part of the system." *Id.* at 863. *See also, Sokol & Co. v. Atlantic Mut. Ins. Co.*, 430 F.3d 417 (7th Cir. 2005) (spoiled peanut butter packets supplied by food products manufacturer to customer for inclusion in customer's cookie mix boxes did not cause "physical injury to tangible property" despite manufacturer having to open each box to remove and replace each packet and experiencing delays in getting cookie mix to the market); *Fidelity & Deposit Co. of Md. v. Hartford Cas. Ins Co.*, 215 F.Supp. 1171, 1181 (D. Kan. 2002) (mere incorporation of the insured's faulty workmanship into a building was not "property damage"); *Amtrol*

Inc. v Tudor Ins. Co., 2002 WL 31194863 (D. Mass. 2002) (leaks from the insured's product, a hot water maker, which resulted in no physical injury to third-party property did not constitute "property damage"); *Seagate Tech., Inc. v. St. Paul Fire & Marine Ins. Co.*, 11 F.Supp.2d 1150 (N.D. Cal. 1998) (insured's supply of defective disk drives that were incorporated into the plaintiff's products were not covered as there was no allegation of "physical injury"); *F&H Constr. v. ITT Hartford Ins. Co. of the Midwest*, 118 Cal. App. 4th 364 (2004) (incorporation of a defective component or product into a larger structure does not constitute property damage unless and until the defective component causes physical injury to tangible property in at least some other part of the system); *Lennar Corp. v. Great Am. Ins. Co.*, 200 S.W. 651 (Tex. Ct. App. 2006) (costs incurred in removing and replacing an exterior stucco used on homes built by the insured to prevent future physical injury to homes that had not yet experienced water damage due to defects in the stucco could not be considered damages because of "property damage").

While the first prong of the definition of "property damage" requires physical injury, the second prong does not. It requires "loss of use of tangible property that is not physically injured." The important element in any claim for "loss of use" is that the loss must be to tangible property. This concept was discussed in *Bituminous Casualty Corp. v. Gust K. Newberg Constr. Co.*, 218 Ill.App.3d 956, 578 N.E.2d 1003 (1st Dist. 1991), appeal denied, 143 Ill.2d 636, 587 N.E.2d 1011 (1992). In *Bituminous*, the insured was sued because of its installation of a faulty heating, air conditioning, and ventilation system. The underlying complaint alleged that high temperatures in the building made employees ill and unable to work. The court found that the allegations in the complaint were insufficient to constitute a "loss of use," since the building was never unoccupied or unused as a result of the allegedly faulty heating, air conditioning, and ventilation systems. Consequently, the court found the insurer had no duty to defend, because there had been no "loss of use" relative to tangible property.

In contrast, where faulty construction or construction delays cause a temporary inability to use a new or existing building, or other structure, a court may find "property damage" under the "loss of use" prong. For example, in *Gibraltar Casualty Co. v. Sargent & Lundy*, 214 Ill.App.3d 768 (1st Dist. 1990), appeal denied 141 Ill.2d 540 (1991), the court held that the delay in the construction of a nuclear power plant and temporary inability to use the property constituted a "loss of use" triggering coverage under the general liability policy. The court noted that "loss of use" is the loss of the right to use property, which is an incident of ownership. Such a loss in "ownership," even if temporary, should trigger an insurer's duty to defend under the "property damage" provision of a CGL policy.

B.   Was the Property Damage Caused by an "Occurrence"?

The next significant limitation to coverage is that the "property damage" must be caused by an "occurrence." That term is defined as: "an accident, including continuous or repeated exposure to substantially the same general harmful conditions." Courts have defined the term "accident" in various ways. For example, in *Kvaerner Metals Division of Kvaerner v. Commercial Union Insurance Co.*, 589 Pa. 317, 908 A.2d 888, 897-88 (Pa. 2006), the Pennsylvania Supreme Court held that an "accident" is "'[a]n unexpected and undesirable event,' or 'something that occurs unexpectedly or unintentionally.'" In *Stoneridge Dev. Co. v. Essex Ins. Co.*, 382 Ill. App. 3d 731 (Ill. App. Ct. 2d Dist. 2008), the Illinois appellate court held that an accident is an "unforeseen occurrence, usually of an untoward or disastrous character or an undesigned, sudden or unexpected event of an inflictive or unfortunate character. The natural and ordinary consequences of an act do not constitute an accident." In *Kalchthaler v. Keller Construction Co.*, 224 Wis. 2d 387, 397, 591 N.W.2d 169 (Ct. App. 1999), the Wisconsin Court of Appeals held that "[a]n accident is an 'event or change occurring without intention or volition through carelessness, unawareness, ignorance, or a combination of causes and producing an unfortunate result.'" This definition was cited with approval in *American Family Mut. Ins. Co. v. American Girl, Inc.*, 268 Weis.2d 16, 673 N.W.2d 54 (2004).

There are four competing lines of authority regarding whether faulty workmanship claims constitute an "occurrence" and thus fall within the scope of the insuring agreement of the policy.

Some courts hold that such claims do not involve "property damage" caused by an "occurrence" because the natural and ordinary consequences of faulty workmanship is the destruction, damage, or failure of the insured's work or the insured's product. This rationale finds particular support where the claims asserted against the insured are solely breach of contract claims and the claims involve solely the insured's own work or product. Claims in which property damage is alleged to have been caused by an insured's breach of contract have often been deemed by courts not to be the result of an "occurrence" because such property damage is viewed as a "normal, expected consequence" of the insured's breach of contract that is "foreign to the risk insured against." Courts have, therefore, held that property damage caused by an insured's failure to perform its contract in a workmanlike manner or its use of inferior materials in the performance of its contract falls outside the insuring agreement because such property damage is not the result of an accident.

This analysis was exemplified in *American States Insurance Co. v. Mathis*, 974 S.W.2d 647 (Mo. App. 1998). In that case, the insured constructed certain trenches and duct banks at the wrong grade and slope. Other contractors had to tear out, retrench, and reinstall the improperly constructed duct banks. The insured was sued for breach of contract, negligence and negligent misrepresentation. The court held that the insured's breach of a construction contract was not an accident, and, thus, was not an "occurrence" within the meaning of the policy at issue. The court upheld the insurer's denial of coverage for the claim, explaining that:

> Such a breach of a defined contractual duty cannot fall within the term "accident." Performance of its contract according to the terms specified therein was within [the insured's] control and management and its failure to perform cannot be described as an undesigned or unexpected event.

Id. at 650.

That view was embraced by the court in *Hotel Roanoke Conference Center Comm. v. Cincinnati Ins. Co.*, 303 F.Supp. 2d 784, 788 (W.D. Va. 2004). In that case, the court held that the word "accident" as used in the definition of "occurrence" "involves a degree of fortuity not present when the insured's defective performance of a contract causes injury to the insured's own work or product." *See also, Norwalk Ready Mixed Concrete v. Travelers Ins. Cos.*, 246 F.3d 1132, 1137 (8th Cir. 2001) (defective workmanship cannot be characterized as an accident under Iowa law); *Union Ins. Co. v. Hottenstein*, 83 P.3d 1196 (Co. Ct. App. 2003) (an "accident" is an unusual or unanticipated result flowing from a commonplace cause; breach of contract following from poor workmanship is no such accident).

This reasoning was also employed by the Pennsylvania Supreme Court in *Kvaerner, supra. Kvaerner* was sued for breach of contract and breach of warranty because the "Coke Oven Battery" it manufactured for Bethlehem Steel was alleged to be damaged, and did not meet contract specifications or applicable industry standards. As a result of property damage to the Battery (including sheared joints, broken outer blocks, spalling walls, bowed housings, etc), Bethlehem Steel sought either "the amount that it will cost to replace the Coke Oven Battery or the difference in value between the defective Coke Oven Battery that it received and the Coke Oven Battery that the insured warranted that it would deliver. The court held that the definition of "accident" required to establish an "occurrence" under the CGL policy cannot be satisfied by claims based upon faulty workmanship. It explained:

> Such claims simply do not present the degree of fortuity con- templated by the ordinary definition of "accident" or its common judicial construction in this context. To hold otherwise would be

to convert a policy for insurance into a performance bond. We are unwilling to do so, especially since such protections are readily available for protection of contractors [through, for example, a builder's risk policy or a professional liability policy, both of which had paid out money on Kvaerner's behalf].

Kvaerner, *supra*, 589 Pa. at 335-36. *Accord, Brosnahan Builders, Inc. v. Harleysville Mut. Ins. Co.*, 137 F. Supp. 2d 517 (D. Del. 2001); *Cincinnati Ins. Co. v. Motorists Mut. Ins. Co.*, 306 S.W.3d 69 (Ky. 2010); *L-J, Inc. and Eagle Creek Const. Co. v. Bituminous Fire & Marine Ins. Co.*, 366 S.C. 117, 621 S.E.2d 33 (2005); *Mello Constr., Inc. v. Acadia Ins. Co.*, 2007 Mass. App. LEXIS 1063 (Mass. App. Ct. 2007); *Pursell Constr., Inc. v. Hawkeye-Security Ins. Co.*, 596 N.W.2d 67 (Iowa 1999).

Contrary authority, however, also exists, and it may now be the majority. Several state courts have retreated from the view that claims sounding in contract and involving faulty workmanship can never involve a covered "occurrence." Even some of the decisions relied upon in *Kvaerner* have now been reversed. More courts are now finding that faulty workmanship may be an "occurrence" under various circumstances.

In *Lamar Homes Inc. v. Mid-Continent Cas. Co.*, 242 S.W.3d 1 (Tex. Sup. Ct. 2007), the Texas Supreme Court held that breach of a contract can constitute an "occurrence" where the defective construction is a product of negligence. That determination, according to the court, is based on the allegations of the complaint. The court noted, with reference to the complaint filed against the insured, that no one alleged that the insured intended or expected its work or its subcontractor's work to damage the claimant's home. *Id.* Accordingly, the court found that an "occurrence" had been alleged. *Accord, American Family Ins. Co. v. American Girl, Inc.*, 673 N.W.2d 65 (Wis. 2004) (property damage to building due to improper soil preparation was caused by an "occurrence").

The court in *Capstone Bldg. Corp. v. Am. Motorists Ins. Co.*, 308 Conn. 760 (Conn. 2013) also determined that a contractual breach can be an "occurrence" in rare instances. In that case, a contractor was hired by a university to build a student housing complex. After the project was finished, the university found multiple defects. The defects were remedied by a subcontractor. The insurer argued that since the defects stemmed from a breach of contract they would not be covered. The court disagreed, citing to the ever expanding definition of what constitutes an "occurrence."

Among those states that have found that faulty workmanship can constitute an "occurrence," three views have emerged on what circumstances must exist in order for faulty workmanship to qualify as an "occurrence." The first view is that an "occurrence" will be found only if the insured did not subjectively intend to perform defective work and the damages were not expected or intended. *K & L Homes, Inc. v. Am. Family Mut. Ins. Co.*, 2013 ND 57 (N.D. 2013), embraced that approach. The court found that if the faulty workmanship was not intentional, and therefore, unexpected, then faulty workmanship may constitute an "occurrence." This subjective intent viewpoint is intended to reinforce the notion that the CGL policy is designed to cover only fortuitous losses. Courts following this view include: *Sheehan Const. Co., Inc. v. Continental Ins. Co.*, 935 N. E. 2d 160 (Ind. 2010); *Capstone Bldg. Corp. v. Am. Motorists Ins. Co.*, 308 Conn. 760 (Conn. 2013); *U.S. Fire Ins. Co. v. J.S.U.B., Inc.*, 979 So. 2d 871 (Fla. 2007); *D.R. Sherry Constr., Ltd. v. Am. Family Mut. Ins. Co.*, 316 S.W.3d 899 (Mo. 2010) (faulty home construction was determined to be unexpected and unforeseeable, and therefore the faulty workmanship could be seen as an "occurrence"); *Corner Const. Co. v. U.S. Fid. & Guar. Co.*, 638 N.W. 2d 887 (S.D. 2002) ("occurrences" need only be undersigned, sudden, and unexpected); *Cherrington v. Erie Prop. & Cas. Co.*, 745 S.E. 2d 508 (W.Va. 2013) (anytime there is damage caused by faulty workmanship that is not deliberate, intentional, expected, desired, or foreseen it is an "occurrence").

Other courts have found that damage caused by the defective work to other non-defective portions of the work or property qualifies as an "occurrence" without focusing on the subjective intent of the insured, but presuming such third party property damage was caused by an accident. *See, e.g., Owners Ins. Co. v. Jim Carr Homebuilder, LLC*, 2014 Ala. LEXIS 44 (Ala. Mar. 28, 2014) (while there is no coverage for the cost of repairing faulty work, there is coverage to fix damage caused by the faulty work); *Auto-Owners Ins. Co. v. Home Pride Cos.*, 268 Neb. 528 (Neb. 2004) (faulty workmanship standing alone is not an occurrence, but an accident caused by faulty workmanship is an occurrence); *Dodson v. St. Paul Ins. Co.*, 812 P.2d 372 (Okla. 1991) (faulty workmanship provides coverage to damage other than that upon which the insured worked); S.C. CODE ANN. §38-61-70 (2011) (definition of "occurrence" may include any damage except that of remedying the faulty workmanship); *Webster v. Acadia Ins. Co.*, 934 A. 2d 567 (N.H. 2007) (unexpected physical injury to other property is an "occurrence"); *Lagastee-Mulder, Inc. v. Consol. Ins. Co.*, 682 F.3d 1054 (7th Cir. 2012) (damage done to other property is an "occurrence" of faulty construction); *Firemen's Fund Ins. Co. of Newark v. National Union Fire Ins. Co.*, 904 A. 2d 754 (N.J. Super Ct. App. Div. 2006) (for faulty workmanship to constitute an "occurrence," there must be damage to other property); *William C. Vick Constr. Co., v Pennsylvania Nat'l Mut. Ins. Co.*, 52 F. Supp. 2d 569 (E.D.N.C. 1999) (faulty construction causing leaks in a building that damaged other property may constitute an "occurrence"), aff'd 213 F. 3d 634 (4th Cir. 2000).

Lastly, some courts consider all faulty workmanship to be an "occurrence," and instead focus on whether the exclusions sufficiently incorporate the business risk doctrine to preclude coverage for the loss. For example, in *U.S. Fire Ins. Co. v. JSUB, Inc.*, 979 So. 2d 871 (2007), the Florida Supreme Court observed:

> In this case, if the insuring provisions do not confer an initial grant of coverage for faulty workmanship, there would be no reason for U.S. Fire to exclude damage to "your work":

> If ... losses actionable in contract are never CGL "occurrences" for purposes of the initial coverage grant, then the business risk exclusions are entirely unnecessary. The business risk exclusions eliminate coverage for liability for property damage to the insured's own work or product-liability that is typically actionable between the parties pursuant to the terms of their contract, not in tort. If the insuring agreement never confers coverage for this type of liability as an original definitional matter, then there is no need to specifically exclude it. Why would the insurance industry exclude damage to the insured's own work or product if the damage could never be considered to have arisen from a covered "occurrence" in the first place?

Id. at 886-887 citing *Am. Fam. Mut. Ins. Co. v. American Girl, Inc.*, 673 N. W. 2d 65, 78 (WI. 2004). *Accord Lamar Homes, supra*, 242 S.W.3d at 12 ("by incorporating the subcontractor exception into the 'your work' exclusion, the insurance industry specifically contemplated coverage for property damage caused by a subcontractor's defective performance"); *Erie Ins. Exch. v. Colony Dev. Corp.*, 2003-Ohio-7232 (Ohio Ct. App., Franklin County Dec. 31, 2003) (failure of a contractor to perform an adequate job is an occurrence, requiring the need for a "your work" exclusion); *Auto Owners Ins. Co. v. Newman*, 385 S.C. 187, 684 S.E. 2d 541 (2009).

It should also be noted that some states have enacted statutes to give more clarity to the meaning of the term "occurrence" or to tacitly overrule jurisdictional law. Those include Ark. Code Ann. §23-79-155 (2011); Colo. Rev. Stat. 13-20-808 (2010); Haw. Rev. Stat. §431:1-217; and S.C. Code Ann. §38-61-70 (2011).

The Business Risk Exclusions

Whether a claim involves "property damage" caused by an "occurrence" and when and how the business risk exclusions apply has generated much misunderstanding and controversy. These issues affect both the design and the implementation of a liability insurance program.

The claims often pose difficult questions of interpretation and involve hundreds and thousands of dollars. As a result, some of the most litigated issues in insurance law have involved the business risk exclusions. Because the business risk exclusions may affect only a portion of the claimed damages in a given case, it is important to understand not only their application, but also their limitations.

In *Grinnell Mutual Reinsurance Ins. v. Lynne*, 686 N.W.2d 118 (2004), the North Dakota Supreme Court noted that the purpose of the business risk exclusions is to prevent policyholders from converting liability insurance into protection from foreseeable business risks. The court noted that insurance companies theorize that a business risk, such as costs resulting from improper performance of a contract, should be built into the price of the product. The court further observed:

> Business risk exclusions are intended to provide coverage for tort liability, but not for contract liability of the insured for loss because the product or completed work was not that for which the other party had bargained.... The exclusions are meant to remove coverage for risks which are subject to manipulation by the insured or a third party.

Id. at 124 (citations omitted).

Not all courts concur with the concept that CGL coverage is limited to tort liability. In *Lamar Homes, Inc. v. Mid-Continent Cas. Co.*, 242 S.W.3d 1, 13 (Tex. 2007), the Texas Supreme Court observed:

> Contrary to the carrier's contentions, the CGL policy makes no distinction between tort and contract damages. The insuring agreement does not mention torts, contracts, or economic losses; nor do these terms appear in the definitions of "property damage" or "occurrence." The CGL's insuring agreement simply asks whether "property damage" has been caused by an "occurrence." Therefore, any preconceived notion that a CGL policy is only for tort liability must yield to the policy's actual language. The duty to defend must be determined here, as in other insurance cases, by comparing the complaint's factual allegations to the policy's actual language.

Id. at 13, citing 2 JEFFREY W. STEMPEL, LAW OF INSURANCE CONTRACT DISPUTES §14.02[d][1] at 14A-10 (2d ed. 1999) ("The language of the CGL policy and the purpose of the CGL insuring agreement will provide coverage for claims sounding in part in breach-of-contract/breach-of-warranty under some circumstances."); *See also*

9 COUCH ON INSURANCE §126:3 at 126-8 (3d ed.1997) ("the legal theory asserted by the claimant is immaterial to the determination of whether the risk is covered").

With that background in mind, the following is a discussion of the individual business risk exclusions.

Exclusion j.—Damage to Property

Exclusion j. states: This insurance does not apply to:

"Property damage" to:

(1)   Property you own, rent, or occupy, including any costs or expenses incurred by you, or any other person, organization or entity, for repair, replacement, enhancement, restoration or maintenance of such property for any reason, including prevention of injury to a person or damage to another's property;

(2)   Premises you sell, give away or abandon, if the "property damage" arises out of any part of those premises;

(3)   Property loaned to you;

(4)   Personal property in the care, custody or control of the insured;

(5)   That particular part of real property on which you or any contractors or subcontractors working directly or indirectly on your behalf are performing operations, if the "property damage" arises out of those operations; or

(6)   That particular part of any property that must be restored, repaired or replaced because "your work" was incorrectly performed on it.

Paragraphs (1), (3), and (4) of this exclusion do not apply to "property damage" (other than damage by fire) to premises, including the contents of such premises, rented to you for a period of 7 or fewer consecutive days. A separate limit of insurance applies to Damage to Premises Rented To You as described in Section III – Limits of Insurance.

Paragraph (2) of this exclusion does not apply if the premises are "your work" and were never occupied, rented or held for rental by you.

Paragraph (3), (4), (5), and (6) of this exclusion do not apply to liability assumed under a sidetrack agreement.

> Paragraph (6) of this exclusion does not apply to "property damage" included in the "products-completed operations hazard".

Exclusion j. generally reinforces the need of the insured to maintain its own premises and personal property in good condition and use reasonable care to prevent damage or injury. The first four paragraphs of exclusion j. apply to the insured's real or personal property. The last two paragraphs of exclusion j. apply to a contractor's business risks.

The exclusions set forth in j.(1) through (4) have three general objectives. First, they are intended to prevent CGL insurance from providing property insurance coverage that is available under other types of insurance coverage such as first-party property or fire and casualty policies. Secondly, they seek to avoid having the policy essentially operate as a guarantor of the insured's property by excluding liability when the only damage results from the property itself. Third, they are designed to prevent an insured from obtaining insurer-funded improvement of its own property as a byproduct of having incurred liability to third parties.

The exclusions encompassed in paragraph j. have undergone modifications over the years. The current version is a combination of the care, custody, or control and alienated premises exclusions contained in the 1973 CGL policy and various exclusions contained in the broad form property damage endorsement commonly included with the 1973 policy form. That endorsement was eventually written into the standard CGL policy in 1986. Additional modifications to the subparts of exclusion j. are noted below.

Exclusion j.(1)

Exclusion j.(1) is commonly referred to as the "owned property" exclusion. It excludes claims for property damage to the named insured's building or real estate that it owns or rents. In 1998, an exception was added to this exclusion that states that the exclusion does not apply "to premises rented to the named insured for seven or fewer consecutive days or to its contents." For example, this exception would permit coverage for "property damage" to hotel room furnishings or to conference facilities rented by the insured on a short–term (seven days or less) basis, provided that such "property damage" was caused by an "occurrence" or accident.

Exclusion j.(1) was enhanced in 2001 to state that this insurance does not apply to "property damage" to property you own, rent, or occupy, *including any costs or expenses incurred by you, or any other person, organization or entity, for repair, replacement, enhancement, restoration or maintenance of such property for any reason, including prevention of injury to a person or damage to another's property."* The significance of this is addressed below.

This exclusion has been most extensively litigated in environmental insurance coverage cases. Typically, environmental contamination is discovered within the boundaries of the named insured's property, including the groundwater beneath the property. Setting aside the pollution exclusion and its potential applicability, many courts have held that exclusion j.(1) does not bar coverage for costs associated with complying with government-ordered cleanup of the groundwater contamination because, according to state law, it is the state, not the individual property owner, that owns the groundwater beneath the property. Thus, since the groundwater is not owned by the named insured, the groundwater would qualify as "property damage" to third party property. The United States District Court for the Western District of Wisconsin adopted this view in *Maryland Cas. Co. v. Wausau Chemical Corp.*, 809 F.Supp 680 (1992). *See also Martin v. State Farm Fire & Cas. Co.*, 146 Ore. App. 270 (Or. Ct. App. 1997).

The enhancement made to the exclusion in 2001 was designed to clarify that prophylactic measures taken to prevent third party property damage are also encompassed within the scope of the "your property" exclusion—irrespective of whether the threat of "property damage" to third party property is "imminent" or "immediate." Previously, some courts interpreting exclusion j.(1) had refused to exclude coverage for the cost of pollution cleanup on a policyholder's own property when the cleanup was alleged to be necessary to prevent the migration of pollutants into groundwater or onto adjacent third-party property. These courts reasoned that if coverage is only triggered when waste seeps onto third-party property, this creates an incentive for the insured to delay cleanup until it affects third-party property. This view was embraced by the courts in *Savoy Med. Supply Co., Inc. v. F & H Mfg. Corp.*, 776 F.Supp. 703, 708 (E.D.N.Y. 1991), and *Claussen v. Aetna Cas. & Sur. Co.*, 754 F.Supp. 1576, 1580 (S.D. Ga. 1990): ("[e]ven if the pollution had not yet damaged the surrounding land and water, the *imminent threat* justified cleaning up the site to prevent damage to the surroundings"). Rulings such as these should no longer occur under the enhanced version of the exclusion.

Exclusion j.(2)

Exclusion j.(2) is commonly referred to as the "alienated premises" exclusion. The alienated premises exclusion narrows the scope of the CGL policy to exclude coverage for "property damage" to premises that the named insured has sold, given away or abandoned, if the "property damage" arises out of any part of those premises. The intent of this exclusion is to preclude coverage for liability that is based on the obligation of a seller of a building or other premises to identify and correct defects in the premises. For example, assume the insured sold a building with defective wiring. If the building subsequently catches fire as a result of the defective wiring and the insured is sued by the new homeowner for the fire loss, the claim against the insured would be barred by the alienated premises exclusion.

There is an exception to this exclusion that states that the exclusion does not apply if the premises are "your work" and were never occupied, rented, or held for rental by you. This exception restores coverage for contractors who never occupied the premises, but whose "work" it was to construct the premises. In other words, in the example cited above, if it was a contractor's faulty wiring during the construction of the building that caused the premises to catch fire, the alienated premises exclusion would not apply if the contractor had never occupied the building.

Fejes v. Alaska Ins. Co., 984 P.2d 519 (Alaska 1999), provides an example of a fact pattern where the court addressed the alienated premises exclusion and its exception. In that case, a contractor was sued by a homeowner when an improperly constructed curtain drain failed and caused a septic system to stop functioning. The insurer denied coverage based, in part, on the alienated premises exclusion. The insured argued that the alienated premises exclusion is limited to cases where the premises was first occupied, rented or held for rental by the insured and was not intended to apply to the completed operations of a contractor. The court agreed. Thus, the alienated premises exclusion did not preclude coverage for the negligence claims against the contractor.

Courts have broadly construed exclusion j.(2) to include any form of occupied housing, even if for a profit. In *Genesis Ins. Co. v. BRE Props.*, 916 F. Supp. 2d 1058 (N.D. Cal. 2013), BRE bought and rented an apartment complex, which it then sold. BRE argued that since they were in the business of selling apartment complexes, they should not be considered as occupying a complex they intended to sell. The court disagreed, and stated that since they rented it out for any length of time, the exclusion applied.

Exclusions j.(3) and (4)

Exclusion j.(3) excludes coverage for property loaned to the named insured. Exclusion j.(4) is known as the "care, custody, or control" exclusion and precludes coverage for personal property in the care, custody or control of any person qualifying as an insured under the terms of the policy.

The purpose of exclusions j.(3) and (4) is to prevent the CGL policy from being tantamount to property insurance when property is in the hands of a bailee or lessee, or is otherwise in the custody and control of the insured and thereby subject to damage or loss due to the insured's acts or omissions.

In 1998, along with exclusion j.(1), both exclusions j.(3) and (4) were revised to preserve coverage for "property damage" to premises, including the contents of such premises, rented to you [the named insured] for a period of seven or fewer consecutive days.

Little case law exists regarding exclusion j.(3), but possession and control would likely be the main factors a court would consider in deciding whether property was "loaned" to the named insured at the time that the "property damage" took place. Those were factors the Supreme Court of Virginia considered in *American Reliance Insurance Co. v. Mitchell*, 385 S.E.2d 583 (Va. 1989), when the court was evaluating whether a truck used by the insured was "loaned" property. The policy at issue excluded "bodily injury arising out of the operation of use of any motorized vehicle *loaned* to any insured." A neighbor volunteered his truck to two farmers to help the farmers load hay. While the farmers were using the truck, a child fell from the truck and was injured. Suit was brought against the farmers for their negligence in causing the minor's injuries. Both farmers had commercial liability insurance policies with the same insurer. The insurance company refused to pay the claims for the minor's injuries, arguing that coverage was excluded because the truck at issue was a loaned vehicle. The court noted that the term "loaned" was not defined in the policy and was susceptible to different interpretations. It could mean a formal bailment or it could be a loose, informal arrangement, such as where a volunteer has offered the use of his truck as a friendly gesture for a specific purpose, never relinquishing possession or control over the vehicle. Adopting the interpretation most favorable to the insured, the court held that the term would be construed as a formal bailment. As the insurer did not establish that the owner of the vehicle had relinquished possession or control over the vehicle, the court refused to apply the exclusion to preclude coverage.

Whether damaged property was in the "care, custody, or control" of the insured has been the subject of much controversy. In resolving this issue, courts have generally considered one or more of the following factors to determine if the insured exercised sufficient control over the property to bring the claim within the scope of the exclusion:

- the role of the insured in supervising and protecting the damaged property at issue;

- whether the insured's control was exclusive;

- whether the damaged property was merely incidental to the insured's work; and

- the amount of time which elapsed between the insured's relinquishment of control over the property and the property damage.

Illinois courts apply a two-part test to determine if property is within the care, custody or control of the insured and thus excluded from coverage. First, the insured must have possessory control of the property at the time of the loss; intimate handling of the product is not a prerequisite to establishing possessory control. Second, the property must be a necessary element of the work performed. *Liberty Mut. Ins. Co. v. Zurich Ins. Co.*, 402 Ill. App. 3d 37 (Ill. App. Ct. 1st Dist. 2010). The control exercised by the insured must be exclusive, but it need not be continuous. If the insured has possessory control at the time the property is damaged, the exclusion will apply.

Country Mutual Ins. Co. v. Waldman Mercantile Co., Inc., 103 Ill. App.3d 39, 43, 430 N.E.2d 606, 610 (5th Dist. 1981), is illustrative of a case applying the "care, custody and control" exclusion. The insured in *Waldman* was a discount store. Its policy excluded "property in the care custody or control of the insured or as to which the insured is for any purpose exercising physical control." The insured leased space in the store to various lessees, who displayed their merchandise within the leased space. The lessees' merchandise was shipped to the store by either their own employees or a commercial carrier. The lessees were responsible for maintaining their own displays and shelves and their employees came to the store about once or twice a week during regular business hours to check and restock the merchandise. The insured charged the third party lessees a percentage of their sales as compensation for its services. The insured was the only business that had keys to the premises. It was responsible for cleaning and maintaining the building and the surrounding area and providing security services. A fire broke out in the store, which destroyed the building and the merchandise located therein. The destroyed merchandise included that which was owned by the lessees.

The Illinois appellate court found that the policy's "care custody or control" exclusion precluded coverage for the claims by the lessees against the discount store owner. The court noted that the fire that destroyed the lessees' property occurred while the insured's employees were, for all practical purposes, in full charge of the property. The court also found it significant that only the insured's personnel had access to the merchandise at all times. The court was unpersuaded by the insured's argument that the exclusion should not apply on grounds that the insured did not have "exclusive control" since the lessees' employees were responsible for taking inventory and restocking the merchandise. The court found the term "limited access" more aptly applied to the lessees, who could only access the product during regular business hours. The court found that such access to the merchandise did not amount to "limited access" on the part of the insured. Accordingly, the court found the exclusion applied since the insured had exclusive possessory control at the time of the loss. The court in *Cashmere Pioneer Growers, Inc. v. Unigard Sec. Ins. Co.*, 77 Wash. App. 436, 439, 891 P.2d 732, 734 (1995) similarly found that the care, custody, or control exclusion barred coverage for "property damage" claimed by the owner of apples stored at the insured's atmosphere controlled storage facility after apples were damaged and deemed unfit due to freezing.

In *Acadia Ins. Co. v. Peerless Ins. Co.*, 679 F. Supp. 2d 229 (D. Mass. 2010), a contractor was storing doors in the home of the woman who hired the contractor to do renovation work. The woman, though never excluded completely from the home, moved out while the work was being completed as all her utilities were turned off. Thus, her home was effectively in the care and custody of the contractor. During this time, the windows were damaged from excessive moisture. The contractor argued that exclusion j.(4) should not preclude coverage for the doors. The court disagreed. Even though the doors were not technically in exclusive control of the contractor (since the homeowner was never officially excluded from the house), it was clear that the contractor effectively exercised exclusive possession of the doors during the time of the damage.

On the other hand, the court in *Crane Serv. & Equip. Corp. v. United States Fid. & Guar. Co.*, 496 N.E.2d 833 (Mass. App. 1986), refused to apply an exclusion for property "rented to," "used by" or in the "care, custody or control" of the insured, where a crane used by the insured was damaged. The crane owner had furnished the insured, a general contractor, with a truck crane, an oiler who drove the crane, and an operator who operated the levers to make lifts. Although operating under the insured's supervision, the crane owner's employees had retained physical control and responsibility over the crane at all times. When an accident occurred that damaged the crane, the crane owner sued the general contractor who, in turn, tendered its defense to its insurance carrier. The insurer denied coverage to the insured based on an exclusion for property "rented to," "used by" or in the "care, custody or control" of the insured. The court disagreed that the exclusion precluded coverage. The court viewed the transaction as involving a service contract as opposed to an equipment lease. Noting that courts look to who has possession and who has control of the property versus a mere reference to a contractual arrangement of a "lease" or "rental," the court concluded that the damage to the crane rented to the general contractor fell outside the scope of the exclusion.

Exclusion j.(5)

Exclusion j.(5) applies to a contractor's business risks. It is commonly referred to as the "performing operations" exclusion. Because this exclusion applies to faulty workmanship, it is often addressed in tandem with the "occurrence" issue. The "performing operations" exclusion precludes recovery for "property damage" to that particular part of real property on which you [the named insured] or any contractors or subcontractors working directly or indirectly on your behalf are performing operations, if the "property damage" arises out of those operations. There are three requirements for this exclusion to apply: 1) there must be "property damage" to a particular part of real property (as opposed to personal property), 2) the "property damage" must occur during ongoing work, and 3) the "property damage" must arise out of those operations or work.

The CGL policy form does not define "that particular part," and so there exists controversy as to the meaning of that phrase. The Wisconsin Court of Appeals in *Acuity v. Society Ins.*, 2012 WI APP 13, 810 N.W.2d 812 (2012), held that the phrase "that particular part" applies only to those parts of a building on which the defective work was performed, which is determined based on the scope of the construction agreement. *Accord, Gore Design Completions, Ltd. v. Hartford Fire Ins.*, 538 F.3d 365 (5th Cir. 2008) (where contract to install entertainment center in airplane, damage to other aspects of the plane, including loss of use, were not excluded). Other courts have held that "the particular part of the property must have been the subject of the incorrectly performed 'work' to be subject to exclusions j.(5) and j.(6). *See Mid-Continent Cas. Co. v. JHP Dev., Inc.*, 557 F3d 207 (5th Cir. 2009)(applying Texas law); *Fortney v. Weygandt, Inc. v. Am. Mfrs. Mut. Ins. Co.*, 595 F.3d 308, 311 (6th Cir. 2010)(applying Ohio law).

Irrespective of whether the exclusion is read with reference to the scope of the construction contract, courts have uniformly held that the exclusion should be applied narrowly. For example, in *Columbia Mutual Insurance Co. v. Schauf*, 967 S.W.2d 74 (Mo. 1998), the insured, a contractor, had been painting kitchen cabinets in a homeowner's house. While he was cleaning his equipment, the pump generator used for applying the paint started a fire that caused extensive damage throughout the house. Giving a narrow construction to "that particular part of real property" on which the insured was performing operations, the court held that exclusion j.(5) precluded coverage solely for damage to the cabinets but not for the damage to the remainder of the house.

The court in *Roaring Lion, LLC v. Nautilus Ins. Co.*, 2011 U.S. Dist. LEXIS 100666 (D. Mont. July 15, 2011), reached a similar conclusion. A subcontractor negligently poured a foundation, which harmed the foundation as well as the frame. The question turned on whether exclusion j (5) excluded both the damage to the foundation and the frame, or just the foundation. The court found that the exclusion only applied to the foundation as "that particular part of real property."

The insured's efforts at obtaining an overly narrow reading of exclusion j.(5), however, were not successful in *Jet Line Services Inc. v. American Employers Ins. Co.*, 404 Mass. 706, 537 N.E.2d 107 (1989). In that case, the insured was hired to clean and repair a large petroleum tank. While the insured's employees were working on the bottom of the tank, it exploded. The tank owners sued the insured, alleging that the insured negligently caused the explosion. The insured sought a defense from its insurer. The insurer denied coverage based on exclusion j.(5). The Massachusetts Supreme Court concluded that this exclusion applied to all of the damages to the tank resulting from the tank explosion even though the insured's employees were working only on the bottom of the tank when the explosion occurred.

The Supreme Court of North Dakota examined this exclusion in *Grinnell Mut. Reinsurance Co. v. Lynne*, 2004 ND 166, 686 N.W.2d 118 (2004), in a case that has become a cautionary tale for insurance practitioners. In that case, the insured, Lynne, contracted with Edward Larson to construct a new foundation for Larson's farmhouse. While the house was lifted, it fell off the support jacks and into the basement approximately three feet. Larson sued the contractor, Lynne, for the expenses incurred in connection with the removal and replacement of the house.

The court held that the claims against the contractor fell squarely within exclusion j.(5). The court held that reasonable persons could not disagree that at the time of the loss: 1) Lynne was performing operations, 2) on real property (owned by Larson), and 3) damage (to the property) arose out of those operations. Accordingly, the court determined that the damage to the house resulting from the contractor's work was not covered. Notably, the court found that the insured waived any argument that work was directed only at the basement and foundation, not to the house proper, by failing to offer any case law or other authority to support that position.

The court in *Mid-Continent Cas. Co. v. JHP Dev., Inc.*, 557 F.3d 207 (5th Cir. Tex. 2009), examined what it means to be performing "ongoing work." A contractor was hired to build five condominium units. After only one was finished, water damage occurred. The project was halted for the foreseeable future, or until the already finished unit sold. Since the work had been stopped for some time, the work was not ongoing. The court stated that rather than the time between workdays, or a specified period needed to complete the work, lack of completion alone is not enough to consider the work ongoing. Therefore the exclusion did not apply.

Exclusion j.(6)

Exclusion j.(6), commonly referred to as the "faulty workmanship" exclusion, states that the policy does not apply to "property damage" to "that particular part of any property that must be restored, repaired or replaced because 'your work' was incorrectly performed on it."

This exclusion contains an exception for "property damage" included within the products-completed operations hazard. The net result is that this exclusion is only applicable if the work is ongoing at the time the "property damage" occurs. Exclusion j.(6) does not apply if the work has been completed. Under the definition of "products-completed operations hazard," work will be deemed completed at the earliest of the following times:

a.   When all of the work called for in your contract has been completed.

b.   When all of the work to be done at the job site has been completed if your contract calls for work at more than one job site.

c.   When that part of the work done at a job site has been put to its intended use by any person or organization other than another contractor or subcontractor working on the same project.

The definition further clarifies that "[w]ork that may need service, maintenance, correction, repair or replacement, but which is otherwise complete, will be treated as completed."

Like exclusion j.(5), exclusion j.(6) is also limited to "that particular part of any property." The discussion of that issue with respect to j.(5) has equal application to j.(6).

It can be a fact intensive inquiry as to whether an insured's work was still ongoing at the time the "property damage" occurred or was discovered. The Supreme Court of Missouri in *Arnold v. Edelman*, 392 S.W.2d 231 (Mo 1965), surveyed many decisions on this issue, although it did not specifically discuss exclusion j.(6). In that case, the insured had contracted to install a revolving door. The door had been installed, but not adjusted, tested, or accepted by the owner at the time an accident occurred. The court held that the job was an incomplete operation and, therefore, did not constitute a products-completed operations hazard.

The court in *Farmington Cas. Co. v. Duggan*, 417 F.3d 1141 (10th Cir. 2005), applied the "faulty workmanship" exclusion to preclude coverage for claims against the insured for the cost of a wall that collapsed. The insured was hired to do masonry work and to clean the walls with a light acid solution. It allowed braces to the masonry walls to be removed prematurely and high winds caused the wall to collapse. The district court refused to apply exclusion j.(6) on the basis that the policy was ambiguous with respect to the term "your work" and also because the insured's work on the building was "substantially completed." The Tenth Circuit Court of Appeals reversed on both grounds. The court noted that the Colorado Court of Appeals in *McGowan v. State Farm Fire and Cas. Co.*, 100 P.3d 521, 526 (Colo. Ct. App. 2004), held that a substantially similar products-completed operations hazard provision was unambiguous and excluded coverage unless all the work called for in the contract was complete when the damage occurred. As the insured in the *Duggan* case had not yet acid washed the wall, it had not completed the work called for in its contract at the time the wall collapsed. Thus, the exclusion applied.

In *McGowan*, the McGowans contracted with Eagle Summit Construction Co., Inc. ("Eagle Summit") to build a house for them. Dissatisfied with the quality of Eagle Summit's work, the McGowans terminated them after rough framing was complete and hired another contractor to finish the project. The McGowans then sued Eagle Summit to recover the costs for completing their home per the original plans. The trial court awarded the McGowans approximately $400,000 in damages for the costs of repairs to correct construction errors and to complete the house according to contract specifications. Eagle Summit's insurer denied coverage for the judgment based on exclusion j.(6).

The Court of Appeals held that the faulty workmanship exclusion clearly applied to the McGowans' claim/judgment against Eagle Summit, as they were seeking to recover the expenditures they were required to make to repair the damage caused by Eagle Summit's faulty and incomplete work. The court held that the "products-completed operations hazard" exception to the faulty workmanship exclusion was inapplicable. By definition, that exception applies only to work that is "deemed completed." Eagle Summit was terminated after rough framing. Thus, its work was *not* completed.

In *Pekin Ins. Co. v. Willett*, 704 N.E.2d 923 (Ill.App.3d 1998), the Illinois Appellate Court applied exclusion j.(6) to preclude coverage for the costs of replacing or repairing a swimming pool. In *Pekin*, the insured was untimely in the performance of painting and maintenance work on a swimming pool. The pool owner sued the insured, alleging negligence and breach of contract. The suit sought damages for the repair of the pool, which had been "pushed out of the ground" as a result of the insured's failure to timely complete its maintenance work and fill the pool. The insurer denied coverage, relying in part on exclusion j.(6). The court agreed with the insurer's position. It reasoned that the underlying complaint alleged that the swimming pool needed to be replaced or repaired because the insured performed his work incorrectly by failing to fill the pool in a timely manner. Thus, it found that exclusion j.(6) clearly applied. It also found that exclusion j.(5) precluded coverage as the underlying complaint alleged that a part of real property, namely, the swimming pool, was damaged while the insured was working on it. *Compare, American Equity Ins. Co. v. Van Ginhoven*, 788 So.2d 388, 391 (Fla. App. 2001) (while damage claim for the pool was excluded, damages to the other property including the plumbing, electrical, deck work, and patio were not excluded, as the insured was neither performing operations on or incorrectly performing work on that other property).

The Supreme Court of Rhode Island discussed exclusion j.(6) in *Employers Mut. Cas. Co. v. Pires*, 723 A.2d 295 (1999). In *Pires*, the court was asked to decide whether the faulty workmanship exclusion should be held inapplicable because it allegedly contravened the insured's objectively reasonable expectations of coverage. Pires had a subcontract with a general contractor to paint replacement windows and doors that the general contractor had installed in a home. The general contractor later found scratches on the windowpanes, which he believed occurred when Pires sanded the frames. The general contractor later sued Pires for the damage to the panes. Pires' insurer refused to defend Pires based on an exclusion in the policy that stated that the insurance did not apply to "[t]hat particular part of any property that must be restored, repaired or replaced because 'your work' was incorrectly performed on it." The court decided that the exclusion was clear and unambiguous and stated that it would apply the exclusion unless doing so would render "illusory" the coverage provided by the policy. The court recognized that other courts not only typically enforced such provisions as written, but ordinarily found that they did not violate an insured's objectively reasonable expectations about a policy's scope of coverage. The court concluded that enforcing the exclusion in the case would not cause the general liability coverage provisions to become "illusory." The court, however, remanded the case to a lower court to determine whether Pires' work was "incorrectly performed", or whether Pires had accidentally damaged the windowpanes when he performed work on the frames. The court additionally outlined possible outcomes of the case on remand by stating that:

> If Pires performed work on the window panes in connection with painting the window frames … and he negligently damaged the

panes as part of such a preparation or cleanup operation, then the damage would fall within the exclusion for incorrectly performed work. If, on the other hand, Pires did not intentionally perform work on the window panes in connection with painting the window frames, but only damaged them accidentally when he was performing work on the frames, then such damage would not fall within the policy's exclusion for 'incorrectly performed' work on such property.

Id. at 299.

The court further noted that if Pires' work caused damage to other property in addition to the property on which he allegedly "incorrectly performed work," the exclusion would not apply to the third-party property. The court emphasized that even if Pires damaged the panes by incorrectly performing work on them, excluded damage would only be limited to the cost of repairing or replacing the damaged panes. This is a similar principle as what was decided in the *Roaring Lions* opinion.

Exclusion k.—Damage to "Your Product"

Exclusion k. reads: This insurance does not apply to:

"Property damage" to "your product" arising out of it or any part of it.

The policy provides that "your product" means:

a.   Any goods or products, other than real property, manufactured, sold, handled, distributed or disposed of by:

    (1)   You;

    (2)   Others trading under your name; or

    (3)   A person or organization whose business or assets you have acquired; and

b.   Containers (other than vehicles), materials, parts or equipment furnished in connection with such goods or products.

"Your product" includes:

a.   Warranties or representations made at any time with respect to the fitness, quality, durability, performance or use of "your product"; and

b.   The providing of or failure to provide warnings or instructions.

"Your product" does not include vending machines or other property rented to or located for the use of others but not sold.

The 1973 CGL policy provided that coverage did not apply "to property damage to the named insured's products arising out of such products or any part of such products." In 1986, the exclusion was revised to its current wording.

The "your product" exclusion precludes coverage for "property damage" arising out of a defect in an insured's product that renders the product useless or less useful. The court in *Fireguard Sprinkler Systems, Inc. v. Scottsdale Ins. Co.*, 864 F.2d 648, 654 (9th Cir. 1988), applied this exclusion to exclude coverage for the costs of upgrading a sprinkler system. The court reasoned that liability insurance should not be considered a warranty or performance bond for general contractors controlling their work. However, the exclusion is not intended to bar coverage for claims arising *from* the insured's products, but for coverage for property damage to the products themselves. For example, if the insured manufactures a stove that later malfunctions, catches on fire, and destroys itself, due to exclusion k., the insured would not be allowed to recover for damage to the stove. Conversely, if the fire spreads to the counter immediately adjacent to the stove, the damages to the counter fall outside the terms of the "your product" exclusion and would be covered.

The "your product" exclusion will not preclude coverage if the insured product was fundamentally changed into a new product prior to the loss. The alteration of the insured's product must be significant. This issue was addressed in *Liberty Mut. Fire Ins. Co. v. MI Windows & Doors, Inc.*, 2013 WL 4734045 (Fla. App. 2 Dist. Sept. 4, 2013). In that case, MI Windows manufactured windows and doors which it sold to All Seasons to install in condominiums along the coast of Alabama. In some of the buildings, All Seasons added a transom to the doors, which made the doors less structurally sound. In other buildings along the coast, All Seasons installed the doors in their original form.

Alabama was hit by Hurricane Ivan. The hurricane severely damaged the buildings in which MI Windows' doors and windows were installed. The condo association sued MI Windows. The issue raised in the declaratory judgment action was whether the doors which were altered by All Seasons still qualified as "your product", *i.e.*, MI Windows' product.

The Appellate Court determined that the "your product" exclusion applied to the doors. The court found that an alteration to the product must be so significant that it fundamentally transformed the insured's product into a completely new product. The court compared this case to *Imperial Casualty & Indem. Co. v. High Concrete Structures, Inc.*, 858 F.2d 128 (3d Cir. Pa. 1988). In *Imperial*, the insured sold sheet metal which was then stamped into individual washers. The court found that the washers were a new product. Comparatively, the *MI Windows* court found that the addition of the transom was too ordinary an addition to fundamentally turn the door into a new product.

In *Valmont Energy Steel, Inc. v. Commercial Union Ins. Co.*, 359 F.3d 770 (2004), the Fifth Circuit held that the "your product" exclusion unambiguously barred coverage for claims against the insured for damages arising out of the failure of the insured's steel flanges to meet contract specifications, and the insured's misrepresentations that such flanges were in compliance with the specifications. In that case, Valmont Energy purchased steel flanges from Continental Manufacturing for the construction of microwave towers. Before installing the flanges, Valmont tested the flanges and discovered they did not meet specifications. It sued and obtained damages from Continental for breach of contract. Continental then went bankrupt. Valmont, as a judgment creditor, sought coverage from Continental's insurers. They denied coverage on the basis that the damages sought were not for "property damage" caused by an "occurrence" and that the "your product" exclusion precluded coverage in any event.

As to the "your product" exclusion, Valmont argued that it was ambiguous when read in conjunction with the policy provisions regarding the limits of insurance for "products-completed operations." Specifically, Valmont maintained that while the "your product" exclusion appeared to preclude coverage, the "products completed operations hazard" as described in the limits of liability provision appeared to extend coverage as long as the "property damage" arose out of the insured's product and occurred off the insured's premises and not while the insured had physical possession of its product.

The Fifth Circuit disagreed. It held that there was no ambiguity because the limits of insurance provision could not be construed as a grant of coverage for "products-completed operations hazard." Rather, it only delineated the amounts that the insurer would pay for such claims. Accordingly, the limits of insurance provision did not conflict with the "your product" exclusion and the exclusion would be enforced.

Numerous other courts have applied the "your product" exclusion where the only property damage was to the insured's own product. *See, e.g., Microvote Corp. v. GRE Ins. Group*, 779 N.E2d 94 (Ind. Ct. App. 2002) (cost of malfunctioning voting machines excluded by the "your product" exclusion); *National Clothing Co. v. Hartford Cas. Ins. Co.*, 135 Wash. App. 578 (Wash. App. 2006) (the insured's cost of reimbursing Costco for the purchase price, lost profits and other costs arising from the insured's sale of counterfeit goods is excluded by the "your product" exclusion);

Hartog Rahal P'ship v. American Motorists Ins. Co., 359 F.Supp. 2d 331 (S.D.N.Y. 2005) (where insured incorporated artificially sweetened juice into a concentrate used in products that were supposed to be 100% pure juice, the cost of replacing the insured's product fell within the "your product" exclusion); *Standard Venetian Blind Co. v. Am. Empire Ins. Co.*, 469 A.2d 563 (Pa. 1983) (coverage excluded by "your product" exclusion where portico manufactured by insured collapsed and purchaser sought reimbursement for the costs of replacing the portico, repairing items stored beneath the portico and labor needed to remove the collapsed structure).

In contrast, where the insured's product causes property damage to third party property, the exclusion will not bar coverage for the third party property damage. That was the case in *Armstrong World Industries, Inc. v. Aetna Cas. & Sur. Co.*, 45 Cal.App.4th 1 (Cal. App. 1996). The insured's asbestos-containing products were installed in various buildings. After the asbestos was discovered, the building owners sued the insured for the cost of the asbestos removal and repair of the building. The court rejected the application of the "your product" exclusion to the suit brought against the insured because it held that the claims involved property damage to the buildings as a result of the insured's product, not merely damages due to the asbestos products themselves.

The definition of "your product" indicates that products do not include real property. This clarification dispels the notion that a building completed by a general contractor is the product of the general contractor, such that any defect in the building would be excluded from coverage by the "your product" exclusion. This issue was addressed in *Scottsdale Ins. Co. v. Tri-State Ins. Co. of Minnesota*, 302 F.Supp.2d 1100 (D. ND 2004). In that case the definition of "your product" included the exception for "real property." The insured, Commercial Group West ("CWG"), manufactured and erected modular buildings. Each unit was custom designed and completed floor to ceiling. Each unit was then encased in reinforced plastic and transported to a construction site for assembly on a foundation prepared by the insured. Once assembled on site, the protective covering was removed and the roof was built over the resulting structure.

CWG contracted to construct modular units and transport them to a site to be assembled to form a motel. After the modules were on site and were affixed to the foundation, a severe rainstorm caused the plastic covering on certain of the unroofed modular units to rupture and each sustained substantial damage. CWG's insurer denied coverage on the basis that the claim was excluded by the "your product" exclusion.

In the declaratory judgment action, the federal district court determined that, based on North Dakota law, the modular units were part of real property once they became affixed to the land. As the modules were attached to the foundation at the time the units sustained water damage, the modules no longer fell within the definition of "your product." Hence, the "your product" exclusion did not preclude coverage.

A similar exclusion of real property was extended to housing materials in *Auto-Owners Ins. Co. v. American Building Materials, Inc.*, 820 F.Supp.2d 1265, 1272 (M.D.Fla. 2011). In that case, the issue was whether drywall was "your product" once it was installed in a home. The court found that, under Florida law, drywall became real property once it was installed and therefore the "your product" exclusion did not apply.

Exclusion I.—Damage to "Your Work"

Exclusion l. provides:

This insurance does not apply to:

> "Property damage" to "your work" arising out of it or any part of it and included in the "products-completed operations hazard." This exclusion does not apply if the damaged work or the work out of which the damage arises was performed on your behalf by a subcontractor.

"Your work" and "products-completed operations hazard" are defined as follows:

"Your Work" means:

a.   Work or operations performed by you or on your behalf; and

b.   Materials, parts or equipment furnished in connection with such work or operations.

"Your work" includes:

a.   Warranties or representations made at any time with respect to the fitness, quality, durability, performance or use of "your work"; and

b.   The providing of or failure to provide warnings or instructions.

"Products-completed operations hazard":

a.   Includes all "bodily injury" and "property damage" occurring away from premises you own or rent and arising out of "your product" or "your work" except:

> (1)   Products that are still in your physical possession; or

    (2)   Work that has not yet been completed or abandoned. However, "your work" will be deemed completed at the earliest of the following times:

        (a)   When all of the work called for in your contract has been completed.

        (b)   When all of the work to be done at the job site has been completed if your contract calls for work at more than one job site.

        (c)   When that part of the work to be done at the job site has been put to its intended use by any person or organization other than another contractor or subcontractor working on the same project.

Work that may need service, maintenance, correction, repair or replacement, but which is otherwise complete, will be treated as completed.

b.   Does not include "bodily injury" or "property damage" arising out of:

    (1)   The transportation of property, unless the injury or damage arises out of a condition in or on a vehicle not owned or operated by you, and that condition was created by the "loading or unloading" of that vehicle by any insured;

    (2)   The existence of tools, uninstalled equipment or abandoned or unused materials; or

    (3)   Products or operations for which the classification, listed in the Declarations or in a policy schedule operations are subject to the General Aggregate Limit.

In 1973, the "your work" exclusion was much broader in scope than the current version. The exclusion in effect in 1973 barred coverage for work performed by the named insured as well as by its subcontractors. Since 1986, however, the CGL policy form specifically provides that the "your work" exclusion does not apply if the damaged work or the work out of which the damage arises was performed on the named insured's behalf by a subcontractor. Post-1986, there have been no other substantive changes to this exclusion.

The "your work" exclusion precludes coverage for "property damage" to "your work" arising out of it or any part of it. "Your work" refers exclusively to the named insured's work, materials used in conjunction therewith and warranties given by the named insured. Courts often address the "your work" exclusion in tandem with the "occurrence" issue in addressing whether "property damage" resulting from faulty workmanship is covered. As discussed in the "occurrence" section, the subcontractor exception set forth in exclusion l. is frequently cited as a significant factor in the court's analysis of whether faulty workmanship can constitute an "occurrence."

The "your work" exclusion requires that the "property damage" be included in the "products-completed operations hazard." In other words, the named insured's work must be completed or this exclusion is not applicable. If the named insured becomes liable for "property damage" to its work before operations are completed, one or more subparts to exclusion j. may apply to the claim. For example, if the insured's faulty electrical work causes the building to burn before completion, paragraphs (5) and (6) of exclusion j. would bar coverage for the faulty electrical work. The justification for requiring a completed operation before exclusion l. is applied involves the notion that while the insured is performing its work, the insured can control the quality of the work done in order to prevent damage. *See*, 2 Allan D. Windt, Insurance Claims & Disputes: Representation of Insurance Companies and Insureds, §11.10 (6th ed. 2008 and Supp. 2014). Exclusion l. is aimed at forcing the insured to internalize the costs of unsatisfactory operations.

The Texas Supreme Court addressed exclusion l. in *Pine Oak Builders, Inc. v. Great American Lloyds Ins. Co.*, 279 S.W.3d 650 (Tex. 2009) in the context of a duty to defend. Pine Oak was a home builder. In one of four suits that had been filed against Pine Oak, the petition sought recovery for damage due to improper design and construction of columns and a balcony. The petition contained claims for breach of contract and warranty, violation of the Residential Construction Liability Act, and negligence based on Pine Oak's alleged failure to perform its work in a good and workmanlike manner and failure to make requested repairs. There were no allegations of defective work by a subcontractor. There were also no allegations of property damage to property other than that upon which Pine Oak had worked. The court, refusing to consider extrinsic evidence, held that the claims fell within the "your work" exclusion. Accordingly, it found that the insurer owed no duty to defend Pine Oak.

The "your work" exclusion only negates coverage if the only property damaged is that upon which the named insured worked. If some other property is damaged, the exclusion will not preclude coverage for that third party's property damage. Thus if a claim involves damages for both the named insured's repair or replacement of faulty workmanship *and* physical injury caused by the insured's work to another's property, coverage will exist for the latter damages, but not for the former.

The subcontractor exception was addressed by the court in *Architex Ass'n v. Scottsdale Ins. Co.*, 27 So. 3d 1148 (Miss. 2010). A real estate company contracted with the general contractor, Architex, to build a hotel. Architex contracted with subcontractors to work on the construction. The real estate company had an issue with the structure of the hotel's foundation. The real estate company sued Architex based on the faulty workmanship of one of Architex's subcontractors. Architex then turned to its insurer for coverage. Its insurer denied coverage relying on the "your work" exclusion. The Supreme Court of Mississippi determined that the faulty work of the subcontractor was an unexpected occurrence which triggered coverage. The court concluded that while there would be no coverage under the policy for work performed by Architex itself, any of the alleged defective work that had been performed by subcontractors would not fall within the terms of the exclusion.

The court in *Pulte Home Corp. v. Fidelity & Guar. Ins. Co.*, 2004 WL 516216 (Va. Cir. Ct. Feb. 6, 2004), addressed the "your work" exclusion in the context of an additional insured's claim for coverage. In that case, Pulte Home Corp. ("Pulte"), a large homebuilder, was sued in numerous lawsuits along with the subcontractor it retained to install allegedly defective Exterior Insulation Finish Systems ("EIFS"). Pulte qualified as an additional insured under the insurance policy issued to its subcontractor. It sought reimbursement of its defense costs and settlement sums from the subcontractor's insurers. They denied coverage for that portion of the damages allocated to the repair and replacement of the EIFS on the basis that: 1) there is no indemnity coverage for repair or replacement of the named insured's own work under the "your work" exclusion, and 2) defective workmanship is not an "occurrence" under the terms of the contract.

The court found the "your work" exclusion to be unambiguous. It held that the exclusion clearly excluded indemnity for repair or replacement of "your work" by the named insured. The court held that the exclusion extended to Pulte as the additional insured under its subcontractor's policy since the subcontractor was the entity that did the work. Thus, the "property damage" was to the named insured's work. In addition, the court agreed that defective workmanship was not an "occurrence."

Interestingly, while the "your work" exclusion precluded coverage for damages allocated to the EIFS installation under the subcontractor's policy, such damages would not have been precluded by the "your work" exclusion in Pulte's own policy. That is because the subcontractor actually performed the work. As mentioned previously, the "your work" exclusion is not applicable to work performed on behalf of the named insured by a subcontractor.

One issue that might arise in the construction of the "your work" exclusion is whether an entity qualifies as a "subcontractor" for the purposes of the subcontractor exclusion. In *Wanzek Constr., Inc. v. Emplrs. Ins.*, 679 N.W.2d 322 (Minn. 2004), a general contractor used a specific manufacturer to provide coping stones for the construction of a public pool. The stones cracked and caused injury to patrons of the pool. The insurer refused to cover the repairs to the pool for the general contractor citing the "your work" exclusion. The general contractor argued that the stone manufacturer was not a subcontractor, and therefore, the "your work" exclusion did not bar coverage. The district court agreed, finding that a subcontractor is one who installs the product, not one who merely provides it. The Minnesota Supreme Court let the policy language decide. It found the policy language to be ambiguous. The court held that the stone manufacturer was a subcontractor for purposes of the policy as the contract between the stone manufacturer and the general contractor required the stone manufacturer to furnish and pay for all supervision, labor, and materials necessary or required to fully prepare, design, fabricate, treat and deliver the coping stones. As such, the stone manufacturer performed work as a subcontractor, thereby implicating the exception to the "your work" exclusion. Accordingly, the insurer could not rely on the "your work" exclusion to preclude coverage.

Exclusion m.—Damage to Impaired Property or Property Not Physically Injured

Exclusion m. states:

This insurance does not apply to:

"Property damage" to "impaired property" or property that has not been physically injured, arising out of:

(1)   A defect, deficiency, inadequacy, or dangerous condition in "your product" or "your work"; or

(2)   A delay or failure by you or anyone acting on your behalf to perform a contract or agreement in accordance with its terms.

This exclusion does not apply to the loss of use of other property arising out of sudden and accidental physical injury to "your product" or "your work" after it has been put to its intended use.

The policy definitions of "your product" and "your work" were provided earlier in this section, in connection with exclusion k. and exclusion l., respectively. As introduced in 1986, the term "impaired property" is defined as follows:

"Impaired Property" means tangible property, other than "your product" or "your work", that cannot be used or is less useful because:

1.   It incorporates "your product" or "your work" that is known or thought to be defective, deficient, inadequate or dangerous; or

2.   You have failed to fulfill the terms of a contract or agreement; if such property can be restored to use by:

   a.   The repair, replacement, adjustment, or removal of "your product" or "your work"; or

   b.   Your fulfilling the terms of the contract or agreement.

The "impaired property" exclusion was first included in CGL policies in 1966 and was later refined in 1973, 1986, and 1990. The 1973 version of the exclusion applied only to the *loss of use* of tangible property not physically injured, while the current version applies to property damage to "impaired property" *or* to property that has not been physically injured.

The court in *Hamlin Inc. v. Hartford Accident & Indem. Co.*, 86 F.3d 93 (7th Cir. 1996), provided an explanation of "impaired property." In that case, the insured manufactured liquid crystal displays ("LCDs") that were incorporated into agricultural machinery. Defects in the LCDs caused the instrument panels on the machinery to work improperly. The court analogized the defect in the LCDs to a malfunctioning clock in an automobile and stated that while such a malfunction would impair the performance of the automobile, it does not physically injure the automobile.

The court in *Pinkerton & Laws, Inc. v. Royal Ins. Co. of America*, 227 F.Supp.2d 1348, 1354 (N.D. Ga. 2004), provided a succinct statement about the purpose and requirements of exclusion m.:

> This exclusion is commonly called the "impaired property" exclusion and is included in a policy to prevent the insured from claiming economic losses resulting from the insured's work or work product. Florida courts have outlined three rules regarding the applicability of exclusions such as exclusion m. The first rule is that if the complaint fails to allege injury to other property, and merely alleges economic loss resulting from injury to the product itself, the exclusion applies, thus precluding coverage. The second rule is that if the complaint alleges or otherwise establishes damage to other property, the exclusion will not apply. The third rule is that the exclusion does not apply to situations arising from a sudden and accidental injury to the product, which results in economic loss.

The first rule articulated in the *Pinkerton* decision is exemplified by *Transcontinental Ins. Co. v. Ice Systems of America*, 847 F. Supp. 947 (M.D. Fla. 1994). In that case, the Tampa Bay National Hockey Group contracted with Ice Systems to set up a portable rink suitable for ice hockey.

The Hockey Group scheduled an exhibition game for its team to be played in the rink, but the ice on the rink never froze properly. The game had to be cancelled, and the Hockey Group sued Ice Systems for recovery of damages in the form of lost business. Ice Systems tendered its defense to its CGL insurer. The insurer denied coverage based on exclusion m. The insured argued that the loss fell within the exception to exclusion m. The court rejected the insured's argument, noting that the exception to exclusion m was not applicable because there was no sudden and accidental injury to property alleged in the complaint. Rather, only purely economic damages were alleged in the complaint for which no coverage was available.

The impaired property exclusion has been applied in other circumstances, as well. For example, in *Sokol & Co. v. Atlantic Mut. Ins. Co.*, 430 F.3d 417, 423 (7th Cir. 2005), the Seventh Circuit held that the "impaired property" exclusion applied where the insured's spoiled peanut butter - encapsulated in its own self-contained packet - was included in a cookie mix, and where the cookie mix could be restored to use by simply removing the insured's product. Thus, the costs associated with the replacement of the spoiled peanut butter was excluded. In *H.E. Davis & Sons, Inc. v. N. Pac. Ins. Co.*, 248 F. Supp. 2d 1079 (D. Utah 2002), the court applied the exclusion to bar coverage for the costs of repairing and re-doing the insured's faulty soil compaction on a construction project for a school district. The school district had to remove and replace concrete footings as a result of the insured's inadequate soil compaction. The court found that, although the concrete footings had to be removed in order to repair the soil compaction problem, the footings themselves were not damaged. Accordingly, it held that the impaired property exclusion barred coverage.

In contrast, where the insured's product is inextricably intertwined with or incorporated into a finished product, such that it is impossible to remove the component from the whole, the impaired property exclusion does not apply. That was the case in *Shade Foods, Inc. v. Innovative Products Sales and Marketing, Inc.*, 78 Cal. App. 4th 847, 93 Cal. Rptr. 2d 364 (2000), where the insured supplied almonds for General Mills' use in cereal. General Mills discovered wood splinters after the almonds had been incorporated into nut clusters, which were composed of congealed syrup and diced nuts. The nut clusters could not be restored to use by removal of the wood splinters. Thus, the impaired property exclusion was not applicable.

The same was true in *Harleysville Worcester Ins. Co. v. Paramount Concrete, Inc.*, 2014 U.S. Dist. LEXIS 43889 (D. Conn. Mar. 31, 2014). In that case, the insured made liquid shotcrete which was applied to concrete in pools. The shotcrete was impure, and its inconsistencies caused the concrete in the pool to not harden correctly, which caused leaks. The court found that the liquid concrete could not be removed from the completed pools as it hardened and became an integral part of the pool walls. Moreover, removal of the faulty concrete portions did not fix the pools and, therefore, the pools could not be considered impaired property.

By its terms, the impaired property exclusion does not apply where there has been physical injury to tangible property. For example, in *Potomac Ins. v. Huang*, 2002 WL 418008 (D. Kan. Mar. 1, 2002), the insured was a window distributor that sold windows to a general contractor to be installed in a home. After the windows leaked and damaged the home, the insured repaired and re-caulked a number of the windows. However, they continued to leak. The court held that the impaired property exclusion was not applicable because the home did not qualify as "impaired property." Specifically, the home could not be restored to its prior condition simply by repairing the windows, as the interior of the home had also sustained physical damage.

Citing the business risk doctrine, the Appeals Court of Massachusetts applied the impaired property exclusion to a claim against a painting contractor for contamination of the inside of a house by lead-based paint chips, which occurred when the contractor was hired to scrape old paint off the house. The owners of the house sued the contractor for recovery of costs incurred in hiring a clean-up company, vacating the premises, and conducting tests to check lead levels in family members. The court in *Dorchester Mut. Fire. Ins. Co. v. First Kostas Corp., Inc.*, 731 N.E.2d 569 (2000), found that the contamination of the inside of the house was a "normal, foreseeable, and expected" business risk in the paint trade that general liability coverage is not designed to cover. In support, it cited the impaired property exclusion as well as the overall purposes of the business risk exclusions.

Exclusion n.—Recall of Products, Work or Impaired Property

Exclusion n. provides:

This insurance does not apply to:

Damages claimed for any loss, cost or expense incurred by you or others for the loss of use, withdrawal, recall, inspection, repair, replacement, adjustment, removal or disposal of:

(1)   "Your product";

(2)   "Your work"; or

(3)   "Impaired property";

> if such product, work or property is withdrawn or recalled from the market or from use by any person or organization because of a known or suspected defect, deficiency, inadequacy or dangerous condition in it.

This exclusion was added to the CGL policy in 1966 and was commonly referred to as the "sistership" exclusion. The exclusion derives its name from an occurrence in the aircraft industry where one plane crashed and its "sister ships" were thereafter grounded and recalled by the manufacturer in order to correct the common defect that had caused the crash. [*See, Arcos Corp. v. American Mutual Liability Ins. Co.*, 350 F.Supp. 380, 384 n.2 (E.D.Pa.1972), *affirmed* 485 F.2d 678 (3rd Cir. 1973).] In 1973, the policy excluded costs to withdraw the insured's products from the market. The 1986 exclusion followed the 1973 version with two amendments intended to strengthen the purpose of the exclusion. One provision expanded the exclusion to exclude not only the costs of the named insured but also those of other parties who were involved in the recall of final work or product. Another provision expanded the exclusion to encompass not only damages claimed for costs due to recall of the named insured's product or work, but also of "impaired property." Since 1986, there have been no further substantive revisions made to this exclusion.

Generally, the "sistership exclusion" applies in cases where because of the actual failure of the insured's product, similar or "sister" products that have not yet failed are withdrawn from use because they are suspected of containing the same defect. *United States Fid. and Guar. Co. v. Wilkin Insulation Co.*, 144 Ill.2d 64, 578 N.E.2d 926, 934 (1991). It does not apply to the product that has already failed while in use and caused damage to the property of a third party. *Id. Armstrong World Indus. v. Aetna Cas. & Sur. Co.*, 45 Cal.App.4th 1, 113, 52 Cal.Rptr.2d 690 (Cal.Ct.App.1996) ("the sistership exclusion operates to exclude coverage for the cost of 'preventative or curative action' when the insured withdraws a product in situations in which a danger is merely apprehended; it does not operate to exclude coverage for actual damage caused by the very product giving rise to such an apprehension.")

The "recall exclusion" as it is currently drafted does not merely exclude sister products that have not yet failed, but it also excludes the costs of recalling "impaired property." In that instance, the product has already failed but because it can be removed without causing property damage to third-party property, it is considered "impaired property." Thus, exclusion n. is more properly referred to as the "recall exclusion" because it is not limited to the recall of products that have not yet failed.

"Impaired property" was the property at issue in *Sokol and Co. v. Atlantic Mut. Ins. Co.*, 430 F.3d 417 (7th Cir. 2005). In that case, the insured sold peanut butter packets to its customer for inclusion in boxes of cookie mix. The customer discovered that the peanut butter had gone rancid and retrieved the cookie mix, substituted fresh peanut butter packets and demanded reimbursement from the insured of its costs associated with the replacement. The insured sought coverage under its CGL policy for that claim. The insurer denied coverage based on exclusion n., among other policy defenses. The court determined that the peanut butter packets qualified as "impaired property" since the cookie mix could be restored to use by the replacement of that product. It found that the recall exclusion squarely applied to the replacement costs at issue as the recall exclusion applied to the costs of or expense incurred by the named insured or others for the withdrawal and replacement of "impaired property." The court further found that the recall or replacement was because the peanut butter was rancid, which constituted a known or suspected "inadequacy." *Id.* at 424.

The court in *Bright Wood Corporation v. Bankers Standard Ins. Co*, 665 N.W.2d 544 (Minn. Ct. App. 2003), addressed the "recall" exclusion in a factual context that demonstrates the magnitude of the damages that can be at issue for this excluded risk. The insured in that case was Bright Wood, a manufacturer of wood sash components for windows. In 1996, Scherer entered into a contract with Bright Wood to supply the wood components that surround the glass in a window sash. Scherer specified that the wood sash components had to be treated with a wood preservative to prevent rot. From October 1996 to November 1997, Bright Wood failed to treat the sash components sold to Scherer. Unaware of the problem, Scherer continued to use both treated and untreated components, installing them in between 50,000 and 90,000 sash units.

In late 1997, Scherer began to receive service requests for windows with problems with discoloration. After it received additional complaints of deteriorating or rotting windows, Scherer embarked on a repair program. Initially, it responded to complaints and replaced visibly defective parts during field visits. It found that it could not reliably determine which sash units would rot, and began on-site replacement of *all* wood sash components manufactured in 1996 and 1997. During these repairs, the windows showed no other damage or deterioration except to the Bright Wood components. However, in order to replace the wood sash components, Scherer technicians necessarily had to remove weather stripping, hardware, and aluminum cladding. The windows also had to be refinished. As the scope of the problem grew, Scherer decided it was more efficient to replace the entire window with a newly manufactured window; although material costs were somewhat higher, labor costs were lower. This again meant that window finishes had to be redone to match. In all the inspections and replacements, no defect or damage was noted in any part of the windows except to the wood sash components provided by Bright Wood. The only damage to non-Bright Wood components occurred during the repair process.

Scherer sued Bright Wood for breach of contract and warranties. Bright Wood settled the claims for $8.2 million, and then filed suit against its insurers who had denied coverage based on the "your product" and "sistership/recall" exclusions. Bright Wood argued that because the repair and replacement process damaged non-Bright Wood components, neither exclusion applied.

Preliminarily, the court observed that the damage at issue was based solely on Bright Wood's defective product. The incidental damage to the finish, hardware, and weather-stripping was incurred *only in order to make repairs*. As those repairs were deliberately undertaken, the resulting damage to other property was not caused by an accident or occurrence.

The court then turned to the sistership/recall exclusion. The court stated:

> "The theory of the sistership exclusion, which excludes coverage when a product is withdrawn, recalled, or replaced because of a known or suspected defect discovered in a similar product, is that the insurer should not be saddled with the cost of preventing such defects or failure any more than it was intended that the insurer would pay the cost of avoiding the defect in the first place or preventing the first failure of the product to have been discovered to be in a defective or dangerous condition before the occurrence."

Atlantic Mut. Ins. Co. v. Judd Co., 380 N.W.2d 122, 124-25 (Minn. 1986) (quoting 2 R. Long, *Law of Liability Insurance* §11.11 (1983)).

The court noted that to qualify under the recall exclusion, the repair or replacement process must include more than the product that has already failed. There is no withdrawal or recall where no attempt is made to prevent future failures. The court held that because Scherer could not identify which wood components would fail, it had to replace all components that could be defective, thus the damages incurred for withdrawing all of the windows fit squarely within the sistership exclusion.

Bright Wood then argued that the sistership/recall exclusion should not apply, because the definition of "impaired property" requires that: 1) the property incorporating the insured's defective product can be restored to use by simply removing the insured's defective product, and 2) "other property" must be essentially undamaged, except for the inclusion of the insured's defective product. The court determined that the windows qualified as impaired property. The court reasoned that the Scherer windows were defective only because they contained Bright Wood's defective product; removal and replacement of Bright Wood's components restored the windows to use. Scherer's business decision to replace its windows with brand-new units in order to lower its labor costs did not change this result.

As the *Bright Wood* decision underscores, the recall exclusion precludes coverage for the damages, costs, or expenses associated with the recall, withdrawal, or repair of sister products that have not yet failed, but are suspected of containing the same defect as a similar failed product, as well as "impaired property." Numerous courts have applied this exclusion to preclude recovery of such recall expenses. *See, e.g., Atlantic Mut. Ins. Co. v. Hillside Bottling Co., Inc.*, 903 A. 2d 513, 387 N. J. Super. 224 (2006) (this exclusion precludes coverage for the cost of a general recall—including recalling apparently undamaged products to search for damaged components otherwise not yet discovered); *Keystone Filler & Mfg. Co. v. Am. Mining Ins. Co.*, 179 F.Supp.2d 432, 439 (M.D. Penn. 2002) ("this exclusion is called the 'sistership exclusion' because it applies where products are recalled because of known defects in their sister products").

Unlike the risks excluded under most of the business risk exclusions, "recall coverage" can be purchased by an insured, as a supplemental coverage. A separate premium is charged for such coverage. Recall coverage, however, is typically subject to a sublimit and may not provide complete funding for the costs or recalling of replacing potentially defective or actually defective products.

Conclusion

In theory, whether damages are sought for "property damage" caused by an "occurrence" in the first instance, as well as whether the loss is precluded by the business risk exclusions should be a matter of interpreting the language of the insurance contract. However, many courts have struggled with interpreting the "property damage" liability coverage of the CGL policy. They have grappled with claims of ambiguity, the "reasonable expectations of the insured" and the concepts underlying the "business risk doctrine." The result has been conflicting case law on whether and when coverage might apply for damages resulting from the insured's faulty work or product.

Section II

Additional Insureds and Contractual Liability

By: Carol P. Keough, Esq.

Risk Shifting–A Critical Part of Commercial Business

Risk shifting continues to be a major issue in risk management for both large and small commercial companies. Policyholders demand broad additional insured coverage and contractual liability coverage in their Commercial General Liability ("CGL") policies. Broad coverage in the CGL policies opens the door for named insured companies to engage in a wide range of complex commercial business contracts. Without the support of additional insured and contractual liability coverage, the policyholder's ability to bid against its competitors and win certain jobs may be lost.

Faced with these demands for broad based coverage for additional insured and for contractual liability, insurance companies have tried to define the CGL insurance company's duties and obligations to additional insureds by the use of certain additional insured and contractual liability limitations endorsements. Further, to meet the demand for primary and noncontributory coverage as part of this risk shifting, new endorsements have been created. All of these endorsements which are crafted to define the risks of the insurance company, policyholder, and additional insured are the source of complex insurance litigation.

A continuing dilemma for policyholders and their agents or brokers is the impact of these coverage extensions to additional insureds and to indemnitees. The policyholder's contractual obligations may assume liability for a property owner, a general contractor, and certain other subcontractors as additional insureds and contractual indemnitees. Another critical area in additional insured coverage involves drilling and offshore coverage for major oil companies by the drilling contractors. A policyholder may not realize that he is putting his own limits of coverage at risk by granting this additional insured status and agreeing to contractual indemnity in the contracts. Conversely, he may agree to contractual terms that are not covered by his insurance policies and unknowingly self-insure these risks. Therefore, a critical part of business decisions involving contractual agreements are the ramifications of insurance.

Regulations for certificates of insurance in a majority of states have altered the risk shifting scheme by preventing misinformation through the use of certificates of insurance. Many contracts have insurance requirements that cannot be met by policies the insurers are willing to provide. To prevent fraud or misinformation, new requirements for certificates of insurance range from the requirement of only approved standard forms to strict guidelines requiring the filing of any nonstandard form with the insurance regulatory authority for approval before the form may be used.

In response to business necessities, contractual liability coverage is included within standard Insurance Services Office (ISO) commercial general liability forms, and a number of standardized additional insured endorsements are available; companies that draft their own forms, called manuscripts, also provide the coverage. So, policyholders and their agents or brokers are faced with a garden-variety of forms that include some early forms from 1973, manuscript forms, and revised forms from 2004. ISO also revised the additional insured endorsements in 2013 to align more closely with the coverage required by the contract terms. This may leave gaps in coverage for a named insured when the policy limits and the contract terms do not align.

The Scope of Additional Insured Endorsements

Insurance companies do a careful analysis of the risk that is being assumed under a CGL policy before offering coverage to a prospective policyholder. However, after a policy is issued, the policyholder may engage in commercial business transactions with any party pursuant to a written contract that expands the risk assessment for that insurance company due to additional insureds. Additional insured endorsements may open the door of insurance coverage to high risk ventures, questionable companies, or even municipalities, all of which may have poor safety records, a long list of recent accidents, or numerous pending lawsuits related to their job sites. Broad based additional insured endorsements continue to extend coverage as additional insureds to these businesses, which may not have been approved for coverage on their own with that insurance company.

The origin of the broad based additional insured endorsements that are used is unclear. The general liability endorsement number, which still is seen on current policies, may have originated with the CGL forms commonly used beginning in 1973. Some insurance carriers have created a manuscript endorsement to complement their proprietary general liability policies. For example, surplus lines carriers that operate in some states are not required to use the same standard or approved forms as carriers registered with the department of insurance. In addition, some carriers simply have replaced the schedule of specifically identified additional insured names with the words *"blanket"* or *"as required by written contract."* Both of these terms make the identity of a specific person or entity impossible to determine when the policy is issued. There are many variations of the additional insured endorsements, but the problems and litigation appear to stem from the *"arising out of"* language that has become standard wording as well as the conflict between what the contract promises to the additional insured and what the policy provides.

Insurance companies have attempted to limit this risk by adding terms to these additional insured endorsements which limit the time of the risk to *"ongoing operations"* or *"completed operations."* Further, some insurance companies have specifically stated in the endorsement that the insurance company is not assuming liability for the additional insured's sole negligence. Additional insured endorsements have attempted to limit the liability for the additional insured by adding the phrase *"caused by the policyholder's acts or omissions."* In 2004, ISO modified these broad-based endorsements with the language *"caused in whole or in part by the named insured."* Further, new endorsements created by ISO in 2013 have substantively changed the scope of additional insured coverage to more closely align with the terms and provisions of the contract which requires coverage. Another significant limitation added in the 2013 ISO endorsements is the statement *"only to the extent permitted by law."* The meaning of these additional insured limitations or exclusions may not yet have been definitively tested by the courts. Therefore, questions remain as to the scope of insurance being provided to the additional insureds since the use of some older forms may continue to be found in some jurisdictions as well as the addition of new 2013 forms.

Contractual Risk-Shifting Common

Construction and other commercial contracts continue to contain risk-shifting provisions with a scope broad enough to protect owners, subcontractors, general contractors, subsidiaries, and even, to some extent, entire cities and towns as additional insureds. Even though the policyholder's background, accident record, and work experience have been carefully examined to determine whether the risks fall within an acceptable range for the insurance company, the additional insured endorsement may greatly expand that risk—to an unknown "who" performing an unknown scope of work in an unknown location.

The additional insured endorsement affects not only the insurance company who writes the risk and the underwriters who determine the scope of the risk. It also impacts the agents of the policyholder who are attempting to make sure that the policyholder has adequate coverage to protect his business in the event of any serious bodily injury or property damage claims. $1 million in primary coverage and $2 million in umbrella coverage may be adequate to protect a policyholder in business as a plumber. However, when that same plumber is performing subcontract work at ten different industrial sites—including chemical plants, refineries, and for cities—and every one of the owners, general contractors, and other subcontractors of the entities are given additional insured status to comply with the contracts, those minimal insurance limits may not provide sufficient protection. The policyholder may have exposed itself to liability in excess of its policy limits. In addition, a policyholder may have inadequate protection to cover both itself and the additional insured for the same occurrence. Therefore, insurance companies, underwriters, agents, and brokers need to be aware of the issues and ramifications that stem from the use of additional insured endorsements since they affect both the scope of coverage and the policyholder's coverage availability.

Typical Additional Insured Endorsements

In an attempt to restrict the broad coverage afforded to numerous unknown entities, insurance companies have created additional insured endorsements with other limiting provisions, including a specific location, additional insured only as provided by written contract, and only for "your work" for that additional insured.

In earlier forms in 1985, additional insured coverage was provided for all operations–while the work was in progress, and when the work was completed. In 2001 the forms used required a separate endorsement for ongoing operations and completed operations. This trend has continued as additional insured endorsements have been modified throughout the years.

In 2004, ISO modified the coverage provided by the "arising out of" language in its CG 20 10 07 04 and CG 20 37 07 04 forms to liability at least caused in whole or in part by the named insured. These modifications are made to the "Who Is An Insured" provision of a CGL policy. If one of these forms is used to provide additional insured coverage, there will be no coverage for the sole negligence of the additional insured.

Some of the policies provide slightly different language in the additional insured endorsement which reads: "Who Is an Insured is amended to include as an insured the person or organization shown in the schedule, but only with respect to liability arising out of 'your work' for the insured or for you." The policy defines "your work" generally as "work or operations" performed by you or on your behalf.

The term "your work" is also found in the ISO form CG 20 37 07 04. The 20 37 form amends the "Who Is An Insured" provision and includes as an insured:

> the identified persons or organizations, "but only with respect to liability for 'bodily injury' or 'property damage' caused in whole or in part, by your work at the location designated and described in the schedule of [the additional insured endorsement] performed for that additional insured in the 'products completed operations hazard.'"

Insurance companies have relied on restrictions in the additional insured endorsements which may attempt to limit liability to vicarious liability and exclude the sole negligence of the additional insured. Such a provision may read:

> Who Is An Insured (Section II) is amended to include as an insured [additional insured], but only with respect to liability arising out of [Named Insured's] ongoing operations, but in no event for [additional insured's] sole negligence.

In ISO form CG 20 10 07 04 created in 2004, the form itself further limits when additional insured coverage may be provided by amending the "Who Is An Insured" provision of the policy to only include as an insured:

> the identified persons or organizations, "but only with respect to liability for 'bodily injury', 'property damage' or 'personal injury' caused, in whole or in part, by: 1) Your acts or omissions, or 2) The acts or omissions of those acting on your behalf; in the performance of your ongoing operations for the additional insured(s) at the locations designated in the endorsement."

Further restrictions placed in the additional insured endorsements include a time limit of "ongoing operations." To ensure complete coverage for the additional insured and to protect the named insured, the policy must contain an endorsement for both ongoing operations and completed operations. Therefore, if ISO forms from 2004 are being used the endorsements should include CG 20 10 07 04 for ongoing operations and CG 20 37 07 04 for completed operations.

Another exclusion placed in the additional insured endorsements excludes coverage for bodily injury or property damage arising out of any act of omission of the additional insured(s) or any of their employees, but allows an exception to that exclusion for the general supervisor or work performed for the additional insured(s) by the named insured.

An ISO form even offers additional insured status for owners, lessees, or contractors on an automatic basis when required in construction agreements with the policyholder through ISO form CG 20 33. However, the automatic feature specifically excludes coverage for professional liability.

In 2013, ISO made substantive changes to the additional insured endorsements. These changes were made to include limitations in states where the state had enacted an anti-indemnity statute. Also the new forms narrow the scope of coverage to what was required by the contract or agreement. Moreover, the policy limits are restricted to what the contract calls for or the applicable limits found in the declarations, whichever is less.

Some of the most significant language in the 2013 provisions is as follows:

> If coverage provided to the additional insured is required by a contract or agreement, the insurance afforded to such additional insured will not be broader than that which you are required by the contract or agreement to provide for such additional insured.

> The insurance provided to such additional insured only applies to the extent permitted by law.

> If coverage to the additional insured is required by a contract or agreement, the most (the insurer) will pay on behalf of the additional insured is the amount of insurance: 1) required by the contract or agreement; or 2) available under the applicable limits of insurance shown in the Declarations, whichever is less. This endorsement shall not increase the applicable limits of insurance shown in the Declarations.

The new 2013 modifications could leave an insured with a gap in insurance coverage if the contract requires a $1 million coverage limit, the policy provides a $2 million coverage limit and the property damage is for $2 million. Instead of paying the full $2 million in damages, the coverage under the endorsement would be limited to whichever is less or to only $1 million; thereby leaving the named insured on the hook for the difference. This places both the language of the contract and the endorsement in play when a determination is being made as to whether a named insured has adequate coverage.

The policyholder commonly is required to agree to risk-shifting provisions in a commercial contract. Additional insured status for the owner or general contractor also is often required from companies that want to bid on construction projects or enter into other commercial contracts as a regular part of their business. For example, a company that contracts to do all the pipe-fitting work in the construction of a chemical plant may be required to provide additional insured status to the general contractor, the owner of the plant, and possibly any number of other subcontractors also working on the job depending on the laws of that state and the type of commercial contract at issue.

Difference between Additional Insured and Contractual Liability Coverage

There is a critical difference between *additional insured* status and *contractual liability coverage* as provided by a CGL policy. An additional insured on the policy has all of the same rights under the policy as the policyholder. This includes both defense and indemnity payments for claims of bodily injury or property damage that may be covered by the policy.

Contractual liability, which is discussed in more detail subsequently, may specifically preclude coverage for the *sole negligence* of the general contractor or may not include liability for a particular category of worker— such as other subcontractors that are hired by the general contractor. Further, contractual liability may limit the potential recovery of defense costs. The terms and conditions of the contract itself may further limit the liability of the policyholder to a certain dollar amount below the actual limits of the policyholder's policy.

Broad based additional insured endorsements may open the door for full coverage under the policy, but only if the accident falls within the parameters of the additional insured endorsement. The sole negligence of the additional insured owner or general contractor must be restricted by the endorsement or specifically excluded to be effective. Only the clear and specific language of the additional insured endorsement itself, coupled with the specific coverage limitations set forth in the terms of the CGL policy, can control and limit the coverage provided to an additional insured. The specific language of additional insured endorsements has been the subject of litigation when the insurance company wants to limit coverage, but the additional insured believes it is entitled to full coverage for both defense and indemnity. Recent litigation focuses on the scope of coverage available to an additional insured when interpreting both the grant of coverage to additional insureds and exclusions or restrictions found in the additional insured endorsements.

In some instances, exclusions which apply to "you", the named insured(s), do not apply to an "insured", giving the additional insured even broader coverage than the named insured. For example, the property damage exclusions of a CGL policy refer to "you" or "your", a term defined in the CGL policy as applying to the "named insured(s)". An analysis of coverage depending on the accident may require a review of the entire policy to determine what is meant by the additional insured endorsement and how much coverage to which an additional insured is entitled.

Courts Broadly Interpret "Arising out of" Wording

Originally, it was thought that additional insured liability was restricted because of the commonly used language, "but only with respect to liability arising out of the policyholder's operations" and/or "liability arising out of 'your work' for the insured or for you" found in additional insured endorsements. The phrase "arising out of" has generally been interpreted to mean "directly from" by insurance carriers.

For example, three employees of a subcontractor are welding sheet metal on the property of the owner of a natural-gas-pipeline plant. Unknown to these employees, certain areas of the plant are being cleared of residue pockets of gas by an employee of the plant's owner. An explosion that is caused by the work being done by the plant employee severely injures the subcontractor's (policyholder's) employees. The employees sue the plant's owner, who claims that he is entitled to defense and indemnity from the subcontractor through the additional insured endorsement attached to the subcontractor's CGL policy. The subcontractor's insurance company determines there is no coverage under the policy because the accident resulted from the *sole negligence of the contractor* and did not arise out of or come directly from the work of the subcontractor.

This type of situation is seen in *Granite Construction Co. v. Bituminous Ins. Co.*, 832 S.W.2d 427 (Tex. Civ. App. 1992, no writ), in which the court determined the additional insured endorsement excluded coverage for the additional insured's own negligence. Granite had contracted with Brown Company to haul asphalt from its construction site. One of Brown's employees was injured while the Granite employees loaded the asphalt onto Brown's truck. The court concluded that, because the loading of the granite was the sole responsibility of Granite and not Brown, the additional insured endorsement with the arising out of language did not provide coverage for Granite under Brown's policy for the accident in question.

Likewise, in *Davis v. LTV Steel Co.*, 716 N.E.2d 766 (Ohio App. 1998), the court reasoned that "the express language of the policy did not afford coverage to LTV for its own negligence." As a result, the court ruled that LTV was not entitled to coverage under the additional insured endorsement contained in the subcontractor's policy.

However, the majority of courts nationwide, including the Texas courts, have given the *"arising out of"* language a much broader interpretation. The courts have expanded coverage beyond simple vicarious liability of the additional insureds for the policyholder's work. The Third Circuit under Pennsylvania law, in *Aetna Casualty and Surety Co. v. Ocean Accident Guaranty Corp.*, 386 F.2d 413(3rd Cir. 1967), stated "arising out of" is very "broad and vague". The court said "it means connected with and not proximately caused by." Generally stated, this broader interpretation is that when the worker's injury occurs while he is on the premises to do the work of his employer, his injury arises out of the policyholder's work, even if the cause of the injury is the additional insured's negligence. In *Admiral Ins. Co. v. Trident N.G.L., Inc.*, 988 S.W.2d 451 (Tex. App.-Houston [1st Dist.] 1999, pet. denied), an explosion injured an employee of the policyholder who was performing maintenance work on Trident's equipment. The court reasoned that the maintenance and resulting explosion arose *from* the policyholder's work but that the policy did not require that the explosion be the *fault* of the policyholder. Other similar cases include *Shell Oil Co. v. AC&S, Inc.*, 649 N.E. 2d 946 (Ill. App. 1995), in which an AC&S employee tripped on Shell's pipes and was injured. The court stated that the arising out of language meant "originating from" or "having its origins in" so that AC&S's insurance company did owe a duty to defend Shell in the suit. In *Marathon Ashland Pipeline LLC v. Maryland Cas. Co.*, 243 F.3d 1232 (10th Cir. 2001), the court also stated that the arising out of language meant the natural and reasonable consequences of the policyholder's operations.

"Arising out of" Equates to Broad Coverage in Many Jurisdictions

The additional insured endorsement and how far the arising out of language can be stretched have been tested across the country. Instead of restricting coverage for the additional insured as originally crafted, this wording expanded coverage to additional insureds because of the legal interpretation by the courts.

In the Tenth Circuit, the court considered these facts: a patron of a city festival was injured when he jumped over a retaining wall when trying to quickly get to a portable toilet. The patron sued the city, which called upon the additional insured endorsement for coverage under the festival company's general liability policy. Although the city stipulated that it alone was negligent, the court held that, because the injury "arose out of" the operation of the festival, the city had coverage under the additional insured endorsement. *See McIntosh v. Scottsdale Ins. Co.*, 992 F.2d 251 (10th Cir. 1993).

Similarly in another case, a subcontractor performing work for the general contractor was required to add the general contractor as an additional insured on its CGL policy. One of the employees of the subcontractor was injured on the job solely as a result of the general contractor's negligence. The court held that, because the injury occurred in the course of and contemporaneously with the subcontractor's work with the general contractor, the general contractor was covered for the employee's negligence claims by virtue of his additional insured status. See *Merchant's Ins. Co. v. U.S. Fid. & Guar. Co.*, 143 F.3d 5 (1st Cir. 1998); *See also Hartford Accid. & Indem. Co. v. U.S. Natural Res. Inc.* 897 F. Supp. 466 (D. Oregon 1995).

A majority of courts now appear to hold that the *"arising out of"* language translates into merely a causal connection between the injury and the work being performed by the policyholder for the additional insured. For example, in *McCarthy Bros. Co. v. Continental Lloyds Ins. Co.*, 7 S.W.3d 725 (Tex. App.–Austin 1999, no pet.), an employee was simply going to get tools for his work as an electrician when he fell on a slippery incline. The court found that because the employee was getting tools to perform his job for the policyholder to do electrical work for McCarthy, the general contractor, there was a causal connection between the injury and the performance of work by the subcontractor for the general contractor. Therefore, the court found that liability "arose out of" the subcontractor's work for the general contractor and that there was coverage pursuant to the additional insured endorsement.

Likewise, in *Saavedra v. Murphy Oil U.S.A*, 930 F.2d. 1104 (5th Cir. 1991), an employee of a subcontractor slipped and was injured on Murphy Oil's premises. The court ruled that the subcontractor's insurance company was obligated to defend and indemnify Murphy as an additional insured on the subcontractor's policy. The court reasoned that the additional insured provision accomplishes two objectives.

> "First, it describes who is included as an additional insured: insureds are covered under this policy as required by written contract. Second, the policy places a single limitation on its obligation to give Murphy (and others) additional insured status. The insured status arises only with respect to operations performed by or for the policyholder. Because the accident Saavedra sues upon is directly related to Lou-Con's work, this clause is satisfied, and the policy extends insured status to Murphy."

Similar cases are *Philadelphia Elec. Co. v. Nationwide Mut. Ins. Co.*, 721 F. Supp. 740 (E.D. Pa. 1989), in which the court ruled that additional insureds are covered for their own negligence as long as the injuries are related to the work of the policyholder, and *Cas. Ins. Co. v. Northbrook Prop. & Casualty. Co.*, 501 N.E. 2d 812 (Ill. App. 1986), in which the court reasoned that the wording, "arising out of operations" performed by the additional insured for the policyholder, covered the additional insured for its own negligence.

Therefore, the "arising out of" language has now generally expanded additional insured coverage to cover the work of the general contractor, the owner, and other subcontractors whom the policyholder makes agreements with in their numerous commercial contracts as long as some causal connection can be made to the named insured's work.

Broad Coverage for An Additional Insured, but Not Unlimited

Courts have disputed the breadth of additional insured endorsements that provide coverage to an additional insured, "but only with respect to acts or omissions of the policyholder in connection with the policyholder's operations...." Some courts have found that even if the policyholder is not negligent, coverage can be afforded to an additional insured. *U.S. Fire Ins. Co. v. Aetna Life Ins. and Cas. Co.*, 291 Ill. App.3d 991, 225 (1st Dist 1997). (Even if the named insured is not negligent, the policy language "acts" is not limited to "negligent" acts. Conversely, The Houston Court of Appeals found that unless the policyholder is named in the suit as a defendant, or allegations are made against the policyholder for negligence, there can be no duty to defend or indemnify a purported additional insured. *D.R. Horton – Texas, Ltd. v. Markel Int'l Ins. Co., Ltd.*, 2006 WL 3040745*4 (Tex.App – Houston [14th Dist.] 2006, no pet.). However, in *Atofina Petrochemicals, Inc. v. Cont. Ins. Co.*, 185 S. W. 3d 440, 442-443(Tex. 2006), the court held that if the plaintiff made allegations against the named insured, even if the named insured was not named as a party, the additional insured could obtain coverage.

Underwriter Evaluations of Risk

Even if the policyholder is a company performing electrical work, and the underwriters for the insurance carrier give careful consideration to the risk for that type of work, the broad expanse of the "arising out of language" poses a real problem for the underwriter's evaluation of the risk. Underwriters and agents should ask more questions about who will perform the electrical work and the location of the site where the policyholder will be performing that work.

Additional insured endorsements can be limited if *potential* additional insureds are specifically named. Prior to the loss, the insurance company and the agent can evaluate the risk by an investigation of any potential additional insureds identified. Insurance companies can use a specific endorsement that excludes the sole negligence of the additional insured from coverage. The use of endorsements with limiting language was reviewed in both *BP Chemicals, Inc. v. First State Ins. Co.*, 226 F.3d 420 (6th Cir. 2000) and *Boise Cascade Corp. v. Reliance*, 129 F. Supp. 2d 41 (D. Maine 2001). In both cases, the courts upheld the limiting language.

However, in recent years many of the additional insured endorsements being used merely state that whoever is listed on the schedule is an additional insured. Even though some schedules do identify specifically named companies or contractors, many simply state: "as required by written contract", "blanket", or other similar language that encompass any person or entity that is required to be named as an additional insured in the contract.

Restrictions such as requiring the policyholder "to add another as an additional insured on the policy under a written contract" are liberally construed in favor of coverage. For example: An employee of A&B was injured unloading steel on FINA's property. FINA was sued and sought coverage from A&B based on A&B's agreement to provide insurance to cover the FINA property. The insurance company argued the contract between FINA and A&B was not definite enough to trigger additional insured coverage. In *Atofina* the Texas Supreme Court disagreed and relied on the relationship between A&B and FINA to show the intent of the parties was to provide FINA with additional insured coverage.

Underwriters have limited the time when coverage is available to additional insureds. The existence of a written contract is also required before additional insured coverage is available. Underwriters have also added exclusions to the additional insured endorsements to control the risks associated with insuring unknown additional insureds. Although the limitations and exclusions have been somewhat helpful, courts continue to allow for broad additional insured coverage based on endorsements added to the CGL policies. Underwriters continue to be challenged to clarify in plain language the coverage which is being provided. In the *Atofina* case above, there was a broad grant of coverage for all liability arising out of A&B's work. However, the second paragraph of the policy attempted to state that there would be no coverage for any acts or omissions on the part of FINA or its employees. The court held this only excluded sole negligence, not "all" conduct of FINA. *Id.*

As observed above, underwriters have tried to develop additional insured provisions which address the broad scope of coverage. At minimum, most insureds have been able to establish that the policy does not cover the sole negligence of the additional insured under a properly worded grant of coverage or exclusion. A sample of a provision the Texas Supreme Court found effective is as follows:

> Who Is An Insured Section II is amended to include as an insured [additional insured,] but only with respect to liability arising out of [Named Insured's] ongoing operations performed for [additional insured] but in no event for [additional insured's] sole negligence.

Evanston Ins. Co. v. Atofina Petrochemicals, 256 S.W. 3d 660 (Tex. 2008).

Further, the court made it clear that the scope of coverage is determined by the policy alone and the scope of the indemnity agreement is not relevant to that determination. *Id.* If an insurance policy does not cover the indemnity obligation, the obligor [Named Insured] remains exposed to liability. *Id.*

Under Florida law, the court looked at allegations in a petition which alleged negligence against the policyholder and independent negligence solely against the additional insured. Homeowners suffered property damage which was caused by excavation of property to build a Home Depot store. Home Depot sought additional insured coverage under the excavation company's insurance policy. The court found Home Depot was an additional insured even though "sole negligence" was excluded because some obligations alleged vicarious liability against Home Depot for the policyholder's operations. *Home Depot U.S.A. v. National Fire Ins. Co. of Hartford*, 2007 WL 846525 (N.D. Tex. 2007).

New Trend to Restrict Additional Insured Coverage

In an effort to provide underwriters with the clear and unambiguous language necessary to limit additional insured coverage, ISO has modified the broad based language in the revised 2004 additional insured form. Moreover, in 2013, the ISO forms substantively changed to limit additional insured coverage even further. The trend in additional insured coverage is to restrict the coverage to liability caused in whole and in part by the Named Insured's ongoing or completed operations.

In 2004, ISO revised its standard ISO form CG 20 10 07 04 for additional insureds. The key change in the language changes the way that the additional insured's ongoing operations are connected to the additional insured's liability. The "arising out of" language is gone from the endorsement. The new language states:

A.   **Section II – Who Is An Insured** is amended to include as an additional insured the person(s) or organization(s) shown in the Schedule, but only with respect to liability for "bodily injury," "property damage," or "personal or advertising injury," caused in whole or in part by:

   1.   Your acts or omissions; or

   2.   The acts or omission of those acting on your behalf; in the performance of your ongoing operations for the additional insured(s) at the location(s) designated above.

The purpose of this endorsement is to focus on an injury *caused in whole or in part* by the policyholder before additional insured coverage is available. The following example demonstrates this principle:

An employee of a roofing manufacturer is injured when the roofing manufacturer's employee delivered roof tiles to the job site of the general contractor. The policyholder roofer is working at the site, but liability is found 60 percent against the general contractor and 40 percent against the manufacturer employee. There is no additional insured coverage for the general contractor under Form CG 20 10 07 04. Under these facts, the sole negligence of the general contractor does not trigger additional insured coverage.

Similarly, a general contractor is sued by the employee of a subcontractor who is working at the job site. There is no allegation that the injury was caused in whole or in part by the named insured subcontractor. The carrier denied coverage in *Schafer v. Paragano Custom Building, Inc.*, 2010 WL 624108 (N.J. Supr. A. D. February 4, 2010). The court held that the policy does not provide coverage for the additional insured's own acts or omissions.

A number of states have now refused to allow subcontractors or insurers through the use of additional insured endorsements to indemnify a contractor for its own negligence. Anti-indemnity statutes not only address indemnity clauses in contracts, but in some instances find it is illegal to use an additional insured endorsement to cover the negligence of a purported additional insured. CA, CO, KS, LA, MT, NM, OK, TN, and TX anti-indemnity statutes also apply to additional insured coverage.

As indicated above, in 2013, ISO moved to fix some of the broad implications from additional insured coverage by requiring that coverage is restricted to the extent allowed by law. This aligns with the state laws that preclude coverage through anti-indemnity statutes.

Further, the 2013 endorsements restrict coverage to that which is required by contract and to the limits that are required by the contract or the policy, whichever is less. These new endorsements keep in place the modifications of 2004 noted above as to "caused in whole or in part" by the named insured's acts or omissions or those of someone acting on behalf of the named insured.

The Policy and The Contract –
Are They Separate and Independent?

One recent issue that has confused the interpretation by the courts of additional insured endorsements is the extent to which the policy of the named insured is separate and independent from the contract that the insured has entered into with the purported additional insured.

The events of the Deepwater Horizon oil spill in the Gulf of Mexico are well known in the country. From that spill, there has been extended litigation regarding the additional insurance coverage owed by the drilling rig owner Transocean, Ltd. to British Petroleum (BP). Although the issue arises under Texas law, additional insured coverage nationwide could be affected by a Texas Supreme Court decision as to whether additional insured coverage is affected by the limitations agreed to in the contract between the named insured and the purported additional insured or whether the policy alone controls what coverage is provided. BP argued that the policy alone controls and any limitation in the contract by Transocean would not affect the additional insurance coverage because the policy and the contract are separate and independent. Transocean argued the contract limited its liability and BP had no coverage as an additional insured. The district court agreed with Transocean and found that BP had no coverage as an additional insured. The case was appealed to the Fifth Circuit Court of Appeals who initially found in favor of BP, but withdrew the decision and sent certified questions to the Texas Supreme Court to determine if the policies of insurance alone determine coverage because the policy and the contract are separate and independent.

In the *Evanston Insurance* case, the Texas Supreme Court found that the policy alone did control coverage for the additional insured. Transocean argued that the contract is referred to and incorporated into the insurance policy and the liability of Transocean is limited by what the contract provides, therefore Evanston does not apply to the Deepwater Horizon oil spill.

The decisions of the Texas Supreme Court are usually followed by the Fifth Circuit Court of Appeals and so will influence insurance coverage decisions in other jurisdictions nationwide.

The 2013 ISO form appears to have been created with this Transocean-type contract limitation in mind by limiting coverage to the additional insured to no broader than that to which the named insured is required to provide by written contract. However, whatever the Texas Supreme Court decides, unless the policy is clear on its face, more litigation nationwide may ensue on the issue of whether the additional insured coverage is limited by specific liability limitations in the contract that do not appear in the additional insured endorsement.

Different Types of Additional Insured Status

Unlike the broad based additional insured endorsements, some endorsements cover more specific risks and generally name the additional insured party. Examples of these are endorsements for vendors, landlords, condominium unit owners, church members, cities, and lessors of leased equipment. Each one of these endorsements should be carefully reviewed to determine the extent of protection that is provided to the additional insured. Although some of these endorsements were created by ISO or some may be manuscript, it is unclear as to whether these endorsements have evolved to the trend for limiting additional insured coverage.

However, when these endorsements rely on the "arising out of" language, careful consideration should be given to who is added as additional insureds. Although these specific endorsements do not seem to be litigated to the same extent as the broad based additional insured endorsements, it appears likely that the "arising out of" language that appears in them would be given the same broad interpretation as on the broad based additional insured endorsements. One can expect from the case law previously cited that this type of language would cover the additional insured for its own negligence if the activity being performed is related to the work of the policyholder. Conversely, additional restrictions to the grant of coverage to additional insureds as well as exclusions for sole negligence will affect the scope of coverage. Therefore, if the insurance company only intends to cover vicarious liability, there should be clear language in the endorsement that sole negligence of the additional insured and its employees is excluded.

Coverage Limits in Primary Policies
Need More Careful Examination

Insureds tend to purchase $1 million in primary CGL coverage. Then, depending upon the type of business and the risk involved, the insured may purchase additional umbrella or excess coverage above the $1 million limit. Within one policy year, the most coverage usually available from the primary policy for any single accident or occurrence will be $1 million despite the number of insureds, suits, or claims. Some policyholders will have an aggregate limit of $2 million for all accidents and occurrences in that policy year, but some aggregate limits are only $1 million.

The additional insured provisions may be important in the consideration of policy limits and the amount of excess coverage that the named insured will need to protect its interests. The 2013 ISO endorsements may leave a gap in the insurance coverage when the contract limits coverage to $1 million, but the accident damages exceed that amount. More careful consideration should be given to the limits both in the contract and the policy if an insured is going to be protected when the new endorsements are used to provide additional insured coverage.

Analysis of the Coverage Needed
Must Include Many Factors

It is standard practice for almost every construction and business contract to contain additional insured provisions requiring that the policyholder (subcontractor) name the other contracting party (owner or general contractor) as an additional insured. Risk managers, insurance agents, underwriters, and insurance carriers need to be more aware of how easily the insured's CGL limits of liability can be eroded through this practice. Additional insureds may expand the insured's risk to cities, chemical plant owners, pipeline owners, oil well operators, manufacturers, and refineries. A standard $1 million primary policy is often very little protection for a policyholder that could face any number of serious bodily injury or property damage claims as a result of this exposure expansion.

For example, the policyholder subcontractor, who performs maintenance work at a chemical plant, is required to name the chemical plant owner as an additional insured. While the subcontractor's workers are at the plant, an explosion kills three of the subcontractor's employees. Within the same policy time frame another accident occurs at another plant at which the policyholder subcontractor is working. Both of the plant owners, who are additional insureds on the subcontractor's CGL policy, are sued after each of the accidents. The potential bodily injury damages from both of these accidents exceed $3 million. A policyholder subcontractor with only $1 million in primary coverage and $2 million in excess coverage may not have adequate limits to handle the expanded risk he has taken on. Without adequate insurance protection, the policyholder's own assets are at risk for any additional bodily injury or property damage claims within that policy year.

Another circumstance that may arise is when a policyholder receives three or four competing claims for "bodily injury" or "property damage" all arising from the same accident or occurrence. Each claim in itself may not exceed the $1 million policy limit or aggregate. However, now the insured is faced with the dilemma that paying any of the claims will erode the policy limit, leaving him with inadequate insurance to pay the remaining— or subsequent—claims.

Finally, the policyholder may face litigation for failing to provide the additional insured coverage which was required by the contract. If a policyholder subcontractor depletes his policy limit on one claim, then if there are subsequent claims under the same policy, and no available funds for additional insureds, the policyholder may face liability for the loss, or a breach of contract claim. For example, the policyholder had only

$1 million of available coverage. The allegations were that six people died as a result of both negligence and a defective product. The additional insured demanded defense and indemnity. The policyholder who was also sued had little or no assets other than a $1 million policy, which only covered the policyholder's liability. The additional insured paid $4 million to settle the case, then sued the policyholder, resulting in a multi-million dollar judgment.

Potential Agent E&O Problem

When the policyholder is faced with inadequate limits for pending claims, the insurance agent or broker who worked with the policyholder to develop the insurance program may be the target of litigation. If the agent or broker has been asked specifically to evaluate the potential risks and recommend both adequate policy limits and coverage, then the policyholder will rely on his professional advice when purchasing coverage. For example, when the agent has recommended an insurance program with $1 million in coverage, and a $1 million aggregate, the following may happen.

A road constructor hires subcontractors to provide proper signage, barrels and road markings at the road construction site. One subcontractor also agreed to assist with traffic control. When a vehicle ran off the road and flipped over, killing one passenger and injuring two others, the general contractor sought additional insured coverage from the subcontractor, who handled traffic control. The same subcontractor also had additional insured coverage for the other subcontractors and the state regulatory department. The available policy limits were wholly inadequate to protect the subcontractor from the multi-million dollar suit.

The agent who fails to recognize the expanded insurance needs that additional insured endorsements have created may make representations that the insured is adequately protected. This agent could find herself (or her errors and omission insurance carrier) picking up the cost for the liability damages outside the policyholder's insurance program.

A policyholder faced with the prospect of inadequate insurance and possible financial ruin will look to the professionals who provided him with insurance coverage to recover losses. Even the insurance company, depending on the state in which the policyholder is located, may face possible liability for the representations of certain agents. Therefore, careful evaluation of the risks faced by a policyholder when additional insured coverage is a part of her insurance program is a critical issue not to be ignored by underwriters, agents, and brokers.

Level of Care

Underwriters generally perform an extensive review and analysis of prior insurance claims, accident record, financial security, and business location when evaluating the risk to providing CGL coverage to a potential insured. However, when using a broad based additional insured endorsement the insured can execute contracts and agreements that put the policy limits at risk without any investigation of the exposures involved. The insurance carrier, in conjunction with the agents who are procuring these policies, needs to determine ways to evaluate the risk when additional insureds are required in the policyholder's insurance program.

One way to better evaluate the risk is to eliminate the broad based additional insured endorsements and replace them with endorsements specifically identifying the name of the person or company that will be additional insureds. Requiring that policyholders request additional insured status for their contractual partners identifies the particular additional insured and puts the agent and insurance company on notice of a new risk that should be evaluated. The insurance company then can investigate more fully the actual risk that is being undertaken before issuing the additional insured endorsement.

Some insureds and agents believe that such review is unnecessarily time-consuming and hampers contractual relationships. Many insureds continue to blindly enter into contracts without analyzing whether they have adequate insurance. It may seem quicker to adopt the broad based additional insured process instead of reviewing each contract individually—until claims occur and the policyholder's limits are put in jeopardy. Additional insureds have added contract language that places liability directly on the named insured even if they are inadequately insured to cover such liability.

Some insurance companies are also requiring that the policyholder require their subcontractors to maintain certain levels of insurance. Unless the policyholder complied with this provision, a premium surcharge will be charged at the end of the policy period to cover the additional risk.

In this vein, some insurance companies have instituted procedures that additional insured status will not be granted unless they are provided with a contract that describes the scope of the work of both the additional insured and the policyholder so the risk can be more adequately assessed. However, once a policy is written, and the premium paid, it is unlikely the insurance company will review the additional insured risk, leaving that analysis to agents and the policyholder.

Finally, additional insured endorsements can limit the scope of coverage provided to the additional insureds by restricting coverage to "ongoing operations" or "completed operations" and "caused in whole or in part by the named insured's work." Additional insured endorsements at a minimum should exclude coverage for the sole negligence of the additional insured and its employees. Further, consideration should be given to more restrictive endorsements or manuscript endorsements which limit liability to only vicarious liability.

A key factor to limit additional insured coverage is to consider what liability the insured is responsible for in the contract. Clear limitations as found in the 2004 and 2013 endorsements will not end litigation if the contracts leave a named insured at risk for millions of dollars in excess of what the policy provides.

Contractual Liability Issues

Contractual liability is controlled to some extent by the terms of the CGL policy. Generally, the policy only provides coverage for liability assumed by an insured under an "insured contract". An "insured contract" is a defined term in the CGL policy that includes six types of contracts. For the purposes of this section, only the sixth type of insured contract is discussed.

Insured Contracts

In the current ISO CGL form, this sixth category is:

f.   That part of any other contract or agreement pertaining to your business (including an indemnification of a municipality in connection with work performed for a municipality) under which you assume the tort liability of another party to pay for "bodily injury" or "property damage" to a third person or organization. Tort liability means a liability that would be imposed by law in the absence of any contract or agreement.

Paragraph f. does not include that part of any contract or agreement:

(1)   That indemnifies a railroad for "bodily injury" or "property damage" arising out of construction or demolition operations, within 50 feet of any railroad property and affecting any railroad bridge or trestle, tracks, road-beds, tunnel, underpass or crossing;

(2)   That indemnifies an architect, engineer or surveyor for injury or damage arising out of:

> (a) Preparing, approving, or failing to prepare or approve, maps, shop drawings, opinions, reports, surveys, field orders, change orders or drawings and specifications; or
>
> (b) Giving directions or instructions, or failing to give them, if that is the primary cause of the injury or damage; or
>
> (3) Under which the insured, if an architect, engineer or surveyor, assumes liability for an injury or damage arising out of the insured's rendering or failure to render professional services, including those listed in (2) above and supervisory, inspection, architectural or engineering activities.

There is now an amended "insured contract" definition under Form CG 24 26 04 13 In the amended endorsement paragraph, it now reads:

> f. That part of any other contract or agreement pertaining to your business (including an indemnification of a municipality in connection with work performed for a municipality) under which you assume the tort liability of another party to pay for "bodily injury" or "property damage" to a third person or organization provided the "bodily injury" or "property damage" is caused, in whole or in part, by you or by those acting on your behalf. However, such part of a contract or agreement shall only be considered an "insured contract" to the extent your assumption of the tort liability is permitted by law. Tort liability means a liability that would be imposed by law in the absence of any contract or agreement.

The amended insured contract definition limits the liability assumed by the insured under the "insured contract." The limiting language is: "provided the 'bodily injury' or 'property damage' is caused in whole or in part by you or by those acting on your behalf." This language appears to eliminate sole negligence and adds the restriction of vicarious liability now found in the amended ISO 2013 additional insured endorsement discussed above. This may leave a policyholder unprotected if the policyholder has promised indemnity to another party for sole negligence. Complex insurance litigation in the future will also determine the meaning of such phrases "in whole or in part" and "caused by" to determine the scope of coverage under the amended "insured contract" definition.

In essence, the tort liability assumed under a contract may expand the policyholder's CGL coverage to the indemnity he promises to a general contractor, an owner, the subsidiaries of the owner, and, possibly, other subcontractors working for the contractor if such liability falls within the policy coverage. The coverage is limited only by the indemnification provisions of the contract itself and the specific terms of the policy.

Contractual Indemnity Wording

A typical construction contract includes this type of indemnity provision:

Named Insured agrees to indemnify, defend, and hold harmless Company WW from any and all claims of every kind and character which may be asserted against Company WW, the owner, the employees, and the subcontractors of Company WW, by the agents and/or employees of the named insured by reason of or in any way connected with the performance of named insured's contract regardless of whether the damages are the result of the sole negligence of the property owner, of Company WW, its employees, agents, or subsidiaries, and/or concurrent negligence with the named insured, its employees, and agents.

According to *Black's Law Dictionary*, "indemnify" means to restore a person in whole or in part by payment, repair or replacement.

Under an indemnity provision, the named insured often agrees to assume both defense costs and damages that result from injury to any employee or agent of the named insured. The indemnity clause may encompass damages that result from the negligence of the named insured, concurrent negligence of the named insured and the general contractor or owner, or even for the sole negligence of the general contractor or owner.

As previously noted, many states have now passed anti-indemnity statutes which affect the enforceability of these indemnity clauses. These anti-indemnity provisions are aimed at the construction, and oil and gas industries in particular to cure the uneven bargaining power of small contractors who want to bid for work with larger general contractors, oil companies, or rig owners. However, not all contracts are so limited and hold harmless indemnity clauses are regularly found in commercial leases, municipal contracts, school district contracts, and other government contracts which are not controlled or may be excluded from the anti-indemnity laws. The statutes may explicitly allow for indemnity if an employee of the subcontractor sues the contractor or the owner. Therefore, contractual liability coverage continues to be a very important part of every named insured's insurance program.

Hold Harmless Wording and Defense Costs

It is important to note that "hold harmless" may mean "to assume all expenses incident to the defense of any claim and to fully compensate an indemnitee for all loss or expense," as the court explained in *Bank El Paso v. Powell*, 550 S.W.2d 383 (Tex. App.–El Paso 1977, no writ) and *Pinney v. Tarpley*, 686 S.W.2d 574 (Tenn. Ct. App. 1985). *Black's Law Dictionary* defines "hold harmless" as an "agreement or contract" in which one party agrees to hold the other without responsibility for *damage* or other *liability* arising out of the transaction invoked (emphasis added).

The standard ISO CGL form provides that defense costs assumed in a contract or agreement are available for parties other than an insured as long as the liability for defense also has been assumed in the insured contract and the insurance applies to the allegations. The Third Circuit in *Kiewit Eastern Co. v. L&R Constr. Co., Inc.*, 44 F.3d 1194 (3rd Cir. 1995), confirmed that defense costs are included as long as the insured assumes those costs in the contract.

However, many insurance companies have limited contractual liability coverage under their CGL policies to damages for "bodily injury" or "property damage" excluding defense costs and litigation expenses, even though the contractual provisions usually require a named insured to "indemnify, defend, and hold harmless" the other party. The basis for the denial of coverage is that the policies will pay only *damages*.

The definition of hold harmless distinguishes *damage* and *loss* from expenses and other liability. Therefore, when the policy only agrees to pay for "bodily injury" or "property damage," the insurance company may argue that defense costs are not included. In addition, the duties to defend and indemnify are generally considered separate obligations of the insurance company.

More recent CGL forms may provide for defense costs to a contractual indemnitee as supplemental payments under the named insured's policy which would be an expense and not damages.

There are a number of variations to the payment of defense costs under contractual liability coverage which continue to evolve. An important consideration is whether the defense costs will erode the policy limits. ISO forms from 1992 forward may specifically identify defense costs under contractual liability coverage as damages. If defense costs are damages, then whenever the insurer pays for the defense costs of the contractual indemnitee the policy limit on damages is reduced. This could ultimately affect the ability of the named insured to pay all of the actual damages in a lawsuit. Eroding limits for defense costs may place the named insured at risk for any remaining unprotected loss that remains after the defense costs are paid. Further, if the defense is within the limits and a settlement is paid for one insured which exhausts the policy limits, the defense will end.

The ISO CGL policy form provides a defense in addition to the limits, but only if the following conditions are all met:

- the subcontractor assumed the general contractor's liability in an insured contract;

- the policy covers the loss;

- there is no conflict of interest between the policyholder and the general contractor;

- both parties ask for a defense from the insurer and agree to the same counsel; and

- the general contractor agrees to cooperate in writing to any settlement of the claim.

This new provision also may pose problems for the named insured if there is a dispute about what person or entity is responsible for the accident. Generally the general contractor or whoever is offering the contracted-for work will demand both contractual liability coverage and additional insured coverage to make sure that a defense is available under the subcontractor's policy if there is a suit.

Assume the Tort Liability of Another

It appears that courts across the country are consistent in the determination that an "insured contract" exists only if the policyholder assumes the tort liability of another. Simply agreeing to provide compensation to a third party for actions against an insured where the third party is added to the suit may not trigger the "insured contract" definition under contractual liability coverage. *Alex Robertson v. Imperial Cas. & Indem. Co.*, 8 Cal. App. 4th 338, 10 Cal. Rptr. 165 (1992). There must be an express provision in the contract which provides that the policyholder assume the other party's liability and the insured must then assume the tort liability of another. *United States Fid. & Guar. Co.*, 120 S.W.3d 556 (Ark. 2003). Contractual liability coverage is limited to a specific assumption by the insured of liability that results from negligence of a third party. Therefore, a poorly worded contractual obligation may not be covered by the contractual liability coverage under a policy.

Potential Conflict

A conflict can develop between the policyholder and the party who has bargained for indemnification when it appears there is no insurance coverage for defense. The insured contract is critical to understanding the risk assumed by the policyholder. However, the risk assumed may conflict with the express terms or exclusions of the policyholder's policy. Often the insurance company will not have seen the "insured contract." After the loss, the insurance company analyzes what is covered and what is not. The policyholder may face what appears to be an unexpected gap in coverage, or, worse, litigation from the party that was indemnified in the contract demanding full defense and indemnity.

State law also may enter the quagmire of coverage for indemnity assumed in an insured contract. For example, as previously discussed, many states have statutes that include anti-indemnity provisions for certain types of contracts and mutual indemnity. In Texas and New Mexico, for example, indemnity-shifting provisions related to oil, gas wells, and construction preclude the assumption of the sole negligence of the owner and/or general contractor by a subcontractor.

Some states have established by case law that the assumption of the sole negligence of one party by another in a contract is against public policy and void. Therefore it is important to be aware of the laws of the state where the contract is executed to determine the type of indemnity that is available.

There also remains an open question as to whether an unenforceable indemnity agreement may still qualify as an "insured contract." *See Mid-Continent Casualty Co. v. Swift Energy Co.*, 206 F.3d 487 (5th Cir. 2000). However, to avoid this dilemma, most indemnitees insist that contracts with policyholders also have an additional insured provision. Additional insured coverage is not dependent on a viable indemnity agreement.

Fair Notice

The majority of states also have imposed strict requirements on fair notice for provisions involving shifting the risk of the sole negligence of one party to another. The origin of conspicuous requirement for commercial contracts and agreements may be found in the Uniform Commercial Code, which has been adopted by a majority of states. Fair notice generally refers to two requirements for shifting the risk through indemnity agreements. The risk-shifting provision: 1) must clearly state that the party is seeking indemnity for its own negligence from the indemnitor, and 2) the indemnity provision must be conspicuous. *See Dresser Industries v. Page Petroleum, Inc.* 853 S.W.2d 505 (Tex. 1993) and *Transpower Constructors v. Grand River Dam*, 905 F.2d 1413 (10th Cir. 1990).

Another factor to consider is whether other insurance may be available under the policy, even if contractual liability for the sole negligence of the contracting party is precluded. Many commercial contracts also have separate provisions requiring that the contracting party be endorsed as an additional insured on the subcontractor or vendor's policy. However, not every party protected by an indemnity provision is also protected as an additional insured.

For example, a company owner executes a contract for electrical work with the policyholder subcontractor. The electrical subcontractor agrees to indemnify the owner and other subcontractors on the job. An employee of the electrical subcontractor is injured through the sole negligence of the plumbing subcontractor on the job. Per public policy, the state in which the accident occurred precludes contractual indemnity for sole negligence. The plumbing subcontractor was not an additional insured on the electrical contractor's policy but was only contractually indemnified. As a result, there may be no insurance coverage for the subcontractor because public policy precludes the assumption of liability for damages arising from the sole negligence of the plumbing subcontractor.

Be aware of any attempts to limit insurance coverage by the terms of the indemnity contract. The terms and conditions of the policy will control the coverage provided. For example, if the policyholder attempts to limit indemnity to $500,000, this will not affect coverage to the indemnitee, who is also an additional insured.

Additional Insureds and Defense Costs

Because contractual liability may not pay for defense costs based only on an indemnity provision in the contract, experienced business entities now generally require separate provisions in a contract that also make the entity, the general contractor, and the owner additional insureds. The difference in insurance coverage is significant.

Consider these facts in determining the difference between additional insured and contractual liability coverage. A large chemical plant is redoing a section of the plant in which a two-story furnace is being refurbished. The general contractor for the job enters into a subcontract with a pipefitting company (the policyholder) but elects to perform the electrical work itself. A heavy tool is accidentally dropped by one of the general contractor's electricians from approximately 100 feet above where the pipefitters are working and severely injures one of them. The pipefitter files suit.

Who Pays First?

With only contractual liability coverage based on an indemnity provision even for the sole negligence of the contractor, the general contractor will be faced with paying its own defense costs unless the policyholder agrees to defend him. Most often, the general contractor will have to pay first, and then try to recover costs from the policyholder and/or the insurance company.

As an additional insured, the story may be different. The CGL policy states that the insurance company owes the contractor the same duty to defend as the insurance company owes to the policyholder. Defense costs are paid until the policy limits are exhausted by the payment of judgments or settlements. They are in addition to payments of policy limits for indemnity for "bodily injury" or "property damage." The contractor as an additional insured is now protected for both defense and indemnity by simply adding a different risk-shifting provision to the insured contract.

Primary and Noncontributory Coverage—CG 20 01 04 13

This new endorsement amends the other insurance provisions in the CGL policy form to make the insurance of the named insured primary and non-contributory with any other insurance. With this endorsement on the primary policy, it is the named insured's policy which will provide a defense to the additional insured and pay any damages before the additional insured's policy is required to pay.

However, this endorsement generally applies only at the primary level of insurance. A review of excess and umbrella policies needs to be conducted to determine if all of the named insured's policies at each level are expected to pay first in accordance with the terms of the contract.

Careful Reading of The Contract: What Is Agreed?

Indemnification/hold harmless clauses may involve the assumption of liabilities that are not covered under the policyholder's CGL policy. As discussed previously, an insured may have agreed to indemnify another party for defense costs in the contract, but those defense costs may not be covered by the policy. However, there are other areas in which an insured, when negotiating the terms of a commercial contract, may agree to indemnify and hold harmless another party for those specific liabilities assumed that are not covered by his CGL policy.

Generally, a breach of contract is excluded under a CGL policy even though a general contractor or a lessor may demand indemnity for a breach.

For example, some liability policies do not cover punitive damages. Others are silent on the issue, but state law often prohibits insurance coverage from paying punitive damages. In some states, courts have held that public policy prohibits the insuring of punitive damages because it defeats the purpose as a punishment for serious offenses.

In addition, intentional and willful conduct that usually is required before punitive damages are assessed generally does not fall within the definition of occurrence. They may be ruled out by the policy's intentional injury exclusion.

The policy may not cover claims for mental anguish unless there are physical manifestations of the injury; claims for sexual harassment and pollution generally fall outside the scope of CGL coverage.

These and other gaps in coverage often are discovered only after a loss, and lead to suits against the policyholder who agreed to indemnify the other party in the contract. The policyholder often believes it has not been properly treated by its insurance carrier when it is left with no insurance for the very liabilities that it thought were insured under its policy. The general contractor who thought it was covered by the policyholder's policy also finds itself forced to pay costs, expenses, and damages and then having to seek recourse in a suit for indemnity against the policyholder and insurance company.

Insurance Company Review of Contracts

Often the assumption is made that, simply because standard ISO CGL forms have been created, all insurance carriers and agents are using them. However, certain states still rely on older forms because of their lengthy approval process. In addition, some states also permit manuscript endorsements, which can change significantly the scope of coverage provided under a CGL policy. Excess and umbrella forms, which are less standardized than the primary CGL forms, may be called upon for coverage even when the primary policy is not triggered.

For the most part, admitted carriers in any state may be required to use only state approved forms for CGL policies, but surplus lines carriers are not restricted in the use of the forms that may be used to create a policy. Since there is no set standard for CGL forms nationwide, the actual policy provided to the named insured may or may not meet the requirements of the named insured's contract. A named insured may have no knowledge of different coverage forms or different types of carriers which may offer to sell the named insured a policy. The named insured usually discovers the policy limitations on insurance coverage after a major loss.

Insurance companies may want to consider, as a condition precedent to granting contractual liability coverage, that the insured provide sample contracts to the carrier for review before activating contractual liability coverage. Contract review can provide insurance carriers, agents, and brokers with the opportunity to determine what risk is being assumed and whether there are potential gaps in coverage before agreeing to provide contractual liability coverage. The generic term "contractual liability coverage" may be misleading when not all contractual liability coverage is the same.

Failing to Add an Additional Insured

Generally, when an insured fails to comply with the contract requirement to add an endorsement for an additional insured, the primary policy will not provide additional insured coverage. However, in a recent decision, the Houston Court of Appeals determined that an umbrella policy in question filled the coverage gaps in the primary policy. The party was not named as an additional insured on the primary policy and, therefore, had no coverage. However, the language of the commercial catastrophe policy was held to provide additional insured coverage to the party because it stated that "any person or organization to whom or to which you are obligated by virtue of a written contract to provide such insurance as afforded by this coverage part is an insured, but only with respect to liability arising out of 'your work,' 'your product' and to property owned or used by you." *See American Motorist Ins. Co. v. Occidental Chemical Corp.*, 16 S.W.3d 140 (Tex. App. – Houston [1st Dist.] 2000, no pet. hist.).

Therefore, although the court did not find coverage under the primary policy because the contracting party was not an additional insured, coverage was found under the umbrella policy. This case illustrates that careful consideration should be given to the full scope of coverage, particularly when the same carrier is providing both primary and umbrella coverage.

Certificate of Insurance Issues

Certificates of insurance generally are used to show the insurance coverage that contracting parties carry. The certificate usually is provided by an insurance agent and simply provides proof that an insurance policy has been written, but it also may include a statement of coverage in general terms. The format of certificates of insurance may vary from state to state, and some contracting parties insist that their proprietary certificate forms be used and signed by the insurance agent to indicate the terms and conditions of coverage.

The use of certificates of insurance to commit fraud has captured the attention of some state legislatures. These states, like Texas, have enacted statutes to control the use and the form of certificates of insurance. Some states only allow the use of a standard ACORD form unless the Department of Insurance has pre-approved the use of a manuscript form. ACORD provides standard certificates of insurance. In 2010, there were substantive changes to the ACORD form 25 in response to challenges from state regulatory agencies and insurance litigation.

The new form begins with some clarification of the purpose of the form and a statement identified as "important". This warning or disclaimer is in capital letters to provide notice to whoever receives the form.

The form states:

> THIS CERTIFICATE IS ISSUED AS A MATTER OF INFORMATION ONLY AND CONFERS NO RIGHTS UPON THE CERTIFICATE HOLDER. THIS CERTIFICATE DOES NOT AFFIRMATIVELY OR NEGATIVELY AMEND, EXTEND OR ALTER THE COVERAGE AFFORDED BY THE POLICIES BELOW. THIS CERTIFICATE OF INSURANCE DOES NOT CONSTITUTE A CONTRACT BETWEEN THE ISSUING INSURERS(S), AUTHORIZED REPRESENTATIVE OR PRODUCER AND THE CERTIFICATE HOLDER.
>
> IMPORTANT: If the certificate holder is an ADDITIONAL INSURED, the policy(ies) must be endorsed. If SUBROGATION IS WAIVED, subject to the terms and conditions of the policy, certain policies may require an endorsement. A statement on this certificate does not confer rights to the certificate holder in lieu of such endorsement(s).

The remaining language emphasizes yet again the informative aspect of the certificate, but a careful reading indicates that all that this certificate tells you is what policies the insured had when the certificate was issued and for the policy period identified. However, a policy that has been financed may cancel for nonpayment long before the end of the policy period. Notice of cancellation cannot be promised to the certificate holder unless the policy explicitly provides for such notice.

The new certificate attempts to prevent litigation regarding misrepresentations concerning the insurance that is identified on the certificate. The broad disclaimers make reliance on the content of the certificate unlikely unless the certificate holder has looked at the actual terms and conditions of the policy.

Problems with Certificates of Insurance and Additional Insured Status

The following type of situation may occur when a certificate identifies a party as an additional insured: A tugboat company had an oral contract with an asbestos-abatement company to strip asbestos from one of its vessels. While climbing down a ladder, an employee of the abatement company fell onto the vessel. The employee sued the tugboat owner for negligence. Relying on a certificate of insurance that indicated the tugboat owner as an additional insured, the tugboat owner demanded a defense from the insurance company of the asbestos-abatement company. The insurance company denied coverage because the policy specifically stated that additional insured status was only available in accordance with a *written* contract. Without a written contract, there is no coverage for the tugboat owner as an additional insured because the terms of the insurance policy take precedence over the general representation in the certificate of insurance that the tugboat owner was an additional insured. This reasoning is illustrated in cases such as *Graceda v. Tagle*, 946 S.W.2d 504 (Tex. App. 1997, pet. denied), in which the court ruled that a certificate of insurance alone conveys no rights on the holder of the certificate, and *American Cas. Co. of Reading. v. Krueger*, 181 F.3d 1113 (9th Cir. 1999), in which the court stated that a certificate of insurance did not provide coverage but agency relationship may result in a claim against the insurance company.

A survey of case law shows the problems certificates of insurance may create. A certificate of insurance will not suffice to create insurance coverage if such coverage is precluded by the terms of the policy. In other words, a certificate of insurance merely shows one's status as an insured, but actual coverage is provided by the terms of the insurance policy. This reasoning is seen in *TIG Ins. Co. v. Sedgwick James of Washington*, 184 F.Supp.2d 591, 598, 604 (S.D. Tex.2001), *aff'd*, 276 F.3d 754 (5th Cir. 2002) (a certificate of insurance will not create insurance coverage if such coverage is precluded by the terms of the policy); *Granite Construction Co., Inc. v. Bituminous Ins. Co.*, 832 S.W.2d 427, 430 (Tex.App.-Amarillo 1992, n.w.h.) (ruling that insurance is provided by an insurance policy, not by a certificate of insurance); *Boyd v. Travelers Ins. Co.*, 421 S.W.2d 929, (Tex. Civ.App. – Houston [14th Dist.] 1967, writ ref'd n.r.e.) (mere possession of a certificate does not constitute coverage); *Wann v. Metropolitan Life Ins. Co.*, 41 S.W.2d 50, 52 (Tex. Com. App. 1931) (a certificate of insurance does "not constitute the complete contract of insurance" and must be construed in connection with underlying insurance policy); *RNA Investments, Inc. v. Employers Ins. of Wausau*, 2000 WL 1708918 (Tex. App. – Dallas 2000, n.w.h.) (certificates of insurance in and of themselves do not create insurance coverage); *C & W Well Service, Inc. v. Sebasta*, 1994 WL 95680, at *7 (Tex. App.-Houston [14th Dist.] 1994, n.w.h.) (insurance coverage is that provided by a policy, and not a certificate of insurance). Thus, the courts view that the purpose of such certificates is just to generally acknowledge that an insurance policy has been written. The Texas Supreme Court recently stated that given the numerous limitations and exclusions that often encumber insurance policies, those who take insurance certificates at face value do so at their own risk. *Via Net v. TIG Ins. Co.*, 211 S.W.3d 310, 314 (Tex. 2006).

Some certificates of insurance contain broad representations of coverage for additional insureds, including the contracting company, its subsidiaries, and invitees. However, this broad coverage may be limited by a notation such as "only as defined in 'the contract' between the insured and the contracting company." So, for example, even if the certificate represents that there is coverage for all subcontractors, if the contract itself does not require such extensive additional insured status, there will be no coverage. This reasoning is seen in *Granite Construction Co., Inc. v. Bituminous Ins. Co.*, 832 S.W.2d 427 (Tex. App. 1992, no writ) and *J.A. Jones Construction Co. v. Hartford Fire Ins. Co.*, 645 N.E.2d 980 (Ill. App. Ct. 1995), in which the court held that a certificate is not evidence of policy coverage when the certificate is subject to the terms of the policy. *See also Benns v. Continental Cas. Co.*, 982 F.2d 461 (10th Cir. 1993) and *Great Lakes Dredge & Dock Co. v. Commercial Union Assur. Co.*, 2000 WL 769782 at *4 (N.D. Ill. Oct. 4, 1999).

Therefore, the policy itself and the contract between the parties may have a chilling effect on representations made in a certificate of insurance about additional insured status.

Disclaimers on the certificate may protect an insurance company and agent from claims of negligent misrepresentation, particularly when the claim of the owner or general contractor is that they "justifiably relied on the certificate," as seen in *T.H.E. Ins. Co.* case, which shows that there is no justifiable reliance when the two disclaimers discussed previously appear on the face of the certificate. However, a certificate of insurance without disclaimers may pose a serious problem for an insurance company or an agent on a negligent misrepresentation claim.

Best Practices for Getting the Right Insurance for the Insured and the Additional Insured

Certificates of insurance are only to be used for general information. In every case where there is a complex indemnity provision in a contract, a request should be made for a copy of the actual policy.

If the potential additional insured receives the actual policy, the additional insured endorsements can be reviewed and issues of coverage can be remedied before a loss. The actual policy can assure the contracting party that it is receiving the coverage he expected as an additional insured.

The insurance agent plays a key role in obtaining copies of the policies for the insured. If there is a question of coverage this should be raised in writing to the underwriter and resolved before the work begins on the contract.

Some courts have held that an insurance agent does not have an affirmative duty to disclose limitations of insurance coverage. The court upheld a lower court's ruling that an agent did not have a duty to disclose limitations in coverage in *Moore v. Whitney-Vahy Ins. Agency*, 966 S.W.2d 690 (Tex. App. – San Antonio 1998, no pet.), a suit involving a lack of coverage for a retaliatory discharge claim. The client had not requested that specific type of coverage and the agent had not misrepresented the coverage provided in the policy he obtained. In *Brinkerhoff v. Campbell*, 994 P.2d 911 (Wash. Ct. App. 2000), the court reasoned that an insurance company did not have an affirmative duty to disclose policy limits in an auto claim, although the claimant's attorney did have a responsibility to ask the company for the information.

Therefore, reviewing the actual policy for the controlling terms and conditions of coverage may afford the greatest protection for a potential additional insured. The insured or the potential additional insured should review the coverage and ask questions if the coverage is in doubt.

Conclusion

The scope of coverage in a CGL policy can be greatly expanded when taking into consideration broad based additional insured endorsements and contractual liability coverage. There is a growing trend to limit the scope of coverage for additional insureds and contractual liability coverage by the 2004 and 2013 ISO endorsements. The intent is to restrict coverage to vicarious liability only. These endorsements will be the source of continued insurance litigation as to the scope of coverage provided. Certificates of insurance also can affect what the policyholder and the parties contracting with the policyholder envision as potential insurance coverage. The trend is to generally limit certificates of insurance to basic information about the type of policy, name of the insured, limits, and policy periods. More than thirty-nine states have adopted statutes or regulations to limit the use of certificates of insurance. Some of the litigation and confusion that results from poorly worded endorsements, indemnity clauses of commercial contracts, and certificates of insurance can be avoided if the agents, brokers, insurance companies, underwriters, and policyholders carefully consider the losses that may arise as a result of the expanded coverage. This evaluation should occur when the insurance program is procured so that everyone involved in the insurance program understands the risks involved and the issues related to the coverage that is extended to additional insureds and contractual partners.

Section III

One Occurrence, Two Occurrences ...

By: Michael F. Aylward, Esq.

An industrial plant explosion causes damage to several adjacent property owners ... an alleged defect in the design of a PVC pipe product causes plumbing systems around the country to leak ... an archdiocese is sued for its negligent failure to protect parishioners from the sexual depredation of a priest ... a municipal housing authority faces a class action for refusing to rent to African Americans ... a food wholesaler negligently processes ground beef, which causes fast food customers in several states to suffer food poisoning.

What do all of these cases have in common? Each presents the question of whether claims arising from them should be treated as arising from separate occurrences or whether the claims share a common cause and, therefore, trigger only a single occurrence limit.

Few issues can have as dramatic an impact on an insured's coverage rights (and an insurer's duty to pay) as the determination of whether a given set of claims involve one occurrence or many. Yet, the rules pertaining to this issue are cloaked in obscurity and difficult to follow. Indeed, few areas of the law seem as result-oriented as this one.

Until recently, cases involving multiple occurrences have been relatively rare. The rarity stems not so much from the obscurity of the issue as from the constellation of circumstances that must come together to produce such a case. Specifically, 1) the insurer must be found to owe coverage, 2) the insured must be liable, 3) the damages in question must be large, and 4) the claims must not be able to be settled within the limits that the insurer concedes are available.

Most often, disputes arise over which, if any, aggregate should be eroded; when excess or umbrella liability coverage should be pierced; whether single or multiple insured retentions should be applied; when the duty to defend ends; and whether the insured's coverage should be maximized. While such disputes typically focus on policy limits, some recent cases have featured efforts by insureds to separate out new occurrences to avoid defenses of late notice or having "expected or intended" the original occurrence.

Unlike occurrence disputes over cases involving the application of policy exclusions, there is no clear right or wrong position on the number of occurrences that reliably will benefit a party. The analysis that maximizes an insured's indemnity recovery in one case may be devastating to an insured with a different profile. Similarly, the position that an insurer might favor in a case in which its policies are primary might be unfavorable to it in another case in which it issued excess policies. Such shifting roles and complications may well explain the relatively small number of reported decisions.

Indemnity issues also are transforming the cast of characters in coverage disputes. Whereas coverage disputes conventionally have pitted primary insurers against policyholders, disputes concerning the number of occurrences may arise in suits between 1) a policyholder and its primary insurers, 2) a primary insurer and an umbrella or excess insurer, or 3) a ceding insurer and its reinsurer(s).

Although the thrust of this section is on commercial general liability (CGL) policies, some of the examples and case citations deal with excess liability coverages. However, even when coverage on the primary liability policy is excluded, the definition of occurrence is important in determining when and how excess coverage is triggered as well as how self-insured retentions and deductibles are applied.

The Role of Occurrence Wordings

Limiting Coverage

The meaning of occurrence is vital to the two main promises in a liability insurance policy: the promise to pay damages on behalf of the insured, whether through judgments or agreed-to settlements (the duty to indemnify), and the promise to defend suits seeking covered damages (the duty to defend). While broadly stated, neither obligation is without limitation; since 1966, most general liability policies have provided that that the insurer's obligation to defend ends when the applicable policy limits are exhausted. This is one situation in which the issue of how many occurrences are triggered can be critical.

Trigger of Coverage Distinguished

An occurrence can play several roles in a CGL policy. Traditionally, general liability policies are triggered by an occurrence that results in bodily injury or property damage during the policy period. The coverage grant in the current ISO CGL form (CG 00 01) provides that coverage only applies if:

1)   the bodily injury or property damage is caused by an occurrence that takes place in the coverage territory; and

2)   the bodily injury cr property damage occurs during the policy period.

Occurrence also measures the insurer's indemnity obligations that affect when the insurer's duty to defend is exhausted. Looking back to the 1973 comprehensive general liability form, the policy provided that:

all bodily injury and property damage arising out of continuous or repeated exposure to substantially the same general conditions shall be considered as arising out of one occurrence.

More recent ISO forms have tweaked this language slightly, defining occurrence as "an accident, including continuous or repeated exposure to substantially the same general harmful conditions."

While this dual usage sometimes has created confusion, an occurrence is not the trigger of coverage under a liability policy. Broadly stated, an occurrence is the source or cause of the insured's liabilities. By contrast, it is the effect of that occurrence that triggers coverage. In short, the cause of the insured's liability determines the number of occurrences, but that cause does not trigger coverage under an occurrence policy. Coverage is triggered by bodily injury or property damage. Thus, it is the effect of the insured's negligence that determines which policies are triggered, not the date of the original causative negligence that set a train of events in motion that culminated in those injuries. The difference between the occurrence and its effects can be seen in different types of cases.

In some cases, cause and effect will coincide, as in the negligent operation of a motor vehicle. Such is not the case, however, if the cause of the auto accident was the negligent design of the vehicle by the auto manufacturer or negligence by a garage in adjusting the brakes of the vehicle. In these cases, the insured's negligence could antedate the injury-causing accident by months or even years.

A similar lag in time between negligent conduct and resulting injuries often occurs in product liability cases. For instance, in *Whittaker Corp. v. Allianz Underwriters*, 14 Cal. Rptr. 2d 659 (1992), a soft drink producer was sued for injuries resulting from exploding containers. Ruling that the cause of these injuries was the insured's decision to change the process by which its bottles were manufactured, the trial court held that coverage was triggered when the formula was changed. This ruling was overturned on appeal. While concurring that the insured's decision to change its product formulation caused the ensuing products liability claims, the Second District held that the policies were triggered by the bodily injury. Since injuries did not occur until the manufactured products actually left the premises, which did not occur until the next policy year, the appeals court held that only those policies in effect when the explosions took place were triggered, not the policies that were in place when the process was changed.

This is not to say that the issue of trigger is entirely removed from determining how many policy limits may be implicated by a given claim or set of claims. A claim that is deemed to trigger coverage through either a manifestation or actual injury approach generally is more likely to tap into only a single policy limit. Conversely, those jurisdictions that follow a continuous injury or injury in fact approach are more likely to permit an insured to recover a separate occurrence limit in each policy year during which injury occurs.

Policy Wordings and Occurrences Determinations

Indemnity Limits

The limits of the insurer's indemnity obligation generally are set forth in the policy declarations. For instance, a policy may provide that coverage is afforded for $1 million each occurrence, $2 million in the general aggregate, and $1 million for the products-completed operations aggregate. These terms are significant because the CGL form's definition of occurrence states that:

> Occurrence means an accident, including continuous or repeated exposure to substantially the same general harmful conditions.

Some policies contain event or happening language that is more commonly found in reinsurance agreements and permits the aggregation of a series of related acts. For example, in *Owens Illinois, Inc. v. United Insurance Co.*, 625 A.2d 1 (N.J. Super. 1993) *reversed on other grounds*, 650 A.2d 974 (N.J. 1994), policy provisions treating "a series of interrelated acts" were considered to be one "occurrence."

The insurer's obligation to pay damages on account of a covered occurrence is capped by the amount stated in the declarations. In the event that other claims are made against the insured, the insurer may owe a further policy limit (and an accompanying duty to defend) unless the additional claims arise out of the same occurrence for which the insurer has paid its limit. Some also may be subject to a policy aggregate or some other indemnity limitation.

Definition of Occurrence

CGL policies have typically provided that "bodily injury and property damage arising out of continuous or repeated exposure to substantially the same general conditions shall be considered as arising out of one occurrence." For the most part, courts have ruled that "conditions" are those that physically cause injury, not negligent acts or omissions that merely set the stage for such losses to occur, such as an insured's failure to warn about a dangerous condition in its products or a failure to prevent injuries from occurring on its premises.

In *Koikos v. Travelers Insurance Company*, 849 So.2d 263 (Fla. 2003), the Florida Supreme Court held that a restaurant's failure to prevent a gang shoot-out that injured several patrons had more than a single "cause." The court refused to find that the "continuous and repeated exposure to conditions" language was relevant in considering the acts or omissions of the policyholder for which it was deemed to be legally responsible, ruling instead that this language was intended to broaden the scope of earlier coverage so as to clearly afford coverage for incidents in which injuries resulted from environmental exposures or other conditions that occurred over an extended period of time:

> We conclude that the inclusion of the "continuous or repeated exposure" language does not restrict the definition of "occurrence" but rather expands it by including ongoing and slowly developing injuries, such as those in the field of toxic torts. Therefore, we reject Travelers' reliance on the "continuous or repeated exposure" language as a basis for concluding that Koikos' negligent failure to provide security constitutes a single occurrence under the terms of the policy. The victims were not "exposed" to the negligent failure to provide security. If the victims were "exposed" to anything, it was the bullets fired from the intruder's gun.

In *London Market Insurers v. Superior Court of Los Angeles County*, 146 Cal. App. 4th 648; 53 Cal. Rptr. 3d 154 (2d Dist. 2007), the California Court of Appeal rejected a primary insurer's contention that a product manufacturer's sale of asbestos products fell within the "continuous or repeated exposure to conditions" language. The court concluded that the failure to protect claimants from asbestos was not a "condition," but the condition was, rather, the asbestos fibers to which the underlying claimants were exposed. *See also Fina, Inc. v. Travelers Ind. Co.*, 184 F.Supp.2d 547 (N.D. Tex. 2002)(rejecting Travelers' argument that insured's failure to protect its employees was a "continuous or repeated exposure to conditions").

The First Department of the Appellate Division of the New York Supreme Court ruled in *Ramirez v. Allstate Ins. Co.*, 2006 NY Slip Op 01356 (App. Div. 2006), that separate claims brought by two infant children who were exposed to lead dust inside the insured's apartment building were subject to the same occurrence limit as presenting claims for bodily injury "resulting from continuous or repeated exposure to the same general conditions." *See also, Accord Allstate Ins. Co. v. Bonn*, 2010 U.S. Dist. LEXIS 43178 (D.R.I. May 3, 2010)(the children's exposure to lead paint in the insured's apartment share the same cause as arising out of continuous or repeated exposure to the same conditions, namely the presence of lead in the premises).

The court ruled in *Western World Ins. Co. v. Wilkie*, 5:06-cv-64 (E.D.N.C. November 1, 2007) that injuries suffered by various children who came into contact with fecal matter while petting animals at the insured's petting zoo over the course of a week arose out of exposure to the same general harmful conditions (the presence of e. coli at the zoo).

Despite an insurer's argument that the building complex had suffered water damage through various different means and therefore involved multiple "occurrences," Division One of the Washington Court of Appeals ruled in *Certain Underwriters at Lloyd's, London v. Valiant Ins. Co.*, 155 Wash. App. 469, 229 P.3d 930 (2010) that the gradual intrusion of water into the building over a five year period involved "continued or repeated exposure to substantially similar conditions" and was therefore only the product of a single "occurrence." Ongoing discharges of dust from the insured's recycling operations were held to involve "continuous exposure or repeated exposure to substantially the same general harmful conditions" despite the plaintiff's argument in *Stonelight Tile, Inc. v. California Insurance Guaranty Association*, 58 Cal. Rptr. 3d 74, 150 Cal. App. 4th 19 (2007) that there were different types of exposure so as to warrant a finding of separate "occurrences."

Rejecting arguments by the policyholder and excess insurers that each individual asbestos claimant is a new occurrence as well as the argument of the primary insurer that all of the underlying asbestos claims were a single occurrence, a federal district court ruled in *LSJ Technologies, Inc. v. U.S. Fire Ins. Co.*, No. 2:07-CV-399 (E.D. Tex. September 2, 2010) that individual claimants could be grouped together as one occurrence if they were all exposed to asbestos-containing gaskets at the same time and location so as to have been exposed to "substantially the same general conditions."

Courts have also refused to find that the "conditions" language supports the aggregation of multiple claims on the basis of a pattern of conduct. *See H.E. Butt Grocery Company v. National Union Fire Ins. Co. of Pittsburgh*, 150 F.3d 526, 533 (5th Cir. 1988)(refusing to combine two sexual assaults on two different children into one occurrence despite the fact that both claims were predicated on the insured employer's negligence in failing to prevent assault by pedophilic employee); *See also, American Red Cross v. Travelers Ind. Co. of Rhode Island*, 816 F. Supp. 755, 761 (D. DC 1993)(refusing to treat insured's "general, negligent practice in handling HIV-contaminated blood" as cause).

Aggregates

Prior to the 1986 edition of the CGL policy, few liability policies contained general aggregates. Even today, many general liability forms restrict aggregates to claims falling within the completed operations or products hazards or to risks that are underwritten on a remuneration basis. *See Weyerhaeuser Co. v. Commercial Union Ins. Co.*, 15 P.3d 115 (Wash. 2000), which noted that the underlying policy aggregate was restricted to claims for products and occupational disease.

Completed Operations and Products Hazards

The 1973 form defines products hazard as including:

> bodily injury and property damage arising out of the named insured's products or reliance upon a representation or warranty made at any time with respect thereto, but only if the bodily injury or property damage occurs away from premises owned by or rented to the named insured and after physical possession of such products has been relinquished to others.

In short, this hazard extends only to suits in which the plaintiff was injured by the insured's product after the insured had relinquished physical control over it. Injuries that occurred while a product was still being installed were therefore not subject to this aggregate limitation. For example, see *Frontier Insulation Contractors, Inc. v. Merchants Mutual Ins. Co.*, 91 N.Y.2d 169 (1997), which deals with asbestos claims.

The completed operations hazard performs a similar function for contractors that the products hazard fulfills for manufacturers. In addition to the question of the location of injury, this hazard requires that the injury take place after the contractor's work at a given location has been completed. Current forms continue these distinctions from premises hazards, even though products and completed operations are combined within one definition.

Occupational Disease

Employer's liability and some general liability policies also contain language setting an indemnity limit for all occupational disease claims against the insured. Such policies typically state:

> The Company's liability shall be further limited to the [aggregate amount] stated with respect to all ultimate net loss because of personal injury which occurs during each annual period while this policy is in force commencing from its effective date and which arises out of occupational diseases of employees of the insured.

Occupational disease is a term that long has been used in Federal Employers' Liability Act (FELA) and workers compensation case law to describe certain types of employment-related injuries that have two characteristics: 1) the impairment must be caused by employment, and 2) the impairment must gradually result from exposure to conditions of work over an extended period of time. These characteristics are explained in cases such as *Urie v. Thompson*, 337 U.S. 163 (1949).

Premium Bases: Remuneration and Otherwise

The 1973 policy provided for an aggregate limit to apply when premium was quoted on a remuneration basis. Remuneration (payroll) can be contrasted with the other standard measures of premium, such as square footage, receipts, or frontage.

In *Allstate v. Dana Corp.* 737 N.E.2d 1177 (Ind. App. 2000), the Indiana Court of Appeals refused to find that remuneration language was ambiguous, noting that a definition in the policy made clear that "operations rated on a remuneration" basis meant "a business' facilities or activities whose policies are rated according to the compensation paid to the insured's owners and employees." Inasmuch as the excess policies were written on a sales basis, and not remuneration, the court ruled that the excess policies did not contain aggregate limits.

Earlier Aggregate Wordings

Prior to the emergence of the CGL policy as the dominant policy form in the early 1970s, many liability policies provided for separate policy aggregates for operations, contractual, protective, and products coverage areas. The limits language in these older "accident" forms provided that:

Limits of Liability: Products

> The limits of bodily injury liability or property damage liability stated in the declarations as "aggregate products" are respectively the total limits of the company's liability for all damages arising out of the products hazard. All such damages arising out of one prepared or acquired lot of goods or products shall be considered as arising out of an accident.

Limits of Liability: Operations

> The limits of property damage liability stated in the declarations as "aggregate operations" is the total limit of the company's liability for all damages arising out of injury to or destruction of property, including the loss of use thereof, caused by the ownership, maintenance or use of premises or operations rated upon a remuneration premium basis or by contractors equipment rated on a receipts premium basis.

Limits of Liability: Protective

> The limits of property damage liability stated in the declarations as "aggregate protective" is the total limit of the company's liability for all damages arising out of injury to or destruction of property, including the loss of use thereof, caused by operations performed for the named insured by independent contractors or omissions or supervisory acts of the insured in connection therewith, except maintenance or ordinary alterations and repairs on premises owned or rented by the named insured.

Limits of Liability: Contractual

> The limits of property damage liability stated in the declarations as "aggregate contractual" is the total limit of the company's liability for all damages arising out of injury to or destruction of property, including the loss of use thereof, with respect to each contract.

> These limits apply separately to each project with respect to operations being performed away from premises owned or rented by the named insured.

Some also allowed aggregation on the basis of "continuous or repeated exposure to substantially the same general condition existing at or emanating from one premises location." Although these forms were used years ago, they are of continued significance in recent environmental cases. *See London Market Insurers v. Superior Court of Los Angeles County*, 146 Cal. App. 4th 648, 53 Cal. Rptr. 3d 154 (2d Dist. 2007).

Stacking and Anti-stacking Clauses

Stacking

In many states, even a single occurrence may trigger multiple policy limits to the extent that the jurisdiction recognizes a continuous trigger of coverage. The insured may recover a separate occurrence limit in each successive year for which bodily injury or property damage is shown to have occurred. In *Ranger Ins. Co. v. Safety-Kleen Corp.*, 814 F. Supp. 744 (N.D. Ill. 1993), a worker's exposure to solvents was held to trigger occurrence limits in successive years over which leukemia developed. In *Allstate v. Dana Corp.*, 737 N.E.2d 1177 (Ind. App. 2000), contamination involved only one occurrence but triggered new indemnity limits in successive policies.

In *State of California v. Continental Ins. Co.*, 281 P.3d 1000 (Cal. 2012), the California Supreme Court ruled that the limits of successive liability insurance policies could be stacked to satisfy the state's legal obligations with respect to the cleanup of the infamous Stringfellow Acid Pits Superfund site. Whereas it had earlier ruled that under an "all sums" analysis an insured could designate a single carrier to pay its loss leaving that insurer free to seek contribution from other insurers whose policies might be applicable, the Supreme Court held in this case that where a single policy year was inadequate to satisfy the insured loss, successive years of coverage could be stacked together. The court declared that, "The all sums with stacking rule means that the insured has immediate access to the insurance it purchased. It does not put the insured in the position of receiving less coverage than it bought. It also acknowledges the uniquely progressive nature of long-tail injuries that cause progressive damage throughout multiple policy periods." The court left the door open to insurers to adopt anti-stacking provisions in the future but declared that under the policies at issue in this case, stacking was permitted.

This is not uniformly the rule, however. In particular, a number of courts have ruled that if there is only one occurrence, the insured is not entitled to more than a single policy limit. To the extent that the occurrence takes place over the span of several years, the available indemnity will be prorated in proportion to the total limits for the years in question. Therefore, if the insured is forced to pay $1 million for loss that occurred over a ten-year period, each policy year will contribute $100,000.

This rule has been followed in several leading asbestos cases. Indeed, both of the federal circuit rulings that respectively devised the *exposure* and *triple trigger* approaches to the trigger issue cautioned that the insured should not be permitted to stack separate limits for the same occurrence. *See Keene v. INA*, 667 F.2d 1034 (D.C. Cir. 1981) and *INA v. Forty-Eight Insulations, Inc.*, 633 F.2d 1212 (6th Cir. 1980). In *Lafarge Corp. v. Hartford Ins. Co.*, 61 F.3d 389 (5th Cir. 1995) *overruled on other grounds*, 241 F. 3d 396 (5th Cir. Tex. 2001), the court ruled that the insurer's deductible must be prorated in the same manner as loss is apportioned among respective years of coverage.

Likewise, the Appellate Court of the New York Supreme Court ruled in *In Re Liquidation of Midland Ins. Co.*, 709 N.Y.S.2d 24 (N.Y. App. Div. 2000) that even though a loss may occur over a period of twenty years, the most that an insurer should owe is the single occurrence limit. "Otherwise, an insurer that issued a $1 million liability policy renewed twenty times could find itself liable for $20 million in damage claims for the same injury," said the court. The court declared that "our reading of the policy at issue indicates that the purpose of defining all exposure as one occurrence is to make clear that only one deductible will apply and that the limit of liability, where an insurer has issued renewal policies, should be the policy limits for one policy, rather than the aggregate for all policies issued." Similar reasoning also is found in *Garcia v. Physicians Insurance Exchange*, 876 S.W.2d 842 (Tex. 1994), in which the Texas Supreme Court ruled in a medical malpractice case that an insured could not recover more than a single occurrence limit for any given occurrence, regardless of the trigger theory that applied.

Anti-Stacking Terms: Noncumulation and Deemer Clauses

Unlike automobile liability forms, which now contain language specifically addressing policyholder efforts to stack limits, CGL policies do not contain specific anti-stacking language. Nevertheless, some policies, notably those issued by Liberty Mutual in earlier years, contained non-cumulation or deemer clauses that are claimed by insurers to have a similar anti-stacking effect.

Non-cumulation and deemer clauses are intended to prevent policyholders from stacking successive limits where an occurrence results in continuing damage during more than one policy issued by that insurance company. Certain policies contain endorsements stipulating that the insurer shall not owe more than a single limit even if the insured is entitled to claim coverage under multiple policies. An example of this wording is:

> Injury, damage or loss might be covered by this policy and also by other policies issued to you by us or any affiliate. When these other policies contain a provision similar to this one, the amount we will pay is limited. The maximum that we will pay under all such policies combined is the highest limit that applies in any one of these policies.

Several courts have relied on such clauses to limit an insured's recovery in a pollution case to a single policy limit, even in "continuous injury" jurisdictions. *See Hercules, Inc. v. AIU Insurance Company*, 784 A.2d 481 (Del. 2001); *Endicott Johnson Corporation v. Liberty Mutual Ins. Co.*, 928 F.Supp. 176, 180 (N.D.N.Y. 1996); and *O-I Brockway Glass Container, Inc. v. Liberty Mutual Ins. Co.*, 1994 WL 910935 (D.N.J. February 9, 1994). *But see Great Lakes Dredge and Dock Company v. The City of Chicago*, 57 F. Supp.2d 525 (N.D. Ill. 1999)(ruling that successive policies are triggered by flooding claims despite non-cumulation clauses).

The Appellate Court of Illinois ruled in *Illinois Central Railroad v. Acc. & Cas. Co. of Winterthur*, 739 N.E.2d 1049 (1st Dist. 2000) that a "deemer" clause in a CGL policy is only meant to apply in cases where an individual suffered injury in more than one policy, in which event the occurrence was assignable to the policy in which the first material damage took place.

The Delaware Supreme Court ruled in *Stonewall Ins. Co. v. E.I. Du Pont De Nemours & Co.*, 996 A.2d 1254 (Del. 2010) that a non-cumulation clause clearly was intended to reduce the available limits by the total amounts paid or due to the insured from earlier excess carriers. However, the court rejected Stonewall's contention that the word "loss" in this clause referred to the entire loss at issue and not merely those claims involving this policy. The court distinguished those claims that might involve multiple years of damage as opposed to those attributable to only a single year. The court also pointed out that Delaware follows an "all-sums" approach wherein the insured is restricted to a single tower of coverage allowing those carriers to seek contribution from insurers in other years. The court ruled that in light of the "in whole or in part" language of the non-cumulation clause, amounts payable to Du Pont that covered the entire loss would reduce Stonewall's liability, but where the amounts paid by prior excess carriers only covered part of the loss, then Stonewall's coverage applied to the remaining portion.

The Third Circuit ruled in a Pennsylvania case that a "non-cumulation" clause limited an excess insurer's duty to pay asbestos claims to a single policy limit despite the fact that the underlying policy's duty to pay would otherwise have been triggered each year that it had been written between 1975 and 1983. *Liberty Mutual Ins. Co. v. Treesdale, Inc.*, 418 F.3d 330 (3rd Cir. 2005). In keeping with *Treesdale*, in *Greene Tweed & Co., Inc. v. Hartford Acc. & Ind.*, No. 03-3637 (E.D. Pa. April 21, 2006), the court refused to find ambiguity in a "non-cumulation" clause in the American Home umbrella policies despite the insurer's objection that this clause was linked to "loss" in contrast to the occurrence language construed by the Third Circuit in Treesdale. Nevertheless, the court refused to give effect to this clause, finding that it was an unenforceable escape clause contrary to Pennsylvania law. Whereas "excess" clauses may be given effect, clauses that purport to entirely defeat coverage are unenforceable. The court also expressed concern that this might result in higher layer excess insurers being able to avoid coverage since this policy was not exhausted and archly noted that the Third Circuit had not even addressed this issue in *Treesdale*.

New York's highest court has upheld a non-cumulation clause in a lead paint poisoning case. In *Hiraldo v. Allstate Ins. Co.*, 5 N.Y.3d 508, 840 N.E.2d 451 (2005), the New York Court of Appeals held that a landlord's liability insurer's obligation to pay damages on account of a tenant's lead poisoning claims was limited to a single policy limit even though the insurer had issued three separate policies during the period of the child's injury. While suggesting that the stacking issue would ordinarily have been difficult to resolve, the court held that in this case the issue was settled by a "non-cumulation clause" in the policy stating that "regardless of the number of insured persons, injured persons, claims, claimants, or policies involved, our total liability under Business Liability Protection coverage for damages resulting from one loss will not exceed the limit of liability for coverage x shown on the declarations page. All bodily injury, personal injury and property damage resulting from one accident or from continuous or repeated exposure to the same general conditions is considered the result of one loss." As a result, the court concluded that Allstate had fully satisfied its liability through the payment of its $300,000 limit in a court notwithstanding the fact that three of its policies were potentially triggered by the child's lead poisoning.

On the whole, courts that follow an "all sums" approach seem more likely to give effect to non-cumulation clauses in long-tail cases, perhaps on the theory that the existence of such clauses is a refutation of the insurers' position that the policies impliedly require "time on the risk" allocation. *Chicago Bridge & Iron Co. v. Certain Underwriters at Lloyd's*, 59 Mass. App. Ct. 646, 797 N.E.2d 424 (2003). Conversely, some states that permit allocation, such as New Jersey, have held that the principles underlying non-cumulation are incompatible with *pro rata* allocation and that insurers should not be allowed to rely on non-cumulation clauses to reduce the "*pro rata*" exposure applicable to any individual year. *See Spaulding Composites Company, Inc. v. Aetna Cas. & Sur. Co.*, 176 N.J. 25, 819 A.2d 410 (2003).

Batch Clauses

A "batch clause states that all losses involving a single lot or batch of the insured's products will be treated as one occurrence." "Batch clauses" date back more than fifty years and were formerly a standard part of CGL forms before 1966.

In *Home Ins. Co. v. Aetna Casualty & Surety Co.*, 528 F.2d 1388 (2nd Cir. 1976), Diamond Shamrock sought coverage for losses involving a super-concentrated Vitamin D3 resin that it produced at a plant in New Jersey. The resin was melted to form a blend—some of which was sold in that form, some of which was mixed in corn oil and sold, and some of which were mixed with corn oil and shipped to plants in other states for the production of dry Vitamin D3 concentrates. As a result of production errors at the New Jersey plant, however, two lots of inactive super-concentrated Vitamin D3 resin were produced, mixed with corn oil and antioxidants, and shipped to Diamond's plant in Kentucky where they were sprayed onto corn cob fractions to make four lots of "Nopdex 200," a livestock food supplement which was sold to Central Soya Corporation to be included in their chicken feed product. In turn, Central Soya sold the feed to numerous chicken farmers who later reported that their chickens had died or been injured as the result of ingesting defective feed.

During the period in question, the general liability policy issued to Diamond Shamrock by Aetna provided coverage up to $250,000 per occurrence with a $100,000 "per occurrence" deductible. The term occurrence was defined as meaning, "an accident, including continuous or repeated exposure to conditions, which results in bodily injury or property damage neither expected nor intended from the standpoint of the insured." An endorsement to the policy set forth the following "batch clause" stating that, "As respects product liability for property damage coverage, all such damage arising out of one lot or goods or products prepared or acquired by the named insured or by another trading under its name shall be considered as arising out of one occurrence." In addition to this primary policy, Home issued a $3 million excess policy over the Aetna coverage.

A dispute arose among the parties with respect to the number of occurrences. Home argued that there were four occurrences, one for each of the "Nopdex 200" lots that had been created at the Diamond Shamrock plant in Kentucky and sold to Central Soya. Home pointed to the fact that this was the last act over which the insured had any control and was the basis for its liability. Diamond Shamrock and Aetna argued that there were only two occurrences, one for each of the two New Jersey lots of Vitamin D3 resin.

Both parties submitted legal arguments and affidavits concerning the history of the "batch clause" and the alleged custom and understanding of the insurance industry with respect to its scope. The U.S. District Court in New York excluded this extrinsic evidence, however, holding that conclusory statements as to intent were irrelevant and granted summary judgment for Home. On review, however, the Second Circuit held that the District Court erred in failing to take into account the custom in the insurance industry concerning the meaning of "batch clauses" and remanded the case for further findings.

Issues with respect to "batch clauses" also surfaced in the context of Agent Orange claims two decades ago. Thus, in *Diamond Shamrock Chemicals v. Aetna Casualty & Surety Co.*, 609 A.2d 167 (1992), the Appellate Division of the New Jersey Supreme Court refused to find that the "batch clause" in Aetna's policy applied, holding instead that it only extended to problems involving manufacturing defects, not design errors. The court found that the intent of the "batch clause" was to maximize the available insurance coverage by preventing the stacking of policy deductibles for each batch of defectively manufactured product. While the court conceded that nothing in the policy itself required a distinction between manufacturing and design defects, it found that this analysis was consistent with the above-stated intent to use the "batch clause" to maximize coverage rather than limiting it.

Not all courts have recognized this distinction between manufacturing and design claims with respect to the intended application of "batch clauses", however. For instance, in *Ruthart v. Underwriters at Lloyd's London*, Suffolk No. 91-7877 (Mass. Super. March 12, 1998), the State Insurance Commissioner brought suit against the reinsurers of the now-insolvent American Mutual Liability Insurance Company to recover sums allegedly owed as the result of AMLICO's settlement of numerous underlying asbestos liability claims. The court ruled that the claims involved separate "occurrences" and that the claims were subject to separate "batch clause" retentions in certain of the treaties, rejecting the Insurance Commissioner's argument on behalf of AMLICO that such clauses are inapplicable to cases involving "design defects" or inherently dangerous products.

Likewise, in *E.R. Squibb & Sons, Inc. v. Accident and Casualty Ins. Co.*, (S.D. February 1997), the court ruled that various DES claims against E.R. Squibb were subject to a "batch clause." Notwithstanding the Appellate Division's ruling in *Diamond Shamrock*, the court agreed with London underwriters that such clauses were applicable to design defect claims and should therefore limit the number of occurrences presented by the underlying DES actions.

In *London Market Insurers v. Superior Court of Los Angeles County*, 146 Cal. App. 4th 648; 53 Cal. Rptr. 3d 154 (2007), the California Court of Appeal held that asbestos liability claims had not arisen out of a single lot of goods or products under various early CGL policies, as there was no evidence that all of the asbestos claims derived from a single lot of the insured's products. The court declined to limit this language to claims involving design defects, declaring that it had equal applicability to non-conforming products. The court rejected the contrary analysis adopted by the Appellate Court in *Diamond Shamrock* in 1992.

Annualization: Multi-Year Policies

Courts have reached conflicting conclusions with respect to whether policies containing three-year limits should be interpreted as involving only a single policy limit or otherwise. Most three-year policies contain an annualization clause that states that the policy limit is refreshed on an annual basis. For instance, Insurance Services Office (ISO) policies commonly provide the following wording:

> The Limits of Insurance of this Coverage Part apply separately to each consecutive annual period and to any remaining period of less than 12 months...

In the absence of an annualization clause, several courts have ruled that the policy limits stretch over the entire term and are not separately available in each year of the policy term. Examples of this reasoning can be found in *Society of Roman Catholic Church of Diocese of Lafayette, Inc. v. Interstate Fire and Cas. Co.*, 126 F.3d 727 (5th Cir. 1997); *Diamond Shamrock Chemicals Co. v. Aetna Cas. & Sur. Co.*, 609 A.2d 440 (N.J. Super. 1992), *disapproved by* 629 A. 2d 885 (N.J. Sup. 1992); *Hercules, Inc. v. Aetna Cas. & Sur. Co.*, 1998 WL 962089 (Del. Super. September 30, 1998); *CSX Transportation, Inc. v. Commercial Union Ins. Co.*, 82 F.3d 478 (D.C. Cir. 1996); *Air Products and Chemical, Inc. v. Hartford Accident and Ind. Co.*, 1989 WL 73656 (E.D. Pa. June 30, 1989); *Asten Johnson v. Columbia Cas. Co.*, No. 03-1552 (E.D. Pa. March 30, 2007) and *Outboard Marine Corp. v. Liberty Mutual Ins. Co.*, 670 N.E.2d 740 (Ill. App. 1996), *appeal denied*, 675 N.E.2d 634 (Ill. 1996). *But see Chemical Lehman Tank Lines, Inc. v. Aetna Cas. & Sur. Co.*, 978 F. Supp. 589 (D.N.J. 1997) *reversed on other grounds*, 177 F.3d 210 (3rd Cir. 1999) and

Mennen Company v. Atlantic Mutual Ins. Co., No. 93-CIV-5273 (D.N.J. October 20, 1999).

In *California Ins. Co. v. Stimson Lumber Co.*, 2004 WL 1173185 (D. Or. May 26, 2004), a lumber manufacturer sought coverage for various claims arising out of an exterior hardwood siding product. In 2004, the federal district court gave effect to a "prior insurance non-cumulation of liability" provision in the National Union policies which stated that if a "loss" covered under the policy was also covered in whole or in part under any earlier excess policy, the amounts due would be reduced by the amounts owed to the insured under that prior insurance. Although the insured argued that "loss" referred only to each individual siding claim paid by Stimson and therefore should not reduce its claims in the aggregate, the federal district court in Oregon held that this analysis was "unreasonable" and rather held that "loss" should be understood as being similar to "ultimate net loss" and therefore applied to the gross amount that the insured is seeking in its claim under the policy. Accordingly, the court ruled that, "To the extent that there is any excess insurance coverage available for the siding loss, the non-cumulation provision applies to reduce National Union's policy limits by the amounts paid in prior policy years as amounts paid by other excess settling insurers."

Note that more recent editions of the CGL form have added language expressly addressing how many limits of coverage apply in the case of so-called "stub" policies that are issued or extended for more than a single twelve month period. Thus, the standard ISO form (CG 00 01) provides:

> The Limits of Insurance of this Coverage Part apply separately to each consecutive annual period and to any remaining period of less than 12 months, starting with the beginning of the policy period shown in the Declarations, unless the policy period is extended after issuance for an additional period of less than 12 months. In that case, the additional period will be deemed part of the last preceding period for purposes of determining the Limits of Insurance.

Combined Single Limits

General liability policies now are written on a combined single limits basis. Instead of the policy providing separate limits for bodily injury and property damage claims, a single limit governs both.

For the most part, such wording should not affect the number of occurrences or the circumstances under which aggregate limits apply. Rather, the main effect of such clauses is simply to make the same limit applicable to claims for bodily injury or property damage that arise out of one occurrence. While payments made under bodily injury claims therefore will reduce the indemnity available for property damage and vice versa, the same rules apply as are ordinarily applicable with respect to whether the claims are to be treated as a single occurrence or otherwise.

The exception to this general statement is language often found in combined single limit *per project* aggregate limit endorsements that state that the applicable limits of liability "shall apply separately to each project with respect to operations being performed away from premises owned by or rented to the insured." Policyholders sometimes have argued in environmental cases that this language requires a separate occurrence limit for each shipment of waste that a transporter disposes of off-site. Despite the fact that there is no further clarification on what project or operations the clause concerns, it does not appear that such a sweeping interpretation was intended. Similar endorsements are available to provide separate general aggregate limits to each of the insured's locations.

Cases in Which Disputes Arise

Disputes concerning how an occurrence should be defined typically involve situations with multiple plaintiffs, multiple insureds, or widespread injuries.

Multiple Plaintiffs

Most disputes involving the number of occurrences involve multiple injured parties. Occasionally, claims will arise involving a single injured party, such as when a patient sues a physician for negligent failure to properly diagnose or treat his condition over the course of several consultations. In such circumstances, the issue is whether the occurrence (typically under a professional liability policy) is the overall course of treatment or the insured's discrete acts of negligence.

For instance, a federal district court ruled in *All Tech Claims Management, LLC v. Philadelphia Indemnity Ins. Co.*, No. 4:10-CV-01657 (S.D. Tex. July 18, 2011) that an insurance adjusting company must pay a separate deductible on each claim arising from its adjustment of Hurricane Ike claims in Texas, rejecting All Tech's argument that it was only responsible for a single deductible for all of its adjusting work arising out of Ike. The court refused to find that the different adjustment claims were all "logically or causally related."

Such claims may be complicated by the introduction of additional claimants through actions for loss of consortium by family members.

Because such claims are derivative in nature and do not allege any independent claim for bodily injury or property damage, most courts treat them as being subject to the same policy limit that would apply to the injured spouse or parent.

Multiple Insureds

Most occurrence disputes involve only a single insured. However, more than one insured may be named in the same suit. This frequently arises in medical malpractice cases in which the insured's partner consults in a diagnosis or actively participates in the patient's treatment. If the policy requires that each insured be treated separately when applying policy limits, the issue again is whether the occurrence was the overall course of treatment or each insured's discrete acts of negligence. Courts are far less likely to find separate causes when one insured's negligence was closely interwoven with the others, such as when one physician negligently relied on his partner's original misdiagnosis in prescribing further treatment.

Widespread Injuries

In cases where multiple plaintiffs have filed suit, such as in widespread asbestos-injury cases, the crucial factor in determining whether their claims may be aggregated is the extent to which their injuries occurred closely together in time and space. Courts are far more likely to find one cause for diverse claimants when the injuries are part of a continuum of physical conduct by the insured or are otherwise closely linked together. By contrast, multiple causes are more likely to be found when the exposures are geographically dispersed or when they occurred months apart.

Parties to Occurrence Disputes

Although many occurrence disputes fit the classic pattern of a dispute between insureds and insurers, such disputes also may arise between insurers and between insurers and reinsurers.

Insured versus Insurer

There are several benefits to keeping primary insurance limits from being exhausted, not the least of which is the fact that defense costs often are paid in addition to the limits—as long as coverage limits remain. In order to maintain these benefits, policyholders typically argue that claims against them involve multiple occurrences and that policy aggregates do not apply to each claim. Insureds also may be forced to take such positions in situations where the available indemnity limits are simply inadequate to pay for the claims against them.

The coverage calculus becomes more complicated, however, when the primary policies contain deductibles or self-insured retentions that are written on a per occurrence basis and are not subject to any ceiling or aggregate. In such cases, a finding of multiple occurrences requires the insured to pay much more of the loss and significantly diminishes the value of its insurance coverage.

For example, a policy with a $25,000 per occurrence self-insured retention (SIR) and a $1 million liability limit may be triggered by claims from multiple victims. If each claim were considered an occurrence, the insured could have access to multiple $1 million settlement limits. However, the insured also could be responsible for the same number of $25,000 SIRs.

Insurer versus Insurer

Disputes also may arise between different layers of insurance, particularly between primary and umbrella insurers. A primary insurer may argue that its duty to provide a defense to mass tort claims against a policyholder ends when it settles some of the claims and exhausts the policy's occurrence limit. An excess insurer may argue that the claims involve more than one occurrence and that the primary insurer should continue to defend and be responsible for indemnity obligations.

Insurer versus Reinsurer

Finally, disputes may arise between insurers and reinsurers with respect to whether related types of claims should be grouped together to penetrate the reinsurance certificate or treaty. Although such disputes generally are based on *event* or *happening* language that is different from conventional occurrence wordings, the disputes often are impacted by decisions that primary insurers make when addressing their policyholders' claims. They also are affected by the manner in which the ceding insurer assigns value to particular claims in the context of a global settlement or policy buyback. Finally, in the absence of reinsurance case law, courts considering such issues may fall back on CGL precedents.

Legal Tests for Counting Occurrences

Courts have devised three rules for determining whether multiple instances of bodily injury or property damage should be treated as arising out of more than one occurrence:

1) **The Cause Test.** The first, and by far the most broadly accepted rule, is the so-called *cause* approach in which all losses arising out of the same source are treated as one occurrence.

2)   **The Event Test.** A related approach that is followed for the most part only in New York is the *unfortunate event* analysis, in which temporal and spatial limitations are applied when determining whether losses have a common cause. In short, injuries that are closely grouped in time and space are more likely to be treated as a single occurrence than those that are more spread out.

3)   **The Effect Test.** Finally, an earlier but now largely discredited approach considered the *effect* of causes in determining whether they presented multiple occurrences.

While most courts have adopted the cause approach, cause has meant different things to different courts. Indeed, its very elasticity has permitted courts to adopt different meanings of cause to maximize coverage for policyholders in different types of cases while still purporting to be true to the cause test.

Cause Meanings

To the extent that applicable case law can be dissected, cause analysis has been accorded one of two different meanings: proximate cause and legal cause.

Immediate Physical Cause of Injuries (Proximate Cause)

The most common meaning of cause is a physical one, that is, the event that is the immediate cause of the plaintiff's injuries. For instance, the Fifth Circuit ruled in *H.E. Butt Grocery Co. v. National Union Fire Ins. Co. of Pittsburgh*, 150 F.3d 526 (5th Cir. 1998) that two separate sexual assaults by a store employee were separate occurrences for the purpose of applying a self-insured retention. Even though the claims were based on the insured's negligent failure to supervise the employee, the court declared that the immediate cause of the underlying injuries was the intervening intentional tort of the employee. Therefore, each separate assault was a separate occurrence. A concurring opinion took issue with the court's immediate cause analysis, arguing instead that the number of occurrences should be based on the event giving rise to liability from the insured's point of view. The outcome of the case would have been the same, however.

In cases where the insured's conduct was the immediate cause of the injuries, courts typically define cause in a manner similar to the tort conception of *proximate cause*. These cases tend to consider the direct, physical cause of the injuries as the yardstick for measuring whether the claims shared a common origin. For example, when the insured physically strikes a plaintiff—whether with fists, a weapon, or a motor vehicle—courts have tended to find that each separate physical act is a new occurrence.

A distinction sometimes is drawn between cases in which the insured literally is out of control, as in the case of a speeding car that ricochets from one collision to the next, and instances in which the insured has the opportunity to stop and gain control of the situation between each act to prevent further injuries. Courts are far more likely to find only one occurrence in the former fact pattern than in the latter.

Event Giving Rise to Insured's Liability (Legal Cause)

The Connecticut Supreme Court has suggested that cause cases may be divided into two separate categories: those that consider the physical cause of the plaintiff's injuries and those that trigger the insured's liability. As seen in *Metropolitan Life Ins. Co. v. Aetna Casualty & Surety Company*, 765 A. 2d 891 (Conn. 2001), the court refused to find that Metropolitan's failure to disclose asbestos risks was the cause of the underlying claimants' asbestos injuries. Instead the court found that each claimant's exposure to asbestos was a separate occurrence, which decreased Metropolitan's ability to trigger excess liability coverage.

In *Mitsui Sumitomo Ins. Co. of America v. Automatic Elevator Co.*, 09-00480 (M.D.N.C. September 13, 2011), *aff'd*, No. 11-2057 (4th Cir. Feb. 11, 2013), a court ruled that allegations that the insured negligently disposed of waste hydraulic fluid that Duke University mistakenly subsequently used to clean hundreds of surgical instruments involved a single occurrence. The court declared that the occurrence in this case was the elevator contractor's negligence in failing to properly dispose of waste created in the course of its maintenance work, rejecting Duke's argument that there is no occurrence until injury occurs and that, as a result, the focus of the limits analysis must be on the individual surgeries that were performed on different individuals at different times in different hospitals over a 60-day period. These findings were affirmed by the Fourth Circuit in an unpublished 2013 opinion. Notwithstanding the insured's argument that the court should have looked to the "most immediate cause" to find multiple occurrences, the Court of Appeals ruled that "looking to the number of surgeries or instances of using hydraulic fluid to wash surgical instruments to determine the number of occurrences would turn the focus from Automatic Elevator's alleged negligence to Duke's actions." Because Automatic Elevator is the insured party, calculating the number of occurrences based on Duke's conduct would contradict other courts' conclusions that it is more appropriate to "focus on the act of the insureds that gave rise to their liability."

Most general liability policies provide that bodily injury and property damage arising out of "continuous or repeated exposure to substantially the same general harmful conditions" is considered as arising out of one occurrence. (This or similar wording may be included in the definition of occurrence or within a limits of liability section in various editions of standard CGL forms.) Some have argued that this *conditions* language should be interpreted in reference to the acts or omissions that form the basis for the insured's legal liability. When the insured acts in direct physical proximity to the plaintiff, as in many preceding examples, these *conditions* coincide. However, when the insured's conduct is remote from the immediate cause of the plaintiff's injuries—as in products liability cases or theories of liability based on negligent training, supervision, or inspection—the direct cause of injury may have little relevance to the legal cause for purposes of ascertaining the number of occurrences.

For instance, a defective product placed in the stream of commerce by a manufacturer typically will pass through numerous middlemen and intervening circumstances before it physically encounters and injures the plaintiff. In such circumstances, courts will look to the last event over which the insured had any control or which otherwise forms the legal basis for the suit against it. As a result, a given set of claims may comprise only one occurrence for the manufacturer but could result in multiple occurrences for the vendor who sold the product to multiple individuals.

A minority view holds that individual legal theories may not form a basis for separate occurrences, however. For example, in *S.F. v. West American Ins. Co.*, 463 S.E.2d 450 (Va. 1995), the court declared that the meaning of occurrence was ambiguous in that it could extend to the insured's hiring, supervision, or negligent retention of the molester. However, in *Danielson v. ABC Ins. Co.*, 623 N.W.2d 182 (Wis. App. 2000), the court decided that the plaintiff was only entitled to a single "occurrence limit" despite a separate theory of liability involving the insured's negligent entrustment of his vehicle. What may be relevant is the act forming the basis for the insured's liability, not the theories of liability themselves.

For the most part, courts have refused to find that the "conditions" language supports the aggregation of multiple claims on the basis of a pattern of conduct. As discussed previously, the court in *H.E. Butt Grocery Company v. National Union Fire Ins. Co. of Pittsburgh*, 150 F.3d 526 (5th Cir. 1988), refused to combine two sexual assaults on two different children into one occurrence despite the fact that both claims were predicated on the insured employer's negligence in failing to prevent the assaults by its pedophilic employee. Similarly, in *American Red Cross v. Travelers Ind. Co. of Rhode Island*, 816 F. Supp. 755 (D. D.C. 1993), the court refused to treat the insured's "general, negligent practice in handling HIV-contaminated blood" as the "cause."

Burden of Proof Issues

An issue that is rarely considered but of considerable significance in many of these cases is whether it is the insurer or policyholder who has the burden of establishing the cause of the underlying loss.

In a case of first impression, the Illinois Supreme Court assigned this burden to a liability insurer. In *Addison Ins. Co. v. Faye*, 2009 Ill. LEXIS 176 (Ill. January 23, 2009), the court ruled that although an insured has the burden of proving that a loss is covered in the first instance, the issue of limits was more of a limitation on coverage for which the insurer had the burden of proof. In keeping with Nicor, the court declared that the losses would be viewed as separate occurrences if they were the result of separate and intervening human acts or each act increased the insured's exposure to liability. The case involved the death of two boys who died of hypothermia after getting trapped outdoors in wet sand on a neighbor's property but were not discovered until days later. While stating that the two deaths might well have involved a single occurrence if the injuries had occurred closely together in time and space, the court found that it was impossible to prove how the boys died. As the insurer had failed in its burden of proof, the court held that the claims must be treated as involving separate occurrences.

External Factors Impacting Occurrence Determinations

Role of Insured

The resolution of these disputes often depends on where the insured stands in relation to how the accident occurred. The distinction may be illustrated by several cases that involved bodily injuries caused by a shooting.

In *American Ind. Co. v. McQuaig*, 435 So. 2d 414 (Fla. App. 1983), a homeowner engaged in a shoot-out with the police, injuring three officers with successive shotgun blasts. The District Court of Appeals held that each shotgun blast was a separate occurrence. Likewise, an incident in which the plaintiff separately shot and killed various family members was held to involve multiple occurrences based upon a claimed ambiguity in the meaning of occurrence in *State Farm Lloyds, Inc. v. Williams*, 960 S.W. 2nd 781 (Tex. Civ. App. 1997). By contrast, in *Travelers Ind. Co. v. Olive's Sporting Goods*, 764 S.W.2d 596 (Ark. 1989), a sporting goods store was sued by several individuals who were injured after a person to whom the store had sold a gun went on a shooting spree. In these circumstances, the Arkansas Supreme Court held that all of the claims against the insured arose out of the same occurrence, which was the insured's sale of the gun.

The courts' seemingly inconsistent analyses in these gunshot cases may be harmonized by taking into account the role of the insured relative to the immediate, direct cause of the plaintiffs' injuries. In the Texas and Florida cases, the insured stood in direct proximity to the plaintiffs' injuries and was able to control the manner of injury as he aimed and fired. By contrast, in the Arkansas case, the insured's role ended at the point of sale, and that insured had no influence over the manner in which the gun caused injury. Thus, the determination of the number of occurrences is significantly affected by whether the insured had any opportunity to control the process of injury after it commenced.

Similarly, when numerous persons are injured as the result of an ongoing physical process, the resulting injuries typically will be treated as one occurrence. In cases involving natural disasters, such as fires, floods, or auto accidents where the vehicle caroms off one car before striking others, courts generally have found only one occurrence. This is illustrated in *American Cas. Co. v. Heary*, 432 F. Supp. 995 (E.D. Va. 1977), where the court ruled that traffic accidents resulting from the collapse of utility lines a minute after the insured ran into a telephone pole all arose out of one occurrence; in *Bish v. Guaranty Nat. Ins. Co.*, 848 P.2d 1057 (Nev. 1993), in which the insured ran over the plaintiff, put the car in reverse and then ran her over again, the court ruled that the claims involved a single occurrence despite the multiple culpable acts of conduct; and in *Miley v. Continental Ins. Co.*, 645 So. 2d 1166 (La. App. 1994), in which two car collisions that occurred fifteen minutes apart were held to arise out of a single occurrence because both were caused by smoke from a controlled burn that the insured was conducting in a forest adjacent to the highway.

Likewise, the U.S. Court of Appeals for the Seventh Circuit ruled in *Auto-Owners Ins. Co. v. Munroe*, 614 F.3d 322 (7th Cir. 2010) that successive collisions involving three trucks that the insured was operating in a convoy only triggered a single $1 million occurrence limit for allegations with respect to the insured's alleged negligence in hiring and training the truck drivers. Applying Illinois law, the court rejected the plaintiff's argument that there were three limits at issue based upon separate negligent acts of each defendant, declaring instead that the case involved a single uninterrupted chain reaction.

In such cases, the insured was the immediate physical cause of the injuries. Absent some intervening cause, courts typically treat all of the resulting claims as one occurrence. Further, when the acts of negligence are interconnected, they will not be examined separately to create new occurrences.

On the other hand, courts sometimes find more than one occurrence in cases where the insured has the opportunity to stop further injury but failed to do so. In such cases, courts are far more likely to treat each new injury as a separate occurrence. However, in at least one case, the Wisconsin Court of Appeals ruled that, even though a motorist drove over a cyclist and then accidentally backed over him again, these separate incidents were part of the same occurrence because they were the single, uninterrupted cause of the cyclist's injuries. *See Welter v. Singer*, 376 N.W.2d 84 (Wis. App. 1985).

Physical Proximity/Continuity of Damage

Where numerous persons are injured as the result of an on-going physical process, the resulting injuries will typically be treated as one occurrence. Thus, in cases involving natural disasters, such as fires or floods, or auto accidents where the vehicle caroms off one car before striking others, courts have generally found only one occurrence. *See USAA v. Baggett*, 209 Cal. App.3d 1387, 258 Cal. Rptr. 52 (1989)(collision that occurred when a third car ran into motorists who had gotten out of their vehicles to talk after they ran into each other held to arise out of the same accident). In such cases, the insured is the immediate physical cause of the resulting injuries. Absent some intervening cause, courts typically treat all of the resulting claims as one occurrence. Further, where the acts of negligence are interconnected, they will not be examined separately to create new occurrences.

On the other hand, courts may sometimes find more than one occurrence in cases where the insured has the opportunity to stop further injury but fails to do so. In such cases, courts are far more likely to treat each new injury as a separate occurrence. *But see, Welter v. Singer*, 376 N.W.2d 84 (Wis. App. 1985) (even though car drove over a cyclist and then accidentally backed over him again, these separate incidents were part of the same occurrence because they were the single, uninterrupted cause of the cyclist's injuries).

Insured's Coverage Profile

Apart from the insured's role relative to the underlying claims, the single most important factor governing the resolution of these disputes is the insured's coverage profile and, in particular, whether the policies in question contain low indemnity limits, deductibles, or self-insured retentions.

In seeking to maximize coverage, courts first will look at the type of claims presented. Does the insured face hundreds of small claims that largely will be absorbed by policy deductibles and retentions? If so, courts are far more likely to treat the claims as involving one occurrence. Alternatively, are the individual suits themselves quite serious, in that they may exceed the insured's individual policy limits? In such circumstances, courts often will maximize the available coverage by treating the claims as separate occurrences.

Small Claims/Large Retentions

A close examination of the cases in which courts have ruled that mass tort liabilities were all one occurrence reveals that a large number of them feature policies containing large self-insured retentions or similar features that would otherwise have adversely impacted coverage availability for the insured. Examples of such an approach when insured retentions affect coverage applicability are *Champion International Corp. v. Continental Cas. Co.*, 546 F.2d 502 (2d Cir. 1976); *Champion International Corp. v. Liberty Mutual Ins. Co.*, 701 F. Supp. 409 (S.D.N.Y. 1988), and *Owens Illinois, Inc. v. United Insurance Co.*, 625 A.2d 1 (N.J. App. 1993) *rev'd on other grounds*, 650 A.2d 974 (N.J. 1994).

Likewise, in *Transport Ins. Co. v. Lee Way Motor Freight, Inc.* 487 F. Supp. 1325 (N.D. Tex. 1980), multiple instances of race discrimination at four separate locations were found to arise out of a single "pattern and practice" and thus constituted one occurrence under a policy that had a $25,000 per occurrence deductible.

In *Washoe County v. Transcontinental Ins. Co.*, 878 P.2d 306 (Nev. 1994), the Nevada Supreme Court declared that dozens of sexual molestation suits against the county for its claimed failure to properly inspect and monitor the operations of a private day-care center constituted a single occurrence. By state law, the county's liability for such claims was $50,000, the same amount as its self-insured retention in its insurance policy. A finding of multiple occurrences would have effectively nullified the value of the coverage. Even though this consideration was not stated in the court's opinion, it surely influenced it.

There are exceptions to every general rule, however. Courts have decided in several hearing loss cases that the individual liabilities may not be aggregated to maximize coverage, even though the rulings have largely vitiated the value of these policies to the insureds. This is illustrated in *Norfolk and Western Railway Co. v. Accident and Cas. Ins. Co. of Winterthur*, 796 F. Supp. 929 (W.D. Va. 1992), *aff'd on other grounds*, 41 F.3d 928 (4th Cir.1994).

Likewise, the Second Circuit has issued a series of rulings in asbestos and environmental cases declaring that an insurer's policy obligations are not triggered until the pro rata share allocable to that policy year exhausts a full self-insured retention for each policy. *See Stonewall Ins. Co. v. Asbestos Claims Management Corp.*, 73 F.3d 1178 (2nd Cir. 1995) and *Maryland Casualty Co. v. Gerling-Konzern Allgemiene Versicherungs-Atiengelsellschaft*, 128 F.3d 794 (2nd Cir. 1997), and *Olin Corp. v. INA*, 221 F.3d 307 (2nd Cir. 2000).

Deductibles and Self-Insured Retentions (SIRs)

Policyholders have vigorously argued that successive policy limits may be triggered for continuing injury claims when the argument is in their best interest to obtain additional coverage. However, they have opposed this analysis when the question of multiple policy deductibles is at stake. In such instances policyholders have contended that, when there is a single occurrence, the most they should pay in the aggregate is a single occurrence deductible, or, alternatively, that their obligations should be prorated over multiple policies because the claims arise out of a single occurrence.

A number of courts that have adopted a single occurrence approach have been influenced by the involvement of per occurrence deductibles or self-insured retentions. These include *U.S. Gypsum Company v. Admiral Ins. Co.*, 643 N.E.2d 1226 (Ill. App. 1994) and *Owens Illinois, Inc. v. United Insurance Co.*, 625 A.2d 1 (N.J. App. 1993) *rev'd on other grounds*, 650 A.2d 974 (N.J. 1994).

These deductible/retention cases fall into two categories: 1) those in which the insured must pay a full deductible for every policy year for which coverage is triggered, and 2) those in which the most an insured may be required to pay is a single deductible, no matter how many policy years are triggered by the occurrence.

One Full Deductible for Each Year. The majority view is that an insured is responsible for a separate retention in each policy year for which it claims coverage.

In *Northern States Power Co. v. Fidelity & Cas. Co.*, 523 N.W.2d 657 (Minn. 1994), the Minnesota Supreme Court ruled that clean up claims involving the insured's MGP sites were a single occurrence that should be pro-rated across the entire period of pollution on a "time on the risk" basis. The Court further ruled that even though the claim was one occurrence the insured must pay a full self-insured retention in each triggered policy year.

In *Owens-Illinois, Inc. v. United Ins. Co.*, 264 N.J. Super. 460, 625 A.2d 1 (1993), *reversed on other grounds*, 138 N.J. 437, 650 A.2d 974 (1994), the Appellate Division ruled that an asbestos manufacturer was obligated to pay a separate $250,000 self-insured retention for each policy under which the insured was claiming coverage for asbestos liabilities. The court rejected the insurers' contention that the insured was responsible for a separate SIR for each underlying suit, however.

Later, the New Jersey Supreme Court ruled in *Benjamin Moore & Co. v. Aetna Casualty & Surety Co.*, 179 N.J. 87, 843 A.2d 1094 (2004) that a policyholder is responsible for a full occurrence deductible in each triggered year. Notwithstanding its recent ruling in *Spalding* that had refused to give effect to a non-cumulation clause that would have limited an insurer's allocated share beyond that otherwise called for in *Owens-Illinois* and *Carter-Wallace*, the Supreme Court ruled that the purpose of *Owens-Illinois* was simply to standardize irregular environmental losses into separate occurrences that could be assigned to individual policy years. After that, so long as the policy terms were not inconsistent with Owens-Illinois, they should be given effect. Two dissenting judges argued that this result rendered the coverage illusory and that Benjamin Moore should have been entitled to pro-rate its deductibles consistent with the overall period of injury.

In *Missouri Pacific Railroad Co. v. International Ins. Co.*, 288 Ill. App.3d 69, 679 N.E.2d 801 (1997), an Illinois trial court had originally permitted the insured railroad to pick and choose the policies under which it wanted coverage for noise induced hearing loss (NIHL) claims. On appeal, however, the Second District of the Appellate Court of Illinois found that coverage for NIHL claims must be allocated over the total period in which the injury was alleged to have occurred. Furthermore, the court reaffirmed the principle of "horizontal exhaustion" under Illinois law, declaring that the insured was responsible for exhausting all self-insured retentions before it could obtain coverage from its excess carriers. The court rejected the insured's argument that self-insurance is not "insurance" to which the excess policies' "other insurance" clauses would apply.

In *Olin Corporation v. INA*, 972 F. Supp. 189, 202 (S.D.N.Y. 1997), *aff'd*, 221 F.3d 307 (2d Cir. 2000), the U.S. District Court declared that most policy periods were potentially triggered by the underlying DDT pollution claims against Olin. Further, under New York law, the court declared that the loss must be apportioned over the years of available insurance coverage. Each of the years in question contained a $300,000 "per occurrence" limit for which Olin was responsible for a $100,000 "per occurrence" deductible. Although Olin contended that it was entitled to multiple $300,000 limits, it argued that the most it should pay pursuant to these deductible provisions was $100,000 in the aggregate. The district court disagreed, declaring that Olin was required to pay a full deductible of $100,000 for each policy year for which indemnity was otherwise required. On appeal, the U.S. Court of Appeals for the Second Circuit affirmed the district court's ruling that Olin was responsible for a full self-insured retention in each year for which coverage was otherwise triggered, rejecting the insured's argument that the most that it owed for all policies was a single SIR.

Likewise, the Second Circuit ruled in *In Re Prudential Lines, Inc.*, 158 F.3d 65 (2nd Cir. 1998) that a "per occurrence" deductible should be applied separately to each asbestos bodily injury claim presented against a bankrupt shipping company. The court's analysis reflected both its view of New York law and the evidence concerning how the parties had anticipated this issue.

In *Ingersoll-Rand Co. v. INA*, Bergen No. L-37910-89 (N.J. Super. November 16, 1995), the insured sought coverage for asbestos liabilities under policies issued by INA between 1954 and 1961. INA took the position that there was only one occurrence and that its policy obligations were therefore restricted to a single policy limit of $1 million. The court ruled to the contrary, however, finding that each policy limit was potentially triggered up to a maximum potential recovery of $8 million. However, the court disagreed with the insured that it would only need to pay one self-insured retention, holding that it must pay a separate SIR for each policy year in which indemnity was owed.

In *Ranger Ins. Co. v. Safety-Kleen Corp.*, 814 F.Supp. 744 (N.D. Ill. 1993), Safety-Kleen sought coverage for a leukemia claim allegedly suffered by a worker as the result of breathing benzene from the insured's de-greasing product from 1978 or 1980 until May 1987. Following a settlement of the claim, Ranger sought reimbursement from Safety-Kleen for $200,000, reflecting the $50,000 deductible in each of four policies. Safety-Kleen argued, however, that the claim involved only a single occurrence and thus only one $50,000 deductible. The court agreed that the claim involved only one occurrence but also ruled that Ranger was entitled to repayment of a deductible for each additional policy year under which coverage might be sought.

The Delaware Supreme Court ruled in *Stonewall Ins. Co. v. E.I. Du Pont De Nemours & Co.*, 996 A.2d 1254 (Del. 2010) that Du Pont was only required to contribute a single $50 million SIR for claims involving alleged defects in polybutylene plumbing systems. The court rejected Stonewall's contention that the underlying claims had two separate and independent causes (chemical degradation and the product's inability to resist mechanical stresses). "Whether the failure resulted from the product's susceptibility to chemical degradation from the inside of the pipe or from its inability to withstand mechanical stress from the outside, or both, the product itself was the source of the leaking polybutylene systems and the resulting property damage," said the court.

One Deductible for Entire Period of Injury. A minority view holds that the insured is only responsible for a single occurrence deductible or SIR no matter how many policies are triggered.

In *Boston Gas Company v. Century Ind. Co.*, 454 Mass. 337, 910 N.E.2d 290 (2009), the Supreme Judicial Court of Massachusetts held in an environmental liability case that where all of the underlying primary policies contained self-insured retentions, the insured was only required to pay a proportional share of the SIR for each triggered policy.

In *Skinner Corp. v. Firemans Fund Ins. Co.*, No. C95-995 WD, 1996 WL 376657 (W.D. Wash. April 2, 1996), the district court ruled that Skinner need only pay a single policy deductible. The ruling was based upon the court's finding that there had only been a single catastrophe or accident for all claims arising out of the presence of asbestos on board any individual vessel.

In *Hercules, Inc. v. Aetna Cas. & Sur. Co.*, Nos. 92C-10-105 and 90C-FE-195-1-CV, 1998 Del. Super. LEXIS 459 (September 30, 1998), the insured sought repayment of $45 million it had spent to clean up an Arkansas manufacturing plant that had manufactured Agent Orange. The court ruled that the insured's loss should be prorated on a "time on the risk" basis. The court also decided that Hercules was only obligated to assume a single self-insured retention for the entire period, rejecting American Home's contention that a $2 million SIR should apply for each of the twenty-four years that property damage took place. Accordingly, the court ruled that the $2 million SIR should only apply once and be spread over the entire period of injury time.

Having ruled that the NIHL claims against the insured railroad all arose out of one occurrence, the court further declared in *Atchison Topeka & Santa Fe Railway Company v. Stonewall Ins. Co.*, Shawnee County Case No. 94-CV-1464 (Kan. Dist. Ct. July 24, 2000), *rev'd* 71 P.3d 1097 (Kan 2003), Santa Fe was only required to pay a single SIR or deductible no matter how many policy years were triggered. The court ruled that Santa Fe was not required to exhaust all of its self-insured retentions before accessing its excess coverage, nor was it required to pay more than a single deductible for a single occurrence that occurred over multiple periods of time before the excess policies were triggered. While conceding that Kansas law requires that all primary coverage be exhausted before excess coverage is triggered, the court declared that this general rule does not apply inasmuch as the self-insured retentions are not primary insurance. Unlike *Missouri-Pacific*, in which the Appellate Court of Illinois had ruled that SIRs are insurance, the court declared that the Santa Fe retentions were not treated in the policies as insurance nor did the policyholder agree contractually to be a primary insurer. This finding was sustained on appeal by the Kansas Supreme Court, which agreed that the cause of the insured's liability was the failure to provide a safe working environment.

Prorated Deductible over Triggered Period. Finally, when insureds have only been permitted to obtain a single occurrence limit regardless of how many policy years were triggered, courts have tended to rule that indemnity obligations owed by the insured because of deductibles or self-insured retentions should be correspondingly prorated. For example, in *Nationwide Mutual Ins. Co. v. Lafarge Corp.*, 1997 U.S. App. LEXIS 22807 * 17 (4th Cir. August 28, 1997) (unpublished), the court affirmed the lower court's ruling that the insurer was entitled to one-twelfth of its deductible when toxic tort claims triggered twelve years of coverage. Likewise, in *Lafarge Corp. v. Hartford Ins. Co.*, 61 F.3d 389 (5th Cir. 1995), the insurer's deductible was prorated in the same manner as loss was apportioned among respective years of coverage. In *Clemtex, Inc. v. Southeastern Fidelity Ins. Co.*, 807 F.2d 1271 (5th Cir. 1987), the Fifth Circuit ruled that an insurer could not demand the protection of a separate per claim deductible when the losses otherwise would be prorated over the total period of injury. Consistent with the overall loss-spreading approach, the court declared that the insurer could only insist on the same fractional share of its deductible as it was otherwise paying in indemnity, stating:

> Thus, for instance, if an insurer must indemnify Clemtex for only one tenth of Clemtex's liability under a silicosis claim, the insurer would be entitled to only one tenth of a $10,000 per claim deductible, in other words $1,000.

The resolution of such disputes is more complicated in states that otherwise have allowed an insured to pick and choose among triggered policies, whether on a theory of *all-sums* or *joint and several* liability. In cases where certain policies contain retentions but others do not, such courts have tended to permit insureds to allocate claims to the policies that lack deductibles or SIRs. In *TPLC, Inc. v. United National Ins. Co.*, 44 F.3d 1484 (10th Cir. 1995) (Pennsylvania law), the circuit court reversed a district court ruling that an insured should pay a share of the cost of defending heart valve claims for that portion of injury that occurred during a self-insured period.

Low Indemnity Limits

Courts often are most likely to find multiple occurrences when the limits of liability are relatively low compared to the insured's total exposure.

In *Slater v. U.S. Fidelity & Guaranty Co.*, 400 N.E.2d 1256 (Mass. 1980), the fidelity portion of USF&G's policy limited coverage to $10,000 per occurrence. The Supreme Judicial Court of Massachusetts ruled that a scheme in which an employee had embezzled funds on several occasions over a period of months involved multiple occurrences because the employee could have stopped his course of illegal conduct at any time.

Similar reasoning likely was behind many courts' treatment of mass tort liabilities when ruling one occurrence per claimant. For example, *see Asbestos Insurance Coverage Cases, Judicial Council Coordination Proceeding No. 1072*, Tentative Decision on Phase IV Issues, 52 Cal. Rptr.2d 690 (Cal. App. 1996) and *Houston v. Avondale Shipyards*, 506 So. 2d 149 (La. App. 1987), which is a silicosis case.

Insurer Insolvency

A somewhat analogous issue involves the obligation of state guaranty funds to indemnify policyholders for mass tort claims for which coverage otherwise would have been owed by insolvent insurers. In general, courts have ruled that the number of "covered claims" should be determined through the number of individual underlying tort claimants, rather than the underlying accident giving rise to the claims. This analysis can be seen in *H.K. Porter v. Pennsylvania Ins. Guaranty Assoc.*, 75 F.3d 137 (3rd Cir. 1996) and *Dickerson v. Thompson*, 624 N.E.2d 784 (Ohio App. 1993), both asbestos cases, and *Connecticut Ins. Guaranty Assoc. v. Union Carbide Corp.*, 585 A.2d 1216 (Conn. 1991), which involved Bhopal toxic tort claimants.

Case Law Survey

Trends by type of claim also can be useful when considering whether single or multiple occurrences affect the application of coverage. The theories discussed are illustrated in the following discussion of claims by type.

Premises Liability Claims

There are a number of occurrences disputes that arise in the context of insured homes or businesses. Many of these involve property damage to unit owners or occupants due to fire or flood. Others involve bodily injuries. For instance, the Arizona Court of Appeals ruled in *Austin Mut. Ins. Co. v. Aldecoa*, 2011 WL 4794736 (Ariz. App. Oct. 11, 2011) that the death of two children who drowned while under their grandparents' care involved separate occurrences. Applying a cause analysis, Division II held that there were separate causative acts of negligence on the part of the grandparents as one left the outside door unlatched after she fell ill whereas the grandfather left the children in another room and went upstairs to watch television where he fell asleep. Since each act could have independently led to the children wandering outside and drowning in their parents' swimming pool, the court held that there were two different causes of the event and therefore separate occurrences.

Applying a cause test, the court ruled in *Western World Ins. Co. v. Wilkie*, 5:06-cv-64 (E.D.N.C. November 1, 2007) that injuries suffered by various children who suffered injury as the result of coming into contact with fecal matter while petting animals at the insured's petting zoo in the course of a week's visit at the state fair all of the claims arose out of exposure to the same general harmful conditions (the presence of *e. coli* at the zoo).

Other cases include:

- *Allied Grand Doll Mfg. Co., Inc. v. Globe Indem. Co.*, 225 N.Y.S.2d 595 (N.Y. App. Div. 1962). Water that damaged many businesses was caused by an open faucet in the insured's business, which was held to be a single accident.

- *Continental Ins. Companies v. Hancock*, 507 S.W.2d 146 (Ky. App. 1973). Claims that were filed against a bar by individuals who were injured in a brawl that began inside the bar and then continued outside all involved the same occurrence.

- *Doria v. INA*, 509 A.2d 220 (N.J. App. Div. 1986). Injuries to two boys that happened when one fell in a swimming pool while trying to rescue the other arose out of one occurrence. The injuries resulted from the same cause and were closely linked in time and space.

- *Evanston Ins. Co. v. Ghillie Suits Com., Inc.*, 2009 U.S. Dist. LEXIS 22256 (N.D. Cal. 2009). Injuries suffered by two U.S. Marines who were burned during a training exercise when the insured's fireproof clothing caught fire triggered two separate occurrences on the theory that the second marine was injured when he went to the aid of the first marine, whose clothing had caught fire as the result of a muzzle flash such that the injuries had two different causes.

- *Kosnoski v. Rogers*, No. 13-0494 (W. Va. February 18, 2014). Personal injuries suffered by various building occupants as the result of a discharge of carbon monoxide fumes from a defective furnace all arose out of the same occurrence.

- *Michaels v. Mutual Marine Office, Inc.*, 472 F. Supp. 26 (S.D.N.Y. 1979). The court found one event when damage to a ship's deck was caused by the continuous and repeated dropping of grab buckets during unloading.

- *Reynolds v. Scottsdale Ins. Co.*, 1995 U.S. Dist. LEXIS 589 (E.D. La. January 18, 1995). Claims from four residents who suffered carbon monoxide poisoning over a twenty-four-hour period were separate occurrences because each was injured in a different way.

- *Scottsdale Ins. Co. v. Robertson*, 338 Ill.App.3d 397, 788 N.E.2d 279 (2003). Carbon monoxide poisoning claims brought by tenants against a landlord were subject to a single occurrence limit notwithstanding the insured's claim that each injured individual had suffered a separate occurrence triggering the aggregate limit of the policy.

- *Ware v. First Specialty Ins. Corp.*, 983 N.E.2d 1115 (Ill. App. 2013). Individuals who were injured when the insured's porch collapsed during a party were subject to a single occurrence limit.

Diverse damage claims also may be aggregated when they individually result from the same physical cause, as in the case of a building fire or train crash.

- *Barrett v. Iowa National Mut. Ins. Co.*, 264 F.2d 224 (9th Cir. 1959). A fire that damaged the property of seven tenants was held to be one accident.

- *Broadhead v. Hartford*, 773 F. Supp. 882 (S.D. Miss. 1991), *aff'd*, 979 F.2d 209 (5th Cir. 1992). Various claims arising from a gas well blowout were ruled a single occurrence.

- *Denham v. La Salle-Madison Hotel Co.*, 168 F.2d 576 (7th Cir. 1948). Claims for fire damage filed by numerous guests in the insured hotel were subject to a single policy limit.

- *Travelers Indemnity Co v. New England Box Co.*, 157 A.2d 765 (N.H. 1960). All damages caused by a fire were held to be a single occurrence.

- *Tri-State Roofing Co. v. New Amsterdam Cas. Co.*, 139 F. Supp. 193 (W.D. Pa. 1955). Fire that began at the insured's job site and subsequently spread to ten other properties was found to be subject to a single policy limit.

Such claims may be contrasted with *Goose Creek Consol. I.S.D. v. Continental Cas. Co.*, 658 S.W.2d 338 (Tex. App. 1983), in which the Texas Court of Appeals ruled that fires set by the same arsonist at two insured locations several hours apart were separate occurrences.

Food Poisoning Claims

A similar analysis has been applied to outbreaks of food poisoning at restaurants. In *John Mason v. The Home Ins. Co. of Illinois*, 532 N.E.2d 526 (Ill. App.1988), the court declared that incidences of botulism among restaurant patrons all were caused by an improperly prepared batch of onions and, therefore, arose out of a single occurrence. The court rejected arguments that the limits of coverage should be determined by the number of portions of contaminated food that were served to customers. Similar reasoning also is seen in *Firemans Fund Ins. Co. v. Scottsdale Ins. Co.*, 968 F. Supp. 444 (E.D. Ark. 1997), in which three separate hepatitis claims involving contaminated food at a Taco Bell outlet all arose out of the same occurrence—the insured's negligent handling and storage of food.

In an Oklahoma case, the Tenth Circuit ruled in *Republic Underwriters, Inc. v. Moore*, 2012 U.S. App. LEXIS 14907 (10th Cir. July 20, 2012) that the E. Coli poisoning of 341 persons who became sick after eating the insured's contaminated food all arose out of a single occurrence, rejecting the finding of an Oklahoma district court that there were two separate occurrences here because some of the food was prepared at the insured's restaurant and other portions at the church where the insured was catering a social event. Notwithstanding the "geographical distinction", the Tenth Circuit ruled that all of the injuries were proximately caused by the restaurant's preparation of contaminated food and that "it did not matter that the food was served with food items prepared at another location because the contamination originated at the restaurant."

Construction Defect and Building Claims

In property damage cases against building contractors, some courts permit aggregation when the claims share a common physical cause as shown in the following cases:

- *Bethpage Water District v. S. Zara & Sons*, 145 A.D.2d 637, 546 N.Y.S.2d 645 (1989). Diverse claims arising out of the insured contractor's negligent backfilling of a municipal sewer system all involved exposure to "substantially the same general conditions". Only a single occurrence deductible was required.

- *Chemstar, Inc. v. Liberty Mut. Ins. Co.*, 797 F. Supp. 1541 (C.D. Cal. 1992), *aff'd*, 41 F.3d 429 (9th Cir. 1994). A contractor's failure to warn homeowners that its plaster product was unsuitable for use was the cause of all ensuing claims involving unsightly blemishes to homes.

- *Owners Ins. Co. v. Salmonsen*, 366 S.C. 336, 622 S.E.2d 525 (S.C. 2005). Construction defect claims arising out of the insured's manufacture and sale of defective stucco products all arise out of a single occurrence as claims were based on the distribution of an inherently defective product and not because of any defect in the distribution process.

- *Wilkinson and Son, Inc. v. Providence Washington Ins. Co.*, 307 A.2d 639 (N.J. Super. 1973). Damage to several apartments constituted a single occurrence when all involved the same cause, which was a contractor tracking paint on carpets.

On the other hand, when the disparate injuries are separated in time or result from variables that are not common to each claim, courts are more likely to find that each job was a separate occurrence. Examples of this reasoning occur in the following cases:

- *Johnson Corp. v. Indemnity Ins. Co. of North America*, 164 N.E.2d 704 (N.Y. 1959). Collapsing walls at a construction site were held to result from separate events when they were negligently constructed by different individuals at different times.

- *Lennar Corp. v. Great American Ins. Co.*, 200 S.W.3d 651 (Tex. App. 2006). Each home that suffered construction defect claims due to EIFS was a separate occurrence.

- *Mid-Continent Cas. Co. v. Basedeo*, 2012 U.S. App. LEXIS 11864 (11th Cir. June 12, 2012). That water damage suffered by a condominium complex as the result of Hurricane Wilma in 2005 involved three different occurrences as the faulty tarping, damage to the building's mansard, and injury to a flat-top roof had different causes.

- *U.S. Fire Ins. Co. v. Safeco Ins. Co.*, 444 So. 2d 844 (Ala. 1983). Property damage resulting separately from a leaking roof and a contractor's subsequent failure to fix the roof had two causes. Therefore, two separate occurrences were involved.

- *Vandenberghe v. Amco Ins. Co.*, No. C-91-3885 MHP, 1992 U.S. Dist. LEXIS 10760 (N.D. Cal. July 10, 1992). Homeowners' claims against a plumber for negligent pipe installations involved diverse occurrences because different physical factors caused each claimant's loss, despite the fact that the work all was performed under one contract.

An intermediate approach is suggested by *Home Ind. Co. v. City of Mobile*, 749 F.2d 659 (11th Cir. 1984), in which the City of Mobile was sued by numerous homeowners for failing to properly maintain the municipal drainage system, which resulted in significant flood damage after three rainstorms. Home contended that the number of occurrences should be determined by the number of storms, while the city argued that the court should look at the specific circumstances of each claim. While agreeing that the cause of the claims (and not the number of claimants) was determinative, the Eleventh Circuit, applying Alabama law, adopted an intermediate position, holding that each discrete causative act of negligence was a separate occurrence. Therefore, if the city's failure to maintain a particular drain had flooded ten homes, those losses would be subject to the same $100,000 occurrence limit. If a separate act of negligence had independently injured a different home or homes, a separate policy limit would apply.

Likewise, in *Kvaerner ES, Inc. v. OneBeacon Ins. Co.*, 2005 Phila. Ct. Con. Pl. LEXIS 377 (Pa. August 19, 2005), the Philadelphia Court of Common Pleas ruled that the various personal injury claims brought against an insured that had constructed various furnaces could be grouped together as an occurrence for each construction site where the exposures had occurred. Although the insurers had argued that all of the asbestos-related claims were caused by a single occurrence, that is to say the continuous or repeated exposure to asbestos fibers, the Court of Common Pleas held that the insured's conduct did not arise from a single negligent practice such as distributing a uniformly defective product, but rather, involved the construction of furnaces at different sites at different times and varying lengths of times. Accordingly, the court ruled that the claimants that were exposed to asbestos at the same location and same time were exposed to "substantially the same general conditions."

In New York, however, the First Department refused to find that a manufacturer must pay a separate per occurrence deductible for each individual asbestos claim against it. In *Mt. McKinley Ins. Co. v. Corning, Inc.*, 2012 NY slip op 04398 (App. Div. June 7, 2012), the Appellate Division found that factual issues remained with respect to whether these claimants could be grouped together as involving exposures in the same time and place and distinguished cases in which courts had found multiple occurrences under policies that didn't define occurrences or lacked language requiring that exposures to similar conditions "shall be considered as arising out of one occurrence."

The California Court of Appeal ruled in *Safeco Ins. Co. of America v. Fireman's Fund Ins. Co.*, B187743 (Cal. App. March 14, 2007) that a neighbor's claim for damage in the loss of his property due to accumulated dirt and debris that had spilled onto his land from the insured's property in the course of a landslide triggered only a single occurrence limit at the time of the landslide notwithstanding the fact that property damage had continued in successive years owing to the insured's failure to clean up the property. The Second District declared that the ensuing damage had only a single cause (the landslide) and that the continuation of the original damage into subsequent policy years, including the plaintiff's loss of use of the property, did not give rise to multiple occurrences. The court therefore rejected the arguments of Safeco, which had provided excess coverage to the homeowner at the time of the landslide, that the insured's loss should be allocated through successive primary policies issued by Fireman's Fund. The court also took note of the potential significance of the distinction between the all sums language in a CGL policy, as construed by the California Supreme Court in *Montrose*, and the homeowner's policies at issue here which merely required the insured to "pay up to our limit of insurance" for each occurrence, "the damages for which the insured is legally liable." In this case, the court held that there was only one occurrence and that the insurer was therefore only obligated to pay a single occurrence limit.

Discrimination Claims: Housing and Employment

Claims involving housing or employment discrimination on the basis of gender or race again raise the issue of the number of occurrences. The question is whether each claimant should be a separate occurrence due to the unique circumstances of her injuries or whether multiple claims may be aggregated because they arise out of ongoing conduct or the operation of a particular practice or guideline.

At times the insured's liability results from the adoption of a particular practice—the signing of a specific contract or some other action that leads inevitably to the resulting claims. Some courts treat this decision or act as the cause of the ensuing claims. Such cases typically arise in actions against employers for race or sex discrimination.

When this is the situation, a number of courts have adopted a *fateful decision* analysis similar to that used in certain products liability cases. This reasoning holds that the insured's promulgation of the offending guideline caused the resulting claims. The leading *guideline* case is *Appalachian Ins. Co. v. Liberty Mutual Ins. Co.*, 676 F.2d 56 (3rd Cir. 1982), in which Liberty Mutual was sued for sex discrimination by a class of female employees. The Third Circuit ruled that the claims all arose out of the insured's adoption of discriminatory employment guidelines and therefore involved a single occurrence in the policy year that the guidelines were adopted. The case involved coverage under an umbrella liability policy.

Similarly, the Eleventh Circuit has issued an unpublished opinion affirming a holding of a federal district court in Florida that allegations that the Broward County Sheriff's Office violated the civil rights of various individuals who were engaging in a mass protest of the Free Trade Area of the Americas involved numerous separate occurrences for which the insured was liable pursuant to self-insured retentions. In *State National Ins. Co. v. Lamberti*, 2010 U.S. App. LEXIS 1455 (11th Cir. January 21, 2010), the court rejected the insured's argument that the occurrence limitations in the State National policy did not apply to the applicable limits of personal injury coverage for offenses. As a result, the court concluded that under Florida law, the claims, which involved separate lawsuits by many different plaintiffs all of whom had their own interactions with members of the sheriff's office, represented more than one occurrence in keeping with cases such as Koikos. The court ruled that the immediate cause of the plaintiffs' injuries was not a single coordinated police action, but rather, individual assaults by police officers at different times and places.

Other guideline cases include:

- *City of Portsmouth v. Colonial Penn Ins. Co.*, 769 F. Supp. 424 (D.N.H. 1990). Separate instances of employment discrimination arose out of a single employment policy guideline and constituted only one occurrence despite the ongoing nature of the damages. This case applies an errors and omissions coverage endorsement.

- *Transport Ins. Co. v. Lee Way Motor Freight Co.*, 487 F. Supp. 1325 (N.D. Tex. 1980). Forty-seven instances of race discrimination at four separate locations over a period of years arose out of a single "pattern and practice" of discrimination and thus involved one occurrence. Note that policy had a $25,000 per occurrence deductible. Again, this case involved an excess umbrella liability policy.

- *Village Management, Inc. v. Hartford Acc. & Ind. Co.*, 662 F. Supp. 1366 (N.D. Ill. 1987). Race discrimination claims against a landlord all arose out of one occurrence, the insured's adoption of a discriminatory policy for selecting tenants. The case involves personal injury coverage on a commercial package policy.

In these cases, the resulting claims often are treated as a single occurrence in the year in which the guideline or practice first harms the plaintiffs. This conclusion is quite striking given the fact that many members of the class may not have been employed when the guideline was first adopted or may have suffered injury in different times and places.

On the other hand, the court ruled in *Illinois Central Railroad Co. v. Acc. & Cas. Co. of Winterthur*, 739 N.E.2d 1049 (Ill. App. 2000) that each individual member of a class action for employment discrimination is a separate occurrence. The court rejected the insured's claim that the class action was based on a single, continuing practice of discrimination and should trigger only a single self-insured retention.

When more than one guideline or practice generates liability, the available limits of coverage may increase. In *Mead Reinsurance v. Granite State Ins. Co.*, 873 F.2d 1185 (9th Cir. 1988), a municipality was named in several police brutality suits. Eleven of the cases were based on the city's alleged policy of condoning excessive force. While ruling that the police brutality claims could be aggregated as a single occurrence because they all arose out of the same policy, the court ruled that a separate claim based on alleged police harassment arose out of a different type of conduct. Therefore, it constituted a different occurrence under California law.

Decisions such as *Mead* should not be interpreted as requiring a new occurrence every time a plaintiff's complaint is amended to add a new cause of action. Alternative legal theories that are based on the same set of causative facts are not new causes. Thus, in *Plante v. Columbia Paints*, 494 N.W.2d 140 (N.D. 1992), an exploding can of paint injured two painters who were both using the paint at the same time. Although the plaintiffs' suits alleged diverse theories of liabilities, the North Dakota Supreme Court (applying Washington law) noted that these legal theories did not cause the plaintiffs' injuries and therefore held that the claims involved only one occurrence.

Similarly, the court refused in *Mid-Century Ins. Co. v. Shutt*, 845 P.2d 86 (Kan. App. 1993) to find that claims against a juvenile for negligent operation of a motor vehicle and against the juvenile's parents for negligent entrustment constituted two occurrences merely because they were based on different legal theories. In *Guaranty National Ins. Co. v. North River Ins. Co.*, 909 F.2d 133 (5th Cir. 1990), a psychiatric patient committed suicide by jumping out of hospital's open window. Even though the hospital was found liable on three theories of liability, the U.S. Court of Appeals for the Fifth Circuit ruled that only one policy limit applied under Kansas law.

As seen from these cases, the fact that different legal theories arise out of the same set of circumstances should not expand the number of occurrences triggered by the claims.

Environmental Liability Claims

In general, waste site disputes concerning the number of occurrences arise in cases in which there are 1) multiple sources of contamination at a single site, 2) multiple sites, or 3) multiple claimants.

Sources of Contamination at a Site

It is not uncommon for a hazardous waste site to become contaminated through intermingled causes. Thus, a site may have pollution from areas where wastes were buried or dumped onto the ground, from spillage or leaks from storage tanks, or from lagoons where liquid wastes were stored. These areas may differ not only in their geography but also in the types of waste involved and the identity of the parties responsible.

Number of Sites. Insureds may seek to aggregate sites based on a common chemical, a common source, or a common transporter.

Identity of Claimants. There may be multiple claimants. This may occur when, for example, property owners sue a facility or different governmental agencies present diverse claims for response costs and natural resource damages at a single site. Alternatively, an effort may be made to aggregate separate sites when they are being treated as a single site for governmental enforcement purposes.

What Is the Cause of Pollution Liabilities?

Single Site Claims. When a claim involves only one site, are the number of occurrences determined by: a) separate spill incidents, b) the type of pollutants involved at the site, c) the number of operable units, or d) the particular areas of contamination? For instance, if a portion of a site is contaminated as the result of ash from a former incinerator and separate contamination exists on the site from underground tanks, should the separate sources generate multiple occurrences? Or should all of the contamination be treated as arising from exposure to the same or substantially similar general conditions?

Multiple Site Claims. If more than one site is at issue, should each site be treated separately? Or should the sites be aggregated based on: a) the disposal of a specific hazardous chemical, b) transshipments from one site to another, c) EPA treatment of the sites as a single investigation or enforcement action, or d) common ownership or operation of the sites?

Case Law Examples

Single Site Cases. Just as courts have tended to treat pollution as a continuous, indivisible injury, most courts have been reluctant to separate out discrete polluting events at a single site as new occurrences. The limited case law that exists tends to concur that waste sites should be treated as a single occurrence. Thus, in *Northern States Power Co. v. St. Paul Fire and Marine Ins. Co.*, 523 N.W.2d 657 (Minn. 1994), the court declared that, because soil and groundwater contamination is a continuous process, the individual discharges of contaminants are so "continuous and repetitive that the unidentifiable individual instances have merged into one continuing occurrence." Similar reasoning is found in *Endicott Johnson Corporation v. Liberty Mutual Ins. Co.*, 928 F. Supp. 176 (N.D.N.Y. 1996); *Consolidated Edison Co. of New York, Inc. v. Employers Ins. Co. of Wausau*, 1997 U.S. Dist. LEXIS 18486 (S.D.N.Y. November 21, 1997); and *Hercules Inc. v. Aetna Cas. & Sur. Co.*, No. 92C-10-105 (Del. Super. August 31, 1999).

The Alabama Supreme Court ruled that PCB contamination due to spills of lubricating fluids at thirteen of thirty-eight compressor stations operated by the insured in conjunction with a gas pipeline that stretches from Georgia to Texas all involve one occurrence. The court ruled in *Certain Underwriters at Lloyd's, London v. Southern Natural Gas Co.*, No. 1110698 (Ala. June 28, 2013) that there was only one cause as the pollution had occurred from the use of the same lubricating fluid (Pydraul) through an integrated, unitary pipeline as the result of uniform plant operations, even though this one occurrence may cause disparate and multiple impacts on individuals and properties extending over time.

In *P.R. Mallory & Co., Inc. v. American Cas. Co.*, 920 N.E.2d 736 (Ind. App. 2010), the Indiana Court of Appeals has declined to hold that different pollution problems involving at the insured's facility involved separate occurrences as to which different notice dates might have applied. As the policies stated that "all bodily injury and property damage arising out of continuous or repeated exposure to substantially the same general condition shall be considered as arising out of one occurrence," the court found that claims involving a local municipality, the U.S. EPA, and various homeowners all arose out of the same occurrence.

A broader view of what constitutes an occurrence in the hazardous waste context was adopted by a federal district court in Pennsylvania. In *Centennial Ins. Co. v. Lumbermens Mut. Cas. Co.*, 677 F. Supp. 342 (E.D. Pa. 1987), the court declared that the insured's dumping of hazardous waste at the same site on sixteen separate occasions was each a new occurrence. The court ruled that the dates of the pollution releases were reasonably identifiable and that the damage resulting from each release was separate and distinct.

Multiple Site Claims. The leading case analyzing this fact pattern remains *Consolidated Edison Co. of New York, Inc. v. Employers Ins. Co. of Wausau*, 1997 U.S. Dist. LEXIS 18486 (S.D.N.Y. November 21, 1997). Consolidated Edison sought coverage for Superfund liabilities arising out of the cleanup of two waste sites near Kansas City. During the period in question, Con Ed had shipped mineral oil and capacitors to the Envirosure site in Kansas City, Missouri, and PCB-contaminated transformers to the Environmental Resource Management site in Kansas City, Kansas. Both sites were operated by subsidiaries of PCB Treatment, Inc. In 1994, the U.S. EPA designated Con Ed as a potentially responsible party (PRP) at both sites. In 1996, Con Ed entered into a single consent agreement to clean up the sites.

Con Ed sought coverage for the cost of undertaking this cleanup under an excess liability policy. The policy provided coverage in the amount of $1.5 million per occurrence in excess of underlying limits of $4 million. The key issue, therefore, was whether the insured's per occurrence liabilities exceeded the $4 million retention. Con Ed argued both claims arose out of the same occurrence because the pollution was caused by the common "mishandling of PCBs" by PCB Treatment, Inc. at both sites. Further, it noted that the EPA had treated both sites as being linked together and that the sites and activities conducted on them were so similar that no meaningful distinction existed between them. The excess carrier disagreed, contending that each site was a separate occurrence.

Applying New York law, where Con Ed was based and where the subject policies had been entered into, the court ruled that the pollution at the two sites had separate causes and, therefore, the claims could not be aggregated for insurance purposes. In reaching this conclusion, the court successively rejected the insured's argument that a finding of one occurrence was mandated by: 1) the government's treatment of the claims, 2) he facts concerning the interrelationship between the sites, or 3) the wording in the excess policy.

The court found that the EPA's linking of the sites together for administrative convenience did not mean that the sites were a "unitary whole for purposes of investigation and cleanup." In fact, the record established that the government had imposed different procedures and requirements for the investigation and cleanup of the two sites and had not treated them as a single facility. Whether the two sites were considered one for purposes of the EPA's investigation was a question of administrative procedure and federal law; the interpretation of the number of occurrences was a function of contract interpretation and state law.

The court also disagreed that the pollution processes at the sites were so similar that they mandated a finding of a common cause. In this case, the insured had used the sites for different purposes and had shipped different wastes that required different treatment to them.

Finally, the court rejected Consolidated Edison's contention that policy language that "damages arising out of exposure to substantially the same general conditions shall be considered as arising out of the same occurrence" applied to the case. The court ruled that the pollution of the two sites did not arise from "substantially the same general conditions" but, rather, was caused by separate contamination and mishandling of PCBs at each site. On the other hand, the court noted that the cited language was significant because it would require aggregation of all the spills at a single site in a given year.

Arguments for aggregation sometimes are advanced by insurers. In *Indiana Gas Co., Inc. v. Aetna Cas. & Sur. Co.*, 951 F. Supp. 773 (N.D. Ind. 1996), a gas utility sought coverage from its liability insurance for nine manufactured gas plants that had developed environmental liabilities. Aetna contended that the most that it could owe in indemnity was a single policy limit, despite the number of plants and the fact that it had issued coverage to Indiana Gas over a period of years. The court denied Aetna's motion for summary judgment, noting that the gas plants had utilized different types of gas manufacturing processes, had employed different structures and materials, and had been operated by different entities. The court refused to find as a matter of law that the cause of the overall environmental liabilities was the insured's "long term business practices in operating its MGP sites."

In *E.I. duPont de Nemours v. Admiral Ins. Co.*, No. 89C-AU-99, 1996 Del. Super. LEXIS 137 (April 9, 1996), a state trial court in Delaware was asked whether environmental liabilities arising out of the insured's legal liability to clean up a manufacturing facility and an off-site landfill could be aggregated as a single occurrence. The landfill was located less than two miles from the factory and had received waste material from it. Nevertheless, the court ruled that the claims involved two separate premises locations and refused to permit aggregation on the basis of "continuous or repeated exposure to substantially the same general condition existing at or emanating from one premises location."

In *City of Seattle v. Certain Underwriters at Lloyds*, King No. 97-2-15939 (Wash. Super. January 28, 1998), a court granted Allstate's motion for partial summary judgment, declaring that Allstate, as an excess insurer, had no duty to drop down over the underlying insolvent policies. Since each site was a separate occurrence, the amounts at issue were less than the retention limit for the excess policy.

In *Endicott Johnson Corp. v. Liberty Mutual Ins. Co.*, 928 F. Supp. 176 (N.D.N.Y. 1996), a waste generator sought recovery for the cost of responding to a PRP letter involving the disposal of waste at the Endicott Landfill and the Tri-Cities Barrel sites in New York between 1957 and 1983. Even though the insured's discrete disposal activity separately caused property damage throughout the period in question, the court ruled that the dumping at each site constituted separate occurrences. On the other hand, the court declined to find that each separate act of disposal was a new occurrence. The court ruled that the cause of the insured's liability was its disposal of waste at each site.

In *Domtar, Inc. v. Niagara Fire Ins. Co.*, A03, 630 (Minn. App. March 2, 2004)(unpublished), the Minnesota Court of Appeals rejected the insured's argument that six separate sites could be aggregated. In an unpublished opinion, the Court of Appeals ruled that the trial court had not erred in refusing to aggregate the six sites as a single occurrence despite the insured's argument that they were an "integrated business unit, with uniform and standardized procedures...." Rather, the court found it more likely that the varied activities at Domtar's "geographically and geologically distinct sites" involved separate occurrences even if the sites were operated by affiliated corporate entities.

In *Caldo Oil Co. v. State Water Resources Control Board*, 44 Cal. App. 4th 1821 (1996), the California Court of Appeal ruled that separate leaking underground storage tanks operated on adjacent parcels by the same insured nonetheless represented two "occurrences" for purposes of obtaining up to $990,000 "per occurrence" reimbursement for the State Water Resources Control Board.

In contrast to these cases, the California Court of Appeal declared in *Garamendi v. Mission Ins. Co.*, 131 Cal.App.4th 30 (2005) that a lower court erred in concluding as a matter of law that two nearby facilities that were both owned and operated by one Rudolph Kraus did not necessarily involve separate occurrences in light of the intermingled means of operation and the fact that even the U.S. EPA viewed the sites as linked. The court did not resolve the number of occurrences issue; however, as it separately concluded that the court had also erred in declaring that aggregate language in the underlying Transamerica Insurance policy (to which the insolvent Mission excess policy followed form) lacked an applicable aggregate. Whereas the lower court had concluded that language in the Mission policy that made it subject to the aggregate listed in the policy Declarations for each annual period during the currency of this policy, separately in respect of Products Liability and in respect of "occupational injury" indicated that only products and occupational injury claims were subject to an aggregate, the Court of Appeal ruled that this language merely indicated that there was a separate annual aggregate limit for those types of claims, and adopted the insured's (Industrial Trucking) contention that the Mission policy should be triggered once all other claim payments, either singly or together, that did not involve products or occupational injuries reached a total of $1.5 million in any year. The California Court of Appeal noted that the only other case in the country that had analyzed these issues was the Washington Supreme Court's 2002 opinion in *Weyerhaeuser*, a case in which the Washington Supreme Court had split 5-4, and adopted the view of the dissenting justices in *Weyerhaeuser* that the underlying property damage insurance coverage was subject to a separate aggregate limit. The analyses was undertaken pursuant to California law, notwithstanding the fact that the sites were located in New Jersey and the insured in Pennsylvania, as the Court of Appeal declared that it was appropriate to apply its own law in the absence of any suggestion that the law of New Jersey or Pennsylvania would lead to a different conclusion. As a result, the court concluded that the Commissioner of Insurance, as the liquidator for Mission, was responsible for all of the liabilities in the subject policy year over the $1.5 million underlying limit, thus avoiding the issue of whether the two underlying claims should be treated as a single occurrence in order to maximize the insured's claim under the excess policy.

A federal district court ruled that various fires, explosions and other pollution incidents occurring over a period of years at the insured's oil refinery in Shreveport, Louisiana did not involve "related Pollution Conditions" and therefore required a separate $2 million deductible as to each incident. In *Pennzoil-Quaker State Co. v. American International Specialty Lines Ins. Co.*, 2009 U.S. Dist. LEXIS 80645 (S.D. Tex. September 4, 2009), the court held that whether the claims were interpreted in accordance with the law of Texas or Louisiana, the allegations of pollution in the five underlying suits alleged distinct kinds of emissions and releases with distinct causes and therefore could not be grouped together. The court noted it could go beyond the conventional "eight corners" test under Texas law but found it unnecessary in order to reach this conclusion because the allegations of the underlying suits made clear that the various losses involved separate occurrences.

In *Indemnity Ins. Co. v. North American City of Tacoma*, 2010 Wash. App. LEXIS 2427 (Wash. App. November 1, 2010)(unpublished), the Washington Court of Appeals rejected the insured's argument that pollution liability claims had resulted from separate occurrences (the building of the dam and the accumulation of sediment), neither of which were expected or anticipated.

Reinsurance Disputes. As might be expected, the substantial sums that insurers have paid and the odd nature of environmental liability claims have prompted disputes between cedents and reinsurers. These mainly deal with the number of retentions that must be satisfied and whether a reinsurer may aggregate multiple site claims to more quickly access a reinsurance recovery.

In *Travelers Cas. & Sur. Co. v. Certain Underwriters at Lloyd's*, 716 N.Y.S.2d 297 (App. Div. 000), *aff'd*, No. 123/124 (N.Y. October 16, 2001), Travelers sued Lloyd's seeking indemnification under reinsurance agreements for pollution-related losses involving 150 hazardous waste sites around the country that had been the subject of a comprehensive settlement between Travelers and its policyholder, Koppers Company. In a separate proceeding, Travelers sued to recover monies that it paid to settle a multi-site pollution case with E.I. duPont.

In both cases, Travelers had treated each individual site as a separate occurrence in allocating the payments among its policies but argued that they could be grouped together for reinsurance purposes because the claims all had a common origin as being traceable to the same error or mistake; namely the insured's company-wide waste disposal practice. The treaties in question called for the payment of "each and every loss" for "disaster and/or casualty" which was defined as "each and every accident, occurrence and/or causative incident, it being further understood that all loss resulting from a series of accidents, occurrences and/or causative incidents having a common origin and/or being traceable to the same act, omission, error and/or mistake shall be considered as having resulted from a single accident, occurrence and/or causative incident."

The Appellate Division of the Supreme Court of New York ruled that Travelers could not aggregate multiple environmental claims for the purpose of a reinsurance cession. The First Department stated that, "The lower court correctly concluded that [Travelers] cannot meet its burden of establishing a single unifying cause for its separate claims to justify the submission of the policyholder's distinct claims as a single loss for purposes of the reinsurance policies."

These findings were affirmed by the New York Court of Appeals on October 16, 2001. The Court of Appeals held that the "series" language required that the "accidents, occurrences and/or causative incidents" have a spatial or temporal relationship to one another as well as a "common origin." In short, the court concluded "that the parties did not intend for the reinsured to simply group together all other losses as a single 'disaster and/or casualty,' but sought to allow aggregation only where the losses are linked spatially or temporally and share a 'common origin.'" Where, as here, "Travelers seeks to attribute events and losses separated spatially by thousands of miles and temporally by decades to a single "disaster and/or casualty," the Court of Appeals ruled that the claim could not be supported by the language of the reinsurance treaties in question. In light of the fact that none of the individual sites claims pierced the retention levels for these reinsurance treaties, the court declared that summary judgment was properly granted in favor of the reinsurers.

To similar effect is *Allstate Ins. Co. v. American Home Assurance Co.*, 2007 N.Y. slip. op. 05170 (App. Div. June 12, 2007), in which the Appellate Division ruled that a facultative reinsurer was not obliged to accept American Home's cession of its payments to United Technologies to resolve environmental liability claims around the country on a "one site/ one occurrence basis where such arguments were inconsistent with the "multiple occurrences" position that the insurer had used against UTC in the original coverage litigation, a case in which AIG had also obtained a ruling for one of the sites that separate operations and contamination at the site involve multiple occurrences. Unlike the trial court, the Appellate Division was not swayed by a single occurrence analysis that had been prepared after the fact by coverage counsel. Rather, the court declared that, "A reinsurer is not bound by the follow the fortunes doctrine where the reinsured's settlement allocation, at odds with its allocation of the loss with its insured, designed to minimize its loss, reflects an effort to maximize unreasonably the amount of collectible reinsurance." The Appellate Division also ruled that American Home's argument that there was an "industry practice of ceding pollution claims to reinsurers on a single occurrence per site basis" was not only unsubstantiated but inconsistent with its own evidence.

Claimed inconsistencies between the manner in which cedents count the number of occurrences for the purpose of resolving claims with their policyholders and in the manner in which they calculate their loss for reinsurance purposes were also presented in *Stonewall Insurance Company v. Argonaut Insurance Company*, 73 F.Supp.2d 893 (N.D. Ill. 1999). Stonewall brought this action against Argonaut seeking a declaration that it did not owe coverage under a reinsurance contract issued to Argonaut for a settlement that Argonaut had entered into with Hughes Aircraft resolving its insurance claim for pollution at the Fullerton site in California. Argonaut had insured Hughes under a 1970-1971 policy that lacked a pollution exclusion as well as a policy in effect from 1972-1975 that contained a pollution exclusion. Stonewall had issued three facultative certificates with respect to this 1972-1975 insurance. Argonaut ceded the claim on the basis of a single occurrence even though another insurer had been found to owe coverage for four occurrences in a separate coverage suit involving the same site. Stonewall disputed this cession, questioning whether it had been entered into reasonably or in good faith. Further, Stonewall contended that Argonaut contended that the settlement should have been entered into on the basis of six occurrences involving discrete causes of contamination at the Fullerton site. These issues were tried before the U.S. District Court in early 1999. On December 3, 1999, following a three week trial, the jury entered a verdict in favor of Argonaut and against Stonewall in the amount of $2.5 million on its breach of contract claim, $6 million for Stonewall's breach of the duty of good faith and fair dealing, and $7 million in punitive damages on its claim that Stonewall had breached its duty of utmost good faith. In particular, the jury made factual findings that Stonewall had not settled on the basis of multiple occurrences or because of its alleged exposure to bad faith liability to Hughes, nor had it acted unreasonably in its cession.

Stonewall argued that Argonaut was collaterally estopped to claim that the settlement was based on a single occurrence in light of the fact that a single issue had been litigated against another insurer of Hughes with the result that the jury had found four separate occurrences. The court agreed with Stonewall that the jury's verdict did not moot Stonewall's motion for summary judgment as the legal issue had to be resolved by the court. While, therefore, rejecting the Magistrate's recommendation that the motion be declared moot, the court nonetheless denied the motion as being without merit. The District Court concluded that Argonaut was not in privity with the insurers in the other coverage case and that the doctrine of collateral estoppel, therefore, did not apply.

The Louisiana Court of Appeal ruled in *Devillier v. Alpine Exploration Co.*, No. 06-0770 (La. App. December 29, 2006) that the "per claim" retention in an insurance policy was ambiguous and therefore only required an oil well operator to pay a single retention despite the fact that numerous individual claims were brought against it for personal injuries and property damage arising out of a well explosion. Despite a trial court's declaration that the policy clearly required the insured to pay a separate $100,000 "per claim" self-insured retention for each individual claimant, the court found that the Limits of Insurance section of the contractor's Pollution Liability Coverage Endorsement was ambiguous as suggesting that the number of claims should be defined by reference to the number of pollution conditions. Where, as here, there was a single pollution condition, the court found that only one claim should apply.

Molestation and Sexual Assault Claims

Sexual molestation claims most frequently have arisen in the context of day-care centers and religious institutions. As the molesters intentional acts generally preclude coverage for them, coverage litigation for such claims has tended to focus on the employers or groups charged with negligence for failing to prevent such assaults. As will be shown, this distinction between perpetrators and supervisors can be crucial in determining the number of available policy limits.

One Occurrence: Failure to Prevent Abuse

In cases where claims have been filed against entities for failing to prevent abuse, courts sometimes have found a single occurrence based on the insured's failure to perform a duty.

In *Interstate Fire & Casualty Co. v. Archdiocese of Portland*, 747 F. Supp. 618 (D. Ore. 1990), *rev'd*, 35 F.3d 1325 (9th Cir. 1994), the court ruled that the number of occurrences was not determined by each act of molestation, but, rather, by the event giving rise to the Archdiocese's liability. This was the continuous negligence in retaining and supervising the priest, which was a single occurrence. On appeal, the Ninth Circuit disagreed, holding that the victim suffered separate injuries from the different acts of molestation and finding a new occurrence in each year that molestation had occurred. On remand, the U.S. District Court held the insured responsible for an individual retention in each of the four triggered policy years. *Interstate Fire & Cas. Co. v. Archdiocese of Portland*, 899 F. Supp. 498 (D. Ore. 1995).

In *Washoe County v. Transcontinental Ins. Co.*, 878 P.2d 306 (Nev. 1994), the Nevada Supreme Court ruled that the county's negligence in licensing a day-care center in which forty children were molested over a three-year-period was only one occurrence. The basis for the insured's liability was its single ongoing failure to perform its legal duty to properly monitor and regulate the center's operations. The court distinguished this case from its earlier ruling in *INA v. Rubin*, 818 P.2d 389 (Nevada 1991), which had held that each occasion on which an insured physician negligently failed to diagnose a young girl's brain tumor was a separate occurrence. In *INA* the county was being held liable for its failure to perform a single duty, not for discrete acts. The fact that the county's policy contained a $50,000 per occurrence retention was perhaps not coincidental to the ruling.

Arguably, a different conclusion might be reached if an institution were held vicariously liable for the torts of its employee. However, courts have been reluctant to find that sexual assaults are within the scope of employment and have not imputed liability to the employer on this basis. For example, *see Houg v. State Farm Fire & Cas. Co.*, 509 N.W.2d 590 (Minn. App. 1993).

Some earlier cases had avoided this issue altogether by adopting the so-called *first encounter* trigger, which restricts coverage to the policy in effect when the first assault or sexual encounter occurred.

By and large, this approach has been rejected in recent years. In particular, the District Court's 1993 ruling in *Lee v. Interstate Fire & Cas. Co.*, 826 F. Supp. 1156 (N.D. Ill. 1993) was rejected on appeal in *Lee v. Interstate Fire & Cas. Co.*, 86 F.3d 101 (7th Cir. 1996). The Seventh Circuit ruled that the claims of negligent supervision against the archdiocese were a separate occurrence in each year that misconduct was alleged. A *first encounter* rule was similarly rejected in *Roman Catholic Diocese of Joliet, Inc. v. Interstate Fire Ins. Co.*, 685 N.E.2d 932 (Ill. App. 1st Div. 1997), which involved claims for negligent supervision constituting an occurrence in each policy period in which molestation continued.

One Occurrence per Policy Year

Most courts have ruled that a separate occurrence limit is triggered in each year when molestation occurred. For example, the U.S. Court of Appeals for the Fifth Circuit held in *Society of Roman Catholic Diocese of Lafayette v. Interstate Fire & Cas. Co.*, 26 F.3d 1359 (5th Cir. 1994), that the molestation of thirty-one children over a period of years should trigger coverage in each year that incidents took place. Only the incidents within a policy year could be aggregated.

The New York Court of Appeals ruled in *Roman Catholic Diocese of Brooklyn v. National Union Fire Ins. Co. of Pittsburgh, PA*, 21 N.Y.3d 139, 991 N.E.2d 666, 969 N.Y.S.2d 808 (2013) that sexual abuse that occurred over a period of many years involved multiple occurrences and should be allocated on a *pro rata* basis among each of the policy years when abuse took place. The court found that there was no single "unfortunate event" as the incidents of sexual abuse had occurred over a span of six years and took place in multiple locations; thus lacking the temporal and spatial closeness necessary to support a finding of one occurrence. In *Safeguard Ins. Co. v. Angel Guardian Home*, 946 F. Supp. 221 (E.D.N.Y. 1996), a federal district court ruled that allegations that foster children were subjected to sexual abuse over a period of years involved an occurrence in each year in which the abuse occurred. The court rejected the insurer's contention that the insured's liability arose solely from its negligent placement of children in the foster home.

In *National Union Fire Ins. Co. v. Lynette C.*, 33 Cal. Rptr.2d 496 (1994), the California Court of Appeals ruled that a foster parent's negligent failure to protect a child from sexual molestation by the other foster parent triggered a separate claim limit in each of the policy years during which the negligent acts occurred.

In *TIG Insurance Company v. San Antonio YMCA*, No. 04-04-00017 (Tex. App. July 13, 2005), the Texas Court of Appeals held that even though TIG had contributed $1 million towards the settlement of various sexual abuse claims involving a YMCA counselor, it had a continuing duty to defend owing to the possibility that certain of the claims might potentially be construed as involving physical abuse that did not contain any "sexual" element. The court rejected the insured's contention that the sexual abuse occurrence endorsement was not meant to supersede the occurrence language and separate limits might therefore be available. To the contrary, the court ruled that all of the claims involving this particular perpetrator were subject to a single occurrence limit for sexual abuse claims.

Multiple Locations or Perpetrators as Separate Occurrences

Several courts have found multiple occurrences based on the number of claimants or the disparate manner in which the assaults occurred.

In a Texas case, the Fifth Circuit ruled in *H.E. Butt Grocery Co. v. National Union Fire Ins. Co.*, 150 F.3d 526 (5th Cir. 1998) that two separate sexual assaults by a store employee were separate occurrences when applying a self-insured retention. Even though the claims were based on the insured's negligent failure to supervise, the court declared that the immediate cause of the underlying injuries was the employee's intervening intentional tort. In addition to its refusal to find ambiguity in the meaning of occurrence in this context, the Fifth Circuit took note of the fact that the insured could have purchased an endorsement that would have aggregated such conduct as a single occurrence.

In *Worcester Ins. Co. v. Fells Acres Day School, Inc.*, 558 N.E.2d 958 (Mass. 1990), the Supreme Judicial Court ruled that claims against a day-care center involved more than one occurrence, since the sexual assaults were by various individuals at diverse locations and times.

Each Child a New Occurrence

Similarly, several courts have ruled that the molestation of each child is a separate occurrence because the process of injury and the circumstances of molestation differ from individual to individual. This is illustrated in *Preferred Risk Mutual Ins. Co. v. Watson*, 937 S.W.2d 148 (Tex. App. 1997), in which allegations that three children were molested by an employee of a day-care center were subject to a separate occurrence limit for each child.

S.F. v. West American Ins. Co., 463 S.E.2d 450 (Va. 1995), involved an apartment building owner who was sued by seven plaintiffs who had been sexually assaulted by the insured's property manager. The Virginia Supreme Court held the meaning of occurrence was ambiguous in that it could extend to the insured's hiring, supervision, or negligent retention of the molester. Under these circumstances, the court ruled that the claims could not be restricted to a single policy limit and were each a separate occurrence. However, the court refused to find that each separate molestation incident was a new occurrence.

Impact of Aggregating Provisions

The occurrences issue may be mooted by more recent policies that provide specific coverage for such claims but insulate the insurer by including a separate indemnity sublimit. Thus, when a policy contains a separate sublimit providing that all acts of sexual misconduct by a single individual would be considered a single occurrence, the U.S. Court of Appeals for the Tenth Circuit held that claims by multiple individuals who were molested must nonetheless all be considered part of the same occurrence. *See Kansas State Bank & Trust v. Midwest Mutual Ins. Co.*, No. 93-3066, 1994 WL 192035 (10th Cir. 1994).

Nursing Home Claims

The U.S. Court of Appeals for the Fifth Circuit, interpreting Texas law, has ruled that various different acts of negligence over the course of several years involved separate occurrences under a policy providing both professional liability and general liability insurance. In *Royal Ins. Co. of America v. Caliber One Indemnity Co.*, 465 F.3d 614 (5th Cir. 2006), the court held that the CGL "conditions" language could not be construed to encompass separate acts of negligence by nurses and doctors at the facility. The court observed that the "continuous or repeated exposure to conditions" language in the policy was designed to deal with physical conditions at the premises rather than the separate negligent acts of caregivers. The court cited a similar holding in an earlier sexual abuse case, declaring that "continuous or repeated exposure to conditions sounds like language designed to deal with asbestos fibers in the air, or lead-based paint on the walls, rather than with priests and choirboys." In this case, the court held that the acts and omissions that caused the patient's stage four pressure sores, pneumonia and other injuries culminating in her death were divisible from the acts and omissions that resulted in earlier bruises and sores.

Shooting and Criminal Assault Claims

Apart from these sexual molestation cases, there are numerous situations in which courts have been called upon to determine whether separate criminal acts involve one or more occurrences. As before, the resolution of this issue sometimes turns on the identity of the insured. In other cases, courts have focused on the specific physical circumstances of the incident in assessing whether the victims' injuries shared a common cause.

In several cases, courts have focused on the nature of the insured's liability in finding that multiple shooting incidents all arose out of the same occurrence.

In *Travelers Ind. Co. v. Olive's Sporting Goods*, 297 Ark. 516, 764 S.W.2d 596 (1989), a sporting goods store was sued by several individuals who were injured after a person to whom the store had sold a gun went on a shooting spree. In these circumstances, the Arkansas Supreme Court held that all of the claims against the insured arose out of the same occurrence, which is to say the insured's sale of the gun.

Likewise, the Massachusetts Appeals Court has ruled that various suits against a college for failing to prevent a shooting spree by a deranged student all arose out of a single occurrence. In *RLI Ins. Co. v. Simon's Rock Early College*, 54 Mass. App. Ct. 286 (2002), the court rejected RLI's contention that its umbrella policy obligations would not arise until the $3 million aggregate limit in American Alliance's primary policy was exhausted, holding instead that the primary insurer only owed a single $1 million occurrence limit. As the claims against the college were for negligence, the Appeals Court held that the cause of the victim's injuries was the insured's negligent failure to keep the student from using his gun to shoot them.

Most recently, the Appellate Division of the New Jersey Superior Court has ruled that claims against a homeowner for injuries suffered in an incident where the insured's adult son shot at various police officers on three occasions, injuring several officers, constitute a single occurrence. In *Bomba v. State Farm Fire & Cas. Co.*, 379 N.J. Super. 589, 879 A.2d 1252 (2005), the court rejected the insured's contention that each separate gunshot was a new occurrence, holding instead that inasmuch as the claims against the insured were based upon their negligence in allowing their son access to gun, the underlying injuries all shared the same cause.

On the other hand, several cases have found multiple occurrences under similar circumstances.

In *American Ind. Co. v. McQuaig*, 435 So.2d 414 (Fla. App. 1983), a homeowner engaged in a shoot-out with the police, injuring three officers with successive shotgun blasts. The District Court of Appeals held that each shotgun blast was a separate occurrence.

In *New Hampshire Insurance Company v. RLI Insurance Company*, 807 So.2d 171 (Fla. DCA 3 2002), a tenant in the insured's apartment building fired three separate shots at different times and places inside the apartment complex, injuring three individuals and killing two. The families of the victims sued the apartment building owner alleging that he had been negligent in failing to provide proper security that might have precluded such events from occurring. The Third Circuit of the Florida District Court of Appeal concluded that each separate incident was a different occurrence. The Florida District Court of Appeals ruled that "the act which causes the damage constitutes the occurrence." The Third District concluded that:

> there were three separate acts of shooting, causing three separate injuries to three separate persons in three separate instances. This is not a case with one proximate, uninterrupted continuing cause resulting in the deaths and injuries but rather three separate causes. New Hampshire did not incur any liability because of the aggressor's residence, but rather liability attached when the aggressor fired three shots which resulted in injury to the three victims.

Relying on *McQuaig* and *RLI*, the Florida Supreme Court ruled in 2003 that allegations of a restaurateur's negligence in failing to prevent an incident in which an aggrieved patron successively shot several patrons constituted multiple occurrences. In the absence of a policy definition of "accident," the Florida Supreme Court answered a certified question for the Eleventh Circuit in *Koikos v. Travelers Insurance Company*, 849 So.2d 263 (Fla. 2003) that the cause of the claims was the physical discharge of the firearm. The court rejected Travelers' contention that the relevant consideration was the single omission of its policyholder in failing to provide proper security. Further, the court refused to find that the "continuous and repeated exposure to conditions" language was relevant in considering the acts or omissions of the policyholder for which it was deemed to be legally responsible, ruling instead that this language was intended to broaden the scope of earlier coverage so as to clearly afford coverage for incidents in which injuries resulted from environmental exposures or other conditions that occurred over an extended period of time.

The court concluded that the inclusion of the "continuous or repeated exposure" language does not restrict the definition of occurrence but rather expands it by including ongoing and slowly developing injuries, such as those in the field of toxic torts. Therefore, the court reject Travelers' reliance on the "continuous or repeated exposure" language as a basis for concluding that Koikos' negligent failure to provide security constitutes a single occurrence under the terms of the policy. The victims were not "exposed" to the negligent failure to provide security. If the victims were "exposed" to anything, it was the bullets fired from the intruder's gun.

The Florida Supreme Court declared that "it is the act that causes the damage, which is neither expected nor intended from the standpoint of the insured that constitutes the occurrence." The court found that "focusing on the immediate cause—that is the act that causes the damage, rather than the underlying tort—that is the insured's negligence, is also consistent with the interpretation of other forms of insurance policies."

Pennsylvania's intermediate appellate court ruled 5-3 in *Donegal Ins. Co. v. Baumhammers*, 2006 PA Super. 32 (Pa. Super. Feb. 2006) that a shooting spree in which the insured's son fatally shot five people and wounded another involved six separate occurrences. On appeal, however, a similarly divided Supreme Court held that the claims involved a single occurrence. In *Donegal Mut. Ins. Co. v. Baumhammers*, 938 A.2d 286 (Pa. 2007), the Supreme Court held that the appropriate focus of a cause analysis was on the act of the insured that gave rise to his or her liability rather than the "immediate injury-producing act." The court held that, "Determining the number of occurrences by looking to the underlying negligence of the insured recognizes that the question of the extent of coverage rests upon the contractual obligation of the insurer to the insured. Since the policy was intended to insure [policyholders] for their liabilities, the occurrence should be an event over which [policyholders] had some control."

Likewise, the Texas Court of Appeals has ruled that an incident in which the plaintiff separately shot and killed various family members involved multiple occurrences based upon a claimed ambiguity in the meaning of occurrence. *State Farm Lloyds, Inc. v. Williams*, 916 S.W. 2nd 781 (Tex. App. - Dallas, 1997).

Finally, some courts have focused on the specific nature of the shooting injuries. For instance, the Alaska Supreme Court ruled in *USAA v. Neary*, 307 P.3d 907 (Ala. 2013) that an incident in which a bullet accidentally fired by insured's teenage son from his father's gun that passed through the body of one friend, fatally wounding him, and then lodged in the spine of another friend resulted from a single occurrence. In rejecting a trial court's determination that the plaintiffs were entitled to three separate occurrence limits under the personal liability provisions of the USAA homeowner's policy, the court ruled that the occurrence limit of liability applied "regardless of the number of insureds, claims made or persons injured" and that the trial court had therefore erred in multiplying the available limits by the number of insureds under the policy. Further, the court refused to find that these claims involved multiple occurrences based on the insureds' respective acts of negligence. The Supreme Court ruled that "There may have been multiple acts of negligence, but it was a single gunshot that caused the plaintiff's damages...." The court rejected the plaintiff's argument that it should adopt an "effects" test that would result in six separate occurrences.

Products Liability Claims

Defendants in products liability cases typically are removed in time and space from the event that physically causes the plaintiff's injuries. As a result, courts considering the number of occurrences for products claims have come to different conclusions on the identity of the event that is the cause of the insured's liabilities. Conversely, the rules that courts have adopted for auto accidents, premises exposure cases, and more common forms of tort liability are not necessarily a reliable basis for predicting the outcome of products-based occurrences disputes.

Single versus Multiple Occurrences

As a general rule, courts are more likely to find a *single* occurrence when a claim arises out of a defectively designed product or an inherent characteristic that is not affected by factors beyond the insured's control. By contrast, courts are more likely to find *multiple* occurrences in products liability cases where the incidence of loss is significantly affected by the manner in which the product is used or applied.

This distinction is illustrated by a brace of decisions from the U.S. District Court for the Eastern District of Michigan involving Dow Chemical's liability insurance policies. In the first of these, the court found multiple occurrences for Dow's Sarabond claims. In the second, all of the claims against the insured involving a defective pipeline were found to involve a single occurrence.

In *Dow Chemical Corp. v. Associated Indemnity Corp.*, 727 F. Supp. 1524 (E.D. Mich. 1989), Dow Chemical faced hundreds of suits for property damage arising out of the installation of Sarabond as a building mortar. The Sarabond caused internal steel to rust, which eventually created cracks. The court ruled that each installation of Sarabond in a separate building was a separate occurrence because the manner of injury differed from site to site and depended to a large extent on how the product had been installed.

By contrast, the same court ruled that a different set of mass products liabilities were one occurrence in *Associated Indemnity Corporation v. Dow Chemical*, 814 F. Supp. 613 (E.D. Mich. 1993). Defects in one of Dow's resin products had required the replacement of a vast natural gas pipeline network in Alberta, Canada. The court ruled that all the claims arose from an inherently defective product and should be grouped as one occurrence. In contrast to its rulings in the Sarabond litigation, the court noted that Dow manufactured the product component and was not directly involved in the installation or operation of the pipeline. Unlike the Sarabond claims in which relatively few of the products had actually failed, the replacement rate for the pipeline product was 100 percent. The judge found, therefore, that the Dow resin product was an "intrinsically harmful" product that had resulted in property damage without regard to subsequent factors.

Where the insured is a product manufacturer and the immediate cause of each plaintiff's injury are circumstances that are beyond the control of the insured (the product having previously been placed in the stream of commerce and having traveled to the plaintiff through a wholesaler, distributor, vendor and customer), courts are more likely to determine the number of occurrences by looking to the last act of the insured that forms the basis of its liability. In most cases, this will be the insured's transfer or delivery of the product to a third party.

In *Maurice Pincoffs Co. v. St. Paul Fire & Marine Ins. Co.*, 447 F.2d 204 (5th Cir. 1971), the U.S. Court of Appeals for the Fifth Circuit ruled in a Louisiana case that where the insured sold contaminated bird seed to eight dealers, who in turn sold the seed to various individual bird owners, it was the insured's sales to the dealers that were the cause of insured's liability, not the number of individual claims by irate bird owners.

This is particularly so in cases where the defect was caused by manufacturing problems, not design defect, and is therefore limited to particular batches of products. In a later Michigan case, the Sixth Circuit ruled in *Michigan Chemical Corp. v. American Home Assur. Corp.*, 728 F.2d 374 (6th Cir. 1984) that it was the insured's negligence in allowing the PBB to contaminate its cattle feed products that was the occurrence. Since contaminants had been introduced into some shipments and not others, the court ruled that shipments of contaminated cattle feed by the manufacturer were each separate occurrences. *See also Home Ins. Co. v. Aetna Cas. & Sur. Co.*, 528 F.2d 1388 (2d Cir. 1976), *remanded*, 1977 Fire & Casualty Cases 9 (S.D.N.Y. 1977)(damage to farm animals caused by the incorporation of contaminated resin into insured's feed supplement involved multiple occurrences since the cause of insured's liability was separate sales to third parties).

Courts have disagreed in these cases whether the insured's defective design or marketing of a product can be an occurrence. In *London Market Insurers v. Superior Court of Los Angeles County*, 146 Cal. App.4th 648, 53 Cal. Rptr.3d 154 (2007), the California Court of Appeal ruled that the insured's manufacture of asbestos products could not be the occurrence since injuries did not occur until the products left the insured's control. In a related vein, a New York trial court ruled in *ExxonMobil Corp. v. Certain Underwriters at Lloyd's*, 2007 WL 1615102 (N.Y. Supr. June 5, 2007) that an insured could not aggregate various products claims because "ExxonMobil's manufacture of these products is more easily characterized as conduct that was conscious and purposeful. There was never any event that took place unexpectedly or without design until the property damage occurred."

The Appellate Division of the New York Supreme Court ruled in *International Flavors and Fragrances, Inc. v. Royal Ins. Co. of America*, No. 11-05-07 (App. Div. October 30, 2007) that toxic tort claims presented by workers in a microwave packaging plant who suffered respiratory injuries as the result of exposure to a popcorn butter flavoring additive were separate occurrences and therefore required the insured to pay separate occurrence deductibles for each claim. In keeping with the New York Court of Appeals' decision in General Electric, the appellate court ruled that these claims could not be grouped as a single occurrence since they involved exposures that occurred in different places over a period of many years.

In *American Red Cross v. The Travelers Ind. Co.*, 816 F.Supp. 755 (D.D.C. 1993), the District Court ruled that claims against the Red Cross for shipping HIV contaminated blood were not based on any single negligent practice and should therefore be based on the number of shipments of contaminated blood.

By contrast, a few products cases have found that because the defect in the insured's product existed when it left the insured's premises, all of the resulting claims share the same cause and should therefore be treated as arising out of a single occurrence. *See Champion International Corp. v. Continental Cas. Co.*, 400 F.Supp. 978 (S.D.N.Y. 1975), *aff'd* 546 F.2d 502 (2nd Cir. 1976)(sale of the insured's defective panels to 26 boat manufacturers which resulted in 1400 separate claims were all found to share one cause and therefore constituted a single occurrence). *Accord, Champion International Corp. v. Liberty Mutual Ins. Co.*, 701 F.Supp. 409 (S.D.N.Y. 1988).

Some courts have ruled that measuring occurrences by the number of shipments is unfair and arbitrary in cases where the number of shipments was predetermined by a procurement contract or where the shipments themselves were a routine, repetitive function. In such cases, courts have looked behind the physical act of shipment towards some more encompassing cause.

In a coverage dispute arising out of the Agent Orange class action the court ruled in *Uniroyal, Inc. v. The Home Ins. Co.*, 707 F.Supp. 1368 (E.D.N.Y. 1988) that looking solely to the number of shipments would result in the amount of coverage being dependent on irrelevant factors, such as the size of the trucks in which the insured's product was shipped. The district court noted that Uniroyal's production volume was preset by its contract with the Pentagon and that the fortuitous circumstance that certain containers were smaller or larger than others (thus determining the number of shipments required to transport the stated product volume) would pointlessly skew these coverage determinations. The district court concluded that Uniroyal's delivery of herbicide to the military was "the conceptual point at which Uniroyal set its contaminated herbicides free upon the world to do their damage." Despite the fact that there were hundreds of deliveries by Uniroyal to the military between October 6, 1966 and March 1, 1968, the court determined that the deliveries were part of a pervasive policy undertaken by the insured over several years and thus constituted only one occurrence in each year that bodily injury had occurred.

In *Nationwide Mutual Ins. Co. v. Lafarge Corp.*, 935 F.Supp. 675 (D. Md. 1996), *aff'd mem.*, 121 F.3d 699 (4th Cir. 1997)(unpublished) (full text available at 1997 WL 532509), LaFarge sought coverage for $11 million that it had paid to resolve certain *Lone Star Steel* claims arising out its sales of allegedly defective cement. The U.S. District Court in Maryland had ruled that the loss should be apportioned throughout the period of injury but was only subject to the $1 million occurrence limit in the underlying primary policies, not the $2 million aggregate as National Union had argued. The court rejected National Union's contention that each shipment of defective cement had constituted a separate occurrence or that the insured had a separate obligation to pay a new deductible for each batch or lot of cement, ruling instead that LaFarge's liability arose out of a single occurrence, namely the "continuous, large scale manufacturing and sale" of its product. These findings were affirmed by the Fourth Circuit in an unpublished opinion.

Applying Pennsylvania law, the Third Circuit has held that 76 of the 77 MTBE suits against a petroleum company resulted from the same occurrence. In an unpublished opinion, the court ruled in *Sunoco, Inc. v. Illinois National Ins. Co.*, No. 05-4922 (3rd Cir. January 31, 2007) that in keeping with its 2005 Treesdale opinion, all but one of the underlying claims was based on the same claimed misconduct of the insured, namely the manufacture of a hazardous product and failure to warn. Accordingly, the court ruled that Illinois National was obligated to defend these cases, since the insured had paid more than a single $250,000 per occurrence SIR. However, the court held that one of the cases was a different occurrence since the claims were premised on Sunoco's negligent maintenance of a gasoline station, rather than some products liability theory. The Third Circuit also ruled that the claims fell within an exception to the policy's pollution exclusion because it involved damage away from the insured's property.

A federal district court ruled in *Dragas Management Corp. v. Hanover Ins. Co.*, No. 2:10CV547 (E.D. Va. July 21, 2011) that a ruling that a residential developer obtained against a drywall subcontractor triggered coverage on the basis that each of the seventy-four homes constituted a separate occurrence, rejecting Hanover's argument that the sole cause of the claims against the insured was its purchase of Chinese Drywall product. Unlike cases where the insured's liability solely arose from its sale or distribution of a defective product, the court found significant the fact that the insured was the party that installed the drywall in each home. The district court held that it was the act of installation that set the chain of events that culminated in damage to each home.

Single Occurrence Products Cases

Examples of single occurrence products liability cases are:

- *American Motorists Ins. Co. v. Trane Co.*, 544 F. Supp. 669 (W.D. Wis. 1982), *aff'd*, 718 F.2d 842 (7th Cir. 1983). All damage at a particular plant was held to be one occurrence because it flowed from the common failure of the insured's heat exchangers.

- *Bartholomew v. INA*, 502 F. Supp. 246 (D.R.I. 1980), *aff'd sub nom*, 655 F.2d 27 (1st Cir. 1981). Damage to car wash customers' vehicles resulted from the same product defect and arose out of one occurrence.

- *Cargill, Inc. v. Liberty Mutual Ins. Co.*, 488 F. Supp. 49 (D. Minn. 1979), *aff'd*, 621 F.2d 275 (8th Cir. 1980). Multiple sales of contaminated nutrient medium were held to constitute one occurrence because all the ensuing claims were caused by a change in the nutrient formula.

- *Carpenter Plastering Co. v. Puritan Ins. Co.*, No. 3-87-2435-R, 1988 WL 156829 (N.D. Tex. August 23, 1988). Damage from installations of asbestos board wall panels in buildings involved exposure to the same conditions and was one occurrence.

- *Cincinnati Ins. Co. v. Devon International, Inc.*, No. 110-5930 (E.D. Pa. February 16, 2013). Chinese drywall claims brought against a Pennsylvania importer all originated from a common source – the insured's single purchase and shipment of defective drywall from Shandong – and therefore are attributable to a single occurrence.

- *Colonial Gas v. Aetna Cas. & Sur. Co.*, 823 F. Supp. 975 (D. Mass. 1993). UFFI claims that were based on off-gassing from the foam insulation that the utility had arranged to have installed in homes constituted one occurrence. Done as a part of an energy conservation program, the insured's insulation program was a single occurrence from which the injuries arose.

- *Household Manuf. Inc. v. Liberty Mutual Ins. Co.*, No. 85-C-8519, 1987 U.S. Dist. LEXIS 10837, (N.D. Ill. February 10, 1987). Claims based upon the same defect in plumbing all arose out of one occurrence.

- *National Union Fire Co. v. Puget Plastics Corp.*, 649 F. Supp.2d 613 (S.D. Tex. 2009). Defective plastic water chambers incorporated into over 800 water heaters constituted a single occurrence, as the cause of the multiple failures was the single manufacturing defect.

- *Sting Security, Inc. v. First Mercury Syndicate, Inc.*, 791 F. Supp. 555 (D. Md. 1992). Separate problems that arose out of a defect in a security system were one occurrence.

- *Westchester Surplus Lines Ins. Co. v. Maverick Tube Corp.*, No. H-07-540 (S.D. Tex. June 28, 2010). Claims against an oil-field pipe manufacturer that sold 1,306 pieces of pipe to a distributor, who in turn sold the pipe to a drilling company, who used the pipe in four different gas wells where the pipe failed due to a manufacturing defect were subject only to a single $350,000 per occurrence self-insured retention.

Multiple Occurrence Products Cases

Examples of multiple occurrence products liability cases are:

- *Affiliated FM Ins. Co. v. Beatrice Foods Co.*, 1986 U.S. Dist. LEXIS 24265 (N.D. Ill. June 16, 1986). The insured's sales of a defective coating product to pool manufacturers constituted separate occurrences.

- *Bausch & Lomb, Inc. v. Lexington Ins. Co.*, 2009 U.S. Dist. LEXIS 120304 (W.D.N.Y. December 28, 2009). Thousands of individual lawsuits brought against the manufacturer of a contact lens cleaning solution were held to involve separate occurrences.

- *Dow Corning v. Continental Cas. Co.*, No. 200143 (Mich. App. October 12, 1999) (unpublished). Suits against silicone-filled breast implant manufacturer arose from multiple occurrences.

- *Dragas Management Corp. v. Hanover Ins. Co.*, No. 2:10CV547 (E.D. Va. July 21, 2011). Each of the homes into which insured installed defective dry wall product deemed a separate occurrence.

- *Honeycomb Systems, Inc. v. Admiral Ins. Co.*, 567 F. Supp. 1400 (D. Me. 1983). When machinery broke down a few years after the original incident because of a different problem, the claims involved two occurrences.

Toxic Tort Litigation

Since the 1970s, insurers have been confronted by policyholder demands for coverage for mass litigation by individuals and property owners who allege injury from the harmful consequences of the insured's products, notably asbestos-containing materials, prosthetic devices, and pharmaceutical products. Mass tort litigation also has emerged from occupational exposures, such as hearing loss.

Courts have developed three classifications for measuring the number of occurrences for toxic tort liabilities: 1) the marketing of the product (one occurrence), 2) the location or particular circumstances to which groups of plaintiffs were exposed (dozens of occurrences), or 3) the specific exposure of each plaintiff (countless occurrences).

Of these three, the most common has been the latter. A large number of courts have recently found that each claimant is a separate occurrence on the theory that the specific etiology of the claimant's asbestosis, mesothelioma, silicosis, or other disease developed through a slightly different process than other claimants' diseases. Even when the insured's coverage profile makes a single occurrence the best means of maximizing coverage, these courts have for the most part refused to look at intermediate unifying factors, such as exposure to common products during particular periods of time or at particular locations, as the cause of the insured's liabilities. Viewed in this way, cause becomes synonymous with effect.

The Illinois Supreme Court ruled in *Nicor, Inc. v. Aegis*, 860 N.E.2d 280 (Ill. 2006) that class action claims against a gas utility for personal injury and property damage resulting from the negligent removal of meter devices that contained mercury did not all result from a single cause so as to only require the insured to pay a single occurrence deductible. Rather, the court ruled that the mercury contamination in the 195 homes for which it submitted claims under the policies that it purchased from London Insurers between 1961 and 1978 required the insured to pay additional occurrence deductibles for each triggered year. After a lengthy and detailed review of Illinois cases over the past two decades in which courts had applied the cause theory to the issue of occurrences, the Supreme Court held that the appellate court had correctly concluded that there was no single underlying cause to these claims as each asserted loss was the result of a separate and intervening human act in contrast to claims against a product manufacturer where the damages are all attributable to the manufacturer's sale of a defective product or a fraudulent sales scheme. The court adopted with favor the cause approach that the appellate court had pioneered in 1988 in the *Mason* case. Despite Nicor's argument that its liability was not tied to any individual spill but rather reflected the overall cost of investigating and remediating the spills in response to the legal actions filed against it, the Supreme Court held that the operative "happening" "event" or "accident" was not the lawsuit brought against the utility but rather the underlying injuries. Likewise, the court rejected the insured's contention that these claims should be viewed as a single occurrence, since they all arose out of a uniform legal proceeding. The court ruled that the consolidation of individual claims as a single action was a question of litigation efficiency and had no bearing on the limits of coverage. Likewise, the court rejected Nicor's argument that interpreting these claims as involving 195 separate occurrences would somehow deny it the benefit of its bargain, the court declined the invitation of certain *amici* to adopt a rule that would preclude the finding of a single occurrence in the absence of a unifying directive in the policy language.

One might well wonder why the occurrences issue arises in the context of products liability claims, whether for toxic torts or otherwise, since most general liability policies contain aggregate protection for claims within the products hazard. Part of the reason is that the aggregate limit may be higher than the per occurrence limit. Also, courts sometimes have refused to give effect to this aggregate protection in toxic tort cases. For instance, negligence claims involving the typing of blood were held to involve services and not products in *American Red Cross v. The Travelers Ind. Co.*, 816 F. Supp. 755 (D.D.C. 1993), which involved the mishandling of HIV-contaminated blood. Alternatively, some courts have ruled that injurious exposures to asbestos fibers that occur while the insured's asbestos-containing product is being installed are outside the scope of the products hazard because the product was still under the insured's control. Examples of this reasoning are found in *Frontier Insulation Contractors, Inc. v. Merchants Mutual Ins.*

Co., 690 N.E. 2d 866 (N.Y. 1997) and *Commercial Union Ins. Co. v. Porter Hayden Co.*, 698 A.2d 1167 (Md. App. 1997), *writ denied* (Md. December 10, 1997). Of course, current editions of standard CGL policies do include general aggregates for nonproducts claims, but these often are higher than the products-completed operations aggregate.

Asbestos Claims

Without surprise, the greatest number of toxic tort occurrences cases involves asbestos claims. Many courts have ruled that each individual asbestos claimant is a new occurrence despite arguments that the cause of the insured's liability was the decision to market asbestos products.

An exception to this one claimant/one occurrence rule are cases in which policies contain high self-insured retentions or deductibles, retrospectively-rated premiums, or other provisions that would limit the insured's recovery if more than one occurrence were found. This line of reasoning can be seen in *Colt Industries, Inc. v. Aetna Cas. & Sur. Co.*, 1989 U.S. Dist. LEXIS 14496 (E.D. Pa. December 5, 1989), which highlights high per occurrence deductibles, and *Morton-Thiokol, Inc. v. Aetna Cas. & Sur. Co.*, 666 N.E.2d 1163 (Sept. 29, 1995), which involves a retrospectively rated premium. In such cases, courts have tended to focus on the insured's decision to market a particular product as the cause of all ensuing liabilities involving that product.

Another notable exception was the Third Circuit's ruling in *Liberty Mutual Ins. Co. v. Treesdale, Inc.*, 418 F.3d 330 (3rd Cir. 2005). Treesdale manufactured and sold a product known as Soffelex that contained asbestos and as a result became the subject of thousands of asbestos bodily injury claims. Liberty Mutual provided a defense to these actions under various policies that it issued between 1975 and 1985 that contained policy limits of $500,000. After exhausting these policies, Liberty agreed to pay a single $5 million umbrella limit notwithstanding the fact that it had issued excess policies to Treesdale between 1975 and 1983. As these policies contained a non-cumulation clause, however, Liberty Mutual contended that the most that it owed was the largest per occurrence limit in the excess layer. A federal district court in the Western District of Pennsylvania agreed. On appeal, the Third Circuit ruled on August 15, 2005 that these claims all involve a single occurrence because the cause of all the underlying claims was the insured's manufacture and sale of products containing asbestos. The court relied in large part on its 1982 opinion in *Appalachian* in which it noted that, "The fact that there are injuries of different magnitudes that occur at different times did not alter the conclusion that there was a similar occurrence as long as they all shared one proximate cause." The court took note of the fact that language in the underlying policies differentiated between persons, claims and occurrences. Additionally, it rejected the insured's various arguments as to why *Appalachian* was no longer good law in Pennsylvania as well as the insured's argument that it should follow alternative sources of authority, such as the Connecticut Supreme Court's analysis in *Metropolitan*, in which the court had ruled that each individual claimant is a new occurrence.

Similarly, in a case applying Illinois law, the New Jersey Supreme Court in *In The Matter of The Liquidation of Integrity Ins. Co.*, 214 N.J. 51, 67 A.3d 587 (2013) ruled that, as a sophisticated insured, Celotex should have realized that its excess layers of coverage were going to be penetrated by its asbestos liabilities and should have given notice to its post-1982 insurers, including Integrity. Although the claims set forth in the Trust's 2009 Proof of Claim had not been extant at the time of the dispositive rulings in the Florida coverage litigation, the court ruled that these later claims were subject to the same outcome that they all arose out of the same occurrence, which it defined under Illinois law as "Celotex's continued manufacture and distribution of asbestos-containing products."

Asbestos Cases Finding One Occurrence. The earlier, but no longer majority view was that the cause of asbestos liability was the insured's decision to market asbestos products. This is illustrated in a number of cases, including:

- *Air & Liquid Systems and Ampco Pittsburgh Corp. v. Allianz Ins., et al.*, No. 11-427 (W.D. Pa. September 30, 2013).

- *Colt Industries, Inc. v. Aetna Cas. & Sur. Co.*, 1989 U.S. Dist. LEXIS 14496 (E.D. Pa. December 5, 1989) The insured's manufacture of asbestos products was a single ongoing occurrence.

- *Greene Tweed & Co., Inc. v. Hartford Accident & Indemnity*, No. 03-3637 (E.D. Pa. April 21, 2006).

- *International Surplus Lines Ins. Co. v. Certain Underwriters at Lloyd's*, 868 F. Supp. 917 (S.D. Ohio 1994) The liability insurer acted reasonably in settling an asbestos coverage dispute on a single occurrence basis, focusing on the insured's decision to manufacture and market asbestos products.

- *In the Matter of The Liquidation of Integrity Ins. Co.*, 214 N.J. 51, 67 A.3d 587 (2013) (applying Illinois law).

- *Liberty Mutual Ins. Co. v. Treesdale, Inc.*, 418 F.3d 330 (3rd Cir. 2005) (applying Pennsylvania law).

- *Morton-Thiokol, Inc. v. Aetna Cas. & Sur. Co.*, 666 N.E.2d 1163 (Sept. 29, 1995). These asbestos personal injury suits against the insured arose out of its corporate decision to manufacture brake components containing asbestos. That decision is the single occurrence that caused all the claims.

- *Owens Illinois, Inc. v. United Insurance Co.*, 625A.2d 1 (N.J. App. 1993) *rev'd on other grounds*, 138 N.J. 437, 650 A.2d 974 (N.J. 1994). Policy provisions treating "a series of interrelated acts" as one occurrence mandate finding the insured's marketing of asbestos products was the sole occurrence for resulting liabilities.

- *Owens Illinois, Inc. v. Aetna Cas. & Sur. Co.*, 597 F. Supp. 1515 (D.D.C. 1984). The decision to manufacture asbestos products was the single cause of all personal injury claims.

- *Truck Ins. Exchange v. Kaiser Cement & Gypsum Corp.*, Los Angeles No. BC249550 (Cal. Super. January 10, 2006) Occurrence interpretation focuses on conduct of manufacturer.

- *U.S. Gypsum Co. v. Admiral Ins. Co.*, 643 N.E.2d 1226 (Ill. App. 1994). Rejecting the trial court's determination that each discovery of damage by a building owner was a separate occurrence requiring the payment of a separate policy deductible by USG, the Appellate Court ruled that these claims were also caused by the "continuing process of the manufacture and sale of asbestos containing products" by the insured and should therefore be treated as involving one occurrence.

Even these "failure to warn" or "decision to manufacture" cases have found separate occurrences when the claims against the manufacturer arise out of different product lines. For instance, in *Westinghouse Electric Corp. v. Aetna Cas. & Sur. Co.*, Union No. L-069351-97 (N.J. Super. August 7, 1998), a New Jersey trial court declared that under Pennsylvania law the various suits involving asbestos, PCB-containing products, and welding rod fumes should be treated as involving three separate occurrences because there was a separate decision to manufacture and sell each product.

Asbestos Cases Finding Multiple Occurrences. More recent cases have tended to take a more expansive view and have ruled that each individual claimant is a new occurrence.

An early but influential ruling in this respect was the Phase IV decision in *Asbestos Insurance Coverage Cases, Judicial Council Coordination*

Proceeding No. 1072 (Cal. Super. August 29, 1988), *aff'd on other grounds*, 52 Cal. Rptr.2d 690 (Cal. App. 1996). The Superior Court agreed with Armstrong and other asbestos manufacturers that had argued that each asbestos bodily injury claimant was a separate accident or occurrence. Various insurers had contended that the number of policy limits should be aggregated by factors that might be common to the exposures suffered by groups of claimants, such as the type of product or location of exposure.

The *Coordinated Asbestos* analysis was largely adopted by the California Court of Appeal in *London Market Insurers v. Superior Court of Los Angeles County*, 146 Cal. App.4th 648, 53 Cal. Rptr.3d 154 (2007). In declaring that a trial court erred in holding that it was a cement manufacturer's productionand distribution of products containing asbestos that was the single occurrence giving rise to its liabilities, the Second District rejected any remote cause analysis of this sort, declaring that the plain language of the various policies at issue, coupled with their drafting history precluded any such finding as a matter of law. In keeping with the *Coordinated Asbestos* and *Fina* opinions, the court concluded that the failure to protect claimants from asbestos was not a condition. Rather, it concluded that the conditions at issue were the asbestos fibers released from Kaiser's product to which the underlying claimants were exposed. The court also refused to find that these claims fell within the products hazard since the manufacture or distribution occurred prior to the relinquishment of the product by the insured. Nor did they fall within the policies deemer clause. Finally, turning to California precedents in non-toxic tort cases, the Court of Appeal refused to find that any of the cited cases suggest that the number of occurrences should be determined by reference to the conduct of the insured which gives rise to liability or any other remote cause. While therefore rejecting the primary insurer's contention that these claims involved a single occurrence, the Court of Appeal further found that separate occurrences were not subject to any applicable policy aggregate. First, the court refused to find that these claims involved injuries arising out of a lot of goods or products under certain earlier policies, observing that there was no evidence that all of the asbestos claims derived from a single lot of the insured's products. The court declined to limit this language to claims involving design defects, declaring that it had equal applicability to non-conforming products. The court rejected the contrary analysis adopted by the Appellate Court in *Diamond Shamrock* in 1992. The court declined to give effect to language in the policies issued after 1974 aggregating losses involving "substantially the same general conditions existing at or emanating from each premises location." In view of the fact that the products at issue were manufactured at ten different facilities at various times, the Court of Appeal held that the claims could not have all emanated from one premises location. However, the court refused to find that this "same general conditions" language applied only to premises coverage, not products liability claims. The case was therefore remanded for the development of a more precise factual record as to whether the facts of each claim would permit the number of occurrences and the insurer's obligations to be limited by separate claims involving individual lots or individual premise locations.

In *Babcock and Wilcox Co. v. Arkwright-Boston Manufacturing Mutual Ins. Co.*, 53 F.3d 762 (6th Cir. 1995), the district court in Ohio ruled that each claimant's exposure to asbestos materials was a separate event for determining the number of occurrences. On appeal, the U.S. Court of Appeals for the Sixth Circuit agreed.

The Connecticut Supreme Court ruled in *Metropolitan Life Ins. Co. v. Aetna Cas. & Sur. Co.*, 255 Conn. 295, 765 A.2d 891 (2001) that the cause of the underlying claimants' asbestos injuries was not Metropolitan's alleged failure to warn but rather each claimant's exposure to asbestos fibers. Metropolitan was sued by thousands of asbestos claimants who alleged that it had concealed knowledge with respect to asbestos risks that it had obtained as a consequence of providing health care insurance to various asbestos manufacturers and distributors. In particular, the evidence was that Metropolitan had engaged in medical research concerning asbestos exposures beginning in the 1930's under the direction of Dr. Anthony Lanza, Metropolitan's medical directors. Metropolitan sought coverage for these claims under primary and excess policies issued to it between 1976 and 1986 by Aetna (Travelers). The excess policies were not triggered until such time as Metropolitan had paid $25 million per occurrence. In order to maximize the benefits of this coverage, therefore, Metropolitan argued that all of the underlying claims could be aggregated as a single occurrence since all asserted that Metropolitan was liable for the same conduct (i.e. its failure to warn the plaintiffs of what it had learned about the dangers of asbestos). Home, Travelers, and other excess carriers contended, however, that whether viewed under the law of Connecticut or New York, the cause of each plaintiff's injury was their exposure to asbestos and that each claimant must be therefore treated as a separate occurrence. The Superior Court agreed with the insurers, stating that "The event of unfortunate character which must occur close in time with no intervening agent must be...each claimant's separate exposure to asbestos." The court declined to alter this analysis merely because excess insurance existed, finding that "this court is not persuaded as a matter of pure social policy that catastrophic insurance was ever meant to cover losses for a collection of underlying lawsuits of dubious merit, no matter how great in number, which are being settled individually for nuisance values."

On appeal, the Connecticut Supreme Court was asked to consider whether an omission, that is to say the insured's failure to warn, might constitute a cause of the plaintiff's injuries. The court ruled that the policy terms could not plausibly be read to combine "hundreds of thousands of exposures that occurred under different circumstances throughout the country over a period of sixty years into one occurrence." Adopting the New York event test, the Supreme Court ruled that the exposures to asbestos constitute several occurrences in view of the fact that they were separated in time, place and circumstances. Rather, the court looked to the "immediate event that caused the claimants' injuries" and therefore ruled that the number of occurrences must be determined by each claimant's individual exposure to asbestos.

In keeping with *Metropolitan*, a state trial court in Connecticut rejected Hartford's contention that the $1.15 billion that it paid to Western McArthur to resolve coverage issues involving 17,000 underlying asbestos suits could be ceded to London reinsurers as arising out of a single accident, happening or occurrence. In *Hartford Accident & Indemnity Co. v. Ace American Reinsurance Co.*, CV03-017822 (Conn. Super. December 13, 2005), *appeal pending* (Conn. 2007), the court granted summary judgment to Hartford's reinsurers holding that they had established beyond any question of fact that the underlying claims failed to exhaust the $25 million per occurrence retentions. The court rejected Hartford's efforts to distinguish the Connecticut Supreme Court's multiple occurrences holding in *Metropolitan*. Under the circumstances, the superior court refused to find that the underlying claims shared a common cause. The court also rejected Hartford's contention that reinsurers were bound to follow its fortune and could only avoid a payment obligation by establishing that Hartford had acted unreasonably or in bad faith in construing these treaties to allow aggregation, holding in stead that the "follow the fortunes" doctrine could not be relied on to trump terms in the underlying policies or to bind a reinsurer to indemnify a cedent whenever it paid a claim regardless of the contractual language defining the loss in the underlying policies.

In *Flintkote Co. v. General Accident Assurance Co. of Canada*, No. C04-01827 (N. D. Cal. January 3, 2006), the court held that in the context of asbestos claims an occurrence is "exposure to asbestos that causes and immediately precedes an injury giving rise to liability under the policy." In rejecting the defendant's argument that the district court should use an equitable approach that might focus on different events depending on discovery such as the insured's decision to mine and sell asbestos or the number of plants receiving the insured's asbestos, the court ruled that equity was not the relevant test and that, applying the terms of the policy the event giving rise to liability that immediately precedes the asbestos-related injury is plainly the exposure to asbestos fibers.

In the most recent opinion to analyze these issues, the California Court of Appeal ruled in *London Market Insurers v. Superior Court*, 146

Cal. App. 4th 648; 53 Cal. Rptr. 3d 154 (2007) that a trial court erred in holding that it was a cement manufacturer's manufacture and distribution of products containing asbestos that was the single occurrence giving rise to its liabilities. In rejecting any remote cause analysis of this sort, the Second District declared that the plain language of the various policies at issue, coupled with their drafting history precluded any such finding as a matter of law. While refusing to find that each individual claim was a separate occurrence, the Court of Appeal remanded the case to the Superior Court for the development of a more precise factual record as to whether the real parties in interest could establish that certain of the claims might be aggregated as arising out of a particular lot or an individual premises location.

Likewise, the New York Court of Appeals has ruled that each individual worker who suffered bodily injury as a consequence of exposure to asbestos-containing products constitutes a separate occurrence for purposes of determining the limits of coverage available to satisfy the third-party claims. The effect of the court's ruling in the matter of *Appalachian Ins. Co. v. General Electric Co.*, No. 11 (N.Y. February 15, 2007) will be to largely preclude General Electric from obtaining any excess coverage for these asbestos claims owing to the fact that its primary liability insurance (which was largely self-insured), only contained per occurrence limits and did not include any aggregate liability limit. The excess insurers had disputed efforts by GE and Emlico to characterize its asbestos liabilities on a more limited basis which, while it varied over time, ultimately focused on the number of product lines manufactured by GE that were resulting in asbestos claims. Whereas GE argued that the cause of its liabilities was its failure to give warnings concerning the presence of asbestos in its turbines, the Court of Appeals agreeing with the trial court and the Appellate Division ruled that in keeping with cases such as *A. Johnson* and *Wesolowski*, claims occurring in different parts of the country in different decades affecting different individuals could not all be aggregated as a single occurrence. The Court of Appeals held that factors to consider in assessing whether there were one or several occurrences included "whether there is a close temporal and spatial relationship between the incidents giving rise to injury or loss, and whether the incidents could be viewed as part of the same causal continuum, without intervening agents or factors." Even though *A. Johnson* had construed the meaning of an accident policy, the Court of Appeals held that the same analysis was true with respect to these occurrence policies since there was no indication that the industry's transition from accident to occurrence-based coverage was intended to have any impact on the limits of coverage. Since the triggering event for purposes of coverage was each individual claimant's exposure to asbestos and in view of the fact that these injurious exposures occurred in widely different locations and times, the court ruled that there were unquestionably multiple occurrences.

This one claim/one occurrence analysis is not limited to bodily injury claims. In *Stonewall Ins. Co. v. Asbestos Claims Management Corp.*, 73 F.3d 1178 (2nd Cir. 1995), National Gypsum sought coverage for hundreds of property claims filed against it that had arisen out of the installation of its asbestos-containing building products. The policies at issue contained a substantial per occurrence deductible. In light of the effect that this deductible would have had on its available insurance coverage if each claim were treated as a separate occurrence, National Gypsum contended that the claims all arose from its manufacture and sale of asbestos-containing products—a single occurrence. The Second Circuit rejected this argument. Applying New York's *unfortunate event* cause analysis, the court declared that the insurable occurrence was not the manufacturer's general decision to manufacture wallboard containing asbestos but rather each installation of wallboards. Accordingly, the court declared that each building constituted a separate occurrence. *Accord, Maryland Cas. Co. v. W.R. Grace and Co.*, 128 F.3d 794 (2nd Cir. 1997).

A divided panel of the U.S. Court of Appeals for the Second Circuit affirmed a New York district court's determination that a per occurrence deductible be applied separately to each asbestos bodily injury claim against a bankrupt shipping company. In *In Re Prudential Lines, Inc.*, 158 F.3d 65 (2nd Cir. 1998), the court noted that New York law would, in any event, likely have resulted in each claim being treated as a separate occurrence. The court quoted with favor decisions from other jurisdictions that had declared that, because the medical history and process of diseases for each asbestos claimant was unique, each exposure must be viewed as a separate occurrence. A dissenting judge, however, warned that the logical outcome of this analysis would require a finding that each subsequent exposure suffered by a claimant also would be a separate occurrence. The court pointed out that the occurrence in such cases is not the same as the claimed injury because one is the cause and the other, the effect.

On a certified question from the Seventh Circuit, the Wisconsin Supreme Court ruled in *Plastics Engineering Co. v. Liberty Mut. Ins. Co.*, 759 N.W.2d 613 (Wis. 2009), that under a cause test, each individual asbestos claimant should be treated as a separate occurrence, rejecting an insurer's argument that it was the insured manufacturer's failure to warn that was the common cause.

In contrast to this each claimant/each occurrence approach, a few courts have adopted an intermediate approach that focuses on occupational exposures in which multiple claimants are injured as the result of exposures to toxic materials in the same time and place.

For instance, a federal district court ruled in *Fina, Inc. v. Travelers Ind. Co.*, 184 F.Supp.2d 547 (N.D. Tex. 2002) that exposure to asbestos at three separate locations all owned by the defendant constituted three separate occurrences. Travelers had argued that the claims all arose out of a single occurrence, namely the insured's failure to protect its employees, which Travelers likened to the "continuous or repeated exposure to conditions" language in its policy.

In keeping with this approach, another federal district court ruled in *LSJ Technologies, Inc. v. U.S. Fire Ins. Co.*, No. 2:07-CV-399 (E.D. Tex. September 2, 2010) that there was no single continuous cause that had resulted in all of the underlying injuries although claimants exposed to asbestos-containing gaskets at the same time and location could be aggregated together since they were "exposed to substantially the same general condition." The court adopted an intermediate approach, however, holding that the cause analysis should focus on the events giving rise to the plaintiffs' injuries, not the injuries themselves and that individual claimants could be grouped together as one occurrence if they were all exposed to asbestos-containing gaskets at the same time and location so as to have been exposed to "substantially the same general conditions."

Hearing Loss Claims. In recent years, railroads have been sued in thousands of FELA cases for alleged hearing loss due to employees' exposure to allegedly unsafe work conditions around the country. Many of these cases involve policyholders with large self-insured retentions who therefore contend that their failure to implement proper protective measures was the single cause of their liabilities. Conversely, insurers have tended to argue that the specific circumstances of the claimants' injuries require a finding of multiple occurrences, or, at a minimum, that only cases involving hearing loss arising out of exposures to substantially similar conditions may be grouped. This includes arguments for grouping employees who worked at a particular site at the same time.

While sharing certain common characteristics with products liability suits, hearing loss claims are a unique area of occurrences case law. As a preliminary matter, they do not arise out of the sale or distribution of a product. Railroads do not manufacture or sell noise. In addition, such claims are influenced by the statutory elements of FELA as well as the fact that many of the policies contain employer's liability insurance features, such as cessation from work clauses and a separate aggregate limit for occupational disease.

Courts have frequently ruled that gradually developed injuries by railroad workers fall within this meaning of occupational disease and therefore are subject to this aggregate limit. Cases that discuss these issues include *Chesapeake & Ohio Ry. Co. v. Certain Underwriters at Lloyd's*, 716 F. Supp. 27 (D.D.C. 1989), *rev'd on other grounds*, 910 F.2d 960 (D.C.

Cir. 1990) (asbestos claims) and *Norfolk & Western Railway Co. v. Accident & Cas. Ins. Co. of Winterthur*, 41 F.3d 928, 931 (4th Cir. 1994) *aff'd in part, rev'd in part*, 41 F.3d 982 (4th Cir. 1994) (NIHL claims).

In *CSX Transportation, Inc. v. Continental Ins. Co.*, 680 A.2d 1082 (Md. 1996), a railroad conglomerate sought coverage from its liability insurers for thousands of hearing loss claims. Each of the 246 policies at issue contained a self-insured retention that ranged from $100,000 to $3 million. The Maryland trial court rejected the insured's contention that there were at most two occurrences: the claimant's exposure to hazardous noise and the failure of the railroad's mandated system-wide hearing protection that would have prevented these exposures. The jury was instructed that the purpose of this self-insurance was to protect against high frequency, low severity losses, without incurring the additional premium expense that the policyholder would otherwise incur. The jury concluded that there were a minimum of 20,235 separate occurrences and found that CSX had failed to prove that the occupational hearing losses at issue were accidents or a series of accidents under the policies. Based upon this verdict, the court entered a judgment in favor of the insurers.

On appeal, the Maryland Court of Appeals declared that the cause instruction to the jury had appropriately stated the test for determining the number of occurrences. Addressing the claims as a whole, the court held that multiple injuries could only be aggregated if the exposure of the claimants occurred at the same place or had been caused by the same source. Otherwise, the court held that there was no commonality between the claims or between the injuries. Conversely, the causes proposed by CSX were too broad in general to be applied.

A different view was adopted by the Kansas Supreme Court in *Atchison, Topeka and Santa Fe Railroad Co. v. Stonewall Ins. Co.*, 71 P.3d 1093 (Kan. 2003). The lower court ruled that noise induced hearing loss claims could be aggregated because they shared a single cause, namely the insured's failure to implement a program to protect its employees from hearing loss. On appeal, the Kansa Supreme Court began with the issue of whether the 3,800 individual NIHL claims should be treated as a single occurrence or not. The railroad had argued that the event was "its negligent failure to timely implement an effective hearing conservation program that would have protected its workers from the excessive noise inherent in railroad operations." The insurers argued, on the other hand, that the event was the exposure to the injurious noise and because each worker had a unique work history, the many exposures to different noises at different times and places required a finding of multiple occurrences. As none of these occurrences exceeded Santa Fe's self-insured retentions, the excess insurers argued that they should be freed from any contractual obligation for these claims. After a lengthy discussion of Kansas precedents as well as out-of-state cases such as *CSX* and *Norfolk & Western*, the Supreme Court concluded with minimal analysis that there was support for the trial court's "single occurrence" decision in the policy language as well as the law of either Kansas or Illinois. To a large extent, the Kansas Supreme Court followed the analysis of the Appellate Court of Illinois in *Missouri Pacific*, particularly as regards the issue of self-insured retentions, number of occurrences, horizontal exhaustion and allocation.

Lead Paint Claims. Although some courts have held that children's' exposure to lead in a single insured apartment or residence involves exposure to similar conditions, others have found that the individualized circumstance of each plaintiff's injury is a new occurrence.

The Maryland Court of Special Appeals has ruled that the exposure of various children to lead paint in a single apartment triggered separate occurrence limits in each of the years in which bodily injury occurred. In *Maryland Casualty Co. v. Hanson*, 902 A.2d 152 (Md. App. 2006), the court rejected the insurer's argument that the children's injuries all arose out of the same cause or that coverage should be limited to the year in which injuries initially arose. In a lengthy opinion, the court declared that in the absence of a non-cumulation clause or limiting language of the sort construed by the New York Court of Appeals in *Hiraldo*, Maryland "trigger of coverage" case law and the Maryland Court of Appeals' recent ruling in *Riley* made clear that successive limits of coverage could be stacked for continuing injury cases and that the insured's recovery was not limited to a single policy year. Unlike the court's ruling in *CSX*, the Court of Special Appeals declared that the number of occurrences was determined by reference to the continuous injury trigger without regard to a cause analysis.

The First Department of the Appellate Division of the New York Supreme Court ruled in *Ramirez v. Allstate Ins. Co.*, 2006 NY Slip Op 01356 (N.Y. App. February 23, 2006), that separate claims brought by two infant children who were exposed to lead dust inside the insured's apartment building were subject to the same occurrence limit as presenting claims for bodily injury "resulting from continuous or repeated exposure to the same general conditions."

Other Job Site Exposures. Efforts to aggregate on the basis of the number of job sites have been rejected by state and federal courts in Louisiana in a series of asbestos and silicosis cases. *See e.g., Ducre v. Mine Safety Appliances Co.*, 645 F. Supp. 708 (E.D. La. 1986), *aff'd*, 833 F.2d 588 (5th Cir. 1987)(silicosis claims); *Cole v. Celotex*, 588 So. 2d 376 (La. App. 1991), *aff'd*, 599 So. 2d 1058 (La. 1992)(asbestos) and *Houston v. Avondale Shipyards, Inc.*, 506 So. 2d 149 (La. App. 1987), *writ denied*, 512 So. 2d 460 (La. 1987) (silicosis).

In *Exxon Corp. v. St. Paul Fire & Marine Ins. Co.*, 1996 U.S. Dist. LEXIS 17278 (E.D. La. November 15, 1996), *aff'd mem.*, 129 F.3d 781 (5th Cir. 1997), several workmen became ill after handling a cargo of soil and petroleum residues that apparently contained trace substances of hazardous materials. St. Paul contended that all of the workers became ill as the result of their exposure over the course of a few days to the contaminated cargo. However, the court ruled that the claimants' exposures, which had occurred at different stages of the cargo's journey over the course of several days, could not be said to all involve the consequences of a single, identifiable event. This was particularly true because the marine policy involved did not contain CGL language that would have aggregated all "continuous or repeated exposure to substantially the same general conditions."

Toxic Tort Claims against Contractors. An effort to trigger multiple occurrence limits based upon separate spraying incidents was rejected by the Texas Court of Appeals in *Foust v. Ranger Ins. Co.*, 975 S.W.2d 329 (Tex. App. 1988). Foust was a cotton farmer whose crop was damaged as a consequence of herbicides that drifted onto his property while being sprayed by the insured crop duster. The crop dusting was performed over the course of three hours on May 14, 1994. During this period, the wind direction changed, and temperature changes may have affected how the herbicides drifted. The insured also had to make numerous passes over the target area and landed to refuel on several occasions. The plaintiffs contended that each time the plane landed, the previously released herbicide dissipated so that each new spraying created a new cloud that was a separate occurrence.

The Ranger policy had limits of $100,000 per occurrence and $200,000 in the aggregate. The policy stated that "...all bodily injury or property damage resulting from the same general conditions will be considered to be caused by one occurrence." Although Ranger agreed to provide a defense, it balked when asked to contribute more than $100,000 toward the settlement. The underlying plaintiffs sought a declaration that they were entitled to $200,000 because more than one occurrence had taken place. The San Antonio trial court entered summary judgment for Ranger, declaring that the insured's application of herbicide on that date constituted a single occurrence.

This finding was affirmed by the Texas Court of Appeals in early 1998. The court stated that "each pass resulted in the creation of the same general conditions" and, therefore, arose out of the same overall occurrence.

Conclusion

The issue of whether one or several occurrences are involved in claim situations has complex implications for both insureds, insurers, and reinsurers. It impacts how and when aggregates are eroded and excess layers pierced, how much insureds will have to pay in retentions or deductibles, and when an insurer's duty to defend ends.

There is no clear right or wrong position for either insureds or insurers because their situations change with the details of the case. A greater understanding of how these needs and roles change, however, will help when establishing insurance programs and analyzing claim situations.

Section IV

Cyber Liability

By: Gregory Deimling, CPCU

The Epidemic of Cybercrime

Cybercrime is criminal activity or a crime relating to, or involving computers or computer networks such as the Internet. The June 2014 report from the Center for Strategic and International Security touts cybercrime as a growth industry: "the returns are great and the risks are low". Interpol recognizes "cybercrime as the fastest growing area of crime. Criminals exploit the speed, convenience and anonymity of the Internet to commit a diverse range of criminal activities that know no borders, either physical or virtual." It equals, and may well surpass, drug trafficking as a criminal moneymaker.

The Internet generates \$2 to \$3 trillion of the global economy and is expected to grow; cybercrime currently extracts some 15 percent of its value. Last year cybercrime cost the global economy approximately \$400 billion; \$100 billion in the United States. These losses will only increase as more economic activity and businesses move online.

PriceWaterhouseCoopers' 2014 *Global Economic Crime Survey* confirms the significant, continuing impact of this crime on business, with now one in four of respondents reporting they have experienced a cybercrime and over 11 percent of these suffering financial losses of more than \$1 million.

Types of Cybercrimes

Cybercrimes are defined as:

1. Attacks that target computer hardware and software, for example, botnets, malware, and network intrusion.

2. Financial crimes, such as online fraud, penetration of online financial services, and phishing.

3. Abuse, especially of young people, in the form of grooming or 'sexploitation'.

The two most common exploitation techniques, both relatively simple and cheap, are social engineering and vulnerability of the equipment, software, installation, or human operator.

Computer-Targeted Crimes

These crimes relate to theft or manipulation of computers, data, or services by hacking or viruses and often result in identity theft, credit card, or bank fraud. It is usually a single event from the perspective of the victim. A virus, or other type of malware, which is unknowingly downloaded, installs a keystroke logger on the computer. The hacker then steals private data such as Internet banking and email passwords. Hackers often carry out these crimes by taking advantage of flaws in a Web browser to place a Trojan horse virus onto the unprotected victim's computer.

Another common form is 'phishing'. The victim receives a supposedly legitimate email (quite often claiming to be a bank or credit card company) with a link that leads to a hostile Web site. Once the link is clicked, the computer can then be infected with a virus.

Financial Crimes

PriceWaterhouseCoopers' 2014 *Global Economic Crime Survey*, stated that 39 percent of financial sector respondents said they had been victims of cybercrime, compared with only 17 percent in other industries. Financial crime is theft of financial assets through cyber intrusions. According to the June 2014 report from the Center for Strategic and International Security, the best data on financial cybercrime comes from the global financial services sector. Because banks, insurers, investment firms, etc., who hold and manage both data and money for their customers, are regulated, they pay attention to cybersecurity and can easily measure loss. Privacy laws that require firms to report losses when personal information is compromised mean that the expense of managing the attack $100 million or more for large incidents can exceed the amount gained by the cyber criminals.

Retailers are favored targets of cybercriminals because they offer access to personally identifiable customer and credit card data (issued and maintained by the banking and credit industries). UK retailers lost $850 million last year and Australian retailers averaged $100 million per company. In the U.S., the Black Friday attack on retailer Target stores cost the banks over $200 million, not including Target's costs or its customers' expenses.

Exploitation Crimes

The computer isn't the target of the attack. The computer is a tool used to commit more serious crimes such as cyber stalking, harassment, child predation, extortion, blackmail, stock market manipulation, complex corporate espionage, and planning or carrying out terrorist activities. These are usually repetitive, involving multiple interactions with the target. Social media, chat rooms, etc., offer opportunities for a predator to interact and establish relationships and then exploit them to commit a crime. Members of criminal and/or terrorist groups use these same social platforms to plan and discuss crimes.

Theft of confidential business information is the third largest cost from cybercrime and cyber espionage because it can be turned into immediate gain. Stock market manipulation is a growth area for cybercrime. Breaking into systems and stealing sensitive revenue reports, contract information, or merger plans gives criminals an advantage in trading.

Cyber theft of intellectual property is of significant concern to businesses. It impacts the ability to competitively manufacture and deliver goods to sustain operations and meet financial commitments. Many companies do not know that their intellectual property has been stolen until after the clones have been manufactured and brought to market.

Opportunity Costs

The value of forgone activities cannot be realized when resources are spent elsewhere. Loss from cybercrimes can result in reduced investment in R&D, increased spending in network defense, and avoidance of Internet use.

Employment

Diversion of resources to combat cybercrime has serious impacts on employment. In the U.S., it could cost as many as 200,000 jobs and in Europe, as many as 150,000.

Cybercrime in the United States

PriceWaterhouseCoopers' *U.S. Cybercrime: Rising Risks, Reduced Readiness* report discloses results of the 2014 U.S. State of Cybercrime Survey. Cybersecurity leaders from PriceWaterhouseCoopers, CSO magazine, the CERT Division of the Software Engineering Institute at Carnegie Mellon University, and the United States Secret Service worked with 500 executives of U.S. businesses, law enforcement services and government agencies. The survey found that in 2013:

- 7% of U.S. organizations lost $1 million or more due to cyber-crime incidents compared with 3% of global organizations.

- 19% of U.S. organizations reported losses of $50,000 to $1 million, compared with 8% of worldwide respondents.

- 77% of respondents detected a security event in the past 12 months; 34% said the number of security incidents detected increased over the previous year.

Significant incidents across industries:

Banking & Finance

No incidents – 20%

Identify theft – 20%

Customer records compromised or stolen – 23%

Financial losses – 23%

Denial of service attacks – 29%

Financial fraud – 36%

Healthcare

Theft of electronic medical data – 15%

Customer records compromised or stolen – 19%

Financial losses – 19%

Email or other applications unavailable – 22%

Private or sensitive data unintentionally exposed – 22%

No incidents – 30%

Insurance

Confidential records (trade secrets or IP) compromised or stolen – 19%

Customer records compromised or stolen – 19%

Financial fraud – 19%

Unauthorized access/use of data, systems, networks – 19%

Financial losses – 29%

No incidents – 38%

- 59% of respondents said that they were more concerned about cybersecurity threats this year than in the past.

- 69% of U.S. executives are worried that cyber threats will impact growth.

- The average number of security incidents detected in 2013 was 135 per organization. This does not account for incidents that go undetected. Last year 3,000 companies were unaware of cyber intrusions until notified by the FBI. (Many discovered through release of WikiLeaks reports.)

- 14% of respondents reported losses increased last year.

- 67% of those who detected a security incident could not estimate the financial costs. Among those that could, the average annual monetary loss was $415,000.

- Organizations that have experienced a cybercrime are more cautious and exhibit more sophisticated security practices than those that have not: 37% of respondents who had not suffered a security incident did not know what groups posed the greatest threat to their organization, compared with 18% of those who had experienced an incident.

Sources of U.S. Cybersecurity Incidents

- 72% of respondents cited outsiders, such as hackers.

- 26% of respondents that had detected a cybersecurity incident could not identify the source of the attack.

- 28% of respondents pointed the finger at insiders, which includes trusted parties such as current and former employees, service providers, and contractors.

- 32% said insider crimes are more costly or damaging than incidents perpetrated by outsiders.

- The larger the business, the more likely it is to consider insiders a threat; larger businesses also are more likely to recognize that insider incidents can be more costly and damaging.

- Despite this, however, only 49% of all respondents have a plan for responding to inside threats.

PriceWaterhouseCoopers' *U.S. Cybercrime: Rising Risks, Reduced Readiness* states, "One thing is very clear: The cybersecurity programs of U.S. organizations do not rival the persistence, tactical skills, and technological prowess of their potential cyber adversaries. Today, common criminals, organized crime rings, and nation-states leverage sophisticated techniques to launch attacks that are highly targeted and very difficult to detect. Particularly worrisome are attacks by tremendously skilled threat actors that attempt to steal highly sensitive—and often very valuable—intellectual property, private communications, and other strategic assets and information."

Correlation of U.S. Cybersecurity Expenditure to Detected Events

Data has revealed a significant correlation between the level of spending on cybersecurity and the number of events detected. Organizations operating in highly-regulated sectors typically have high-performing cybersecurity programs. They also invest considerably more in cybersecurity than organizations from other sectors. Banking and finance respondents spent as much as $2,500 per employee on cybersecurity, while retail and consumer products businesses invested up to $400 per employee and education respondents invested a maximum of $200 per employee. According to a recent Global Economic Crime Survey by PricewaterhouseCoopers:

> Even when organizations are generally aware of the types of cyber-threats they face, many do not truly understand the capabilities of cybercriminals, what they might target, and what the value of those targets might be. Yet companies continue to make their critical data available to management, employees, vendors, and clients on a multitude of platforms, including high-risk platforms such as mobile devices and the cloud because the economic and competitive benefits appear so compelling. Ultimately, cybercrime is not strictly speaking a technology problem. It is a strategy problem, a human problem and a process problem. After all, organizations are not being attacked by computers, but by people attempting to exploit human frailty as much as technical vulnerability.

Curbing Cybercrime

Acceptable Losses from Cybercrime

The June 2014 report from the Center for Strategic and International Security suggests that "countries will tolerate malicious activity as long as it stays at acceptable levels – less than 2% of the national income." It compared losses from cybercrime to those from other types of crime and mishaps.

ACTIVITY	COST IN PERCENTAGE OF GBD
Car Crashes	1.0% (U.S.)
Counterfeiting/Piracy	0.89% (global)
Cybercrime	0.8% (global)
Maritime Piracy	0.02% (global)
Narcotics	0.9% (global)
Pilferage	0.5% (U.S.)
Transnational Crime	1.2% (global)

Societies absorb the costs of cybercrime as a part of doing business. But money may not be the best metric. Consumer confidence and national security are examples of other costs.

The Internet has become the forefront of commercial endeavors affecting all facets of commerce. There are no existing entities, for profit or not-for-profit, governmental or quasi-governmental, or individually owned which are not touched in some form by the computer and the Internet.

Large enterprises are constantly evaluating their cyber exposures; however, small and medium enterprises are just beginning to awaken to the new reality. That reality is that the cyber-criminal now has the tools to easily hack into any system that ever attaches to the information highway, the Internet.

The Cost of a Data Breach

For the past nine years, the Ponemon Institute has conducted research into the direct first-party cost of a data breach. The report issued in May of 2014 provides data covering 250 organizations representing ten countries besides the United States. The costs incurred by organizations experiencing a data breach are significant regardless of the size of the organization. In relative terms whether the breach involves 1,000 or 100,000 at-risk records, the organization will experience direct, indirect, and opportunity costs emanating from the cyber-event. The overall cost of a cyber-event is influenced by regulation. Those industries which are highly-regulated find their cost to be much greater than those with lesser regulatory and compliance requirements. Therefore, industries such as healthcare, financial services, pharmaceuticals, transportation, and communications experience a higher cost from cybercrimes.

One of the biggest challenges facing business entities is the retention of their customer's loyalty and the development of the means and methods to restore confidence in the organizations ability to protect the customer's personal data. One method is to have in place a crisis management plan to handle the reputational damage inflicted by the cybercrime. It is important that these plans be driven by the top-down with the CEO, board chairman, or owner fully committed to immediately begin a planned response and remediation to the loss of personal or private information.

Direct Cost

The direct cost of a data breach includes all identifiable items of cost which are measureable from an accounting standpoint. Detection and repair of the breach, notification cost, ongoing notification and monitoring cost, and legal and administrative cost are examples of direct cost.

The Ponemon study found that the average expenditures per record for the cost of detection and escalation were $10; notification cost $20; and post notification cost, $49.

Indirect Cost

Indirect costs are those associated with the loss of business, i.e., customer-retention programs. Also included in the indirect cost are those expenses associated with potential third-party liability claims such as defense cost from law suits, credit card reissuance cost, consumer redress funds, and other fines and penalties. According to the Ponemon study, the loss business cost was $105 for each record compromised.

Opportunity Cost

The opportunity costs are financial resources that must be directed away from business activities that create value and growth to handle the costs of managing the cybercrime. The ultimate case would be where the breach was so consuming that the business or entity attacked by the cyber-criminal was forced into bankruptcy or closure. (While the opportunity costs have been separated for our treatment, most researchers include missed opportunity cost as an additional indirect cost. Regardless of where these cost are shown it is important to recognize them in the total cost of cyber risk.)

Most of the available data regarding direct, indirect and opportunity costs support the point that the costs of handling a data breach or system attack continues to rise. The current study released in May 2014 indicates an average response cost of $5.4 million and an average number of records compromised of 28,742.

Individual elements of the cost are becoming more predictable and therefore, from a risk management perspective, more manageable. Those entities with response plans in place are experiencing cost reductions in some areas of both direct and indirect costs.

Large attacks on well-known and respected organizations make headline news. Target stores experienced a data breach in the fourth quarter of 2013. On February 26, 2014 Target released their fourth quarter earnings report which indicated a revenue loss of 5.3% and a reduction of profit by 46%. The report also identified $61 million dollars in breach related expenses and a $17 million dollar reduction in the bottom line. Moreover, it was reported within days of the breach that several multi-million dollar lawsuits had been filed. At the company's first quarter Earnings Call on May 21, 2014, in addressing the data breach:

> Expenses may include payments associated with potential claims by the payment card networks for alleged counterfeit fraud losses and non-ordinary course operating expenses (such as card re-issuance costs), REDcard fraud and card re-issuance expense, payments associated with civil litigation, governmental investigations and enforcement proceedings, expenses for legal, investigative and consulting fees, and incremental expenses and capital investments for remediation activities. These costs may have a material adverse effect on Target's results of operations in second quarter and full-year 2014 and future periods.

However, at the other end of the cyber spectrum are thousands of small businesses who are experiencing an increasing number of cyber-attacks. With new tools that make it easier for hackers to prey on small businesses, these entities have become an easy target for the criminal cartels operating in Russia, Ukraine and the China rim.

While there are many such events happening every day, the Wall Street Journal reported the Burger Me LLC incident. In 2006 and 2007, Burger Me, a small restaurant business owned by Rich Griffith of Bellington, Washington, had a computerized cash register system often referred to as a point-of-sale system. Burger Me accepted credit cards. The system was hacked. Unknown to Burger Me, the criminals made fraudulent charges to its customers' credit cards. As the fraud began to unravel, and the source traced to Burger Me, the firm's credit card services provider shut down the Burger Me account and froze payment transfers, drying up the cash flow needed to support the business activity. Unable to accept credit cards, shrinking customer flows and mounting debt forced the business to close and liquidate. The hacker was never identified. While large organizations like Target may recover, small business may not completely rebound, if at all.

Small businesses, defined as those employing fewer than 250 employees, are facing a growing assault from cyber criminals all over the world. This means that any organization is a potential target.

A Change of Culture

The acceleration of change and the amount of change occurring from the technological advances being thrust upon the global economy are causing a radical shift in organizational cultures.

In order to win in the current cyber-crime assault the determination must be driven from the top-down. Thus, it is everyone's task to be vigilant and relentlessly protect the intangible assets of the enterprise. The size of the organization does not matter. The type of organization does not matter. Network security and privacy efforts will fail if everyone does not embrace the task at hand.

Everybody Is a Publisher

The risk and exposures associated with words, communication, advertising, and a host of other produced material are exacerbated by the speed at which communication can be sent and by the overwhelming ability to keep and store that communication over time. Additionally, the geographical boundaries of space and time have effectively been eliminated. What once lasted only for the life of the document and was contained in a defined space can be sent around the world in seconds and remain forever. Content liability exposures are now expanding like never before with communication platforms, such as Facebook, LinkedIn, Twitter, blogs, instant messaging, video conferencing, online transactions, RSS feeds, and a host of others. With this technology also comes malware, intrusion software, phishing, spy bots, and other dangerous criminal activity. Anyone can be a publisher.

Producer Involvement

Historically, the commercial insurance marketplace has been dominated by the producer whether employed directly by the insurer or acting as an independent agent/producer representing a single company or a number of independent companies. Early on each of the insurance companies offered an insurance product line covering many different lines of business: the personal lines of automobile and dwelling coverage to the commercial lines automobile, property, general liability, malpractice, and many other lines of needed coverage. When the multiline companies became prevalent in the late sixties, carriers offered as many different lines of business that their clients required. As the insurance industry continued to evolve in the early eighties, the individual companies began to leave those lines of business which required special expertise or unusual amounts of capital and resources to maintain, i.e. malpractice and professional liability. Maintaining open markets on such a large number of business lines was becoming more demanding upon the insurer's limited resources, both human and financial. Other outside forces were also at play which greatly affected the financial stability of the insurance industry. Litigation was on the rise especially as the country began dealing with pollution and the changing economy from industrial based to services based. All of these changes resulted in changing the insurance markets forever.

By the mid-eighties many carriers had shrunk their available product lines. Insurers willing to write a specific line of business began to consolidate their offerings and policy forms. The effect of this marketing shift was to leave the average producer with a narrowing product mix. Thus specialist and specialty producers began to appear by the 1990s. Those retail producers not connecting with the excess, surplus and specialty lines markets were left without access to many of the products and resources needed to provide coverage for the changing risk and exposures facing the commercial client.

The importance of these market changes became painfully evident as the industry moved into the twenty-first century. Technology has moved the industry faster and farther than anyone could have imagined back in the late nineties when insurance coverage for cyber exposures first began to appear. These early "cyber policies" were stand-alone products and mostly offered through the specialty insurance markets to larger, more sophisticated entities. Those commercial clients, who through risk management were able to identify and somewhat quantify the cost to their firm from a data breach, demanded products that would address these increasing exposures.

Cyber Liability

Historically, improvements in communication methods have directly benefited commerce. Today, the Internet, computer networks, and technology have enabled mass communication of ideas, information, and marketing with the ability of direct purchase of goods at vastly reduced costs. No paper, no phone calls, no visits to the business establishment are required. The Internet is not bound by time or space. It allows commerce to operate 24/7 without geographic boundaries and unlike paper; the information does not fade away but often indefinitely remains. It allows business to store customer/client data that can be used for improved products, services and ordering processes. The Internet and technology provides "the ease of doing business" for both the seller and the buyer.

Utilizing technology can create significant benefits for businesses. Likewise, the use of technology can create for the business new risk exposures called cyber risks. Cyber risks differ from the traditional risk exposures in types, form, detection, liability, regulation, and most importantly costs. Traditionally, businesses have utilized the commercial general liability (CGL) policy as a tool to manage business liability risks. Today's businesses, however, may find that the CGL policy does not provide the coverages to adequately manage cyber liabilities, and instead must utilize stand-alone cyber liability insurance policies or specifically designed add on endorsements to their traditional policies.

Applicability of the CGL Policy to Cyber Risk Exposures

The comprehensive general liability (CGL) policy was first introduced in 1941. Correspondence was produced on manual typewriters and mailed through the postal service. Information was manually recorded on paper and filed in filing cabinets. These represented the standard business processes at the time. In 1986 Insurance Service Offices (ISO) introduced the commercial general liability forms and endorsements to replace the comprehensive general liability forms. By 1986 larger businesses were at the early stages of today's technology with large main frame computers, priority software, CRT or dumb terminals directly connected to the main frame, storing only the necessary data as storage space was both limited and expensive for business processes. Smaller businesses had moved to electronic typewriters. There was no Internet. The CGL forms were created prior to the advent of today's cyber-related exposures.

Traditionally many businesses have managed their liability exposures with the purchase of a commercial general liability (CGL) policy. Since 1986 ISO has regularly updated the CGL forms and endorsements. The updates generally clarify the intent of the coverages afforded in response to legal decisions. As cyber liability risks have emerged, the revised CGL forms and endorsements have developed progressively restrictive language and exclusions to clarify the coverage (or non-coverage) intent for the ever evolving business cyber risks exposures. At the same time stand-alone cyber liability forms have been created by ISO and a number of insurers.

The following information discusses the evolution of the CGL form pertaining to cyber risks. For a more detailed analysis of the CGL form, the reader is referred to *Commercial General Liability Coverage Guide, 10th Edition*, by Donald S. Malecki, CPCU, and founder of Malecki, Deimling, Nielander & Associates, published by The National Underwriter Company.

In the Beginning–Y2K

The first cyber liability exposure to garner a CGL policy revision was the Y2K (Year 2000) issue. There was general concern that massive computer generated issues would occur when the world moved from the year 1999 to 2000 at midnight December 31, 1999. Due to the high cost of data storage when proprietary computer programs were created in the 1960s, 70s and into the 80s only a two digit code was used for the year; 99 would turn to 00. ISO introduced in 1998 endorsement CG 04 31 Year 2000 Computer-Related and Other Electronic Problems Limited Coverage Options. This is now past history. Some problems did develop though not on the massive scale as anticipated. It is still in use today.

Covered Territory

One element for coverage to apply is that the damages or offenses take place in specific territory. The CGL form, 2001 edition, revised the scope of covered territory for personal and advertising injury offenses coverage with a change to the definition of coverage territory under c.

4.   "Coverage territory" means:

   a.   The United States of America (including its territories and possessions), Puerto Rico and Canada;

   b.   International waters or airspace, but only if the injury or damage occurs in the course of travel or transportation between any places included in a. above; or

    c.   All other parts of the world if the injury or damage arises out of:

          1)   Goods or products made or sold by you in the territory described in a. above;

          2)   The activities of a person whose home is in the territory described in a. above, but is away for a short time on your business; or

          3)   "Personal and advertising injury" offenses that take place through the Internet or similar electronic means of communication provided the insured's responsibility to pay damages is determined in a "suit" on the merits, in the territory described in a. above or in a settlement we agree to.

Prior to the 2001 edition, if the injury had been sustained outside of the territories listed in "a", then no coverage existed. Otherwise, it needed to be determined that the offense took place in the territories listed in "a". As the Internet or other electronic means of communication is worldwide with no geographic boundaries, this would be very difficult. Now it can take place worldwide, provided the offense is one meeting the definition of personal and advertising injury, and through the Internet or similar electronic means of communication. However, the insured's responsibility to pay damages must be determined in a suit in the territories listed in "a". The policy will also pay damages when the insurer agrees to a settlement.

Tangible Property

The CGL policy provides coverage for physical damage to tangible property and its resulting loss of use. Businesses commonly have two types of property: tangible and intangible. Generally, property to be classified as tangible should possess attributes that allow it to be viewed and touched while intangible does not. Questions arose if electronic data was tangible property or not, as data when displayed can be viewed; it can be printed on paper that can be touched. To clarify that electronic data was not intended to be treated as tangible property under the policy, the 2001 edition modified the definition of property damage.

"Property damage" means:

    a.   Physical injury to tangible property, including all resulting loss of use of that property. All such loss of use shall be deemed to occur at the time of the physical injury that caused it; or

    b.   Loss of use of tangible property that is not physically injured. All such loss of use shall be deemed to occur at the time of the "occurrence" that caused it.

For the purposes of this insurance, electronic data is not tangible property.

As used in this definition, electronic data means information, facts or programs stored as or on, created or used on, or transmitted to or from computer software, including systems and applications software, hard or floppy disks, CD-ROMS, tapes, drives, cells, data processing devices, or any other media which are used with electronically controlled equipment.

Therefore, electronic data does not meet the definition of property damage as defined in the 2001 and subsequent editions of the CGL form.

Personal and Advertising Injury

Historically, advertising liability coverage has been available to businesses since the early 1940s. Personal injury liability coverage has been available since the late 1950s. In the 1998 CGL edition the two coverages were combined as personal and advertising injury coverage. Personal and advertising injury coverage concepts originated prior to the Internet, personal computers, chat rooms, blogs, mobile devices, apps, and other modern modes of instantaneous communications. As business Internet activities increasingly became a method of conducting business, ISO introduced the 2001 CGL form that contained significant revisions addressing Internet activities.

The 2001 edition modified slightly offenses d. and e. with the addition of the words "in any manner" that many understand to include Internet, cyber type activities.

"Personal and advertising injury" means injury, including consequential "bodily injury", arising out of one or more of the following offenses:

    a.   False arrest, detention or imprisonment;

    b.   Malicious prosecution;

    c.   The wrongful eviction from, wrongful entry into, or invasion of the right of private occupancy of a room, dwelling or premises that a person occupies, committed by or on behalf of its owner, landlord or lessor;

    d.   Oral or written publication, in any manner, of material that slanders or libels a person or organization or disparages a person's or organization's goods, products or services;

    e.   Oral or written publication, in any manner, of material that violates a person's right of privacy;

    f.   The use of another's advertising idea in your "advertisement"; or

g.   Infringing upon another's copyright, trade dress or slogan in your "advertisement".

Offenses f. and g. concern risks in the insured's "advertisement". The 2001 edition modified the definition of advertisement.

1.   "Advertisement" means a notice that is broadcast or published to the general public or specific market segments about your goods, products or services for the purpose of attracting customers or supporters. For the purposes of this definition:

a.   Notices that are published include material placed on the Internet or on similar electronic means of communication; and

b.   Regarding Web sites, only that part of a web site that is about your goods, products or services for the purposes of attracting customers or supporters is considered an advertisement.

The definition was expanded to include the Internet and similar electronic communication means and then placed restrictions concerning Web sites. Only parts of a business Web site may be considered advertisement. Other definitions modified in the 2001 edition to address cyber-type activities are "covered territory" and "property damage" discussed above.

ISO also made some changes to personal and advertising injury coverage exclusions b. and c. in the 2013 edition incorporating the words "in any manner". This was consistent with the change made to offenses d. and e. in the definition of "personal and advertising injury".

b.   Material Published With Knowledge of Falsity

"Personal and advertising injury" arising out of oral or written publication, in any manner, of material, if done by or at the direction of the insured with knowledge of its falsity.

c.   Material Published Prior To Policy Period

"Personal and advertising injury" arising out of oral or written publication, in any manner, of material whose first publication took place before the beginning of the policy period.

Historically, advertising injury coverage has excluded the insured's liability when in the business of advertising, publishing, and broadcasting— as this is more appropriately insured under a separate advertiser's or media liability policy. In the 2001 edition of the CGL form, the exclusion was expanded to specifically include Web site design and content development for others and Internet search, access, content or service provider businesses. For these businesses a separate advertiser's or media liability policy is necessary to address these exposures.

j.   Insureds in Media and Internet Type Businesses

"Personal and advertising injury" committed by an insured whose business is:

1)   Advertising, broadcasting, publishing or telecasting;

2)   Designing or determining content of web sites for others; or

3)   An Internet search, access, content or service provider.

However, this exclusion does not apply to Paragraphs 14.a., b., and c. of "personal and advertising injury" under the Definitions Section.

For the purposes of this exclusion, the placing of frames, borders or links, or advertising, for you or others anywhere on the Internet, is not by itself, considered the business of advertising, broadcasting, publishing or telecasting.

Note that businesses that have online bulletin boards and chat rooms should also be aware of the 2001 CGL revision adding exclusion k.

k.   Electronic Chatrooms or Bulletin Boards

"Personal and advertising injury" arising out of an electronic chatroom or bulletin board the insured hosts, owns, or over which the insured exercises control.

ISO continued in its 2001 CGL edition to exclude e-commerce risks with the addition of exclusion l.

l.   Unauthorized Use of Another's Name or Product

"Personal and advertising injury" arising out of the unauthorized use of another's name or product in your e-mail address, domain name or metatag, or any other similar tactics to mislead another's potential customers.

A final cyber risk related exclusion added in the 2001 CGL edition is exclusion p.–Distribution of Material in Violation of Statutes that is the same as under Coverage A Bodily Injury and Property Damage discussed below.

The 2001 CGL edition contained numerous changes, many of which restricted cyber risk coverage.

Electronic Data

The 2004 edition of the CGL form from ISO provided additional support to the 2001 property definition modification that electronic data was not tangible property by adding under Section I Coverages; Coverage A Bodily Injury and Property Damage Liability, Exclusion p. "Electronic

Data" Damages arising out of the loss of, loss of use of, damage to, corruption of, inability to access, or inability to manipulate electronic data.

As used in this exclusion, electronic data means information, facts or programs stored as or on, created or used on, or transmitted to or from computer software, including systems and applications software, hard or floppy disks, CD-ROMS, tapes, drives, cells, data processing devices or any other media which are used with electronically controlled equipment.

Exclusions c. through n. do not apply to damage by fire to premises while rented to you or temporarily occupied by you with permission of the owner. A separate limit of insurance applies to this coverage as described in Section III – Limits of Insurance.

In 2004, ISO also introduced an Electronic Data Liability Coverage Form (CG 00 65). Insureds that faced the risk of such damage could purchase a stand-alone policy.

In the 2013 edition of the CGL form, ISO added this language:

"However, this exclusion does not apply to liability for damages because of bodily injury."

Recording and Distribution of Material or Information in Violation of Law

In response to the TCPA and CAN-SPAM Act of 2003 including statutes, ordinances, or regulations that prohibits or limits the sending, transmitting, communicating or distribution of material or information, ISO created an exclusionary endorsement (CG 00 67) in 2005 to prevent coverage from being provided in the CGL form. In the 2007 CGL filing, ISO incorporated the endorsement as exclusions under both Section I Coverages, Coverage A Bodily Injury and Property Damage Liability, and Coverage B Personal and Advertising Injury Liability.

Distribution of Material in Violation of Statutes

"Bodily injury" or "property damage" arising directly or indirectly out of any action or omission that violates or is alleged to violate:

1) The Telephone Consumer Protection Act (TCPA), including any amendment of or addition to such law; or

2) The CAN-SPAM Act of 2003, including any amendment of or addition to such law; or

3) Any statute, ordinance or regulation, other than the TCPA or CAN-SPAM Act of 2003, that prohibits or limits the sending, transmitting, communicating or distribution of material or information.

Exclusions c. through n. do not apply to damage by fire to premises while rented to you or temporarily occupied by you with permission of the owner. A separate limit of insurance applies to this coverage as described in Section III – Limits of Insurance.

The exclusion was revised in the 2013 edition of the CGL form with the addition of further restrictive 4) language.

4)   Any federal, state or local statute, ordinance or regulation, other than the TCPA, CAN-SPAM Act of 2003 or FCRA and their amendments and additions, that addresses, prohibits, or limits the printing, dissemination, disposal, collecting, recording, sending, transmitting, communicating or distribution of material or information.

Absolute Exclusion

ISO provided further evidence that the intent of the CGL is to provide minimal coverage, if any, for cyber liability and associated risks with the introduction of a series of exclusionary endorsements on the access or disclosure of confidential or personal information and data-related liability. These endorsements significantly reduce if not eliminate coverage should a business receive a claim or lawsuit resulting from a data breach.

The frequency of the occurrence of data breaches has grown exponentially in the last few years and the trend will only continue to increase. Data breach claims can result in large legal fees and/or payment of large fines, plus additional costs in forensic system detection, notification, and credit monitoring services. There continues to be two camps of thought regarding the intent of coverage provided under the commercial general liability coverage part for cyber risk. One side believes that the coverage construction provides coverage, even though when this coverage part was developed there was not much "cyber" risk to consider. The other side has consistently recognized that certain cybercrimes such as data breaches and network security failures are new exposures driven by technology for which the CGL form never contemplated providing coverage. With the recent changes of filing CG 21 06 05 14 the point is mute. Regardless of whose interpretation is correct, the CGL form provides only a minor exception to an exclusion for bodily injury, otherwise, cyber risks are excluded in both coverage A and coverage B.

Endorsement CG 21 06 05 14

The Exclusion Access or Disclosure of Confidential or Personal Information and Data-Related Liability With Limited Bodily Injury Exception endorsement (CG 21 06 05 14) modifies insurance provided under the CGL Section I Coverage A Bodily Injury and Property Damage Liability by replacing exclusion 2 p. Electronic Data.

p.   Access or Disclosure of Confidential or Personal Information and Data-related Liability

Damages arising out of:

1)   Any access to or disclosure of any person's or organization's confidential or personal information, including patents, trade secrets, processing methods, customer lists, financial information, credit card information, health information or any other type of nonpublic information; or

2)   The loss of, loss of use of, damage to, corruption of, inability to access, or inability to manipulate electronic data.

This exclusion applies even if damages are claimed for notification costs, credit monitoring expenses, forensic expenses, public relations expenses or any other loss, cost or expense incurred by you or others arising out of that which is described in Paragraph 1) or 2) above.

However, unless Paragraph 1) above applies, this exclusion does not apply to damages because of "bodily injury".

As used in this exclusion, electronic data means information, facts or programs stored as or on, created or used on, or transmitted to or from computer software, including systems and applications software, hard or floppy disks, CD-ROMs, tapes, drives, cells, data processing devices or any other media which are used with electronically controlled equipment.

B.   The following is added to Paragraph 2. Exclusions of Section I – Coverage B – Personal and Advertising Injury Liability:

2.   Exclusions

This insurance does not apply to:

Access or Disclosure of Confidential or Personal Information

"Personal and advertising injury" arising out of any access to or disclosure of any person's or organization's confidential or personal information, including patents, trade secrets, processing methods, customer lists, financial information, credit card information, health information or any other type of nonpublic information.

This exclusion applies even if damages are claimed for notification costs, credit monitoring expenses, forensic expenses, public relations expenses or any other loss, cost or expense incurred by you or others arising out of any access to or disclosure of any person's or organization's confidential or personal information.

Endorsement CG 21 07 05 14

The endorsement–Exclusions Access or Disclosure of Confidential or Personal Information and Data-Related Liability Limited Bodily Injury Exception Not Included (CG 21 07 05 14) is almost the same as (CG 21 06 05 14) but without the wording that the exclusion does not apply to damages because of bodily injury under Coverage A Bodily Injury and Property Damage. Therefore, bodily injury damages are not excluded.

The endorsement Exclusion Access or Disclosure of Confidential or Personal Information (Coverage B Only) (CG 21 08 05 14) applies only to Coverage B, Personal and Advertising Injury Liability and leaves Coverage A Bodily Injury and Property Damage in the CGL policy as is.

Effectually, these three endorsements reduce coverage in both part A and part B of CG 00 01, commercial general liability form. In general, these endorsements are further evidence that the CGL coverage part was not intended to provide coverage for cyber related events. The types of damages related to data breaches and other data related liabilities including the cost of remediation, notification, credit reporting and other associated loss costs are more appropriately covered under specific stand-alone cyber policies or specific coverage endorsements attached to the traditional policies. This reduction of coverage is further reinforced by the fact CG 21 06 05 14 is a mandatory endorsement under the rules and rates as promulgated by Insurance Services Office. While only these three endorsements have been highlighted, the filing contains additional endorsements affecting the electronic data coverage part, the commercial umbrella coverage part, the commercial excess liability coverage part, owners and contractors protected liability, and products completed operations coverage parts. All of these endorsements are consistent and reinforce the coverage intent as respects damages related to data breaches and data related liabilities. Coverage is not afforded.

Over the course of fourteen years the industry has witnessed the removal and restriction of previously offered cyber coverage and is now entering an era where the commercial general liability policy can no longer be called "general". Similar to the total and absolute pollution exclusion in previous years, the narrowing of coverage and expansion of exclusions for cyber exposures has come full circle with the May 2014 filing of endorsements by ISO leaving cyber liability, electronic, and a host of defined electronic activities without any coverage within the current CGL policy. That said, the new group of endorsements will tend to confuse the producers and clients as there are carve out and specific exceptions still allowed. It is too soon to know whether the carriers will escalate the endorsements to the point of absolute cyber liability exclusion.

It does beg the question, did ISO go far enough? It would appear that a single mandatory absolute exclusion would serve both the carriers and the insurance buying consumers attempting to find coverage for known cyber exposures. The prediction is that the die is cast and both producers and consumers alike need to understand that just like pollution, employer's liability and other liability insurance, coverage needs are not to be found nor relied upon to exist in the CGL policy.

Complex Underwriting

It is extremely difficult to determine how large the cyber insurance market currently is in the United States. This is due to the fact that many carriers do not separate the coverage line for reporting purposes as is done for the traditional coverage lines of business. The conventional wisdom is that the annual premium volume is in excess of a $1.2 billion and may be as high as $1.5 billion. In either event the potential market is huge and expanding. From a revenue stand point, cyber coverages could rise to those of the CGL policy, especially in the small to medium sized risk sector as everyone has a need for some cyber liability products. The question still to be answered: "Are the producers who control much of this marketplace able to provide the necessary selling skills to penetrate the market?" Market penetration is the biggest challenge facing the insurers.

Cyber exposures still present a challenge to the insurers because of the difficulty to understand and then create a pricing model that can actually handle the losses generated. Those models determine the capital and resources that the carrier must commit in order to support the product. A real challenge is the catastrophic nature of the exposures. Cost information still shows an average incident cost of approximately a half million dollars. Currently, available individual limits highlight the caution carriers are taking in offering the coverage. It is also why so much capital is being spent on add-on services and benefits. Controlling the outcomes of the loss as it develops offers huge returns in mitigating the loss cost. Looking forward this coverage may find pretesting vulnerabilities and prevention has the greatest potential. Much like engineering and inspection has done for the mechanical breakdown exposures.

In the trench, the submission process is fairly simple and would not be referenced as complex by most standards. While applications are not standardized, most carriers will underwrite and rate based upon most of the major carriers' applications. Then as a condition to placing coverage, the carrier places the requirement of providing their own completed and signed application. Underwriters may ask for supplemental applications based upon reported risk characteristics and here again, this does really cause additional complexity to the submission.

The amount of time to actually receive an offer of terms and conditions with pricing varies greatly. It depends solely upon the resources which the carrier places upon the policy acquisition side and the appetite for new policies. It is further dependent upon whether the product line has technology support or if the product is manually produced. Regardless, a producer should expect the carrier to be responsive in less than thirty calendar days.

The level of complexity is not on the underwriting side, but does exist on the acquisition or selling side. Since cyber liability is a sold product and there are so many variables in exposure and need, the producer must put forth a great amount of effort to know what he/she is selling. This is especially true in the small to medium marketplace where the producer is looked upon as an advisor to the insurance buyer. The structure of the marketplace causes the retail agent/broker to establish a relationship with an excess, surplus, and specialty broker in order to obtain access to the product and/or a specific market. Additionally, most excess, surplus, and specialty lines brokers require some type of producer representation agreement which further delays and frustrate the acquisition process at the retail level. This market structure removes significant amounts of compensation from the retail producer who does most of the heavy lifting during acquisition. The redundancy of functions including the movement of information causes such inefficiency that it has become a hindrance to market penetration. Much of the cyber liability market is only offered through the specialty markets. While some carriers do provide the coverage on admitted paper, much of this market is only available on non-admitted paper in the individual state. Thus, the retail producer must contend with the state's excess and surplus lines tax laws upon non admitted carriers providing the insurance coverage.

The Coverage Availability

Today the available cyber liability policies provide coverage for a host of exposures facing firms with network security and privacy exposures. In 2008, the Insurance Services Office unveiled its E-Commerce program. The program was recently updated with a country-wide filing showing forms dated 01 2014. The program provides for eight independent coverage agreements which the insured can choose to buy based upon his risk and exposure needs. The basic policy is The Information Security Protection Policy, EC 00 10 01 14. There is a specific program for financial institutions issued under EC 00 11 01 14, Financial Institution Information Security Protection Policy. In addition, there are specific policies for entities engaged in media, the Media and Information Security Protection Policy, EC 00 12 and EC 00 13 01 14. The Media policy has two coverage forms: one providing coverage on an "occurrence basis" and the other providing coverage on a "claims-made basis".

New Optional Coverage

In addition, ISO is expanding coverage by adding new endorsements. EC 20 09 provides coverage for defense expenses and fines or penalties assessed by regulatory proceedings. Endorsement EC 20 12 provides coverage for payment card industry (PCI) compliance violations. Also, coverage can be added for computer and fund transfer fraud, computer fraud, and telephone toll fraud through the use of new endorsements, EC 20 13, EC 20 14, and EC 20 15 respectfully.

Producers and insureds alike need to be aware that only those coverages shown (chosen) in the declaration are applicable. Another important aspect of this program is to recognize that defense cost is inside the policy limit. (Unlike the commercial general liability coverage part where defense cost is generally outside of the coverage limit that is available to indemnify the third party.) This means that the cost of defense will lower the dollars available for indemnity. Thus, a limit of $1 million and a loss having $300,000 in defense cost only leaves $700,000 for indemnity to the third-party. This is particularly important when choosing individual policy limits.

Within each of the forms, there are eight insuring agreements The eight insuring agreements cover both first-party losses as well as third-party liability. The eight agreements are:

1. Web site Publishing Liability

2. Security Breach Liability

3. Programming Errors and Omissions Liability

4. Replacement or Restoration of Electronic Data

5. Extortion Threats

6. Business Income and Extra Expense

7. Public Relations Expense

8. Security Breach Expense

Section VII Definitions provides for the policy definition of thirty-five terms as used within the policy. It is important for anyone dealing with cyber coverage to make themselves aware of these terms. Cyber encompasses such a large number of terms with multiple meanings that definitions are lost. Yet when a claim occurs these defined terms will decide to what and how the coverage will respond. Producers are cautioned to take the time to learn what cyber coverage encompasses so that they can be proactive to an insured's request for coverage using the requisite skills and knowledge to respond appropriately. The market is expansive for these types of coverage. As of 2013, in the U.S. market alone there were a total of 14.72 million self-employed businesses, including 9.41 million unincorporated self-employed and 5.31 million incorporated self-employed individuals. What stands out about this group is that an overwhelming majority of these entrepreneurs utilize the Internet and many third-party vendors in their business and personal activities. More directly, most have the exposure to cybercrime and a growing need for cyber liability coverage.

While ISO established a standard cyber policy in the marketplace, there is a large variation among the carriers providing stand-alone policies. There is an even wider disparity among those insurance carriers providing add-on cyber coverage by endorsement to a traditional policy.

The chart below points out that not all policies are created equal nor is the risk appetite standardized.

SPECIFICATIONS	MEETS SPECIFICATIONS (YES/NO)			
	Company A	Company B	Company C	Company D
Note any positive or negative variations from the definitions of the individual coverages in the specifications				
$3,000,000 content injury liability	Yes	Yes	Yes	Yes
$3,000,000 Privacy Injury Liability and Privacy Regulation Proceeding	Yes	Yes	Yes	No
$3,000,000 Network Security Liability	Yes	Yes	Yes	Yes
$1,000,000 Public Relations Event Expense	Yes	No	No	No
$1,000,000 Network Extortion	Yes	Yes	Yes	Yes

(continued)

SPECIFICATIONS	MEETS SPECIFICATIONS (YES/NO)			
	Company A	Company B	Company C	Company D
Claims-Made Form	Yes	Yes	Yes	Yes
Prior Acts for Content Injury, Privacy Injury, and Network Security Liability is 3/15/2006	Yes	Yes	Yes	Yes
$75,000 Deductible for Content Injury, Privacy Injury, Privacy Regulation and Network Security Liability	Yes	Yes	No	Yes
30% Coinsurance (No Deductible) for Public Relations Expense	Yes	No	No	No
$25,000 Deductible for Network Extortion	Yes	Yes	No	Yes
Support Network in the Event of an Occurrence	Yes	Yes	Yes	Yes
Special Exclusion Endorsements		No	No	No
Broadening Endorsements	Yes	Yes	Yes	
Conditions	Yes	Yes		Yes

More importantly, add-on risk management services really differentiated the carriers' offerings. These value added risk control and management services can easily justify the premium differences among the carriers. Most of these additional resources are being develop by specialists in the field of cyber security and then being made available to the policyholder at no additional or a very nominal charge. Such services as call center and notification response, cyber specialist attorneys, crisis management assistance, forensic assistance, training, testing for system vulnerability and credit monitoring are only a few of the offerings provided. There are also pre-loss services such as a help desk or information portals to assist the insured in managing the cyber exposure.

Third-Party Outsourcing

Technology has given rise to an economy where businesses in a particular industry want to compete above the line in the marketplace where their products or services stand out for the best in class, in design, features, functions, benefits, or services. Below the line where all the administrative functions and business needs are met, these same managers only want the best in service at an ever decreasing cost. What has occurred is that outsourcing and third-party specialist have begun to dominate these functional but necessary areas.

For small and medium sized organizations it allows access to skills and services that would be out of reach if they had to provide and support those functions on their own. Most would not survive the added overhead and burden.

These highly skilled providers usually operate under a contractual relationship. Generally, these contracts or service level agreements (SLA's) containing page upon page of legalese are quickly dispatched with a hasty signature. The devil is in the small print. Most of these agreements contain language which leave businesses without recourse should the vendor cause a problem. The latest of which has been a limitation of liability clause in the event that the vendor was indeed held liable for the occurrence of an adverse event. These clauses cap the limit of potential liability to some percentage of the contract price or value of one year's service payments. For example, assume your business involves a third-party vendor and that vendor's negligence allowed a data breach of your network security system. The loss amounted to $100,000. You paid the vendor $200 a month for its services. A liability limitation clause with a one year limit means your business would receive $2,400 as compensation from the vendor.

When considering these types of agreements, at the very least, read them before signing. It is difficult to have these providers change their agreements but it can be done. If these agreements address services regarding information assets, then a simple vetting of the vendor could potentially save your business future losses. Ask questions and discuss what service levels will be provided.

Some common questions when outsourcing:

1.   What is the data privacy and security of the vendor?

2.   What happens if the vendor files for bankruptcy?

3.   What is your data availability in a natural disaster?

4.   Where will your data be stored?

5.   What are the service reliability and compliance standards?

6.   Are backups tested for operational readiness?

7.   Is information commingled?

By being proactive the entity can mitigate potential problems encountered by third-party vendors and service providers' contracts and SLA's.

A Risk Management Approach to Cyber

Risk management is a process whereby there is a formal plan in place to assess and evaluate exposures to financial loss, protection of balance sheet, and the development of recovery plans in the event that a loss does occur. The steps in a risk management plan are:

1.   Identify and assess the exposures facing the entity.

2.   Establish loss levels in terms of financial both direct and indirect costs of the exposures identified.

3.   Evaluate various methods of handling the loss exposures; i.e. mitigate the exposure, eliminate the exposure, transfer the exposure to a first-party, i.e., insurance.

4.   Select and implement the best option.

5.   Continually monitor and evaluate the effectiveness of the option selected.

During the risk assessment phase, information is classified such that all categories of information assets are identified, both automated and non-automated, i.e. payment information, personal customer information, employee information, etc. Once classified, and knowledge of the assets involved is known, it can be established what threats and vulnerabilities exist to the entity that would cause a financial loss should these events occur. Information assets can mean many things. It is important to identify where the assets exist, and which vulnerability or threat may cause losses.

For intellectual property it is often helpful to also identify or categorize the information assets as to the type of information being evaluated: for example confidential versus nonconfidential information, restricted versus nonrestricted, or public versus nonpublic. It is also helpful to have in place a systematic approach to classifying the information itself. These policies and procedures also form the basis upon which loss prevention and transference can be evaluated as the information value changes over time.

There are a number of methods that an entity can develop in order to quantify the value of measuring the risk of loss. One method is to establish an acceptable risk level and an associate value for a given risk level. Therefore, risk levels of high, medium, and low can be established with value levels for high greater than $100,000, for medium greater than $50,000 and for low less than $50,000. By quantifying in financial terms, it becomes easy to determine the entity's propensity for risk. For a small entity, propensity for risk may equate to a deductible, as the majority of exposures will be transferred through various insurance mechanisms. For a large entity, these values may be many times greater than the example.

Once it has been established which assets should be protected and at what level, the entity is then able to evaluate the options for mitigating risks. There are four standard options:

1. *Accept the risk.* The entity would choose to accept the risk if the value of the asset is low and the threats/vulnerabilities are also low. Generally, in this situation, the cost of using another method is greater than the acceptable risk level.

2. *Transfer the risk.* Also known as sharing the risk. This method allows the entity to transfer their exposure to risk to a third-party either partially or totally. This is commonly done using traditional insurance where the premiums paid represent the cost of transfer to the entity. Another example for transfer is to find a third-party vendor who is willing or more capable than the transferring entity to accept the risk of the activity. Examples would be cloud computing, offsite storage, Web hosting.

3. *Limit the risk.* Often times there is not a third-party to transfer the risk to or the activity is such that it is not possible to place it in the hands of a third-party vendor. The cost of limiting the risk may be inexpensive, though situations where automatic updates to systems or security patches are a part of the software vendor's services. Other times there may be significant costs involved in limiting a risk; for example, providing redundancy and hot spot facilities for recovery services due to the risk of natural disasters.

4.   *Avoid the risk*. Avoidance of risk requires the understanding that the entity has decided that the risk of continuing the business activity is too great of a threat for the financial stability of the business. Therefore, risk avoidance means to no longer perform such activities. One way to avoid network security issues is to disconnect the network from the information highway.

The heavy lifting is now complete and only the choice of an option remains. In general, implementation of a risk mitigation option is not completed in a vacuum. It involves engaging the executive team the owner, or the individual(s) responsible for taking the risk management recommendation, and determining the best possible decision in light of the information assets being protected. When actually implemented, for most entities regardless of size, it is a combination of mitigation methods that are employed in the plan's execution. Often additional loss control methodologies are employed to continually monitor and update the plan such that the risk levels and methods for handling continue to meet the plan goals.

Conclusions and Trends

Cybercrime is the new norm and possesses threats that are estimated to divert 15-20% of the economic value of all Internet and cyber activities. This is a global war on crime and is not isolated to one country or one economy. While states continue to address these cybercrimes from a notification and regulation perspective, there is a mess of overlapping jurisdictional issues and a general lack of consistency. The insurance sector has for all intents and purposes announced that the commercial general liability policy will no longer provide coverage or defense cost for most anything cyber. As the new endorsements to the CGL policy reach the courts, courts will likely side with the policy language and determine no coverage exists for cyber events, as has been the trend.

A healthy sector within the industry is continuing to develop insurance products addressing the various exposures to loss that modern technology has created. While these are traditional insurance policies and a transfer of risk for a known cost, there is much innovation going on to provide preventative tools and resources to lessen the impact of intellectual property asset management and security for informational data and privacy matters. Individual insurers will continue to be innovative as greater knowledge is gained as to the core risk characteristics and exposures. Thus, the future direction will be toward mitigation of cyber exposures. Such tools as call center services, notification systems and controls, as well as crisis management resources will continue to be provided at the carrier level and expanded.

The number of small business entities and other smaller organizations is increasing each year. Cyber insurance products are currently available for these entities. However, most products are in a stand-alone policy solution and not offered through the normal or standard delivery systems. Producers are not fully engaged in the selling of these cyber products. The challenge facing the industry is to make these products available to the owners and managers of these small concerns. Educating the insurance producer segment on cyber exposures and the available coverages, whether in a separate policy or an additional endorsement, will continue to slow the penetration of this important and needed coverage for all types of insurance buyers.

International cooperation and sharing of resources, skills, and information exchange will accelerate at an alarming pace. Today's cyber threat is multi-national and therefore will require a multinational response to curb, reduce, and eliminate the global threat to the personal and economic security of the global community. Investor demands are increasing for more information on the exposure to market value loss due to a cyber-breach event. Both individual and institutional investors will want greater disclosure by public companies of their managements' assessment of the exposure to a material risk of data breach. This pressure may cause the Security and Exchange Commission to further the need for reporting in this critical area of public company operations.

Legal cost associated with data and security of networks will increase. Are the courts going to align with the plaintiffs' bar as the general public continues to be frustrated with the size, cost and life changing events caused by the inadequate protection given to personal and private information? Will this frustration end in a flood of lawsuits? The indications are that it is on the horizon.

Appendices

Appendix A: ISO Forms

Commercial General Liability Coverage Form	CG 00 01 04 13
Additional Insured–Owners, Lessees or Contractors–Scheduled Person or Organization	CG 20 10 04 13
Additional Insured–Owners, Lessees or Contractors–Completed Operations	CG 20 37 04 13
Additional Insured–Owners, Lessees or Contractors–Automatic Status When Required in Construction Agreement with You	CG 20 33 04 13
Amendment of Insured Contract Definition	CG 24 26 04 13
Primary and Noncontributory–Other Insurance Condition	CG 20 01 04 13
Year 2000 Computer-Related and Other Electronic Problems–Limited Coverage Options	CG 04 31 09 98
Exclusion–Violation of Statutes that Govern E-mails, Fax, Phone Call or Other Methods of Sending Material or Information	CG 00 67 03 05
Exclusion–Access or Disclosure of Confidential or Personal Information and Data-Related Liability–With Limited Bodily Injury Exception	CG 21 06 05 14
Exclusion–Access or Disclosure of Confidential or Personal Information and Data-Related Liability–Limited Bodily Injury Exception Not Included	CG 21 07 05 14
Exclusion–Access or Disclosure of Confidential or Personal Information (Coverage B Only)	CG 21 08 05 14
Information Security Protection Policy	EC 00 10 01 14
Media and Information Security Protection Policy	EC 00 12 01 14
Media and Information Security Protection Policy	EC 00 13 01 14

Amend Defense and Settlement Provision   EC 20 09 01 14

Payment Card Industry (PCI)–Provide Coverage for   EC 20 12 01 14
Defense Expenses and Fine or Penalties

Computer and Funds Transfer Fraud   EC 20 13 01 14

Computer Fraud   EC 20 14 01 14

Telephone Toll Fraud   EC 20 15 01 14

Appendix B: The Status of Data Breach Notification Laws in the United States

COMMERCIAL GENERAL LIABILITY COVERAGE FORM

Various provisions in this policy restrict coverage. Read the entire policy carefully to determine rights, duties and what is and is not covered.

Throughout this policy the words "you" and "your" refer to the Named Insured shown in the Declarations, and any other person or organization qualifying as a Named Insured under this policy. The words "we", "us" and "our" refer to the company providing this insurance.

The word "insured" means any person or organization qualifying as such under Section **II** – Who Is An Insured.

Other words and phrases that appear in quotation marks have special meaning. Refer to Section **V** – Definitions.

SECTION I – COVERAGES

COVERAGE A – BODILY INJURY AND PROPERTY DAMAGE LIABILITY

1. Insuring Agreement

  a. We will pay those sums that the insured becomes legally obligated to pay as damages because of "bodily injury" or "property damage" to which this insurance applies. We will have the right and duty to defend the insured against any "suit" seeking those damages. However, we will have no duty to defend the insured against any "suit" seeking damages for "bodily injury" or "property damage" to which this insurance does not apply. We may, at our discretion, investigate any "occurrence" and settle any claim or "suit" that may result. But:

    (1) The amount we will pay for damages is limited as described in Section **III** – Limits Of Insurance; and

    (2) Our right and duty to defend ends when we have used up the applicable limit of insurance in the payment of judgments or settlements under Coverages **A** or **B** or medical expenses under Coverage **C**.

    No other obligation or liability to pay sums or perform acts or services is covered unless explicitly provided for under Supplementary Payments – Coverages **A** and **B**.

  b. This insurance applies to "bodily injury" and "property damage" only if:

    (1) The "bodily injury" or "property damage" is caused by an "occurrence" that takes place in the "coverage territory";

    (2) The "bodily injury" or "property damage" occurs during the policy period; and

    (3) Prior to the policy period, no insured listed under Paragraph **1.** of Section **II** – Who Is An Insured and no "employee" authorized by you to give or receive notice of an "occurrence" or claim, knew that the "bodily injury" or "property damage" had occurred, in whole or in part. If such a listed insured or authorized "employee" knew, prior to the policy period, that the "bodily injury" or "property damage" occurred, then any continuation, change or resumption of such "bodily injury" or "property damage" during or after the policy period will be deemed to have been known prior to the policy period.

  c. "Bodily injury" or "property damage" which occurs during the policy period and was not, prior to the policy period, known to have occurred by any insured listed under Paragraph **1.** of Section **II** – Who Is An Insured or any "employee" authorized by you to give or receive notice of an "occurrence" or claim, includes any continuation, change or resumption of that "bodily injury" or "property damage" after the end of the policy period.

  d. "Bodily injury" or "property damage" will be deemed to have been known to have occurred at the earliest time when any insured listed under Paragraph **1.** of Section **II** – Who Is An Insured or any "employee" authorized by you to give or receive notice of an "occurrence" or claim:

    (1) Reports all, or any part, of the "bodily injury" or "property damage" to us or any other insurer;

    (2) Receives a written or verbal demand or claim for damages because of the "bodily injury" or "property damage"; or

    (3) Becomes aware by any other means that "bodily injury" or "property damage" has occurred or has begun to occur.

  e. Damages because of "bodily injury" include damages claimed by any person or organization for care, loss of services or death resulting at any time from the "bodily injury".

2. Exclusions

This insurance does not apply to:

a. Expected Or Intended Injury

"Bodily injury" or "property damage" expected or intended from the standpoint of the insured. This exclusion does not apply to "bodily injury" resulting from the use of reasonable force to protect persons or property.

b. Contractual Liability

"Bodily injury" or "property damage" for which the insured is obligated to pay damages by reason of the assumption of liability in a contract or agreement. This exclusion does not apply to liability for damages:

(1) That the insured would have in the absence of the contract or agreement; or

(2) Assumed in a contract or agreement that is an "insured contract", provided the "bodily injury" or "property damage" occurs subsequent to the execution of the contract or agreement. Solely for the purposes of liability assumed in an "insured contract", reasonable attorneys' fees and necessary litigation expenses incurred by or for a party other than an insured are deemed to be damages because of "bodily injury" or "property damage", provided:

(a) Liability to such party for, or for the cost of, that party's defense has also been assumed in the same "insured contract"; and

(b) Such attorneys' fees and litigation expenses are for defense of that party against a civil or alternative dispute resolution proceeding in which damages to which this insurance applies are alleged.

c. Liquor Liability

"Bodily injury" or "property damage" for which any insured may be held liable by reason of:

(1) Causing or contributing to the intoxication of any person;

(2) The furnishing of alcoholic beverages to a person under the legal drinking age or under the influence of alcohol; or

(3) Any statute, ordinance or regulation relating to the sale, gift, distribution or use of alcoholic beverages.

This exclusion applies even if the claims against any insured allege negligence or other wrongdoing in:

(a) The supervision, hiring, employment, training or monitoring of others by that insured; or

(b) Providing or failing to provide transportation with respect to any person that may be under the influence of alcohol;

if the "occurrence" which caused the "bodily injury" or "property damage", involved that which is described in Paragraph **(1)**, **(2)** or **(3)** above.

However, this exclusion applies only if you are in the business of manufacturing, distributing, selling, serving or furnishing alcoholic beverages. For the purposes of this exclusion, permitting a person to bring alcoholic beverages on your premises, for consumption on your premises, whether or not a fee is charged or a license is required for such activity, is not by itself considered the business of selling, serving or furnishing alcoholic beverages.

d. Workers' Compensation And Similar Laws

Any obligation of the insured under a workers' compensation, disability benefits or unemployment compensation law or any similar law.

e. Employer's Liability

"Bodily injury" to:

(1) An "employee" of the insured arising out of and in the course of:

(a) Employment by the insured; or

(b) Performing duties related to the conduct of the insured's business; or

(2) The spouse, child, parent, brother or sister of that "employee" as a consequence of Paragraph **(1)** above.

This exclusion applies whether the insured may be liable as an employer or in any other capacity and to any obligation to share damages with or repay someone else who must pay damages because of the injury.

This exclusion does not apply to liability assumed by the insured under an "insured contract".

            © Insurance Services Office, Inc., 2012   **CG 00 01 04 13**

f. Pollution

(1) "Bodily injury" or "property damage" arising out of the actual, alleged or threatened discharge, dispersal, seepage, migration, release or escape of "pollutants":

(a) At or from any premises, site or location which is or was at any time owned or occupied by, or rented or loaned to, any insured. However, this subparagraph does not apply to:

(i) "Bodily injury" if sustained within a building and caused by smoke, fumes, vapor or soot produced by or originating from equipment that is used to heat, cool or dehumidify the building, or equipment that is used to heat water for personal use, by the building's occupants or their guests;

(ii) "Bodily injury" or "property damage" for which you may be held liable, if you are a contractor and the owner or lessee of such premises site or location has been added to your policy as an additional insured with respect to your ongoing operations performed for that additional insured at that premises, site or location and such premises, site or location is not and never was owned or occupied by, or rented or loaned to, any insured, other than that additional insured; or

(iii) "Bodily injury" or "property damage" arising out of heat, smoke or fumes from a "hostile fire";

(b) At or from any premises, site or location which is or was at any time used by or for any insured or others for the handling, storage, disposal, processing or treatment of waste;

(c) Which are or were at any time transported, handled, stored, treated, disposed of, or processed as waste by or for:

(i) Any insured; or

(ii) Any person or organization for whom you may be legally responsible; or

(d) At or from any premises, site or location on which any insured or any contractors or subcontractors working directly or indirectly on any insured's behalf are performing operations if the "pollutants" are brought on or to the premises, site or location in connection with such operations by such insured, contractor or subcontractor. However, this subparagraph does not apply to:

(i) "Bodily injury" or "property damage" arising out of the escape of fuels, lubricants or other operating fluids which are needed to perform the normal electrical, hydraulic or mechanical functions necessary for the operation of "mobile equipment" or its parts, if such fuels, lubricants or other operating fluids escape from a vehicle part designed to hold, store or receive them. This exception does not apply if the "bodily injury" or "property damage" arises out of the intentional discharge, dispersal or release of the fuels, lubricants or other operating fluids, or if such fuels, lubricants or other operating fluids are brought on or to the premises, site or location with the intent that they be discharged, dispersed or released as part of the operations being performed by such insured, contractor or subcontractor;

(ii) "Bodily injury" or "property damage" sustained within a building and caused by the release of gases, fumes or vapors from materials brought into that building in connection with operations being performed by you or on your behalf by a contractor or subcontractor; or

(iii) "Bodily injury" or "property damage" arising out of heat, smoke or fumes from a "hostile fire".

(e) At or from any premises, site or location on which any insured or any contractors or subcontractors working directly or indirectly on any insured's behalf are performing operations if the operations are to test for, monitor, clean up, remove, contain, treat, detoxify or neutralize, or in any way respond to, or assess the effects of, "pollutants".

(2) Any loss, cost or expense arising out of any:

(a) Request, demand, order or statutory or regulatory requirement that any insured or others test for, monitor, clean up, remove, contain, treat, detoxify or neutralize, or in any way respond to, or assess the effects of, "pollutants"; or

(b) Claim or suit by or on behalf of a governmental authority for damages because of testing for, monitoring, cleaning up, removing, containing, treating, detoxifying or neutralizing, or in any way responding to, or assessing the effects of, "pollutants".

However, this paragraph does not apply to liability for damages because of "property damage" that the insured would have in the absence of such request, demand, order or statutory or regulatory requirement, or such claim or "suit" by or on behalf of a governmental authority.

g. Aircraft, Auto Or Watercraft

"Bodily injury" or "property damage" arising out of the ownership, maintenance, use or entrustment to others of any aircraft, "auto" or watercraft owned or operated by or rented or loaned to any insured. Use includes operation and "loading or unloading".

This exclusion applies even if the claims against any insured allege negligence or other wrongdoing in the supervision, hiring, employment, training or monitoring of others by that insured, if the "occurrence" which caused the "bodily injury" or "property damage" involved the ownership, maintenance, use or entrustment to others of any aircraft, "auto" or watercraft that is owned or operated by or rented or loaned to any insured.

This exclusion does not apply to:

(1) A watercraft while ashore on premises you own or rent;

(2) A watercraft you do not own that is:

(a) Less than 26 feet long; and

(b) Not being used to carry persons or property for a charge;

(3) Parking an "auto" on, or on the ways next to, premises you own or rent, provided the "auto" is not owned by or rented or loaned to you or the insured;

(4) Liability assumed under any "insured contract" for the ownership, maintenance or use of aircraft or watercraft; or

(5) "Bodily injury" or "property damage" arising out of:

(a) The operation of machinery or equipment that is attached to, or part of, a land vehicle that would qualify under the definition of "mobile equipment" if it were not subject to a compulsory or financial responsibility law or other motor vehicle insurance law where it is licensed or principally garaged; or

(b) The operation of any of the machinery or equipment listed in Paragraph **f.(2)** or **f.(3)** of the definition of "mobile equipment".

h. Mobile Equipment

"Bodily injury" or "property damage" arising out of:

(1) The transportation of "mobile equipment" by an "auto" owned or operated by or rented or loaned to any insured; or

(2) The use of "mobile equipment" in, or while in practice for, or while being prepared for, any prearranged racing, speed, demolition, or stunting activity.

i. War

"Bodily injury" or "property damage", however caused, arising, directly or indirectly, out of:

(1) War, including undeclared or civil war;

(2) Warlike action by a military force, including action in hindering or defending against an actual or expected attack, by any government, sovereign or other authority using military personnel or other agents; or

(3) Insurrection, rebellion, revolution, usurped power, or action taken by governmental authority in hindering or defending against any of these.

j. Damage To Property

"Property damage" to:

(1) Property you own, rent, or occupy, including any costs or expenses incurred by you, or any other person, organization or entity, for repair, replacement, enhancement, restoration or maintenance of such property for any reason, including prevention of injury to a person or damage to another's property;

(2) Premises you sell, give away or abandon, if the "property damage" arises out of any part of those premises;

(3) Property loaned to you;

        CG 00 01 04 13

(4) Personal property in the care, custody or control of the insured;

(5) That particular part of real property on which you or any contractors or subcontractors working directly or indirectly on your behalf are performing operations, if the "property damage" arises out of those operations; or

(6) That particular part of any property that must be restored, repaired or replaced because "your work" was incorrectly performed on it.

Paragraphs **(1)**, **(3)** and **(4)** of this exclusion do not apply to "property damage" (other than damage by fire) to premises, including the contents of such premises, rented to you for a period of seven or fewer consecutive days. A separate limit of insurance applies to Damage To Premises Rented To You as described in Section **III** – Limits Of Insurance.

Paragraph **(2)** of this exclusion does not apply if the premises are "your work" and were never occupied, rented or held for rental by you.

Paragraphs **(3)**, **(4)**, **(5)** and **(6)** of this exclusion do not apply to liability assumed under a sidetrack agreement.

Paragraph **(6)** of this exclusion does not apply to "property damage" included in the "products-completed operations hazard".

k. Damage To Your Product

"Property damage" to "your product" arising out of it or any part of it.

l. Damage To Your Work

"Property damage" to "your work" arising out of it or any part of it and included in the "products-completed operations hazard".

This exclusion does not apply if the damaged work or the work out of which the damage arises was performed on your behalf by a subcontractor.

m. Damage To Impaired Property Or Property Not Physically Injured

"Property damage" to "impaired property" or property that has not been physically injured, arising out of:

(1) A defect, deficiency, inadequacy or dangerous condition in "your product" or "your work"; or

(2) A delay or failure by you or anyone acting on your behalf to perform a contract or agreement in accordance with its terms.

This exclusion does not apply to the loss of use of other property arising out of sudden and accidental physical injury to "your product" or "your work" after it has been put to its intended use.

n. Recall Of Products, Work Or Impaired Property

Damages claimed for any loss, cost or expense incurred by you or others for the loss of use, withdrawal, recall, inspection, repair, replacement, adjustment, removal or disposal of:

(1) "Your product";

(2) "Your work"; or

(3) "Impaired property";

if such product, work, or property is withdrawn or recalled from the market or from use by any person or organization because of a known or suspected defect, deficiency, inadequacy or dangerous condition in it.

o. Personal And Advertising Injury

"Bodily injury" arising out of "personal and advertising injury".

p. Electronic Data

Damages arising out of the loss of, loss of use of, damage to, corruption of, inability to access, or inability to manipulate electronic data.

However, this exclusion does not apply to liability for damages because of "bodily injury".

As used in this exclusion, electronic data means information, facts or programs stored as or on, created or used on, or transmitted to or from computer software, including systems and applications software, hard or floppy disks, CD-ROMs, tapes, drives, cells, data processing devices or any other media which are used with electronically controlled equipment.

q. Recording And Distribution Of Material Or Information In Violation Of Law

"Bodily injury" or "property damage" arising directly or indirectly out of any action or omission that violates or is alleged to violate:

(1) The Telephone Consumer Protection Act (TCPA), including any amendment of or addition to such law;

(2) The CAN-SPAM Act of 2003, including any amendment of or addition to such law;

(3) The Fair Credit Reporting Act (FCRA), and any amendment of or addition to such law, including the Fair and Accurate Credit Transactions Act (FACTA); or

(4) Any federal, state or local statute, ordinance or regulation, other than the TCPA, CAN-SPAM Act of 2003 or FCRA and their amendments and additions, that addresses, prohibits, or limits the printing, dissemination, disposal, collecting, recording, sending, transmitting, communicating or distribution of material or information.

Exclusions **c.** through **n.** do not apply to damage by fire to premises while rented to you or temporarily occupied by you with permission of the owner. A separate limit of insurance applies to this coverage as described in Section **III** – Limits Of Insurance.

COVERAGE B – PERSONAL AND ADVERTISING INJURY LIABILITY

1. Insuring Agreement

a. We will pay those sums that the insured becomes legally obligated to pay as damages because of "personal and advertising injury" to which this insurance applies. We will have the right and duty to defend the insured against any "suit" seeking those damages. However, we will have no duty to defend the insured against any "suit" seeking damages for "personal and advertising injury" to which this insurance does not apply. We may, at our discretion, investigate any offense and settle any claim or "suit" that may result. But:

(1) The amount we will pay for damages is limited as described in Section **III** – Limits Of Insurance; and

(2) Our right and duty to defend end when we have used up the applicable limit of insurance in the payment of judgments or settlements under Coverages **A** or **B** or medical expenses under Coverage **C**.

No other obligation or liability to pay sums or perform acts or services is covered unless explicitly provided for under Supplementary Payments – Coverages **A** and **B**.

b. This insurance applies to "personal and advertising injury" caused by an offense arising out of your business but only if the offense was committed in the "coverage territory" during the policy period.

2. Exclusions

This insurance does not apply to:

a. Knowing Violation Of Rights Of Another

"Personal and advertising injury" caused by or at the direction of the insured with the knowledge that the act would violate the rights of another and would inflict "personal and advertising injury".

b. Material Published With Knowledge Of Falsity

"Personal and advertising injury" arising out of oral or written publication, in any manner, of material, if done by or at the direction of the insured with knowledge of its falsity.

c. Material Published Prior To Policy Period

"Personal and advertising injury" arising out of oral or written publication, in any manner, of material whose first publication took place before the beginning of the policy period.

d. Criminal Acts

"Personal and advertising injury" arising out of a criminal act committed by or at the direction of the insured.

e. Contractual Liability

"Personal and advertising injury" for which the insured has assumed liability in a contract or agreement. This exclusion does not apply to liability for damages that the insured would have in the absence of the contract or agreement.

f. Breach Of Contract

"Personal and advertising injury" arising out of a breach of contract, except an implied contract to use another's advertising idea in your "advertisement".

g. Quality Or Performance Of Goods – Failure To Conform To Statements

"Personal and advertising injury" arising out of the failure of goods, products or services to conform with any statement of quality or performance made in your "advertisement".

h. Wrong Description Of Prices

"Personal and advertising injury" arising out of the wrong description of the price of goods, products or services stated in your "advertisement".

i. Infringement Of Copyright, Patent, Trademark Or Trade Secret

"Personal and advertising injury" arising out of the infringement of copyright, patent, trademark, trade secret or other intellectual property rights. Under this exclusion, such other intellectual property rights do not include the use of another's advertising idea in your "advertisement".

However, this exclusion does not apply to infringement, in your "advertisement", of copyright, trade dress or slogan.

j. Insureds In Media And Internet Type Businesses

"Personal and advertising injury" committed by an insured whose business is:

(1) Advertising, broadcasting, publishing or telecasting;

(2) Designing or determining content of web sites for others; or

(3) An Internet search, access, content or service provider.

However, this exclusion does not apply to Paragraphs **14.a., b.** and **c.** of "personal and advertising injury" under the Definitions section.

For the purposes of this exclusion, the placing of frames, borders or links, or advertising, for you or others anywhere on the Internet, is not by itself, considered the business of advertising, broadcasting, publishing or telecasting.

k. Electronic Chatrooms Or Bulletin Boards

"Personal and advertising injury" arising out of an electronic chatroom or bulletin board the insured hosts, owns, or over which the insured exercises control.

l. Unauthorized Use Of Another's Name Or Product

"Personal and advertising injury" arising out of the unauthorized use of another's name or product in your e-mail address, domain name or metatag, or any other similar tactics to mislead another's potential customers.

m. Pollution

"Personal and advertising injury" arising out of the actual, alleged or threatened discharge, dispersal, seepage, migration, release or escape of "pollutants" at any time.

n. Pollution-related

Any loss, cost or expense arising out of any:

(1) Request, demand, order or statutory or regulatory requirement that any insured or others test for, monitor, clean up, remove, contain, treat, detoxify or neutralize, or in any way respond to, or assess the effects of, "pollutants"; or

(2) Claim or suit by or on behalf of a governmental authority for damages because of testing for, monitoring, cleaning up, removing, containing, treating, detoxifying or neutralizing, or in any way responding to, or assessing the effects of, "pollutants".

o. War

"Personal and advertising injury", however caused, arising, directly or indirectly, out of:

(1) War, including undeclared or civil war;

(2) Warlike action by a military force, including action in hindering or defending against an actual or expected attack, by any government, sovereign or other authority using military personnel or other agents; or

(3) Insurrection, rebellion, revolution, usurped power, or action taken by governmental authority in hindering or defending against any of these.

p. Recording And Distribution Of Material Or Information In Violation Of Law

"Personal and advertising injury" arising directly or indirectly out of any action or omission that violates or is alleged to violate:

(1) The Telephone Consumer Protection Act (TCPA), including any amendment of or addition to such law;

(2) The CAN-SPAM Act of 2003, including any amendment of or addition to such law;

(3) The Fair Credit Reporting Act (FCRA), and any amendment of or addition to such law, including the Fair and Accurate Credit Transactions Act (FACTA); or

(4) Any federal, state or local statute, ordinance or regulation, other than the TCPA, CAN-SPAM Act of 2003 or FCRA and their amendments and additions, that addresses, prohibits, or limits the printing, dissemination, disposal, collecting, recording, sending, transmitting, communicating or distribution of material or information.

COVERAGE C – MEDICAL PAYMENTS

1. Insuring Agreement

a. We will pay medical expenses as described below for "bodily injury" caused by an accident:

   (1) On premises you own or rent;

   (2) On ways next to premises you own or rent; or

   (3) Because of your operations;

   provided that:

      (a) The accident takes place in the "coverage territory" and during the policy period;

      (b) The expenses are incurred and reported to us within one year of the date of the accident; and

      (c) The injured person submits to examination, at our expense, by physicians of our choice as often as we reasonably require.

b. We will make these payments regardless of fault. These payments will not exceed the applicable limit of insurance. We will pay reasonable expenses for:

   (1) First aid administered at the time of an accident;

   (2) Necessary medical, surgical, X-ray and dental services, including prosthetic devices; and

   (3) Necessary ambulance, hospital, professional nursing and funeral services.

2. Exclusions

We will not pay expenses for "bodily injury":

a. **Any Insured**

   To any insured, except "volunteer workers".

b. **Hired Person**

   To a person hired to do work for or on behalf of any insured or a tenant of any insured.

c. **Injury On Normally Occupied Premises**

   To a person injured on that part of premises you own or rent that the person normally occupies.

d. **Workers' Compensation And Similar Laws**

   To a person, whether or not an "employee" of any insured, if benefits for the "bodily injury" are payable or must be provided under a workers' compensation or disability benefits law or a similar law.

e. **Athletics Activities**

   To a person injured while practicing, instructing or participating in any physical exercises or games, sports, or athletic contests.

f. **Products-Completed Operations Hazard**

   Included within the "products-completed operations hazard".

g. **Coverage A Exclusions**

   Excluded under Coverage **A**.

SUPPLEMENTARY PAYMENTS – COVERAGES A AND B

1. We will pay, with respect to any claim we investigate or settle, or any "suit" against an insured we defend:

   a. All expenses we incur.

   b. Up to $250 for cost of bail bonds required because of accidents or traffic law violations arising out of the use of any vehicle to which the Bodily Injury Liability Coverage applies. We do not have to furnish these bonds.

   c. The cost of bonds to release attachments, but only for bond amounts within the applicable limit of insurance. We do not have to furnish these bonds.

   d. All reasonable expenses incurred by the insured at our request to assist us in the investigation or defense of the claim or "suit", including actual loss of earnings up to $250 a day because of time off from work.

   e. All court costs taxed against the insured in the "suit". However, these payments do not include attorneys' fees or attorneys' expenses taxed against the insured.

   f. Prejudgment interest awarded against the insured on that part of the judgment we pay. If we make an offer to pay the applicable limit of insurance, we will not pay any prejudgment interest based on that period of time after the offer.

    CG 00 01 04 13

g. All interest on the full amount of any judgment that accrues after entry of the judgment and before we have paid, offered to pay, or deposited in court the part of the judgment that is within the applicable limit of insurance.

These payments will not reduce the limits of insurance.

2. If we defend an insured against a "suit" and an indemnitee of the insured is also named as a party to the "suit", we will defend that indemnitee if all of the following conditions are met:

a. The "suit" against the indemnitee seeks damages for which the insured has assumed the liability of the indemnitee in a contract or agreement that is an "insured contract";

b. This insurance applies to such liability assumed by the insured;

c. The obligation to defend, or the cost of the defense of, that indemnitee, has also been assumed by the insured in the same "insured contract";

d. The allegations in the "suit" and the information we know about the "occurrence" are such that no conflict appears to exist between the interests of the insured and the interests of the indemnitee;

e. The indemnitee and the insured ask us to conduct and control the defense of that indemnitee against such "suit" and agree that we can assign the same counsel to defend the insured and the indemnitee; and

f. The indemnitee:

(1) Agrees in writing to:

(a) Cooperate with us in the investigation, settlement or defense of the "suit";

(b) Immediately send us copies of any demands, notices, summonses or legal papers received in connection with the "suit";

(c) Notify any other insurer whose coverage is available to the indemnitee; and

(d) Cooperate with us with respect to coordinating other applicable insurance available to the indemnitee; and

(2) Provides us with written authorization to:

(a) Obtain records and other information related to the "suit"; and

(b) Conduct and control the defense of the indemnitee in such "suit".

So long as the above conditions are met, attorneys' fees incurred by us in the defense of that indemnitee, necessary litigation expenses incurred by us and necessary litigation expenses incurred by the indemnitee at our request will be paid as Supplementary Payments. Notwithstanding the provisions of Paragraph **2.b.(2)** of Section **I** – Coverage **A** – Bodily Injury And Property Damage Liability, such payments will not be deemed to be damages for "bodily injury" and "property damage" and will not reduce the limits of insurance.

Our obligation to defend an insured's indemnitee and to pay for attorneys' fees and necessary litigation expenses as Supplementary Payments ends when we have used up the applicable limit of insurance in the payment of judgments or settlements or the conditions set forth above, or the terms of the agreement described in Paragraph **f.** above, are no longer met.

SECTION II – WHO IS AN INSURED

1. If you are designated in the Declarations as:

a. An individual, you and your spouse are insureds, but only with respect to the conduct of a business of which you are the sole owner.

b. A partnership or joint venture, you are an insured. Your members, your partners, and their spouses are also insureds, but only with respect to the conduct of your business.

c. A limited liability company, you are an insured. Your members are also insureds, but only with respect to the conduct of your business. Your managers are insureds, but only with respect to their duties as your managers.

d. An organization other than a partnership, joint venture or limited liability company, you are an insured. Your "executive officers" and directors are insureds, but only with respect to their duties as your officers or directors. Your stockholders are also insureds, but only with respect to their liability as stockholders.

e. A trust, you are an insured. Your trustees are also insureds, but only with respect to their duties as trustees.

2. Each of the following is also an insured:

  a. Your "volunteer workers" only while performing duties related to the conduct of your business, or your "employees", other than either your "executive officers" (if you are an organization other than a partnership, joint venture or limited liability company) or your managers (if you are a limited liability company), but only for acts within the scope of their employment by you or while performing duties related to the conduct of your business. However, none of these "employees" or "volunteer workers" are insureds for:

  (1) "Bodily injury" or "personal and advertising injury":

  (a) To you, to your partners or members (if you are a partnership or joint venture), to your members (if you are a limited liability company), to a co-"employee" while in the course of his or her employment or performing duties related to the conduct of your business, or to your other "volunteer workers" while performing duties related to the conduct of your business;

  (b) To the spouse, child, parent, brother or sister of that co-"employee" or "volunteer worker" as a consequence of Paragraph **(1)(a)** above;

  (c) For which there is any obligation to share damages with or repay someone else who must pay damages because of the injury described in Paragraph **(1)(a)** or **(b)** above; or

  (d) Arising out of his or her providing or failing to provide professional health care services.

  (2) "Property damage" to property:

  (a) Owned, occupied or used by;

  (b) Rented to, in the care, custody or control of, or over which physical control is being exercised for any purpose by;

  you, any of your "employees", "volunteer workers", any partner or member (if you are a partnership or joint venture), or any member (if you are a limited liability company).

  b. Any person (other than your "employee" or "volunteer worker"), or any organization while acting as your real estate manager.

  c. Any person or organization having proper temporary custody of your property if you die, but only:

  (1) With respect to liability arising out of the maintenance or use of that property; and

  (2) Until your legal representative has been appointed.

  d. Your legal representative if you die, but only with respect to duties as such. That representative will have all your rights and duties under this Coverage Part.

3. Any organization you newly acquire or form, other than a partnership, joint venture or limited liability company, and over which you maintain ownership or majority interest, will qualify as a Named Insured if there is no other similar insurance available to that organization. However:

  a. Coverage under this provision is afforded only until the 90th day after you acquire or form the organization or the end of the policy period, whichever is earlier;

  b. Coverage **A** does not apply to "bodily injury" or "property damage" that occurred before you acquired or formed the organization; and

  c. Coverage **B** does not apply to "personal and advertising injury" arising out of an offense committed before you acquired or formed the organization.

No person or organization is an insured with respect to the conduct of any current or past partnership, joint venture or limited liability company that is not shown as a Named Insured in the Declarations.

SECTION III – LIMITS OF INSURANCE

1. The Limits of Insurance shown in the Declarations and the rules below fix the most we will pay regardless of the number of:

  a. Insureds;

  b. Claims made or "suits" brought; or

  c. Persons or organizations making claims or bringing "suits".

2. The General Aggregate Limit is the most we will pay for the sum of:

  a. Medical expenses under Coverage **C**;

  b. Damages under Coverage **A**, except damages because of "bodily injury" or "property damage" included in the "products-completed operations hazard"; and

  c. Damages under Coverage **B**.

3. The Products-Completed Operations Aggregate Limit is the most we will pay under Coverage **A** for damages because of "bodily injury" and "property damage" included in the "products-completed operations hazard".

4. Subject to Paragraph **2.** above, the Personal And Advertising Injury Limit is the most we will pay under Coverage **B** for the sum of all damages because of all "personal and advertising injury" sustained by any one person or organization.

5. Subject to Paragraph **2.** or **3.** above, whichever applies, the Each Occurrence Limit is the most we will pay for the sum of:

   a. Damages under Coverage **A;** and

   b. Medical expenses under Coverage **C**

   because of all "bodily injury" and "property damage" arising out of any one "occurrence".

6. Subject to Paragraph **5.** above, the Damage To Premises Rented To You Limit is the most we will pay under Coverage **A** for damages because of "property damage" to any one premises, while rented to you, or in the case of damage by fire, while rented to you or temporarily occupied by you with permission of the owner.

7. Subject to Paragraph **5.** above, the Medical Expense Limit is the most we will pay under Coverage **C** for all medical expenses because of "bodily injury" sustained by any one person.

The Limits of Insurance of this Coverage Part apply separately to each consecutive annual period and to any remaining period of less than 12 months, starting with the beginning of the policy period shown in the Declarations, unless the policy period is extended after issuance for an additional period of less than 12 months. In that case, the additional period will be deemed part of the last preceding period for purposes of determining the Limits of Insurance.

SECTION IV – COMMERCIAL GENERAL LIABILITY CONDITIONS

1. Bankruptcy

Bankruptcy or insolvency of the insured or of the insured's estate will not relieve us of our obligations under this Coverage Part.

2. Duties In The Event Of Occurrence, Offense, Claim Or Suit

a. You must see to it that we are notified as soon as practicable of an "occurrence" or an offense which may result in a claim. To the extent possible, notice should include:

   (1) How, when and where the "occurrence" or offense took place;

   (2) The names and addresses of any injured persons and witnesses; and

   (3) The nature and location of any injury or damage arising out of the "occurrence" or offense.

b. If a claim is made or "suit" is brought against any insured, you must:

   (1) Immediately record the specifics of the claim or "suit" and the date received; and

   (2) Notify us as soon as practicable.

   You must see to it that we receive written notice of the claim or "suit" as soon as practicable.

c. You and any other involved insured must:

   (1) Immediately send us copies of any demands, notices, summonses or legal papers received in connection with the claim or "suit";

   (2) Authorize us to obtain records and other information;

   (3) Cooperate with us in the investigation or settlement of the claim or defense against the "suit"; and

   (4) Assist us, upon our request, in the enforcement of any right against any person or organization which may be liable to the insured because of injury or damage to which this insurance may also apply.

d. No insured will, except at that insured's own cost, voluntarily make a payment, assume any obligation, or incur any expense, other than for first aid, without our consent.

3. Legal Action Against Us

No person or organization has a right under this Coverage Part:

a. To join us as a party or otherwise bring us into a "suit" asking for damages from an insured; or

b. To sue us on this Coverage Part unless all of its terms have been fully complied with.

A person or organization may sue us to recover on an agreed settlement or on a final judgment against an insured; but we will not be liable for damages that are not payable under the terms of this Coverage Part or that are in excess of the applicable limit of insurance. An agreed settlement means a settlement and release of liability signed by us, the insured and the claimant or the claimant's legal representative.

4. Other Insurance

If other valid and collectible insurance is available to the insured for a loss we cover under Coverages **A** or **B** of this Coverage Part, our obligations are limited as follows:

a. Primary Insurance

This insurance is primary except when Paragraph **b.** below applies. If this insurance is primary, our obligations are not affected unless any of the other insurance is also primary. Then, we will share with all that other insurance by the method described in Paragraph **c.** below.

b. Excess Insurance

(1) This insurance is excess over:

(a) Any of the other insurance, whether primary, excess, contingent or on any other basis:

(i) That is Fire, Extended Coverage, Builder's Risk, Installation Risk or similar coverage for "your work";

(ii) That is Fire insurance for premises rented to you or temporarily occupied by you with permission of the owner;

(iii) That is insurance purchased by you to cover your liability as a tenant for "property damage" to premises rented to you or temporarily occupied by you with permission of the owner; or

(iv) If the loss arises out of the maintenance or use of aircraft, "autos" or watercraft to the extent not subject to Exclusion **g.** of Section I – Coverage **A** – Bodily Injury And Property Damage Liability.

(b) Any other primary insurance available to you covering liability for damages arising out of the premises or operations, or the products and completed operations, for which you have been added as an additional insured.

(2) When this insurance is excess, we will have no duty under Coverages **A** or **B** to defend the insured against any "suit" if any other insurer has a duty to defend the insured against that "suit". If no other insurer defends, we will undertake to do so, but we will be entitled to the insured's rights against all those other insurers.

(3) When this insurance is excess over other insurance, we will pay only our share of the amount of the loss, if any, that exceeds the sum of:

(a) The total amount that all such other insurance would pay for the loss in the absence of this insurance; and

(b) The total of all deductible and self-insured amounts under all that other insurance.

(4) We will share the remaining loss, if any, with any other insurance that is not described in this Excess Insurance provision and was not bought specifically to apply in excess of the Limits of Insurance shown in the Declarations of this Coverage Part.

c. Method Of Sharing

If all of the other insurance permits contribution by equal shares, we will follow this method also. Under this approach each insurer contributes equal amounts until it has paid its applicable limit of insurance or none of the loss remains, whichever comes first.

If any of the other insurance does not permit contribution by equal shares, we will contribute by limits. Under this method, each insurer's share is based on the ratio of its applicable limit of insurance to the total applicable limits of insurance of all insurers.

5. Premium Audit

a. We will compute all premiums for this Coverage Part in accordance with our rules and rates.

b. Premium shown in this Coverage Part as advance premium is a deposit premium only. At the close of each audit period we will compute the earned premium for that period and send notice to the first Named Insured. The due date for audit and retrospective premiums is the date shown as the due date on the bill. If the sum of the advance and audit premiums paid for the policy period is greater than the earned premium, we will return the excess to the first Named Insured.

c. The first Named Insured must keep records of the information we need for premium computation, and send us copies at such times as we may request.

6. Representations

By accepting this policy, you agree:

a. The statements in the Declarations are accurate and complete;

b. Those statements are based upon representations you made to us; and

c. We have issued this policy in reliance upon your representations.

7. Separation Of Insureds

Except with respect to the Limits of Insurance, and any rights or duties specifically assigned in this Coverage Part to the first Named Insured, this insurance applies:

a. As if each Named Insured were the only Named Insured; and

b. Separately to each insured against whom claim is made or "suit" is brought.

8. Transfer Of Rights Of Recovery Against Others To Us

If the insured has rights to recover all or part of any payment we have made under this Coverage Part, those rights are transferred to us. The insured must do nothing after loss to impair them. At our request, the insured will bring "suit" or transfer those rights to us and help us enforce them.

9. When We Do Not Renew

If we decide not to renew this Coverage Part, we will mail or deliver to the first Named Insured shown in the Declarations written notice of the nonrenewal not less than 30 days before the expiration date.

If notice is mailed, proof of mailing will be sufficient proof of notice.

SECTION V – DEFINITIONS

1. "Advertisement" means a notice that is broadcast or published to the general public or specific market segments about your goods, products or services for the purpose of attracting customers or supporters. For the purposes of this definition:

a. Notices that are published include material placed on the Internet or on similar electronic means of communication; and

b. Regarding web sites, only that part of a web site that is about your goods, products or services for the purposes of attracting customers or supporters is considered an advertisement.

2. "Auto" means:

a. A land motor vehicle, trailer or semitrailer designed for travel on public roads, including any attached machinery or equipment; or

b. Any other land vehicle that is subject to a compulsory or financial responsibility law or other motor vehicle insurance law where it is licensed or principally garaged.

However, "auto" does not include "mobile equipment".

3. "Bodily injury" means bodily injury, sickness or disease sustained by a person, including death resulting from any of these at any time.

4. "Coverage territory" means:

a. The United States of America (including its territories and possessions), Puerto Rico and Canada;

b. International waters or airspace, but only if the injury or damage occurs in the course of travel or transportation between any places included in Paragraph **a.** above; or

c. All other parts of the world if the injury or damage arises out of:

(1) Goods or products made or sold by you in the territory described in Paragraph **a.** above;

(2) The activities of a person whose home is in the territory described in Paragraph **a.** above, but is away for a short time on your business; or

(3) "Personal and advertising injury" offenses that take place through the Internet or similar electronic means of communication;

provided the insured's responsibility to pay damages is determined in a "suit" on the merits, in the territory described in Paragraph **a.** above or in a settlement we agree to.

5. "Employee" includes a "leased worker". "Employee" does not include a "temporary worker".

6. "Executive officer" means a person holding any of the officer positions created by your charter, constitution, bylaws or any other similar governing document.

7. "Hostile fire" means one which becomes uncontrollable or breaks out from where it was intended to be.

8. "Impaired property" means tangible property, other than "your product" or "your work", that cannot be used or is less useful because:

a. It incorporates "your product" or "your work" that is known or thought to be defective, deficient, inadequate or dangerous; or

b. You have failed to fulfill the terms of a contract or agreement;

if such property can be restored to use by the repair, replacement, adjustment or removal of "your product" or "your work" or your fulfilling the terms of the contract or agreement.

9. "Insured contract" means:

  a. A contract for a lease of premises. However, that portion of the contract for a lease of premises that indemnifies any person or organization for damage by fire to premises while rented to you or temporarily occupied by you with permission of the owner is not an "insured contract";

  b. A sidetrack agreement;

  c. Any easement or license agreement, except in connection with construction or demolition operations on or within 50 feet of a railroad;

  d. An obligation, as required by ordinance, to indemnify a municipality, except in connection with work for a municipality;

  e. An elevator maintenance agreement;

  f. That part of any other contract or agreement pertaining to your business (including an indemnification of a municipality in connection with work performed for a municipality) under which you assume the tort liability of another party to pay for "bodily injury" or "property damage" to a third person or organization. Tort liability means a liability that would be imposed by law in the absence of any contract or agreement.

  Paragraph **f.** does not include that part of any contract or agreement:

  (1) That indemnifies a railroad for "bodily injury" or "property damage" arising out of construction or demolition operations, within 50 feet of any railroad property and affecting any railroad bridge or trestle, tracks, road-beds, tunnel, underpass or crossing;

  (2) That indemnifies an architect, engineer or surveyor for injury or damage arising out of:

  (a) Preparing, approving, or failing to prepare or approve, maps, shop drawings, opinions, reports, surveys, field orders, change orders or drawings and specifications; or

  (b) Giving directions or instructions, or failing to give them, if that is the primary cause of the injury or damage; or

  (3) Under which the insured, if an architect, engineer or surveyor, assumes liability for an injury or damage arising out of the insured's rendering or failure to render professional services, including those listed in **(2)** above and supervisory, inspection, architectural or engineering activities.

10. "Leased worker" means a person leased to you by a labor leasing firm under an agreement between you and the labor leasing firm, to perform duties related to the conduct of your business. "Leased worker" does not include a "temporary worker".

11. "Loading or unloading" means the handling of property:

  a. After it is moved from the place where it is accepted for movement into or onto an aircraft, watercraft or "auto";

  b. While it is in or on an aircraft, watercraft or "auto"; or

  c. While it is being moved from an aircraft, watercraft or "auto" to the place where it is finally delivered;

  but "loading or unloading" does not include the movement of property by means of a mechanical device, other than a hand truck, that is not attached to the aircraft, watercraft or "auto".

12. "Mobile equipment" means any of the following types of land vehicles, including any attached machinery or equipment:

  a. Bulldozers, farm machinery, forklifts and other vehicles designed for use principally off public roads;

  b. Vehicles maintained for use solely on or next to premises you own or rent;

  c. Vehicles that travel on crawler treads;

  d. Vehicles, whether self-propelled or not, maintained primarily to provide mobility to permanently mounted:

  (1) Power cranes, shovels, loaders, diggers or drills; or

  (2) Road construction or resurfacing equipment such as graders, scrapers or rollers;

  e. Vehicles not described in Paragraph **a.**, **b.**, **c.** or **d.** above that are not self-propelled and are maintained primarily to provide mobility to permanently attached equipment of the following types:

  (1) Air compressors, pumps and generators, including spraying, welding, building cleaning, geophysical exploration, lighting and well servicing equipment; or

  (2) Cherry pickers and similar devices used to raise or lower workers;

  f. Vehicles not described in Paragraph **a.**, **b.**, **c.** or **d.** above maintained primarily for purposes other than the transportation of persons or cargo.

          CG 00 01 04 13

However, self-propelled vehicles with the following types of permanently attached equipment are not "mobile equipment" but will be considered "autos":

(1) Equipment designed primarily for:

(a) Snow removal;

(b) Road maintenance, but not construction or resurfacing; or

(c) Street cleaning;

(2) Cherry pickers and similar devices mounted on automobile or truck chassis and used to raise or lower workers; and

(3) Air compressors, pumps and generators, including spraying, welding, building cleaning, geophysical exploration, lighting and well servicing equipment.

However, "mobile equipment" does not include any land vehicles that are subject to a compulsory or financial responsibility law or other motor vehicle insurance law where it is licensed or principally garaged. Land vehicles subject to a compulsory or financial responsibility law or other motor vehicle insurance law are considered "autos".

13. "Occurrence" means an accident, including continuous or repeated exposure to substantially the same general harmful conditions.

14. "Personal and advertising injury" means injury, including consequential "bodily injury", arising out of one or more of the following offenses:

a. False arrest, detention or imprisonment;

b. Malicious prosecution;

c. The wrongful eviction from, wrongful entry into, or invasion of the right of private occupancy of a room, dwelling or premises that a person occupies, committed by or on behalf of its owner, landlord or lessor;

d. Oral or written publication, in any manner, of material that slanders or libels a person or organization or disparages a person's or organization's goods, products or services;

e. Oral or written publication, in any manner, of material that violates a person's right of privacy;

f. The use of another's advertising idea in your "advertisement"; or

g. Infringing upon another's copyright, trade dress or slogan in your "advertisement".

15. "Pollutants" mean any solid, liquid, gaseous or thermal irritant or contaminant, including smoke, vapor, soot, fumes, acids, alkalis, chemicals and waste. Waste includes materials to be recycled, reconditioned or reclaimed.

16. "Products-completed operations hazard":

a. Includes all "bodily injury" and "property damage" occurring away from premises you own or rent and arising out of "your product" or "your work" except:

(1) Products that are still in your physical possession; or

(2) Work that has not yet been completed or abandoned. However, "your work" will be deemed completed at the earliest of the following times:

(a) When all of the work called for in your contract has been completed.

(b) When all of the work to be done at the job site has been completed if your contract calls for work at more than one job site.

(c) When that part of the work done at a job site has been put to its intended use by any person or organization other than another contractor or subcontractor working on the same project.

Work that may need service, maintenance, correction, repair or replacement, but which is otherwise complete, will be treated as completed.

b. Does not include "bodily injury" or "property damage" arising out of:

(1) The transportation of property, unless the injury or damage arises out of a condition in or on a vehicle not owned or operated by you, and that condition was created by the "loading or unloading" of that vehicle by any insured;

(2) The existence of tools, uninstalled equipment or abandoned or unused materials; or

(3) Products or operations for which the classification, listed in the Declarations or in a policy Schedule, states that products-completed operations are subject to the General Aggregate Limit.

17. "Property damage" means:

a. Physical injury to tangible property, including all resulting loss of use of that property. All such loss of use shall be deemed to occur at the time of the physical injury that caused it; or

b. Loss of use of tangible property that is not physically injured. All such loss of use shall be deemed to occur at the time of the "occurrence" that caused it.

For the purposes of this insurance, electronic data is not tangible property.

As used in this definition, electronic data means information, facts or programs stored as or on, created or used on, or transmitted to or from computer software, including systems and applications software, hard or floppy disks, CD-ROMs, tapes, drives, cells, data processing devices or any other media which are used with electronically controlled equipment.

18. "Suit" means a civil proceeding in which damages because of "bodily injury", "property damage" or "personal and advertising injury" to which this insurance applies are alleged. "Suit" includes:

a. An arbitration proceeding in which such damages are claimed and to which the insured must submit or does submit with our consent; or

b. Any other alternative dispute resolution proceeding in which such damages are claimed and to which the insured submits with our consent.

19. "Temporary worker" means a person who is furnished to you to substitute for a permanent "employee" on leave or to meet seasonal or short-term workload conditions.

20. "Volunteer worker" means a person who is not your "employee", and who donates his or her work and acts at the direction of and within the scope of duties determined by you, and is not paid a fee, salary or other compensation by you or anyone else for their work performed for you.

21. "Your product":

a. Means:

(1) Any goods or products, other than real property, manufactured, sold, handled, distributed or disposed of by:

(a) You;

(b) Others trading under your name; or

(c) A person or organization whose business or assets you have acquired; and

(2) Containers (other than vehicles), materials, parts or equipment furnished in connection with such goods or products.

b. Includes:

(1) Warranties or representations made at any time with respect to the fitness, quality, durability, performance or use of "your product"; and

(2) The providing of or failure to provide warnings or instructions.

c. Does not include vending machines or other property rented to or located for the use of others but not sold.

22. "Your work":

a. Means:

(1) Work or operations performed by you or on your behalf; and

(2) Materials, parts or equipment furnished in connection with such work or operations.

b. Includes:

(1) Warranties or representations made at any time with respect to the fitness, quality, durability, performance or use of "your work"; and

(2) The providing of or failure to provide warnings or instructions.

          CG 00 01 04 13

COMMERCIAL GENERAL LIABILITY
CG 20 10 04 13

POLICY NUMBER:

THIS ENDORSEMENT CHANGES THE POLICY. PLEASE READ IT CAREFULLY.

ADDITIONAL INSURED – OWNERS, LESSEES OR CONTRACTORS – SCHEDULED PERSON OR ORGANIZATION

This endorsement modifies insurance provided under the following:

COMMERCIAL GENERAL LIABILITY COVERAGE PART

SCHEDULE

Name Of Additional Insured Person(s) Or Organization(s)	Location(s) Of Covered Operations

Information required to complete this Schedule, if not shown above, will be shown in the Declarations.

A. Section II – Who Is An Insured is amended to include as an additional insured the person(s) or organization(s) shown in the Schedule, but only with respect to liability for "bodily injury", "property damage" or "personal and advertising injury" caused, in whole or in part, by:

1. Your acts or omissions; or

2. The acts or omissions of those acting on your behalf;

in the performance of your ongoing operations for the additional insured(s) at the location(s) designated above.

However:

1. The insurance afforded to such additional insured only applies to the extent permitted by law; and

2. If coverage provided to the additional insured is required by a contract or agreement, the insurance afforded to such additional insured will not be broader than that which you are required by the contract or agreement to provide for such additional insured.

B. With respect to the insurance afforded to these additional insureds, the following additional exclusions apply:

This insurance does not apply to "bodily injury" or "property damage" occurring after:

1. All work, including materials, parts or equipment furnished in connection with such work, on the project (other than service, maintenance or repairs) to be performed by or on behalf of the additional insured(s) at the location of the covered operations has been completed; or

2. That portion of "your work" out of which the injury or damage arises has been put to its intended use by any person or organization other than another contractor or subcontractor engaged in performing operations for a principal as a part of the same project.

C. With respect to the insurance afforded to these additional insureds, the following is added to **Section III – Limits Of Insurance:**

If coverage provided to the additional insured is required by a contract or agreement, the most we will pay on behalf of the additional insured is the amount of insurance:

1. Required by the contract or agreement; or

2. Available under the applicable Limits of Insurance shown in the Declarations;

whichever is less.

This endorsement shall not increase the applicable Limits of Insurance shown in the Declarations.

POLICY NUMBER:

COMMERCIAL GENERAL LIABILITY
CG 20 37 04 13

THIS ENDORSEMENT CHANGES THE POLICY. PLEASE READ IT CAREFULLY.

ADDITIONAL INSURED – OWNERS, LESSEES OR CONTRACTORS – COMPLETED OPERATIONS

This endorsement modifies insurance provided under the following:

COMMERCIAL GENERAL LIABILITY COVERAGE PART
PRODUCTS/COMPLETED OPERATIONS LIABILITY COVERAGE PART

SCHEDULE

Name Of Additional Insured Person(s) Or Organization(s)	Location And Description Of Completed Operations

Information required to complete this Schedule, if not shown above, will be shown in the Declarations.

A. **Section II – Who Is An Insured** is amended to include as an additional insured the person(s) or organization(s) shown in the Schedule, but only with respect to liability for "bodily injury" or "property damage" caused, in whole or in part, by "your work" at the location designated and described in the Schedule of this endorsement performed for that additional insured and included in the "products-completed operations hazard".

However:

1. The insurance afforded to such additional insured only applies to the extent permitted by law; and

2. If coverage provided to the additional insured is required by a contract or agreement, the insurance afforded to such additional insured will not be broader than that which you are required by the contract or agreement to provide for such additional insured.

B. With respect to the insurance afforded to these additional insureds, the following is added to **Section III – Limits Of Insurance:**

If coverage provided to the additional insured is required by a contract or agreement, the most we will pay on behalf of the additional insured is the amount of insurance:

1. Required by the contract or agreement; or

2. Available under the applicable Limits of Insurance shown in the Declarations;

whichever is less.

This endorsement shall not increase the applicable Limits of Insurance shown in the Declarations.

THIS ENDORSEMENT CHANGES THE POLICY. PLEASE READ IT CAREFULLY.

ADDITIONAL INSURED – OWNERS, LESSEES OR CONTRACTORS – AUTOMATIC STATUS WHEN REQUIRED IN CONSTRUCTION AGREEMENT WITH YOU

This endorsement modifies insurance provided under the following:

COMMERCIAL GENERAL LIABILITY COVERAGE PART

A. Section II – Who Is An Insured is amended to include as an additional insured any person or organization for whom you are performing operations when you and such person or organization have agreed in writing in a contract or agreement that such person or organization be added as an additional insured on your policy. Such person or organization is an additional insured only with respect to liability for "bodily injury", "property damage" or "personal and advertising injury" caused, in whole or in part, by:

1. Your acts or omissions; or

2. The acts or omissions of those acting on your behalf;

in the performance of your ongoing operations for the additional insured.

However, the insurance afforded to such additional insured:

1. Only applies to the extent permitted by law; and

2. Will not be broader than that which you are required by the contract or agreement to provide for such additional insured.

A person's or organization's status as an additional insured under this endorsement ends when your operations for that additional insured are completed.

B. With respect to the insurance afforded to these additional insureds, the following additional exclusions apply:

This insurance does not apply to:

1. "Bodily injury", "property damage" or "personal and advertising injury" arising out of the rendering of, or the failure to render, any professional architectural, engineering or surveying services, including:

a. The preparing, approving, or failing to prepare or approve, maps, shop drawings, opinions, reports, surveys, field orders, change orders or drawings and specifications; or

b. Supervisory, inspection, architectural or engineering activities.

This exclusion applies even if the claims against any insured allege negligence or other wrongdoing in the supervision, hiring, employment, training or monitoring of others by that insured, if the "occurrence" which caused the "bodily injury" or "property damage", or the offense which caused the "personal and advertising injury", involved the rendering of or the failure to render any professional architectural, engineering or surveying services.

2. "Bodily injury" or "property damage" occurring after:

   a. All work, including materials, parts or equipment furnished in connection with such work, on the project (other than service, maintenance or repairs) to be performed by or on behalf of the additional insured(s) at the location of the covered operations has been completed; or

   b. That portion of "your work" out of which the injury or damage arises has been put to its intended use by any person or organization other than another contractor or subcontractor engaged in performing operations for a principal as a part of the same project.

C. With respect to the insurance afforded to these additional insureds, the following is added to **Section III – Limits Of Insurance:**

The most we will pay on behalf of the additional insured is the amount of insurance:

   1. Required by the contract or agreement you have entered into with the additional insured; or

   2. Available under the applicable Limits of Insurance shown in the Declarations;

whichever is less.

This endorsement shall not increase the applicable Limits of Insurance shown in the Declarations.

COMMERCIAL GENERAL LIABILITY
CG 24 26 04 13

THIS ENDORSEMENT CHANGES THE POLICY. PLEASE READ IT CAREFULLY.

AMENDMENT OF INSURED CONTRACT DEFINITION

This endorsement modifies insurance provided under the following:

COMMERCIAL GENERAL LIABILITY COVERAGE PART
PRODUCTS/COMPLETED OPERATIONS LIABILITY COVERAGE PART

The definition of "insured contract" in the **Definitions** section is replaced by the following:

"Insured contract" means:

a. A contract for a lease of premises. However, that portion of the contract for a lease of premises that indemnifies any person or organization for damage by fire to premises while rented to you or temporarily occupied by you with permission of the owner is not an "insured contract";

b. A sidetrack agreement;

c. Any easement or license agreement, except in connection with construction or demolition operations on or within 50 feet of a railroad;

d. An obligation, as required by ordinance, to indemnify a municipality, except in connection with work for a municipality;

e. An elevator maintenance agreement;

f. That part of any other contract or agreement pertaining to your business (including an indemnification of a municipality in connection with work performed for a municipality) under which you assume the tort liability of another party to pay for "bodily injury" or "property damage" to a third person or organization, provided the "bodily injury" or "property damage" is caused, in whole or in part, by you or by those acting on your behalf. However, such part of a contract or agreement shall only be considered an "insured contract" to the extent your assumption of the tort liability is permitted by law. Tort liability means a liability that would be imposed by law in the absence of any contract or agreement.

Paragraph **f.** does not include that part of any contract or agreement:

(1) That indemnifies a railroad for "bodily injury" or "property damage" arising out of construction or demolition operations, within 50 feet of any railroad property and affecting any railroad bridge or trestle, tracks, road-beds, tunnel, underpass or crossing;

(2) That indemnifies an architect, engineer or surveyor for injury or damage arising out of:

    (a) Preparing, approving, or failing to prepare or approve, maps, shop drawings, opinions, reports, surveys, field orders, change orders or drawings and specifications; or

    (b) Giving directions or instructions, or failing to give them, if that is the primary cause of the injury or damage; or

(3) Under which the insured, if an architect, engineer or surveyor, assumes liability for an injury or damage arising out of the insured's rendering or failure to render professional services, including those listed in **(2)** above and supervisory, inspection, architectural or engineering activities.

COMMERCIAL GENERAL LIABILITY
CG 20 01 04 13

THIS ENDORSEMENT CHANGES THE POLICY. PLEASE READ IT CAREFULLY.

PRIMARY AND NONCONTRIBUTORY – OTHER INSURANCE CONDITION

This endorsement modifies insurance provided under the following:

COMMERCIAL GENERAL LIABILITY COVERAGE PART
PRODUCTS/COMPLETED OPERATIONS LIABILITY COVERAGE PART

The following is added to the **Other Insurance** Condition and supersedes any provision to the contrary:

Primary And Noncontributory Insurance

This insurance is primary to and will not seek contribution from any other insurance available to an additional insured under your policy provided that:

(1) The additional insured is a Named Insured under such other insurance; and

(2) You have agreed in writing in a contract or agreement that this insurance would be primary and would not seek contribution from any other insurance available to the additional insured.

POLICY NUMBER:

COMMERCIAL GENERAL LIABILITY
CG 04 31 09 98

THIS ENDORSEMENT CHANGES THE POLICY. PLEASE READ IT CAREFULLY.

YEAR 2000 COMPUTER-RELATED AND OTHER ELECTRONIC PROBLEMS – LIMITED COVERAGE OPTIONS

This endorsement modifies insurance provided under the following:

COMMERCIAL GENERAL LIABILITY COVERAGE PART

SCHEDULES

SCHEDULE A – COVERAGES TO BE PROVIDED
(SUBJECT TO THE DESCRIPTION IN SCHEDULE B)

Check any one or more of the following:

☐   Bodily Injury
☐   Property Damage
☐   Personal and Advertising Injury

SCHEDULE B – DESCRIPTION OF LOCATION,
OPERATIONS, PRODUCTS OR SERVICES TO BE COVERED
(TO WHICH SCHEDULE A APPLIES)

Description of location(s),
operation(s), product(s) or
service(s)
____
____
____
____
____

SCHEDULE C – PREMIUM

Premium $ _____________, if any.

The following exclusion is added to Paragraph **2.,** **Exclusions** of **Section I – Coverage A – Bodily Injury And Property Damage Liability** and Paragraph **2., Exclusions** of **Section I – Coverage B – Personal And Advertising Injury Liability:**

2. Exclusions

This insurance does not apply to "bodily injury", "property damage" or "personal injury" and "advertising injury" (or "personal and advertising injury" if defined as such in your policy) arising directly or indirectly out of:

a. Any actual or alleged failure, malfunction or inadequacy of:

(1) Any of the following, whether belonging to any insured or to others:

(a) Computer hardware, including microprocessors;

(b) Computer application software;

(c) Computer operating systems and related software;

(d) Computer networks;

(e) Microprocessors (computer chips) not part of any computer system; or

(f) Any other computerized or electronic equipment or components; or

(2) Any other products, and any services, data or functions that directly or indirectly use or rely upon, in any manner, any of the items listed in Paragraph **2.a.(1)** of this endorsement

due to the inability to correctly recognize, process, distinguish, interpret or accept the year 2000 and beyond.

b. Any advice, consultation, design, evaluation, inspection, installation, maintenance, repair, replacement or supervision provided or done by you or for you to determine, rectify or test for, any potential or actual problems described in Paragraph **2.a.** of this endorsement.

This exclusion does not apply to the types of injury or damage indicated in Schedule **A** – Coverages To Be Provided of this endorsement arising out of any operations, products or services, or any operations or services at or from any specific location, described in Schedule **B** – Description Of Location, Operations, Products Or Services To Be Covered of this endorsement.

COMMERCIAL GENERAL LIABILITY
CG 00 67 03 05

THIS ENDORSEMENT CHANGES THE POLICY. PLEASE READ IT CAREFULLY.

EXCLUSION – VIOLATION OF STATUTES THAT GOVERN E-MAILS, FAX, PHONE CALLS OR OTHER METHODS OF SENDING MATERIAL OR INFORMATION

This endorsement modifies insurance provided under the following:

COMMERCIAL GENERAL LIABILITY COVERAGE PART

A. The following exclusion is added to Paragraph **2., Exclusions** of **Section I – Coverage A – Bodily Injury And Property Damage Liability:**

   2. Exclusions

   This insurance does not apply to:

   DISTRIBUTION OF MATERIAL IN VIOLATION OF STATUTES

   "Bodily injury" or "property damage" arising directly or indirectly out of any action or omission that violates or is alleged to violate:

   a. The Telephone Consumer Protection Act (TCPA), including any amendment of or addition to such law; or

   b. The CAN-SPAM Act of 2003, including any amendment of or addition to such law; or

   c. Any statute, ordinance or regulation, other than the TCPA or CAN-SPAM Act of 2003, that prohibits or limits the sending, transmitting, communicating or distribution of material or information.

B. The following exclusion is added to Paragraph **2., Exclusions** of **Section I – Coverage B – Personal And Advertising Injury Liability:**

   2. Exclusions

   This insurance does not apply to:

   DISTRIBUTION OF MATERIAL IN VIOLATION OF STATUTES

   "Personal and advertising injury" arising directly or indirectly out of any action or omission that violates or is alleged to violate:

   a. The Telephone Consumer Protection Act (TCPA), including any amendment of or addition to such law; or

   b. The CAN-SPAM Act of 2003, including any amendment of or addition to such law; or

   c. Any statute, ordinance or regulation, other than the TCPA or CAN-SPAM Act of 2003, that prohibits or limits the sending, transmitting, communicating or distribution of material or information.

COMMERCIAL GENERAL LIABILITY
CG 21 06 05 14

THIS ENDORSEMENT CHANGES THE POLICY. PLEASE READ IT CAREFULLY.

EXCLUSION – ACCESS OR DISCLOSURE OF CONFIDENTIAL OR PERSONAL INFORMATION AND DATA-RELATED LIABILITY – WITH LIMITED BODILY INJURY EXCEPTION

This endorsement modifies insurance provided under the following:

COMMERCIAL GENERAL LIABILITY COVERAGE PART

A. Exclusion **2.p.** of **Section I – Coverage A – Bodily Injury And Property Damage Liability** is replaced by the following:

2. Exclusions

This insurance does not apply to:

p. Access Or Disclosure Of Confidential Or Personal Information And Data-related Liability

Damages arising out of:

(1) Any access to or disclosure of any person's or organization's confidential or personal information, including patents, trade secrets, processing methods, customer lists, financial information, credit card information, health information or any other type of nonpublic information; or

(2) The loss of, loss of use of, damage to, corruption of, inability to access, or inability to manipulate electronic data.

This exclusion applies even if damages are claimed for notification costs, credit monitoring expenses, forensic expenses, public relations expenses or any other loss, cost or expense incurred by you or others arising out of that which is described in Paragraph **(1)** or **(2)** above.

However, unless Paragraph **(1)** above applies, this exclusion does not apply to damages because of "bodily injury".

As used in this exclusion, electronic data means information, facts or programs stored as or on, created or used on, or transmitted to or from computer software, including systems and applications software, hard or floppy disks, CD-ROMs, tapes, drives, cells, data processing devices or any other media which are used with electronically controlled equipment.

B. The following is added to Paragraph **2. Exclusions** of **Section I – Coverage B – Personal And Advertising Injury Liability:**

2. Exclusions

This insurance does not apply to:

Access Or Disclosure Of Confidential Or Personal Information

"Personal and advertising injury" arising out of any access to or disclosure of any person's or organization's confidential or personal information, including patents, trade secrets, processing methods, customer lists, financial information, credit card information, health information or any other type of nonpublic information.

This exclusion applies even if damages are claimed for notification costs, credit monitoring expenses, forensic expenses, public relations expenses or any other loss, cost or expense incurred by you or others arising out of any access to or disclosure of any person's or organization's confidential or personal information.

COMMERCIAL GENERAL LIABILITY
CG 21 07 05 14

THIS ENDORSEMENT CHANGES THE POLICY. PLEASE READ IT CAREFULLY.

EXCLUSION – ACCESS OR DISCLOSURE OF CONFIDENTIAL OR PERSONAL INFORMATION AND DATA-RELATED LIABILITY – LIMITED BODILY INJURY EXCEPTION NOT INCLUDED

This endorsement modifies insurance provided under the following:

COMMERCIAL GENERAL LIABILITY COVERAGE PART

A. Exclusion **2.p.** of **Section I – Coverage A – Bodily Injury And Property Damage Liability** is replaced by the following:

2. Exclusions

This insurance does not apply to:

p. Access Or Disclosure Of Confidential Or Personal Information And Data-related Liability

Damages arising out of:

(1) Any access to or disclosure of any person's or organization's confidential or personal information, including patents, trade secrets, processing methods, customer lists, financial information, credit card information, health information or any other type of nonpublic information; or

(2) The loss of, loss of use of, damage to, corruption of, inability to access, or inability to manipulate electronic data.

This exclusion applies even if damages are claimed for notification costs, credit monitoring expenses, forensic expenses, public relations expenses or any other loss, cost or expense incurred by you or others arising out of that which is described in Paragraph **(1)** or **(2)** above.

As used in this exclusion, electronic data means information, facts or programs stored as or on, created or used on, or transmitted to or from computer software, including systems and applications software, hard or floppy disks, CD-ROMs, tapes, drives, cells, data processing devices or any other media which are used with electronically controlled equipment.

B. The following is added to Paragraph **2. Exclusions** of **Section I – Coverage B – Personal And Advertising Injury Liability:**

2. Exclusions

This insurance does not apply to:

Access Or Disclosure Of Confidential Or Personal Information

"Personal and advertising injury" arising out of any access to or disclosure of any person's or organization's confidential or personal information, including patents, trade secrets, processing methods, customer lists, financial information, credit card information, health information or any other type of nonpublic information.

This exclusion applies even if damages are claimed for notification costs, credit monitoring expenses, forensic expenses, public relations expenses or any other loss, cost or expense incurred by you or others arising out of any access to or disclosure of any person's or organization's confidential or personal information.

COMMERCIAL GENERAL LIABILITY
CG 21 08 05 14

THIS ENDORSEMENT CHANGES THE POLICY. PLEASE READ IT CAREFULLY.

EXCLUSION – ACCESS OR DISCLOSURE OF CONFIDENTIAL OR PERSONAL INFORMATION (COVERAGE B ONLY)

This endorsement modifies insurance provided under the following:

COMMERCIAL GENERAL LIABILITY COVERAGE PART

The following is added to Paragraph **2. Exclusions** of **Section I – Coverage B – Personal And Advertising Injury Liability:**

2. Exclusions

This insurance does not apply to:

Access Or Disclosure Of Confidential Or Personal Information

"Personal and advertising injury" arising out of any access to or disclosure of any person's or organization's confidential or personal information, including patents, trade secrets, processing methods, customer lists, financial information, credit card information, health information or any other type of nonpublic information.

This exclusion applies even if damages are claimed for notification costs, credit monitoring expenses, forensic expenses, public relations expenses or any other loss, cost or expense incurred by you or others arising out of any access to or disclosure of any person's or organization's confidential or personal information.

INFORMATION SECURITY PROTECTION POLICY

INSURING AGREEMENTS 1., 2. AND 3. OF THIS POLICY PROVIDE CLAIMS-MADE COVERAGE. DEFENSE EXPENSES ARE PAYABLE WITHIN, AND NOT IN ADDITION TO, THE LIMIT OF INSURANCE. PAYMENT OF DEFENSE EXPENSES UNDER THIS POLICY WILL REDUCE THE LIMIT OF INSURANCE.

PLEASE READ THE ENTIRE POLICY CAREFULLY.

Various provisions in this Policy restrict coverage. Read the entire Policy carefully to determine rights, duties and what is and is not covered.

Throughout this Policy the words "you" and "your" refer to the "named insured" shown in the Declarations. The words "we", "us" and "our" refer to the company providing this insurance.

Other words and phrases that appear in quotation marks have special meaning. Refer to Section **VII** – Definitions.

SECTION I – INSURING AGREEMENTS

Coverage is provided under the following Insuring Agreements for which an Aggregate Limit Of Insurance is shown in the Declarations:

1. Web Site Publishing Liability

We will pay for both "loss" that the "insured" becomes legally obligated to pay and "defense expenses" as a result of a "claim" first made against the "insured" during the "policy period" or during the applicable Extended Reporting Period, for a "wrongful act" or a series of "interrelated wrongful acts" taking place on or after the Retroactive Date, if any, shown in the Declarations and before the end of the "policy period".

2. Security Breach Liability

a. We will pay for both "loss" that the "insured" becomes legally obligated to pay and "defense expenses" as a result of a "claim" first made against the "insured" during the "policy period" or during the applicable Extended Reporting Period, for a "wrongful act" or a series of "interrelated wrongful acts" taking place on or after the Retroactive Date, if any, shown in the Declarations and before the end of the "policy period".

b. We will pay for both "loss" and "defense expenses" as a result of a "claim" in the form of a "regulatory proceeding" first made against the "insured" during the "policy period" or during the applicable Extended Reporting Period, in response to a "wrongful act" or a series of "interrelated wrongful acts" covered under Paragraph **2.a.**

3. Programming Errors And Omissions Liability

We will pay for both "loss" that the "insured" becomes legally obligated to pay and "defense expenses" as a result of a "claim" first made against the "insured" during the "policy period" or during the applicable Extended Reporting Period, for a "wrongful act" or a series of "interrelated wrongful acts" taking place on or after the Retroactive Date, if any, shown in the Declarations and before the end of the "policy period".

4. Replacement Or Restoration Of Electronic Data

We will pay for "loss" of "electronic data" or "computer programs" stored within the "computer system" resulting directly from an "e-commerce incident" sustained during the "policy period".

5. Extortion Threats

We will pay for "loss" resulting directly from an "extortion threat" communicated to you during the "policy period".

However, we will not pay for "extortion expenses" or "ransom payments" which are part of a series of related threats that began prior to the "policy period".

6. Business Income And Extra Expense

We will pay for "loss" due to an "interruption" resulting directly from an "e-commerce incident" sustained during the "policy period" or an "extortion threat" communicated to you during the "policy period".

7. Public Relations Expense

We will pay for "loss" due to "negative publicity" resulting directly from an "e-commerce incident" or a "security breach" sustained during the "policy period".

8. Security Breach Expense

We will pay for "loss" resulting directly from a "security breach" sustained during the "policy period".

SECTION II – LIMITS OF INSURANCE

1. Policy Aggregate Limit Of Insurance

The most we will pay for all "loss", and "defense expenses" if covered, under this Policy is the Policy Aggregate Limit Of Insurance shown in the Declarations. The Policy Aggregate Limit of Insurance shall be reduced by the amount of any payment made under the terms of this Policy. Upon exhaustion of the Policy Aggregate Limit of Insurance by such payments, we will have no further obligations or liability of any kind under this Policy.

2. Insuring Agreement Aggregate Limit Of Insurance

a. Subject to the Policy Aggregate Limit of Insurance, the most we will pay for all "loss", and "defense expenses" if covered, under each Insuring Agreement, is the Insuring Agreement Aggregate Limit Of Insurance shown in the Declarations:

(1) The Insuring Agreement Aggregate Limit of Insurance shall be reduced by the amount of any payment for "loss", and "defense expenses" if covered, under that Insuring Agreement; and

(2) Upon exhaustion of the Insuring Agreement Aggregate Limit of Insurance by such payments, we will have no further obligations or liability of any kind under that Insuring Agreement.

b. If coverage for "regulatory proceedings" is being provided under Paragraph **b.** of Insuring Agreement **2.** Security Breach Liability, the Limit of Insurance shall be part of, not in addition to, the Aggregate Limit of Insurance for the Insuring Agreement.

SECTION III – DEDUCTIBLE

1. Subject to Section **II** – Limits Of Insurance:

a. Under Insuring Agreements **1.** Web Site Publishing Liability, **2.** Security Breach Liability and **3.** Programming Errors And Omissions Liability:

We will pay only the amount of "loss" and "defense expenses" which are in excess of the applicable Deductible Amount shown in the Declarations resulting from the same "wrongful act" or "interrelated wrongful acts". Such Deductible Amount will be borne by you self-insured, and at your own risk.

b. Under Insuring Agreements **4.** Replacement Or Restoration Of Electronic Data, **5.** Extortion Threats, **7.** Public Relations Expense and **8.** Security Breach Expense:

We will pay only the amount of "loss" which is in excess of the applicable Deductible Amount shown in the Declarations.

c. Under Insuring Agreement **6.** Business Income And Extra Expense:

We will pay only the amount of "loss" which exceeds the greater of:

(1) The Deductible Amount shown in the Declarations; or

(2) The amount of "loss" incurred during the Waiting Period shown in the Declarations.

2. In the event a "loss" is covered under more than one Insuring Agreement, only the highest Deductible Amount applicable to the "loss" shall be applied.

SECTION IV – DEFENSE AND SETTLEMENT

The provisions contained within this section apply only to Insuring Agreements **1.** Web Site Publishing Liability, **2.** Security Breach Liability and **3.** Programming Errors And Omissions Liability:

1. We shall have the right and duty to select counsel and defend the "insured" against any "claim" covered under Insuring Agreements **1.** Web Site Publishing Liability, **2.** Security Breach Liability and **3.** Programming Errors And Omissions Liability, even if the allegations of such "claim" are groundless, false or fraudulent. However, we shall have the right but not the duty to defend the "insured" against a "claim" covered under Paragraph **b.** of Insuring Agreement **2.** Security Breach Liability, and we shall have no duty to defend the "insured" against any "claim" which is not covered under any of these Insuring Agreements.

2. We may, upon the written consent of the "insured", make any settlement of a "claim" which we deem reasonable. If the "insured" withholds consent to such settlement, our liability for all "loss" resulting from such "claim" will not exceed the amount for which we could have settled such "claim", plus "defense expenses" incurred, as of the date we proposed such settlement in writing to the "insured". Upon refusing to consent to a settlement we deem reasonable, the "insured" shall, at its sole expense, assume all further responsibility for its defense, including all additional costs associated with the investigation, defense and/or settlement of such "claim".

        EC 00 10 01 14

SECTION V – EXCLUSIONS

We will not be liable for "loss" or "defense expenses":

1. Based upon, attributable to or arising out of lightning, earthquake, hail, volcanic action or any other act of nature.

2. Based upon, attributable to or arising out of:

   a. War, including undeclared or civil war or civil unrest;

   b. Warlike action by military force, including action hindering or defending against an actual or expected attack, by any government, sovereign or other authority using military personnel or other agents; or

   c. Insurrection, rebellion, revolution, usurped power, or action taken by government authority in hindering or defending against any of these.

3. Based upon, attributable to or arising out of the dispersal or application of pathogenic or poisonous biological or chemical materials, nuclear reaction, nuclear radiation or radioactive contamination, or any related act or incident, however caused.

4. Based upon, attributable to or arising out of bodily injury or physical damage to or destruction of tangible property, including loss of use thereof.

   Bodily injury means bodily injury, sickness or disease sustained by a person, including death resulting from any of these at any time.

5. Based upon, attributable to or arising out of any unexplained or indeterminable failure, malfunction or slowdown of the "computer system" including "electronic data" and the inability to access or properly manipulate the "electronic data".

6. Based upon, attributable to or arising out of any "interruption" in normal computer function or network service or function due to insufficient capacity to process transactions or due to an overload of activity on the "computer system" or network. However, this exclusion shall not apply if such "interruption" is caused by an "e-commerce incident".

7. Based upon, attributable to or arising out of a complete or substantial failure, disablement or shutdown of the Internet, regardless of the cause.

8. Based upon, attributable to or arising out of any failure of, reduction in or surge of power.

9. Based upon, attributable to or arising out of any actual or alleged violation of the Racketeer Influenced and Corrupt Organizations Act (RICO) and its amendments, or similar provisions of any federal, state or local statutory or common law.

10. Based upon, attributable to or arising out of any malfunction or failure of any satellite.

11. Based upon, attributable to or arising out of any oral or written publication of material, if done by an "insured" or at an "insured's" direction with knowledge of its falsity.

12. Based upon, attributable to or arising out of an "insured's" assumption of liability by contract or agreement, whether oral or written. However, this exclusion shall not apply to any liability that an "insured" would have incurred in the absence of such contract or agreement.

13. Based upon, attributable to or arising out of any actual or alleged patent or trade secret violation, including any actual or alleged violation of the Patent Act, the Economic Espionage Act of 1996 or the Uniform Trade Secrets Act and their amendments.

14. Based upon, attributable to or arising out of:

   a. The actual, alleged or threatened discharge, dispersal, seepage, migration, release or escape of "pollutants" at any time;

   b. Any request, demand, order or statutory or regulatory requirement that any "insured" or others test for, monitor, clean up, remove, contain, treat, detoxify or neutralize, or in any way respond to, or assess the effects of, "pollutants"; or

   c. Any "claim" or "suit" brought by, or on behalf of, any governmental authority for damages because of testing for, monitoring, cleaning up, removing, containing, treating, detoxifying or neutralizing, or in any way responding to, or assessing the effects of, "pollutants".

15. Based upon, attributable to or arising out of any "claim", "suit" or other proceeding against an "insured" which was pending or existed prior to the "policy period", or arising out of the same or substantially the same facts, circumstances or allegations which are the subject of, or the basis for, such "claim", "suit" or other proceeding.

16. Based upon, attributable to or arising out of an "insured's" employment practices including, but not limited to, termination of employment, demotion, reassignment, discipline, harassment, coercion or refusal to employ regardless of whether the "insured" is liable as an employer or in any other capacity.

17. Based upon, attributable to or arising out of any "wrongful act" or "interrelated wrongful acts" that occurred before the Retroactive Date, if any, shown in the Declarations.

18. Based upon, attributable to or arising out of the same facts, "wrongful acts" or "interrelated wrongful acts" alleged or contained in any "claim" which has been reported, or in any circumstances of which notice has been given, under any insurance policy of which this Policy is a renewal or replacement.

19. Based upon, attributable to or arising out of any criminal, dishonest, malicious or fraudulent act or any willful violation of any statute or regulation committed by an "insured", acting alone or in collusion with others. However, this exclusion shall not apply to dishonest, malicious or fraudulent acts committed by an "employee" which give rise to a "claim" or "loss" covered under Insuring Agreement **2.** Security Breach Liability.

With the exception of "claims" excluded under Exclusion **13.**, we will defend "claims" first made against an "insured" alleging such acts or violations until final adjudication is rendered against that "insured". Final adjudication rendered against one "insured" shall not be imputed to any other "insured".

We will not provide indemnification for any "claim" to which any "insured" enters a guilty plea or pleads no contest and we will not provide a defense from the time we become aware that any "insured" intends to so plead.

20. Based upon, attributable to or arising out of any action or proceeding brought by, or on behalf of, any governmental authority or regulatory agency including, but not limited to:

    a. The seizure or destruction of property by order of a governmental authority; or

    b. Regulatory actions or proceedings brought by, or on behalf of, the Federal Trade Commission, Federal Communications Commission or other regulatory agency, except when covered under Paragraph **b.** of Insuring Agreement **2.** Security Breach Liability.

    However, this exclusion shall not apply to actions or proceedings brought by a governmental authority or regulatory agency acting solely in its capacity as a customer of the "named insured" or of a "subsidiary".

21. Based upon, attributable to or arising out of costs associated with upgrading or improving the "computer system" regardless of the reason for the upgrade.

22. Based upon, attributable to or arising out of any "claim" brought or alleged by one "insured" against another, except for a "claim" brought or alleged by an "employee" against an "insured" as a result of a "security breach".

23. Based upon, attributable to or arising out of unintentional errors or omissions in the entry of "electronic data" into the "computer system".

SECTION VI – CONDITIONS

1. Cancellation

    a. The first "named insured" shown in the Declarations may cancel this Policy by mailing or delivering to us advance written notice of cancellation.

    b. We may cancel this Policy by mailing or delivering to the first "named insured" written notice of cancellation at least:

        (1) 10 days before the effective date of cancellation if we cancel for nonpayment of premium; or

        (2) 30 days before the effective date of cancellation if we cancel for any other reason.

    c. We will mail or deliver our notice to the first "named insured's" last mailing address known to us.

    d. Notice of cancellation will state the effective date of cancellation. The "policy period" will end on that date.

    e. If this Policy is canceled, we will send the first "named insured" any premium refund due. If we cancel, the refund will be prorated. If the first "named insured" cancels, the refund may be less than pro rata. The cancellation will be effective even if we have not made or offered a refund.

    f. If notice is mailed, proof of mailing will be sufficient proof of notice.

2. Changes

This Policy contains all the agreements between you and us concerning the insurance afforded. The first "named insured" shown in the Declarations is authorized to make changes in the terms of this Policy with our consent. This Policy's terms can be amended or waived only by endorsement issued by us and made a part of this Policy.

3. Examination Of Your Books And Records

We may examine and audit your books and records as they relate to this Policy at any time during the "policy period" and up to three years afterward.

4. Inspections And Surveys

a. We have the right to:

(1) Make inspections and surveys at any time;

(2) Give you reports on the conditions we find; and

(3) Recommend changes.

b. We are not obligated to make any inspections, surveys, reports or recommendations, and any such actions we do undertake relate only to insurability and the premiums to be charged. We do not make safety inspections. We do not undertake to perform the duty of any person or organization to provide for the health or safety of workers or the public. And we do not warrant that conditions:

(1) Are safe or healthful; or

(2) Comply with laws, regulations, codes or standards.

c. Paragraphs **4.a.** and **4.b.** of this condition apply not only to us, but also to any rating, advisory, rate service or similar organization which makes insurance inspections, surveys, reports or recommendations.

5. Premiums

The first "named insured" shown in the Declarations:

a. Is responsible for the payment of all premiums; and

b. Will be the payee for any return premiums we pay.

6. Transfer Of Your Rights And Duties Under This Policy

Your rights and duties under this Policy may not be transferred without our written consent, except in the case of death of an individual "named insured".

If you are a sole proprietor and you die, your rights and duties will be transferred to your legal representative but only while acting within the scope of duties as your legal representative. Until your legal representative is appointed, anyone having proper temporary custody of your property will have your rights and duties but only with respect to that property.

7. Subrogation

With respect to any payment made under this Policy on behalf of any "insured", we shall be subrogated to the "insured's" rights of recovery to the extent of such payment. The "insured" shall execute all papers required and shall do everything necessary to secure and preserve such rights, including the execution of such documents necessary to enable us to bring suit in the "insured's" name. Any recoveries, less the cost of obtaining them, will be distributed as follows:

a. To you, until you are reimbursed for any "loss" you sustain that exceeds the sum of the applicable Aggregate Limit of Insurance and the Deductible Amount, if any;

b. Then to us, until we are reimbursed for the payment made under this Policy; and

c. Then to you, until you are reimbursed for that part of the payment equal to the Deductible Amount, if any.

8. Bankruptcy

Your bankruptcy, or the bankruptcy of your estate if you are a sole proprietor, will not relieve us of our obligations under this Policy.

9. Representations

You represent that all information and statements contained in the "application" are true, accurate and complete. All such information and statements are the basis for our issuing this Policy and shall be considered as incorporated into and shall constitute a part of this Policy. Misrepresentation of any material fact may be grounds for the rescission of this Policy.

10. Changes In Exposure

a. Acquisition Or Creation Of Another Organization

If before or during the "policy period":

(1) You acquire securities or voting rights in another organization or create another organization which, as a result of such acquisition or creation, becomes a "subsidiary"; or

(2) You acquire any organization through merger or consolidation;

then such organization will be covered under this Policy but only with respect to "wrongful acts" or "loss" which occurred after the effective date of such acquisition or creation provided, with regard to Paragraphs **10.a.(1)** and **10.a.(2),** you:

    (a) Give us written notice of the acquisition or creation of such organization within 90 days after the effective date of such action;

    (b) Obtain our written consent to extend the coverage provided by this Policy to such organization; and

    (c) Upon obtaining our consent, pay us an additional premium.

b. **Acquisition Of Named Insured**

If during the "policy period":

(1) The "named insured" merges into or consolidates with another organization, such that the "named insured" is not the surviving organization; or

(2) Another organization, or person or group of organizations and/or persons acting in concert, acquires securities or voting rights which result in ownership or voting control by the other organization(s) or person(s) of more than 50% of the outstanding securities or voting rights representing the present right to vote for the election of directors, trustees or managers (if a limited liability company) of the "named insured";

then the coverage afforded under this Policy will continue until the end of the "policy period", but only with respect to "claims" arising out of "wrongful acts" or "loss" which occurred prior to the effective date of such merger, consolidation or acquisition.

The full annual premium for the "policy period" will be deemed to be fully earned immediately upon the occurrence of such merger, consolidation or acquisition of the "named insured".

The "named insured" must give written notice of such merger, consolidation or acquisition to us as soon as practicable, together with such information as we may reasonably require.

c. **Cessation Of Subsidiaries**

If before or during the "policy period" an organization ceases to be a "subsidiary", the coverage afforded under this Policy with respect to such "subsidiary" will continue until the end of the "policy period" but only with respect to "claims" arising out of "wrongful acts" or "loss" which occurred prior to the date such organization ceased to be a "subsidiary".

11. **Other Insurance**

    a. If any covered "claim" or "loss" is insured by any other valid policy, then this Policy shall apply only in excess of the amount of any deductible, retention and limit of insurance under such other policy, whether such other policy is stated to be primary, contributory, excess, contingent or otherwise, unless such other policy is written specifically excess of this Policy by reference in such other policy to this Policy's policy number.

    b. When this Policy is excess, we shall have no duty under Insuring Agreement **1.** Web Site Publishing Liability, **2.** Security Breach Liability or **3.** Programming Errors And Omissions Liability to defend the "insured" against any "suit" if any other insurer has a duty to defend the "insured" against that "suit". If no other insurer defends, we will undertake to do so, but we will be entitled to the "insured's" rights against all those other insurers.

12. **Legal Action Against Us**

    a. No person or organization has a right:

        (1) To join us as a party or otherwise bring us into a "suit" asking for damages from an "insured"; or

        (2) To sue us under this Policy unless all of its terms have been fully complied with.

A person or organization may sue us to recover on an agreed settlement or on a final judgment against an "insured", but we will not be liable for damages that are not payable under Insuring Agreement **1.** Web Site Publishing Liability, **2.** Security Breach Liability or **3.** Programming Errors And Omissions Liability, or that are in excess of the applicable Aggregate Limit of Insurance. An agreed settlement means a settlement and release of liability signed by us, the first "named insured" and the claimant or the claimant's legal representative.

    b. You may not bring any legal action against us involving "loss":

        (1) Unless you have complied with all the terms of this Policy;

        (2) Until 90 days after you have filed proof of loss with us; and

        (3) Unless brought within two years from the date you reported the "loss" to us.

If any limitation in this condition is prohibited by law, such limitation is amended so as to equal the minimum period of limitation provided by such law.

13. Separation Of Insureds

Except with respect to the applicable Aggregate Limit of Insurance, and any rights or duties specifically assigned in Insuring Agreement **1.** Web Site Publishing Liability, **2.** Security Breach Liability or **3.** Programming Errors And Omissions Liability to the first "named insured", this Policy applies separately to each "insured" against whom "claim" is made.

14. Duties In The Event Of Claim Or Loss

In the event of either an occurrence or offense that may result in a "claim" against an "insured" or a "loss" or situation that may result in a "loss" covered under this Policy, you must notify us in writing as soon as practicable, but not to exceed 30 days, and cooperate with us in the investigation and settlement of the "claim" or "loss". Additionally:

a. Under Insuring Agreements **1.** Web Site Publishing Liability, **2.** Security Breach Liability and **3.** Programming Errors And Omissions Liability, you must:

(1) Immediately record the specifics of the "claim" and the date received;

(2) Immediately send us copies of any demands, notices, summonses or legal papers received in connection with the "claim";

(3) Authorize us to obtain records and other information; and

(4) Assist us, upon our request, in the enforcement of any right against any person or organization which may be liable to you because of an occurrence or offense to which this Policy may also apply.

You will not, except at your own cost, voluntarily make a payment, assume any obligation or incur any expense without our consent.

A "claim" brought by a person or organization seeking damages will be deemed to have been made when the "claim" is received by an "insured".

b. Under Insuring Agreements **4.** Replacement Or Restoration Of Electronic Data and **5.** Extortion Threats, you must:

(1) Notify local law enforcement officials;

(2) Submit to examination under oath at our request and give us a signed statement of your answers; and

(3) Give us a detailed, sworn proof of loss within 120 days.

(4) In addition, under Insuring Agreement **5.** Extortion Threats, you must:

(a) Determine that the "extortion threat" has actually occurred;

(b) Make every reasonable effort to immediately notify an associate and the security firm, if any, before making any "ransom payment" based upon the "extortion threat"; and

(c) Approve any "ransom payment" based upon the "extortion threat".

15. Valuation – Settlement

a. All premiums, Aggregate Limits of Insurance, Deductible Amounts, "loss" and any other monetary amounts under this Policy are expressed and payable in the currency of the United States of America. If judgment is rendered, settlement is agreed to or another component of "loss" under this Policy is expressed in any currency other than United States of America dollars, payment under this Policy shall be made in United States dollars at the rate of exchange published in The Wall Street Journal on the date the final judgment is entered, settlement amount is agreed upon or the other component of "loss" is due, respectively.

b. With respect to "loss" covered under Insuring Agreement **6.** Business Income And Extra Expense:

(1) The amount of "business income" will be determined based on consideration of:

(a) The net income generated from your "e-commerce activities" before the "interruption" occurred;

(b) The likely net income generated by your "e-commerce activities" if no "interruption" had occurred, but not including any net income that would likely have been earned as a result of an increase in the volume of business due to favorable business conditions caused by the impact of the "e-commerce incident" on customers or on other businesses;

(c) The operating expenses, including payroll, necessary to resume your "e-commerce activities" with the same quality of service that existed before the "interruption"; and

(d) Other relevant sources of information, including your financial records and accounting procedures, bills, invoices and other vouchers, and debts, liens and contracts.

However, the amount of "business income" will be reduced to the extent that the reduction in the volume of business from the affected "e-commerce activities" is offset by an increase in the volume of business from other channels of commerce such as via telephone, mail or other sources.

(2) The amount of "extra expense" will be determined based on:

(a) Necessary expenses that exceed the normal operating expenses that would have been incurred in the course of your "e-commerce activities" during the period of coverage if no "interruption" had occurred. We will deduct from the total of such expenses the salvage value that remains of any property bought for temporary use during the period of coverage once your "e-commerce activities" are resumed; and

(b) Necessary expenses that reduce the "business income" "loss" that otherwise would have been incurred during the period of coverage.

16. Extended Reporting Periods

The provisions contained within this condition apply only to Insuring Agreements **1.** Web Site Publishing Liability, **2.** Security Breach Liability and **3.** Programming Errors And Omissions Liability.

a. Basic Extended Reporting Period

(1) A Basic Extended Reporting Period is automatically provided without additional charge. This period starts with the end of the "policy period" and lasts for 30 days. A "claim" first made and reported by the "insured" during this 30-day period will be considered to have been received within the "policy period". However, the 30-day Basic Extended Reporting Period does not apply to "claims" that are covered under any subsequent insurance purchased by the "insured", or that would be covered but for exhaustion of the Aggregate Limit of Insurance applicable to such "claims".

(2) The Basic Extended Reporting Period does not extend the "policy period" or change the scope of coverage provided. It applies only to "claims" to which the following applies:

(a) The "claim" is first made and reported to us during the Basic Extended Reporting Period; and

(b) The "claim" arose out of either a "wrongful act" or the first of a series of "interrelated wrongful acts" which occurred on or after the Retroactive Date, if any, shown in the Declarations and before the end of the "policy period".

b. Supplemental Extended Reporting Period

(1) A Supplemental Extended Reporting Period is available if this Policy is canceled or not renewed by either you or us, but only by endorsement and for an extra charge. The Supplemental Extended Reporting Period starts when the Basic Extended Reporting Period set forth in Paragraph **16.a.** ends. The Supplemental Extended Reporting Period is available unless:

(a) We cancel this Policy for nonpayment of premium; or

(b) You fail to pay any amounts owed us.

(2) In order to obtain a Supplemental Extended Reporting Period, you must give us a written request for the Supplemental Extended Reporting Period Endorsement together with the full payment of the additional premium for the endorsement within 30 days after the end of the "policy period". The Supplemental Extended Reporting Period will not go into effect unless you pay the additional premium promptly when due.

(3) The Supplemental Extended Reporting Period does not extend the "policy period" or change the scope of coverage provided. It applies only to "claims" to which the following applies:

(a) The "claim" is first made and reported to us during the Supplemental Extended Reporting Period; and

(b) The "claim" arose out of either a "wrongful act" or the first of a series of "interrelated wrongful acts" which occurred on or after the Retroactive Date, if any, shown in the Declarations and before the end of the "policy period".

     © Insurance Services Office, Inc., 2013   EC 00 10 01 14

(4) Once in effect, the Supplemental Extended Reporting Period may not be canceled. The premium for the Supplemental Extended Reporting Period Endorsement will be deemed to be fully earned as of the date it is purchased.

c. There is no separate or additional Aggregate Limit of Insurance for the Basic Extended Reporting Period or the Supplemental Extended Reporting Period. The limit of insurance available during the Basic Extended Reporting Period, and the Supplemental Extended Reporting Period if purchased, shall be the remaining amount, if any, of the Aggregate Limit of Insurance of the respective Insuring Agreement, subject to the remaining amount of the Policy Aggregate Limit of Insurance at the time this Policy was canceled or nonrenewed.

17. Confidentiality

Under Insuring Agreement **5.** Extortion Threats, "insureds" must make every reasonable effort not to divulge the existence of this coverage.

18. Territory

This Policy covers "wrongful acts" which occurred anywhere in the world. However, "suits" must be brought in the United States of America (including its territories and possessions), Puerto Rico or Canada.

SECTION VII – DEFINITIONS

1. "Application" means the signed application for this Policy, including any attachments and other materials submitted in conjunction with the signed application.

2. "Business income" means the:

a. Net income (net profit or loss before income taxes) that would have been earned or incurred; and

b. Continuing normal operating expenses incurred, including payroll.

3. "Claim" means:

a. A written demand for monetary or nonmonetary damages, including injunctive relief;

b. A civil proceeding commenced by the service of a complaint or similar proceeding; or

c. Under Paragraph **b.** of Insuring Agreement **2.** Security Breach Liability, a "regulatory proceeding" commenced by the filing of a notice of charges, formal investigative order, service of summons or similar document;

against any "insured" for a "wrongful act", including any appeal therefrom.

4. "Computer program" means a set of related electronic instructions, which direct the operation and function of a computer or devices connected to it, which enables the computer or devices to receive, process, store or send "electronic data".

5. "Computer system" means the following which are owned, leased or operated by you:

a. Computers, including Personal Digital Assistants (PDAs) and other transportable or handheld devices, electronic storage devices and related peripheral components;

b. Systems and applications software; and

c. Related communications networks;

by which "electronic data" is collected, transmitted, processed, stored or retrieved.

6. "Defense expenses" means the reasonable and necessary fees (attorneys' and experts' fees) and expenses incurred in the defense or appeal of a "claim", including the cost of appeal, attachment or similar bonds (without any obligation on our part to obtain such bonds) but excluding wages, salaries, benefits or expenses of your "employees".

7. "E-commerce activities" means those activities conducted by you in the normal conduct of your business via your web site or your e-mail system.

8. "E-commerce incident" means a:

a. "Virus";

b. Malicious code; or

c. Denial of service attack;

introduced into or enacted upon the "computer system" (including "electronic data") or a network to which it is connected, that is designed to damage, destroy, delete, corrupt or prevent the use of or access to any part of the "computer system" or otherwise disrupt its normal operation.

Recurrence of the same "virus" after the "computer system" has been restored shall constitute a separate "e-commerce incident".

9. "Electronic data" means digital information, facts, images or sounds stored as or on, created or used on, or transmitted to or from computer software (including systems and applications software) on electronic storage devices including, but not limited to, hard or floppy disks, CD-ROMs, tapes, drives, cells, data processing devices or any other media which are used with electronically controlled equipment. "Electronic data" is not tangible property.

"Electronic data" does not include your "electronic data" that is licensed, leased, rented or loaned to others.

10. "Employee" means any natural person who was, now is or will be:

a. Employed on a full- or part-time basis;

b. Furnished temporarily to you to substitute for a permanent employee on leave or to meet seasonal or short-term workload conditions;

c. Leased to you by a labor leasing firm under an agreement between you and the labor leasing firm to perform duties related to the conduct of your business, but does not mean a temporary employee as defined in Paragraph **10.b.;**

d. An officer;

e. A director, trustee or manager (if a limited liability company);

f. A volunteer worker; or

g. A partner or member (if a limited liability company);

of the "named insured" and those of any organization qualifying as a "subsidiary" under the terms of this Policy, but only while acting within the scope of their duties as determined by the "named insured" or such "subsidiary".

11. "Extortion expenses" means:

a. Fees and costs of:

(1) A security firm; or

(2) A person or organization;

hired with our consent to determine the validity and severity of an "extortion threat" made against you;

b. Interest costs paid by you for any loan from a financial institution taken by you to pay a ransom demand;

c. Reward money paid by you to an "informant" which leads to the arrest and conviction of parties responsible for "loss"; and

d. Any other reasonable expenses incurred by you with our written consent, including:

(1) Fees and costs of independent negotiators; and

(2) Fees and costs of a company hired by you, upon the recommendation of the security firm, to protect your "electronic data" from further threats.

12. "Extortion threat" means a threat or series of related threats:

a. To perpetrate an "e-commerce incident";

b. To disseminate, divulge or utilize:

(1) Your proprietary information; or

(2) Weaknesses in the source code;

within the "computer system" by gaining unauthorized access to the "computer system";

c. To destroy, corrupt or prevent normal access to the "computer system" by gaining unauthorized access to the "computer system";

d. To inflict "ransomware" on the "computer system" or a network to which it is connected; or

e. To publish your client's "personal information".

13. "Extra expense" means necessary expenses you incur:

a. During an "interruption" that you would not have incurred if there had been no "interruption"; or

b. To avoid or minimize the suspension of your "e-commerce activities".

"Extra expense" does not include any costs or expenses associated with upgrading, maintaining, improving, repairing or remediating any "computer system".

14. "Informant" means a person, other than an "employee", providing information not otherwise obtainable, solely in return for a reward offered by you.

15. "Insured" means any "named insured" and its "employees".

16. "Interrelated wrongful acts" means all "wrongful acts" that have as a common nexus any:

a. Fact, circumstance, situation, event, transaction or cause; or

b. Series of causally connected facts, circumstances, situations, events, transactions or causes.

17. "Interruption" means:

a. With respect to an "e-commerce incident":

(1) An unanticipated cessation or slowdown of your "e-commerce activities"; or

(2) Your suspension of your "e-commerce activities" for the purpose of avoiding or mitigating the possibility of transmitting a "virus" or malicious code to another person or organization;

and, with regard to Paragraphs **17.a.(1)** and **17.a.(2),** shall be deemed to begin when your "e-commerce activities" are interrupted and ends at the earliest of:

(a) 90 days after the "interruption" begins;

(b) The time when your "e-commerce activities" are resumed; or

    (c) The time when service is restored to you.

b. With respect to an "extortion threat", your voluntary suspension of your "e-commerce activities":

    (1) Based upon clear evidence of a credible threat; or

    (2) Based upon the recommendation of a security firm, if any;

and, with regard to Paragraphs **17.b.(1)** and **17.b.(2),** shall be deemed to begin when your "e-commerce activities" are interrupted and ends at the earliest of:

    (a) 14 days after the "interruption" begins;

    (b) The time when your "e-commerce activities" are resumed; or

    (c) The time when service is restored to you.

18. "Loss" means:

a. With respect to Insuring Agreements **1.** Web Site Publishing Liability, **2.** Security Breach Liability and **3.** Programming Errors And Omissions Liability:

    (1) Compensatory damages, settlement amounts and costs awarded pursuant to judgments or settlements;

    (2) Punitive and exemplary damages to the extent such damages are insurable by law; or

    (3) Under Paragraph **b.** of Insuring Agreement **2.** Security Breach Liability, fines or penalties assessed against the "insured" to the extent such fines or penalties are insurable by law.

With regard to Paragraphs **18.a.(1)** through **18.a.(3),** "loss" does not include:

    (a) Civil or criminal fines or penalties imposed by law, except civil fines or penalties as provided under Paragraph **18.a.(3);**

    (b) The multiplied portion of multiplied damages;

    (c) Taxes;

    (d) Royalties;

    (e) The amount of any disgorged profits; or

    (f) Matters that are uninsurable pursuant to law.

b. With respect to Insuring Agreement **4.** Replacement Or Restoration Of Electronic Data:

The cost to replace or restore "electronic data" or "computer programs" as well as the cost of data entry, reprogramming and computer consultation services.

"Loss" does not include the cost to duplicate research that led to the development of your "electronic data" or "computer programs". To the extent that any "electronic data" cannot be replaced or restored, we will pay the cost to replace the media on which the "electronic data" was stored with blank media of substantially identical type.

c. With respect to Insuring Agreement **5.** Extortion Threats:

"Extortion expenses" and "ransom payments".

d. With respect to Insuring Agreement **6.** Business Income And Extra Expense:

The actual loss of "business income" you sustain and/or "extra expense" you incur.

e. With respect to Insuring Agreement **7.** Public Relations Expense:

"Public relations expenses".

f. With respect to Insuring Agreement **8.** Security Breach Expense:

"Security breach expenses".

19. "Named insured" means the entity or entities shown in the Declarations and any "subsidiary".

20. "Negative publicity" means information which has been made public that has caused, or is reasonably likely to cause, a decline or deterioration in the reputation of the "named insured" or of one or more of its products or services.

21. "Personal information" means any information not available to the general public for any reason through which an individual may be identified including, but not limited to, an individual's:

a. Social security number, driver's license number or state identification number;

b. Protected health information;

c. Financial account numbers;

d. Security codes, passwords, PINs associated with credit, debit or charge card numbers which would permit access to financial accounts; or

e. Any other nonpublic information as defined in "privacy regulations".

22. "Policy period" means the period of time from the inception date of this Policy shown in the Declarations to the expiration date shown in the Declarations, or its earlier cancellation or termination date.

23. "Pollutants" means any solid, liquid, gaseous or thermal irritant or contaminant, including smoke, vapor, soot, fumes, acids, alkalis, chemicals and waste. Waste includes materials to be recycled, reconditioned or reclaimed.

24. "Privacy regulations" means any of the following statutes and regulations, and their amendments, associated with the control and use of personally identifiable financial, health or other sensitive information including, but not limited to:

   a. The Health Insurance Portability and Accountability Act of 1996 (HIPAA) (Public Law 104-191);

   b. The Health Information Technology for Economic and Clinical Health Act (HITECH) (American Recovery and Reinvestment Act of 2009);

   c. The Gramm-Leach-Bliley Act of 1999;

   d. Section 5(a) of the Federal Trade Commission Act (15 U.S.C. 45(a)), but solely for alleged unfair or deceptive acts or practices in or affecting commerce;

   e. The Identity Theft Red Flags Rules under the Fair and Accurate Credit Transactions Act of 2003; or

   f. Any other similar state, federal or foreign identity theft or privacy protection statute or regulation.

25. "Public relations expenses" means:

   a. Fees and costs of a public relations firm; and

   b. Any other reasonable expenses incurred by you with our written consent;

   to protect or restore your reputation solely in response to "negative publicity".

26. "Ransom payment" means a payment made in the form of cash.

27. "Ransomware" means any software that encrypts "electronic data" held within the "computer system" and demands a "ransom payment" in order to decrypt and restore such "electronic data".

28. "Regulatory proceeding" means an investigation, demand or proceeding brought by, or on behalf of, the Federal Trade Commission, Federal Communications Commission or other administrative or regulatory agency, or any federal, state, local or foreign governmental entity in such entity's regulatory or official capacity.

29. "Security breach" means the acquisition of "personal information" held within the "computer system" or in nonelectronic format while in the care, custody or control of the "insured" or authorized "third party" by a person:

   a. Who is not authorized to have access to such information; or

   b. Who is authorized to have access to such information but whose access results in the unauthorized disclosure of such information.

30. "Security breach expenses" means:

   a. Costs to establish whether a "security breach" has occurred or is occurring;

   b. Costs to investigate the cause, scope and extent of a "security breach" and to identify any affected parties;

   c. Costs to determine any action necessary to correct or remediate the conditions that led to or resulted from a "security breach";

   d. Costs to notify all parties affected by a "security breach";

   e. Overtime salaries paid to "employees" assigned to handle inquiries from the parties affected by a "security breach";

   f. Fees and costs of a company hired by you for the purpose of operating a call center to handle inquiries from the parties affected by a "security breach";

   g. Post-event credit monitoring costs for the parties affected by a "security breach" for up to one year from the date of notification to those affected parties of such "security breach"; and

   h. Any other reasonable expenses incurred by you with our written consent.

   "Security breach expenses" do not include any costs or expenses associated with upgrading, maintaining, improving, repairing or remediating any "computer system" as a result of a "security breach".

31. "Subsidiary" means any organization in which more than 50% of the outstanding securities or voting rights representing the present right to vote for the election of directors, trustees, managers (if a limited liability company) or persons serving in a similar capacity is owned, in any combination, by one or more "named insured(s)".

32. "Suit" means a civil proceeding in which damages to which this Policy applies are claimed against the "insured". "Suit" includes:

   a. An arbitration proceeding in which such damages are claimed and to which the "insured" submits with our consent; or

        EC 00 10 01 14

b. Any other alternative dispute resolution proceeding in which such damages are claimed and to which the "insured" submits with our consent.

"Suit" does not include a civil proceeding seeking recognition and/or enforcement of a foreign money judgment.

33. "Third party" means any entity that you engage under the terms of a written contract to perform services for you.

34. "Virus" means any kind of malicious code designed to damage or destroy any part of the "computer system" (including "electronic data") or disrupt its normal functioning.

35. "Wrongful act" means:

a. With respect to Insuring Agreement **1.** Web Site Publishing Liability:

Any actual or alleged error, misstatement or misleading statement posted or published by an "insured" on its web site that results in:

(1) Any type of infringement of another's copyright, title, slogan, trademark, trade name, trade dress, service mark or service name;

(2) Any form of defamation against a person or organization; or

(3) A violation of a person's right of privacy.

b. With respect to Insuring Agreement **2.** Security Breach Liability:

Any actual or alleged neglect, breach of duty or omission by an "insured" that results in:

(1) A "security breach"; or

(2) A "computer system" transmitting, by e-mail or other means, a "virus" to another person or organization.

c. With respect to Insuring Agreement **3.** Programming Errors And Omissions Liability:

Any actual or alleged programming error or omission that results in the disclosure of your client's "personal information" held within the "computer system".

MEDIA AND INFORMATION
SECURITY PROTECTION POLICY

INSURING AGREEMENTS 2. AND 3. OF THIS POLICY PROVIDE CLAIMS-MADE COVERAGE. DEFENSE EXPENSES ARE PAYABLE WITHIN, AND NOT IN ADDITION TO, THE LIMIT OF INSURANCE. PAYMENT OF DEFENSE EXPENSES UNDER THIS POLICY WILL REDUCE THE LIMIT OF INSURANCE.

PLEASE READ THE ENTIRE POLICY CAREFULLY.

Various provisions in this Policy restrict coverage. Read the entire Policy carefully to determine rights, duties and what is and is not covered.

Throughout this Policy the words "you" and "your" refer to the "named insured" shown in the Declarations. The words "we", "us" and "our" refer to the company providing this insurance.

Other words and phrases that appear in quotation marks have special meaning. Refer to Section **VII** – Definitions.

SECTION I – INSURING AGREEMENTS

Coverage is provided under the following Insuring Agreements for which an Aggregate Limit Of Insurance is shown in the Declarations:

1. Media Liability

We will pay for both "loss" that the "insured" becomes legally obligated to pay and "defense expenses" as a result of a "wrongful act" or a series of "interrelated wrongful acts" that occur during the "policy period" which gives rise to a "claim", regardless of when the "claim" is made.

2. Security Breach Liability

a. We will pay for both "loss" that the "insured" becomes legally obligated to pay and "defense expenses" as a result of a "claim" first made against the "insured" during the "policy period" or during the applicable Extended Reporting Period, for a "wrongful act" or a series of "interrelated wrongful acts" taking place on or after the Retroactive Date, if any, shown in the Declarations and before the end of the "policy period".

b. We will pay for both "loss" and "defense expenses" as a result of a "claim" in the form of a "regulatory proceeding" first made against the "insured" during the "policy period" or during the applicable Extended Reporting Period, in response to a "wrongful act" or a series of "interrelated wrongful acts" covered under Paragraph **2.a.**

3. Programming Errors And Omissions Liability

We will pay for both "loss" that the "insured" becomes legally obligated to pay and "defense expenses" as a result of a "claim" first made against the "insured" during the "policy period" or during the applicable Extended Reporting Period, for a "wrongful act" or a series of "interrelated wrongful acts" taking place on or after the Retroactive Date, if any, shown in the Declarations and before the end of the "policy period".

4. Replacement Or Restoration Of Electronic Data

We will pay for "loss" of "electronic data" or "computer programs" stored within the "computer system" resulting directly from an "e-commerce incident" sustained during the "policy period".

5. Extortion Threats

We will pay for "loss" resulting directly from an "extortion threat" communicated to you during the "policy period".

However, we will not pay for "extortion expenses" or "ransom payments" which are part of a series of related threats that began prior to the "policy period".

6. Business Income And Extra Expense

We will pay for "loss" due to an "interruption" resulting directly from an "e-commerce incident" sustained during the "policy period" or an "extortion threat" communicated to you during the "policy period".

7. Public Relations Expense

We will pay for "loss" due to "negative publicity" resulting directly from an "e-commerce incident" or a "security breach" sustained during the "policy period".

8. Security Breach Expense

We will pay for "loss" resulting directly from a "security breach" sustained during the "policy period".

SECTION II – LIMITS OF INSURANCE

1. Policy Aggregate Limit Of Insurance

The most we will pay for all "loss", and "defense expenses" if covered, under this Policy is the Policy Aggregate Limit Of Insurance shown in the Declarations. The Policy Aggregate Limit of Insurance shall be reduced by the amount of any payment made under the terms of this Policy. Upon exhaustion of the Policy Aggregate Limit of Insurance by such payments, we will have no further obligations or liability of any kind under this Policy.

2. Insuring Agreement Aggregate Limit Of Insurance

a. Subject to the Policy Aggregate Limit of Insurance, the most we will pay for all "loss", and "defense expenses" if covered, under each Insuring Agreement, is the Insuring Agreement Aggregate Limit Of Insurance shown in the Declarations:

(1) The Insuring Agreement Aggregate Limit of Insurance shall be reduced by the amount of any payment for "loss", and "defense expenses" if covered, under that Insuring Agreement; and

(2) Upon exhaustion of the Insuring Agreement Aggregate Limit of Insurance by such payments, we will have no further obligations or liability of any kind under that Insuring Agreement.

b. If coverage for "regulatory proceedings" is being provided under Paragraph **b.** of Insuring Agreement **2.** Security Breach Liability, the Limit of Insurance shall be part of, not in addition to, the Aggregate Limit of Insurance for the Insuring Agreement.

SECTION III – DEDUCTIBLE

1. Subject to Section **II** – Limits Of Insurance:

a. Under Insuring Agreements **1.** Media Liability, **2.** Security Breach Liability and **3.** Programming Errors And Omissions Liability:

We will pay only the amount of "loss" and "defense expenses" which are in excess of the applicable Deductible Amount shown in the Declarations resulting from the same "wrongful act" or "interrelated wrongful acts". Such Deductible Amount will be borne by you, self-insured, and at your own risk.

b. Under Insuring Agreements **4.** Replacement Or Restoration Of Electronic Data, **5.** Extortion Threats, **7.** Public Relations Expense and **8.** Security Breach Expense:

We will pay only the amount of "loss" which is in excess of the applicable Deductible Amount shown in the Declarations.

c. Under Insuring Agreement **6.** Business Income And Extra Expense:

We will pay only the amount of "loss" which exceeds the greater of:

(1) The Deductible Amount shown in the Declarations; or

(2) The amount of "loss" incurred during the Waiting Period shown in the Declarations.

2. In the event a "loss" is covered under more than one Insuring Agreement, only the highest Deductible Amount applicable to the "loss" shall be applied.

SECTION IV – DEFENSE AND SETTLEMENT

The provisions contained within this section apply only to Insuring Agreements **1.** Media Liability, **2.** Security Breach Liability and **3.** Programming Errors And Omissions Liability:

1. We shall have the right and duty to select counsel and defend the "insured" against any "claim" covered under Insuring Agreements **1.** Media Liability, **2.** Security Breach Liability and **3.** Programming Errors And Omissions Liability, even if the allegations of such "claim" are groundless, false or fraudulent. However, we shall have the right but not the duty to defend the "insured" against a "claim" covered under Paragraph **b.** of Insuring Agreement **2.** Security Breach Liability, and we shall have no duty to defend the "insured" against any "claim" which is not covered under any of these Insuring Agreements.

2. We may, upon the written consent of the "insured", make any settlement of a "claim" which we deem reasonable. If the "insured" withholds consent to such settlement, our liability for all "loss" resulting from such "claim" will not exceed the amount for which we could have settled such "claim", plus "defense expenses" incurred, as of the date we proposed such settlement in writing to the "insured". Upon refusing to consent to a settlement we deem reasonable, the "insured" shall, at its sole expense, assume all further responsibility for its defense, including all additional costs associated with the investigation, defense and/or settlement of such "claim".

  EC 00 12 01 14

SECTION V – EXCLUSIONS

We will not be liable for "loss" or "defense expenses":

1. Based upon, attributable to or arising out of lightning, earthquake, hail, volcanic action or any other act of nature.

2. Based upon, attributable to or arising out of:

    a. War, including undeclared or civil war or civil unrest;

    b. Warlike action by military force, including action hindering or defending against an actual or expected attack, by any government, sovereign or other authority using military personnel or other agents; or

    c. Insurrection, rebellion, revolution, usurped power, or action taken by government authority in hindering or defending against any of these.

3. Based upon, attributable to or arising out of the dispersal or application of pathogenic or poisonous biological or chemical materials, nuclear reaction, nuclear radiation or radioactive contamination, or any related act or incident, however caused.

4. Based upon, attributable to or arising out of bodily injury or physical damage to or destruction of tangible property, including loss of use thereof.

    Bodily injury means bodily injury, sickness or disease sustained by a person, including death resulting from any of these at any time.

5. Based upon, attributable to or arising out of any unexplained or indeterminable failure, malfunction or slowdown of the "computer system", including "electronic data" and the inability to access or properly manipulate the "electronic data".

6. Based upon, attributable to or arising out of any "interruption" in normal computer function or network service or function due to insufficient capacity to process transactions or due to an overload of activity on the "computer system" or network. However, this exclusion shall not apply if such "interruption" is caused by an "e-commerce incident".

7. Based upon, attributable to or arising out of a complete or substantial failure, disablement or shutdown of the Internet, regardless of the cause.

8. Based upon, attributable to or arising out of any failure of, reduction in or surge of power.

9. Based upon, attributable to or arising out of any actual or alleged violation of the Racketeer Influenced and Corrupt Organizations Act (RICO) and its amendments, or similar provisions of any federal, state or local statutory or common law.

10. Based upon, attributable to or arising out of any malfunction or failure of any satellite.

11. Based upon, attributable to or arising out of any oral or written publication of material, if done by an "insured" or at an "insured's" direction with knowledge of its falsity.

12. Based upon, attributable to or arising out of an "insured's" assumption of liability by contract or agreement, whether oral or written. However, this exclusion shall not apply to:

    a. Any liability that an "insured" would have incurred in the absence of such contract or agreement; or

    b. Breach of any written, oral or implied-in-fact indemnification or hold harmless agreement between an "insured" and any person or organization distributing "content" by or on behalf of the "insured".

13. Based upon, attributable to or arising out of any actual or alleged patent or trade secret violation, including any actual or alleged violation of the Patent Act, the Economic Espionage Act of 1996 or the Uniform Trade Secrets Act and their amendments.

14. Based upon, attributable to or arising out of:

    a. The actual, alleged or threatened discharge, dispersal, seepage, migration, release or escape of "pollutants" at any time;

    b. Any request, demand, order or statutory or regulatory requirement that any "insured" or others test for, monitor, clean up, remove, contain, treat, detoxify or neutralize, or in any way respond to, or assess the effects of, "pollutants"; or

    c. Any "claim" or "suit" brought by, or on behalf of, any governmental authority for damages because of testing for, monitoring, cleaning up, removing, containing, treating, detoxifying or neutralizing, or in any way responding to, or assessing the effects of, "pollutants".

15. Based upon, attributable to or arising out of any "claim", "suit" or other proceeding against an "insured" which was pending or existed prior to the "policy period", or arising out of the same or substantially the same facts, circumstances or allegations which are the subject of, or the basis for, such "claim", "suit" or other proceeding.

16. Based upon, attributable to or arising out of an "insured's" employment practices including, but not limited to, termination of employment, demotion, reassignment, discipline, harassment, coercion or refusal to employ regardless of whether the "insured" is liable as an employer or in any other capacity.

17. Based upon, attributable to or arising out of any "wrongful act" or "interrelated wrongful acts" that occurred before the Retroactive Date, if any, shown in the Declarations.

18. Based upon, attributable to or arising out of the same facts, "wrongful acts" or "interrelated wrongful acts" alleged or contained in any "claim" which has been reported, or in any circumstances of which notice has been given, under any insurance policy of which this Policy is a renewal or replacement.

19. Based upon, attributable to or arising out of any criminal, dishonest, malicious or fraudulent act or any willful violation of any statute or regulation committed by an "insured", acting alone or in collusion with others. However, this exclusion shall not apply to dishonest, malicious or fraudulent acts committed by an "employee" which give rise to a "claim" or "loss" covered under Insuring Agreement **2.** Security Breach Liability.

With the exception of "claims" excluded under Exclusion **13.,** we will defend "claims" first made against an "insured" alleging such acts or violations until final adjudication is rendered against that "insured". Final adjudication rendered against one "insured" shall not be imputed to any other "insured".

We will not provide indemnification for any "claim" to which any "insured" enters a guilty plea or pleads no contest, and we will not provide a defense from the time we become aware that any "insured" intends to so plead.

20. Based upon, attributable to or arising out of any action or proceeding brought by, or on behalf of, any governmental authority or regulatory agency including, but not limited to:

    a. The seizure or destruction of property by order of a governmental authority; or

    b. Regulatory actions or proceedings brought by, or on behalf of, the Federal Trade Commission, Federal Communications Commission or other regulatory agency, except when covered under Paragraph **b.** of Insuring Agreement **2.** Security Breach Liability.

    However, this exclusion shall not apply to actions or proceedings brought by a governmental authority or a regulatory agency acting solely in its capacity as a customer of the "named insured" or of a "subsidiary".

21. Based upon, attributable to or arising out of costs associated with upgrading or improving the "computer system" regardless of the reason for the upgrade.

22. Based upon, attributable to or arising out of any "claim" brought or alleged by one "insured" against another, except for a "claim" brought or alleged by an "employee" against an "insured" as a result of a "security breach".

23. Based upon, attributable to or arising out of unintentional errors or omissions in the entry of "electronic data" into the "computer system".

24. Based upon, attributable to or arising out of any actual or alleged violation of price fixing, restraint of trade, monopolization or unfair trade or any violation of the Sherman Act, the Clayton Act or any similar provision of any federal, state or local statutory or common law not related to a "wrongful act" as defined in Paragraphs **39.a.(6)** and **39.a.(7)** of the definition of "wrongful act".

25. Based upon, attributable to or arising out of any direct or indirect publicity or promotion of tickets, coupons or prizes for any contest, lottery, sweepstakes, promotion or game of chance, including "over-redemption" relating therefrom.

26. Based upon, attributable to or arising out of any "claim" brought by, or on behalf of, the ASCAP, SESAC, BMI, RIAA or any similar licensing organization.

27. Based upon, attributable to or arising out of any unauthorized or unsolicited transmission or dissemination of electronic mail, telefacsimile or telephone call.

28. Based upon, attributable to or arising out of any "claim" brought by, or on behalf of, an independent contractor for or resulting from a dispute over the ownership of "content" or services supplied by the independent contractor.

SECTION VI – CONDITIONS

1. Cancellation

    a. The first "named insured" shown in the Declarations may cancel this Policy by mailing or delivering to us advance written notice of cancellation.

    b. We may cancel this Policy by mailing or delivering to the first "named insured" written notice of cancellation at least:

       (1) 10 days before the effective date of cancellation if we cancel for nonpayment of premium; or

       (2) 30 days before the effective date of cancellation if we cancel for any other reason.

    c. We will mail or deliver our notice to the first "named insured's" last mailing address known to us.

d. Notice of cancellation will state the effective date of cancellation. The "policy period" will end on that date.

e. If this Policy is canceled, we will send the first "named insured" any premium refund due. If we cancel, the refund will be prorated. If the first "named insured" cancels, the refund may be less than pro rata. The cancellation will be effective even if we have not made or offered a refund.

f. If notice is mailed, proof of mailing will be sufficient proof of notice.

2. Changes

This Policy contains all the agreements between you and us concerning the insurance afforded. The first "named insured" shown in the Declarations is authorized to make changes in the terms of this Policy with our consent. This Policy's terms can be amended or waived only by endorsement issued by us and made a part of this Policy.

3. Examination Of Your Books And Records

We may examine and audit your books and records as they relate to this Policy at any time during the "policy period" and up to three years afterward.

4. Inspections And Surveys

a. We have the right to:

   (1) Make inspections and surveys at any time;

   (2) Give you reports on the conditions we find; and

   (3) Recommend changes.

b. We are not obligated to make any inspections, surveys, reports or recommendations and any such actions we do undertake relate only to insurability and the premiums to be charged. We do not make safety inspections. We do not undertake to perform the duty of any person or organization to provide for the health or safety of workers or the public. And we do not warrant that conditions:

   (1) Are safe or healthful; or

   (2) Comply with laws, regulations, codes or standards.

c. Paragraphs **4.a.** and **4.b.** of this condition apply not only to us, but also to any rating, advisory, rate service or similar organization which makes insurance inspections, surveys, reports or recommendations.

5. Premiums

The first "named insured" shown in the Declarations:

a. Is responsible for the payment of all premiums; and

b. Will be the payee for any return premiums we pay.

6. Transfer Of Your Rights And Duties Under This Policy

Your rights and duties under this Policy may not be transferred without our written consent, except in the case of death of an individual "named insured".

If you are a sole proprietor and you die, your rights and duties will be transferred to your legal representative but only while acting within the scope of duties as your legal representative. Until your legal representative is appointed, anyone having proper temporary custody of your property will have your rights and duties but only with respect to that property.

7. Subrogation

With respect to any payment made under this Policy on behalf of any "insured", we shall be subrogated to the "insured's" rights of recovery to the extent of such payment. The "insured" shall execute all papers required and shall do everything necessary to secure and preserve such rights, including the execution of such documents necessary to enable us to bring suit in the "insured's" name. Any recoveries, less the cost of obtaining them, will be distributed as follows:

a. To you, until you are reimbursed for any "loss" you sustain that exceeds the sum of the applicable Aggregate Limit of Insurance and the Deductible Amount, if any;

b. Then to us, until we are reimbursed for the payment made under this Policy; and

c. Then to you, until you are reimbursed for that part of the payment equal to the Deductible Amount, if any.

8. Bankruptcy

Your bankruptcy, or the bankruptcy of your estate if you are a sole proprietor, will not relieve us of our obligations under this Policy.

9. Representations

You represent that all information and statements contained in the "application" are true, accurate and complete. All such information and statements are the basis for our issuing this Policy and shall be considered as incorporated into and shall constitute a part of this Policy. Misrepresentation of any material fact may be grounds for the rescission of this Policy.

10. Changes In Exposure

a. Acquisition Or Creation Of Another Organization

If before or during the "policy period":

(1) You acquire securities or voting rights in another organization or create another organization which, as a result of such acquisition or creation, becomes a "subsidiary"; or

(2) You acquire any organization through merger or consolidation;

then such organization will be covered under this Policy but only with respect to "wrongful acts" or "loss" which occurred after the effective date of such acquisition or creation provided, with regard to Paragraphs **10.a.(1)** and **10.a.(2),** you:

(a) Give us written notice of the acquisition or creation of such organization within 90 days after the effective date of such action;

(b) Obtain our written consent to extend the coverage provided by this Policy to such organization; and

(c) Upon obtaining our consent, pay us an additional premium.

b. Acquisition Of Named Insured

If during the "policy period":

(1) The "named insured" merges into or consolidates with another organization, such that the "named insured" is not the surviving organization; or

(2) Another organization, or person or group of organizations and/or persons acting in concert, acquires securities or voting rights which result in ownership or voting control by the other organization(s) or person(s) of more than 50% of the outstanding securities or voting rights representing the present right to vote for the election of directors, trustees or managers (if a limit liability company) of the "named insured";

then the coverage afforded under this Policy will continue until the end of the "policy period", but only with respect to "claims" arising out of "wrongful acts" or "loss" which occurred prior to the effective date of such merger, consolidation or acquisition.

The full annual premium for the "policy period" will be deemed to be fully earned immediately upon the occurrence of such merger, consolidation or acquisition of the "named insured".

The "named insured" must give written notice of such merger, consolidation or acquisition to us as soon as practicable, together with such information as we may reasonably require.

c. Cessation Of Subsidiaries

If before or during the "policy period" an organization ceases to be a "subsidiary", the coverage afforded under this Policy with respect to such "subsidiary" will continue until the end of the "policy period" but only with respect to "claims" arising out of "wrongful acts" or "loss" which occurred prior to the date such organization ceased to be a "subsidiary".

11. Other Insurance

a. If any covered "claim" or "loss" is insured by any other valid policy, then this Policy shall apply only in excess of the amount of any deductible, retention and limit of insurance under such other policy, whether such other policy is stated to be primary, contributory, excess, contingent or otherwise, unless such other policy is written specifically excess of this Policy by reference in such other policy to this Policy's policy number.

b. When this Policy is excess, we shall have no duty under Insuring Agreement **1.** Media Liability, **2.** Security Breach Liability or **3.** Programming Errors And Omissions Liability to defend the "insured" against any "suit" if any other insurer has a duty to defend the "insured" against that "suit". If no other insurer defends, we will undertake to do so, but we will be entitled to the "insured's" rights against all those other insurers.

12. Legal Action Against Us

a. No person or organization has a right:

(1) To join us as a party or otherwise bring us into a "suit" asking for damages from an "insured"; or

(2) To sue us under this Policy unless all of its terms have been fully complied with.

A person or organization may sue us to recover on an agreed settlement or on a final judgment against an "insured", but we will not be liable for damages that are not payable under Insuring Agreement **1.** Media Liability, **2.** Security Breach Liability or **3.** Programming Errors And Omissions Liability, or that are in excess of the applicable Aggregate Limit of Insurance. An agreed settlement means a settlement and release of liability signed by us, the first "named insured" and the claimant or the claimant's legal representative.

b. You may not bring any legal action against us involving "loss":

(1) Unless you have complied with all the terms of this Policy;

(2) Until 90 days after you have filed proof of loss with us; and

(3) Unless brought within two years from the date you reported the "loss" to us.

If any limitation in this condition is prohibited by law, such limitation is amended so as to equal the minimum period of limitation provided by such law.

13. Separation Of Insureds

Except with respect to the applicable Aggregate Limit of Insurance, and any rights or duties specifically assigned in Insuring Agreement **1.** Media Liability, **2.** Security Breach Liability or **3.** Programming Errors And Omissions Liability to the first "named insured", this Policy applies separately to each "insured" against whom "claim" is made.

14. Duties In The Event Of Claim Or Loss

In the event of either an occurrence or offense that may result in a "claim" against an "insured" or a "loss" or situation that may result in a "loss" covered under this Policy, you must notify us in writing as soon as practicable, but not to exceed 30 days, and cooperate with us in the investigation and settlement of the "claim" or "loss". Additionally:

a. Under Insuring Agreements **1.** Media Liability, **2.** Security Breach Liability and **3.** Programming Errors And Omissions Liability, you must:

(1) Immediately record the specifics of the "claim" and the date received;

(2) Immediately send us copies of any demands, notices, summonses or legal papers received in connection with the "claim";

(3) Authorize us to obtain records and other information; and

(4) Assist us, upon our request, in the enforcement of any right against any person or organization which may be liable to you because of an occurrence or offense to which this Policy may also apply.

You will not, except at your own cost, voluntarily make a payment, assume any obligation or incur any expense without our consent.

A "claim" brought by a person or organization seeking damages will be deemed to have been made when the "claim" is received by an "insured".

b. Under Insuring Agreements **4.** Replacement Or Restoration Of Electronic Data and **5.** Extortion Threats, you must:

(1) Notify local law enforcement officials;

(2) Submit to examination under oath at our request and give us a signed statement of your answers; and

(3) Give us a detailed, sworn proof of loss within 120 days.

(4) In addition, under Insuring Agreement **5.** Extortion Threats, you must:

(a) Determine that the "extortion threat" has actually occurred;

(b) Make every reasonable effort to immediately notify an associate and the security firm, if any, before making any "ransom payment" based upon the "extortion threat"; and

(c) Approve any "ransom payment" based upon the "extortion threat".

15. Valuation – Settlement

a. All premiums, Aggregate Limits of Insurance, Deductible Amounts, "loss" and any other monetary amounts under this Policy are expressed and payable in the currency of the United States of America. If judgment is rendered, settlement is agreed to or another component of "loss" under this Policy is expressed in any currency other than United States of America dollars, payment under this Policy shall be made in United States dollars at the rate of exchange published in The Wall Street Journal on the date the final judgment is entered, settlement amount is agreed upon or the other component of "loss" is due, respectively.

b. With respect to "loss" covered under Insuring Agreement **6.** Business Income And Extra Expense:

(1) The amount of "business income" will be determined based on consideration of:

(a) The net income generated from your "e-commerce activities" before the "interruption" occurred;

(b) The likely net income generated by your "e-commerce activities" if no "interruption" had occurred, but not including any net income that would likely have been earned as a result of an increase in the volume of business due to favorable business conditions caused by the impact of the "e-commerce incident" on customers or on other businesses;

(c) The operating expenses, including payroll, necessary to resume your "e-commerce activities" with the same quality of service that existed before the "interruption"; and

(d) Other relevant sources of information, including your financial records and accounting procedures, bills, invoices and other vouchers, and debts, liens and contracts.

However, the amount of "business income" will be reduced to the extent that the reduction in the volume of business from the affected "e-commerce activities" is offset by an increase in the volume of business from other channels of commerce such as via telephone, mail or other sources.

(2) The amount of "extra expense" will be determined based on:

(a) Necessary expenses that exceed the normal operating expenses that would have been incurred in the course of your "e-commerce activities" during the period of coverage if no "interruption" had occurred. We will deduct from the total of such expenses the salvage value that remains of any property bought for temporary use during the period of coverage once your "e-commerce activities" are resumed; and

(b) Necessary expenses that reduce the "business income" "loss" that otherwise would have been incurred during the period of coverage.

16. Extended Reporting Periods

The provisions contained within this condition apply only to Insuring Agreements **2.** Security Breach Liability and **3.** Programming Errors And Omissions Liability.

a. Basic Extended Reporting Period

(1) A Basic Extended Reporting Period is automatically provided without additional charge. This period starts with the end of the "policy period" and lasts for 30 days. A "claim" first made and reported by the "insured" during this 30-day period will be considered to have been received within the "policy period". However, the 30-day Basic Extended Reporting Period does not apply to "claims" that are covered under any subsequent insurance purchased by the "insured", or that would be covered but for exhaustion of the Aggregate Limit of Insurance applicable to such "claims".

(2) The Basic Extended Reporting Period does not extend the "policy period" or change the scope of coverage provided. It applies only to "claims" to which the following applies:

(a) The "claim" is first made and reported to us during the Basic Extended Reporting Period; and

(b) The "claim" arose out of either a "wrongful act" or the first of a series of "interrelated wrongful acts" which occurred on or after the Retroactive Date, if any, shown in the Declarations and before the end of the "policy period".

b. Supplemental Extended Reporting Period

(1) A Supplemental Extended Reporting Period is available if this Policy is canceled or not renewed by either you or us, but only by endorsement and for an extra charge. The Supplemental Extended Reporting Period starts when the Basic Extended Reporting Period set forth in Paragraph **16.a.** ends. The Supplemental Extended Reporting Period is available unless:

(a) We cancel this Policy for nonpayment of premium; or

(b) You fail to pay any amounts owed us.

(2) In order to obtain a Supplemental Extended Reporting Period, you must give us a written request for the Supplemental Extended Reporting Period Endorsement together with the full payment of the additional premium for the endorsement within 30 days after the end of the "policy period". The Supplemental Extended Reporting Period will not go into effect unless you pay the additional premium promptly when due.

(3) The Supplemental Extended Reporting Period does not extend the "policy period" or change the scope of coverage provided. It applies only to "claims" to which the following applies:

(a) The "claim" is first made and reported to us during the Supplemental Extended Reporting Period; and

(b) The "claim" arose out of either a "wrongful act" or the first of a series of "interrelated wrongful acts" which occurred on or after the Retroactive Date, if any, shown in the Declarations and before the end of the "policy period".

(4) Once in effect, the Supplemental Extended Reporting Period may not be canceled. The premium for the Supplemental Extended Reporting Period Endorsement will be deemed to be fully earned as of the date it is purchased.

c. There is no separate or additional Aggregate Limit of Insurance for the Basic Extended Reporting Period or the Supplemental Extended Reporting Period. The limit of insurance available during the Basic Extended Reporting Period, and the Supplemental Extended Reporting Period if purchased, shall be the remaining amount, if any, of the Aggregate Limit of Insurance of the respective Insuring Agreement, subject to the remaining amount of the Policy Aggregate Limit of Insurance at the time this Policy was canceled or nonrenewed.

17. Confidentiality

No "insured" shall be prejudiced by any "insured's" refusal to maintain or divulge the identity of a source or the failure to portray a source in a certain manner or light.

Under Insuring Agreement **5.** Extortion Threats, "insureds" must make every reasonable effort not to divulge the existence of this coverage.

18. Territory

This Policy covers "wrongful acts" which occurred anywhere in the world. However, "suits" must be brought in the United States of America (including its territories and possessions), Puerto Rico or Canada.

SECTION VII – DEFINITIONS

1. "Advertising" means the use of "media" to persuade an audience to purchase or take some action upon products, services or ideas.

2. "Application" means the signed application for this Policy, including any attachments and other materials submitted in conjunction with the signed application.

3. "Business income" means the:

a. Net income (net profit or loss before income taxes) that would have been earned or incurred; and

b. Continuing normal operating expenses incurred, including payroll.

4. "Claim" means:

a. A written demand for monetary or nonmonetary damages, including injunctive relief;

b. A civil proceeding commenced by the service of a complaint or similar proceeding;

c. A written demand for retraction of "content" posted, published, disseminated or released by an "insured";

d. A subpoena seeking "content" or the identity of an external source that supplies information or "content" to an "insured" in confidence; or

e. Under Paragraph **b.** of Insuring Agreement **2.** Security Breach Liability, a "regulatory proceeding" commenced by the filing of a notice of charges, formal investigative order, service of summons or similar document;

against any "insured" for a "wrongful act", including any appeal therefrom.

5. "Computer program" means a set of related electronic instructions, which direct the operation and function of a computer or devices connected to it, which enables the computer or devices to receive, process, store or send "electronic data".

6. "Computer system" means the following which are owned, leased or operated by you:

a. Computers, including Personal Digital Assistants (PDAs) and other transportable or handheld devices, electronic storage devices and related peripheral components;

b. Systems and applications software; and

c. Related communications networks;

by which "electronic data" is collected, transmitted, processed, stored or retrieved.

7. "Content" means any type of communicative or informational material, regardless of its nature or form, including material disseminated electronically, such as via a web site or electronic mail.

8. "Defense expenses" means the reasonable and necessary fees (attorneys' and experts' fees) and expenses incurred in the defense or appeal of a "claim", including the cost of appeal, attachment or similar bonds (without any obligation on our part to obtain such bonds) but excluding wages, salaries, benefits or expenses of your "employees".

9. "E-commerce activities" means those activities conducted by you in the normal conduct of your business via your web site or your e-mail system.

10. "E-commerce incident" means a:

   a. "Virus";

   b. Malicious code; or

   c. Denial of service attack;

introduced into or enacted upon the "computer system" (including "electronic data") or a network to which it is connected, that is designed to damage, destroy, delete, corrupt or prevent the use of or access to any part of the "computer system" or otherwise disrupt its normal operation.

Recurrence of the same "virus" after the "computer system" has been restored shall constitute a separate "e-commerce incident".

11. "Electronic data" means digital information, facts, images or sounds stored as or on, created or used on, or transmitted to or from computer software (including systems and applications software) on electronic storage devices including, but not limited to, hard or floppy disks, CD-ROMs, tapes, drives, cells, data processing devices or any other media which are used with electronically controlled equipment. "Electronic data" is not tangible property.

"Electronic data" does not include your "electronic data" that is licensed, leased, rented or loaned to others.

12. "Employee" means any natural person who was, now is or will be:

   a. Employed on a full- or part-time basis;

   b. Furnished temporarily to you to substitute for a permanent employee on leave or to meet seasonal or short-term workload conditions;

   c. Leased to you by a labor leasing firm under an agreement between you and the labor leasing firm to perform duties related to the conduct of your business, but does not mean a temporary "employee" as defined in Paragraph **12.b.**;

   d. An officer;

   e. A director, trustee or manager (if a limited liability company);

   f. A volunteer worker; or

   g. A partner or member (if a limited liability company);

of the "named insured" and those of any organization qualifying as a "subsidiary" under the terms of this Policy, but only while acting within the scope of their duties as determined by the "named insured" or such "subsidiary".

13. "Extortion expenses" means:

   a. Fees and costs of:

      (1) A security firm; or

      (2) A person or organization;

   hired with our consent to determine the validity and severity of an "extortion threat" made against you;

   b. Interest costs paid by you for any loan from a financial institution taken by you to pay a ransom demand;

   c. Reward money paid by you to an "informant" which leads to the arrest and conviction of parties responsible for "loss"; and

   d. Any other reasonable expenses incurred by you with our written consent, including:

      (1) Fees and costs of independent negotiators; and

      (2) Fees and costs of a company hired by you, upon the recommendation of the security firm, to protect your "electronic data" from further threats.

14. "Extortion threat" means a threat or series of related threats:

   a. To perpetrate an "e-commerce incident";

   b. To disseminate, divulge or utilize:

      (1) Your proprietary information; or

      (2) Weaknesses in the source code;

   within the "computer system" by gaining unauthorized access to the "computer system";

   c. To destroy, corrupt or prevent normal access to the "computer system" by gaining unauthorized access to the "computer system";

d. To inflict "ransomware" on the "computer system" or a network to which it is connected; or

e. To publish your client's "personal information".

15. "Extra expense" means necessary expenses you incur:

a. During an "interruption" that you would not have incurred if there had been no "interruption"; or

b. To avoid or minimize the suspension of your "e-commerce activities".

"Extra expense" does not include any costs or expenses associated with upgrading, maintaining, improving, repairing or remediating any "computer system".

16. "Informant" means a person, other than an "employee", providing information not otherwise obtainable, solely in return for a reward offered by you.

17. "Insured" means any "named insured" and its "employees".

18. "Interrelated wrongful acts" means all "wrongful acts" that have as a common nexus any:

a. Fact, circumstance, situation, event, transaction or cause; or

b. Series of causally connected facts, circumstances, situations, events, transactions or causes.

19. "Interruption" means:

a. With respect to an "e-commerce incident":

(1) An unanticipated cessation or slowdown of your "e-commerce activities"; or

(2) Your suspension of your "e-commerce activities" for the purpose of avoiding or mitigating the possibility of transmitting a "virus" or malicious code to another person or organization;

and, with regard to Paragraphs **19.a.(1)** and **19.a.(2)**, shall be deemed to begin when your "e-commerce activities" are interrupted and ends at the earliest of:

(a) 90 days after the "interruption" begins;

(b) The time when your "e-commerce activities" are resumed; or

(c) The time when service is restored to you.

b. With respect to an "extortion threat", your voluntary suspension of your "e-commerce activities":

(1) Based upon clear evidence of a credible threat; or

(2) Based upon the recommendation of a security firm, if any;

and, with regard to Paragraphs **19.b.(1)** and **19.b.(2)**, shall be deemed to begin when your "e-commerce activities" are interrupted and ends at the earliest of:

(a) 14 days after the "interruption" begins;

(b) The time when your "e-commerce activities" are resumed; or

(c) The time when service is restored to you.

20. "Loss" means:

a. With respect to Insuring Agreements **1.** Media Liability, **2.** Security Breach Liability and **3.** Programming Errors And Omissions Liability:

(1) Compensatory damages, settlement amounts and costs awarded pursuant to judgments or settlements;

(2) Punitive and exemplary damages to the extent such damages are insurable by law; or

(3) Under Paragraph **b.** of Insuring Agreement **2.** Security Breach Liability, fines or penalties assessed against the "insured" to the extent such fines or penalties are insurable by law.

With regard to Paragraphs **20.a.(1)** through **20.a.(3)**, "loss" does not include:

(a) Civil or criminal fines or penalties imposed by law, except civil fines or penalties as provided under Paragraph **20.a.(3)**;

(b) The multiplied portion of multiplied damages;

(c) Taxes;

(d) Royalties;

(e) The amount of any disgorged profits; or

(f) Matters that are uninsurable pursuant to law.

b. With respect to Insuring Agreement **4.** Replacement Or Restoration Of Electronic Data:

The cost to replace or restore "electronic data" or "computer programs" as well as the cost of data entry, reprogramming and computer consultation services.

"Loss" does not include the cost to duplicate research that led to the development of your "electronic data" or "computer programs". To the extent that any "electronic data" cannot be replaced or restored, we will pay the cost to replace the media on which the "electronic data" was stored with blank media of substantially identical type.

c. With respect to Insuring Agreement **5.** Extortion Threats:

"Extortion expenses" and "ransom payments".

d. With respect to Insuring Agreement **6.** Business Income And Extra Expense:

The actual loss of "business income" you sustain and/or "extra expense" you incur.

e. With respect to Insuring Agreement **7.** Public Relations Expense:

"Public relations expenses".

f. With respect to Insuring Agreement **8.** Security Breach Expense:

"Security breach expenses".

21. "Media" means communication outlets such as newspapers, magazines, television, radio, billboards, direct mail, telephone, telefacsimile or the Internet through which news, entertainment, education, data or promotional messages are disseminated.

22. "Named insured" means the entity or entities shown in the Declarations and any "subsidiary".

23. "Negative publicity" means information which has been made public that has caused, or is reasonably likely to cause, a decline or deterioration in the reputation of the "named insured" or of one or more of its products or services.

24. "Over-redemption" means price discounts, prizes, awards or other valuable consideration given in excess of the total contracted or expected amount.

25. "Personal information" means any information not available to the general public for any reason through which an individual may be identified including, but not limited to, an individual's:

a. Social security number, driver's license number or state identification number;

b. Protected health information;

c. Financial account numbers;

d. Security codes, passwords, PINs associated with credit, debit or charge card numbers which would permit access to financial accounts; or

e. Any other nonpublic information as defined in "privacy regulations".

26. "Policy period" means the period of time from the inception date of this Policy shown in the Declarations to the expiration date shown in the Declarations, or its earlier cancellation or termination date.

27. "Pollutants" means any solid, liquid, gaseous or thermal irritant or contaminant, including smoke, vapor, soot, fumes, acids, alkalis, chemicals and waste. Waste includes materials to be recycled, reconditioned or reclaimed.

28. "Privacy regulations" means any of the following statutes and regulations, and their amendments, associated with the control and use of personally identifiable financial, health or other sensitive information including, but not limited to:

a. The Health Insurance Portability and Accountability Act of 1996 (HIPAA) (Public Law 104-191);

b. The Health Information Technology for Economic and Clinical Health Act (HITECH) (American Recovery and Reinvestment Act of 2009);

c. The Gramm-Leach-Bliley Act of 1999;

d. Section 5(a) of the Federal Trade Commission Act (15 U.S.C. 45(a)), but solely for alleged unfair or deceptive acts or practices in or affecting commerce;

e. The Identity Theft Red Flags Rules under the Fair and Accurate Credit Transactions Act of 2003; or

f. Any other similar state, federal or foreign identity theft or privacy protection statute or regulation.

29. "Public relations expenses" means:

a. Fees and costs of a public relations firm; and

b. Any other reasonable expenses incurred by you with our written consent;

to protect or restore your reputation solely in response to "negative publicity".

30. "Ransom payment" means a payment made in the form of cash.

31. "Ransomware" means any software that encrypts "electronic data" held within the "computer system" and demands a "ransom payment" in order to decrypt and restore such "electronic data".

32. "Regulatory proceeding" means an investigation, demand or proceeding brought by, or on behalf of, the Federal Trade Commission, Federal Communications Commission or other administrative or regulatory agency, or any federal, state, local or foreign governmental entity in such entity's regulatory or official capacity.

33. "Security breach" means the acquisition of "personal information" held within the "computer system" or in nonelectronic format while in the care, custody or control of the "insured" or authorized "third party" by a person:

   a. Who is not authorized to have access to such information; or

   b. Who is authorized to have access to such information but whose access results in the unauthorized disclosure of such information.

34. "Security breach expenses" means:

   a. Costs to establish whether a "security breach" has occurred or is occurring;

   b. Costs to investigate the cause, scope and extent of a "security breach" and to identify any affected parties;

   c. Costs to determine any action necessary to correct or remediate the conditions that led to or resulted from a "security breach";

   d. Costs to notify all parties affected by a "security breach";

   e. Overtime salaries paid to "employees" assigned to handle inquiries from the parties affected by a "security breach";

   f. Fees and costs of a company hired by you for the purpose of operating a call center to handle inquiries from the parties affected by a "security breach";

   g. Post-event credit monitoring costs for the parties affected by a "security breach" for up to one year from the date of notification to those affected parties of such "security breach"; and

   h. Any other reasonable expenses incurred by you with our written consent.

   "Security breach expenses" do not include any costs or expenses associated with upgrading, maintaining, improving, repairing or remediating any "computer system" as a result of a "security breach".

35. "Subsidiary" means any organization in which more than 50% of the outstanding securities or voting rights representing the present right to vote for the election of directors, trustees, managers (if a limited liability company) or persons serving in a similar capacity is owned, in any combination, by one or more "named insured(s)".

36. "Suit" means a civil proceeding in which damages to which this Policy applies are claimed against the "insured". "Suit" includes:

   a. An arbitration proceeding in which such damages are claimed and to which the "insured" submits with our consent; or

   b. Any other alternative dispute resolution proceeding in which such damages are claimed and to which the "insured" submits with our consent.

   "Suit" does not include a civil proceeding seeking recognition and/or enforcement of a foreign money judgment.

37. "Third party" means any entity that you engage under the terms of a written contract to perform services for you.

38. "Virus" means any kind of malicious code designed to damage or destroy any part of the "computer system" (including "electronic data") or disrupt its normal functioning.

39. "Wrongful act" means:

   a. With respect to Insuring Agreement **1.** Media Liability:

   Any actual or alleged error, misstatement or misleading statement arising out of the gathering, recording, collecting, writing, editing, publishing, exhibiting, broadcasting or releasing of "content" that results in:

   (1) Any type of defamation, disparagement or harm to the character, reputation or feelings of a person or organization, including libel, slander, product disparagement or trade libel;

   (2) Any type of negligent or intentional infliction of emotional distress, outrage or outrageous conduct;

   (3) Any actual or alleged negligent act, error or omission, misstatement or misleading statement committed by, or on behalf of, the "named insured";

   (4) Any type of invasion, infringement or interference with the right of privacy or publicity, including:

   (a) Eavesdropping;

   (b) False light;

   (c) Public disclosure of private facts;

   (d) Misappropriation of name or likeness; or

   (e) Trespassing or wrongful entering;

   (5) False arrest, detention or imprisonment, abuse of process or malicious prosecution;

   (6) Any type of infringement of copyright, plagiarism or misappropriation of ideas or information; or

   (7) Any type of infringement or dilution of title, slogan, trademark, trade name, trade dress, service mark or service name.

b. With respect to Insuring Agreement **2.** Security Breach Liability:

Any actual or alleged neglect, breach of duty or omission by an "insured" that results in:

(1) A "security breach"; or

(2) A "computer system" transmitting, by e-mail or other means, a "virus" to another person or organization.

c. With respect to Insuring Agreement **3.** Programming Errors And Omissions Liability:

Any actual or alleged programming error or omission that results in the disclosure of your client's "personal information" held within the "computer system".

E-COMMERCE
EC 00 13 01 14

MEDIA AND INFORMATION
SECURITY PROTECTION POLICY

INSURING AGREEMENTS 1., 2. AND 3. OF THIS POLICY PROVIDE CLAIMS-MADE COVERAGE. DEFENSE EXPENSES ARE PAYABLE WITHIN, AND NOT IN ADDITION TO, THE LIMIT OF INSURANCE. PAYMENT OF DEFENSE EXPENSES UNDER THIS POLICY WILL REDUCE THE LIMIT OF INSURANCE.

PLEASE READ THE ENTIRE POLICY CAREFULLY.

Various provisions in this Policy restrict coverage. Read the entire Policy carefully to determine rights, duties and what is and is not covered.

Throughout this Policy the words "you" and "your" refer to the "named insured" shown in the Declarations. The words "we", "us" and "our" refer to the company providing this insurance.

Other words and phrases that appear in quotation marks have special meaning. Refer to Section **VII** – Definitions.

SECTION I – INSURING AGREEMENTS

Coverage is provided under the following Insuring Agreements for which an Aggregate Limit Of Insurance is shown in the Declarations:

1. Media Liability

We will pay for both "loss" that the "insured" becomes legally obligated to pay and "defense expenses" as a result of a "claim" first made against the "insured" during the "policy period" or during the applicable Extended Reporting Period, for a "wrongful act" or a series of "interrelated wrongful acts" taking place on or after the Retroactive Date, if any, shown in the Declarations and before the end of the "policy period".

2. Security Breach Liability

a. We will pay for both "loss" that the "insured" becomes legally obligated to pay and "defense expenses" as a result of a "claim" first made against the "insured" during the "policy period" or during the applicable Extended Reporting Period, for a "wrongful act" or a series of "interrelated wrongful acts" taking place on or after the Retroactive Date, if any, shown in the Declarations and before the end of the "policy period".

b. We will pay for both "loss" and "defense expenses" as a result of a "claim" in the form of a "regulatory proceeding" first made against the "insured" during the "policy period" or during the applicable Extended Reporting Period, in response to a "wrongful act" or a series of "interrelated wrongful acts" covered under Paragraph **2.a.**

3. Programming Errors And Omissions Liability

We will pay for both "loss" that the "insured" becomes legally obligated to pay and "defense expenses" as a result of a "claim" first made against the "insured" during the "policy period" or during the applicable Extended Reporting Period, for a "wrongful act" or a series of "interrelated wrongful acts" taking place on or after the Retroactive Date, if any, shown in the Declarations and before the end of the "policy period".

4. Replacement Or Restoration Of Electronic Data

We will pay for "loss" of "electronic data" or "computer programs" stored within the "computer system" resulting directly from an "e-commerce incident" sustained during the "policy period".

5. Extortion Threats

We will pay for "loss" resulting directly from an "extortion threat" communicated to you during the "policy period".

However, we will not pay for "extortion expenses" or "ransom payments" which are part of a series of related threats that began prior to the "policy period".

6. Business Income And Extra Expense

We will pay for "loss" due to an "interruption" resulting directly from an "e-commerce incident" sustained during the "policy period" or an "extortion threat" communicated to you during the "policy period".

7. Public Relations Expense

We will pay for "loss" due to "negative publicity" resulting directly from an "e-commerce incident" or a "security breach" sustained during the "policy period".

8. Security Breach Expense

We will pay for "loss" resulting directly from a "security breach" sustained during the "policy period".

   © Insurance Services Office, Inc., 2013

SECTION II – LIMITS OF INSURANCE

1. Policy Aggregate Limit Of Insurance

The most we will pay for all "loss", and "defense expenses" if covered, under this Policy is the Policy Aggregate Limit Of Insurance shown in the Declarations. The Policy Aggregate Limit of Insurance shall be reduced by the amount of any payment made under the terms of this Policy. Upon exhaustion of the Policy Aggregate Limit of Insurance by such payments, we will have no further obligations or liability of any kind under this Policy.

2. Insuring Agreement Aggregate Limit Of Insurance

a. Subject to the Policy Aggregate Limit of Insurance, the most we will pay for all "loss", and "defense expenses" if covered, under each Insuring Agreement, is the Insuring Agreement Aggregate Limit Of Insurance shown in the Declarations:

(1) The Insuring Agreement Aggregate Limit of Insurance shall be reduced by the amount of any payment for "loss", and "defense expenses" if covered, under that Insuring Agreement; and

(2) Upon exhaustion of the Insuring Agreement Aggregate Limit of Insurance by such payments, we will have no further obligations or liability of any kind under that Insuring Agreement.

b. If coverage for "regulatory proceedings" is being provided under Paragraph **b.** of Insuring Agreement **2.** Security Breach Liability, the Limit of Insurance shall be part of, not in addition to, the Aggregate Limit of Insurance for the Insuring Agreement.

SECTION III – DEDUCTIBLE

1. Subject to Section **II** – Limits Of Insurance:

a. Under Insuring Agreements **1.** Media Liability, **2.** Security Breach Liability and **3.** Programming Errors And Omissions Liability:

We will pay only the amount of "loss" and "defense expenses" which are in excess of the applicable Deductible Amount shown in the Declarations resulting from the same "wrongful act" or "interrelated wrongful acts". Such Deductible Amount will be borne by you, self-insured, and at your own risk.

b. Under Insuring Agreements **4.** Replacement Or Restoration Of Electronic Data, **5.** Extortion Threats, **7.** Public Relations Expense and **8.** Security Breach Expense:

We will pay only the amount of "loss" which is in excess of the applicable Deductible Amount shown in the Declarations.

c. Under Insuring Agreement **6.** Business Income And Extra Expense:

We will pay only the amount of "loss" which exceeds the greater of:

(1) The Deductible Amount shown in the Declarations; or

(2) The amount of "loss" incurred during the Waiting Period shown in the Declarations.

2. In the event a "loss" is covered under more than one Insuring Agreement, only the highest Deductible Amount applicable to the "loss" shall be applied.

SECTION IV – DEFENSE AND SETTLEMENT

The provisions contained within this section apply only to Insuring Agreements **1.** Media Liability, **2.** Security Breach Liability and **3.** Programming Errors And Omissions Liability:

1. We shall have the right and duty to select counsel and defend the "insured" against any "claim" covered under Insuring Agreements **1.** Media Liability, **2.** Security Breach Liability and **3.** Programming Errors And Omissions Liability, even if the allegations of such "claim" are groundless, false or fraudulent. However, we shall have the right but not the duty to defend the "insured" against a "claim" covered under Paragraph **b.** of Insuring Agreement **2.** Security Breach Liability, and we shall have no duty to defend the "insured" against any "claim" which is not covered under any of these Insuring Agreements.

2. We may, upon the written consent of the "insured", make any settlement of a "claim" which we deem reasonable. If the "insured" withholds consent to such settlement, our liability for all "loss" resulting from such "claim" will not exceed the amount for which we could have settled such "claim", plus "defense expenses" incurred, as of the date we proposed such settlement in writing to the "insured". Upon refusing to consent to a settlement we deem reasonable, the "insured" shall, at its sole expense, assume all further responsibility for its defense, including all additional costs associated with the investigation, defense and/or settlement of such "claim".

                    EC 00 13 01 14

SECTION V – EXCLUSIONS

We will not be liable for "loss" or "defense expenses":

1. Based upon, attributable to or arising out of lightning, earthquake, hail, volcanic action or any other act of nature.

2. Based upon, attributable to or arising out of:

    a. War, including undeclared or civil war or civil unrest;

    b. Warlike action by military force, including action hindering or defending against an actual or expected attack, by any government, sovereign or other authority using military personnel or other agents; or

    c. Insurrection, rebellion, revolution, usurped power, or action taken by government authority in hindering or defending against any of these.

3. Based upon, attributable to or arising out of the dispersal or application of pathogenic or poisonous biological or chemical materials, nuclear reaction, nuclear radiation or radioactive contamination, or any related act or incident, however caused.

4. Based upon, attributable to or arising out of bodily injury or physical damage to or destruction of tangible property, including loss of use thereof.

    Bodily injury means bodily injury, sickness or disease sustained by a person, including death resulting from any of these at any time.

5. Based upon, attributable to or arising out of any unexplained or indeterminable failure, malfunction or slowdown of the "computer system" including "electronic data" and the inability to access or properly manipulate the "electronic data".

6. Based upon, attributable to or arising out of any "interruption" in normal computer function or network service or function due to insufficient capacity to process transactions or due to an overload of activity on the "computer system" or network. However, this exclusion shall not apply if such "interruption" is caused by an "e-commerce incident".

7. Based upon, attributable to or arising out of a complete or substantial failure, disablement or shutdown of the Internet, regardless of the cause.

8. Based upon, attributable to or arising out of any failure of, reduction in or surge of power.

9. Based upon, attributable to or arising out of any actual or alleged violation of the Racketeer Influenced and Corrupt Organizations Act (RICO) and its amendments, or similar provisions of any federal, state or local statutory or common law.

10. Based upon, attributable to or arising out of any malfunction or failure of any satellite.

11. Based upon, attributable to or arising out of any oral or written publication of material, if done by an "insured" or at an "insured's" direction with knowledge of its falsity.

12. Based upon, attributable to or arising out of an "insured's" assumption of liability by contract or agreement, whether oral or written. However, this exclusion shall not apply to:

    a. Any liability that an "insured" would have incurred in the absence of such contract or agreement; or

    b. Breach of any written, oral or implied-in-fact indemnification or hold harmless agreement between an "insured" and any person or organization distributing "content" by or on behalf of the "insured".

13. Based upon, attributable to or arising out of any actual or alleged patent or trade secret violation, including any actual or alleged violation of the Patent Act, the Economic Espionage Act of 1996 or the Uniform Trade Secrets Act and their amendments.

14. Based upon, attributable to or arising out of:

    a. The actual, alleged or threatened discharge, dispersal, seepage, migration, release or escape of "pollutants" at any time;

    b. Any request, demand, order or statutory or regulatory requirement that any "insured" or others test for, monitor, clean up, remove, contain, treat, detoxify or neutralize, or in any way respond to, or assess the effects of, "pollutants"; or

    c. Any "claim" or "suit" brought by, or on behalf of, any governmental authority for damages because of testing for, monitoring, cleaning up, removing, containing, treating, detoxifying or neutralizing, or in any way responding to, or assessing the effects of, "pollutants".

15. Based upon, attributable to or arising out of any "claim", "suit" or other proceeding against an "insured" which was pending or existed prior to the "policy period", or arising out of the same or substantially the same facts, circumstances or allegations which are the subject of, or the basis for, such "claim", "suit" or other proceeding.

16. Based upon, attributable to or arising out of an "insured's" employment practices including, but not limited to, termination of employment, demotion, reassignment, discipline, harassment, coercion or refusal to employ regardless of whether the "insured" is liable as an employer or in any other capacity.

17. Based upon, attributable to or arising out of any "wrongful act" or "interrelated wrongful acts" that occurred before the Retroactive Date, if any, shown in the Declarations.

18. Based upon, attributable to or arising out of the same facts, "wrongful acts" or "interrelated wrongful acts" alleged or contained in any "claim" which has been reported, or in any circumstances of which notice has been given, under any insurance policy of which this Policy is a renewal or replacement.

19. Based upon, attributable to or arising out of any criminal, dishonest, malicious or fraudulent act or any willful violation of any statute or regulation committed by an "insured", acting alone or in collusion with others. However, this exclusion shall not apply to dishonest, malicious or fraudulent acts committed by an "employee" which give rise to a "claim" or "loss" covered under Insuring Agreement **2.** Security Breach Liability.

    With the exception of "claims" excluded under Exclusion **13.**, we will defend "claims" first made against an "insured" alleging such acts or violations until final adjudication is rendered against that "insured". Final adjudication rendered against one "insured" shall not be imputed to any other "insured".

    We will not provide indemnification for any "claim" to which any "insured" enters a guilty plea or pleads no contest, and we will not provide a defense from the time we become aware that any "insured" intends to so plead.

20. Based upon, attributable to or arising out of any action or proceeding brought by, or on behalf of, any governmental authority or regulatory agency including, but not limited to:

    a. The seizure or destruction of property by order of a governmental authority; or

    b. Regulatory actions or proceedings brought by, or on behalf of, the Federal Trade Commission, Federal Communications Commission or other regulatory agency, except when covered under Paragraph **b.** of Insuring Agreement **2.** Security Breach Liability.

    However, this exclusion shall not apply to actions or proceedings brought by a governmental authority or a regulatory agency acting solely in its capacity as a customer of the "named insured" or of a "subsidiary".

21. Based upon, attributable to or arising out of costs associated with upgrading or improving the "computer system" regardless of the reason for the upgrade.

22. Based upon, attributable to or arising out of any "claim" brought or alleged by one "insured" against another, except for a "claim" brought or alleged by an "employee" against an "insured" as a result of a "security breach".

23. Based upon, attributable to or arising out of unintentional errors or omissions in the entry of "electronic data" into the "computer system".

24. Based upon, attributable to or arising out of any actual or alleged violation of price fixing, restraint of trade, monopolization or unfair trade or any violation of the Sherman Act, the Clayton Act or any similar provision of any federal, state or local statutory or common law not related to a "wrongful act" as defined in Paragraphs **39.a.(6)** and **39.a.(7)** of the definition of "wrongful act".

25. Based upon, attributable to or arising out of any direct or indirect publicity or promotion of tickets, coupons or prizes for any contest, lottery, sweepstakes, promotion or game of chance, including "over-redemption" relating therefrom.

26. Based upon, attributable to or arising out of any "claim" brought by, or on behalf of, the ASCAP, SESAC, BMI, RIAA or any similar licensing organization.

27. Based upon, attributable to or arising out of any unauthorized or unsolicited transmission or dissemination of electronic mail, telefacsimile or telephone call.

28. Based upon, attributable to or arising out of any "claim" brought by, or on behalf of, an independent contractor for or resulting from a dispute over the ownership of "content" or services supplied by the independent contractor.

SECTION VI – CONDITIONS

1. Cancellation

    a. The first "named insured" shown in the Declarations may cancel this Policy by mailing or delivering to us advance written notice of cancellation.

    b. We may cancel this Policy by mailing or delivering to the first "named insured" written notice of cancellation at least:

        (1) 10 days before the effective date of cancellation if we cancel for nonpayment of premium; or

        (2) 30 days before the effective date of cancellation if we cancel for any other reason.

    c. We will mail or deliver our notice to the first "named insured's" last mailing address known to us.

d. Notice of cancellation will state the effective date of cancellation. The "policy period" will end on that date.

e. If this Policy is canceled, we will send the first "named insured" any premium refund due. If we cancel, the refund will be prorated. If the first "named insured" cancels, the refund may be less than pro rata. The cancellation will be effective even if we have not made or offered a refund.

f. If notice is mailed, proof of mailing will be sufficient proof of notice.

2. Changes

This Policy contains all the agreements between you and us concerning the insurance afforded. The first "named insured" shown in the Declarations is authorized to make changes in the terms of this Policy with our consent. This Policy's terms can be amended or waived only by endorsement issued by us and made a part of this Policy.

3. Examination Of Your Books And Records

We may examine and audit your books and records as they relate to this Policy at any time during the "policy period" and up to three years afterward.

4. Inspections And Surveys

a. We have the right to:

  (1) Make inspections and surveys at any time;

  (2) Give you reports on the conditions we find; and

  (3) Recommend changes.

b. We are not obligated to make any inspections, surveys, reports or recommendations, and any such actions we do undertake relate only to insurability and the premiums to be charged. We do not make safety inspections. We do not undertake to perform the duty of any person or organization to provide for the health or safety of workers or the public. And we do not warrant that conditions:

  (1) Are safe or healthful; or

  (2) Comply with laws, regulations, codes or standards.

c. Paragraphs **4.a.** and **4.b.** of this condition apply not only to us, but also to any rating, advisory, rate service or similar organization which makes insurance inspections, surveys, reports or recommendations.

5. Premiums

The first "named insured" shown in the Declarations:

a. Is responsible for the payment of all premiums; and

b. Will be the payee for any return premiums we pay.

6. Transfer Of Your Rights And Duties Under This Policy

Your rights and duties under this Policy may not be transferred without our written consent, except in the case of death of an individual "named insured".

If you are a sole proprietor and you die, your rights and duties will be transferred to your legal representative but only while acting within the scope of duties as your legal representative. Until your legal representative is appointed, anyone having proper temporary custody of your property will have your rights and duties but only with respect to that property.

7. Subrogation

With respect to any payment made under this Policy on behalf of any "insured", we shall be subrogated to the "insured's" rights of recovery to the extent of such payment. The "insured" shall execute all papers required and shall do everything necessary to secure and preserve such rights, including the execution of such documents necessary to enable us to bring suit in the "insured's" name. Any recoveries, less the cost of obtaining them, will be distributed as follows:

a. To you, until you are reimbursed for any "loss" you sustain that exceeds the sum of the applicable Aggregate Limit of Insurance and the Deductible Amount, if any;

b. Then to us, until we are reimbursed for the payment made under this Policy; and

c. Then to you, until you are reimbursed for that part of the payment equal to the Deductible Amount, if any.

8. Bankruptcy

Your bankruptcy, or the bankruptcy of your estate if you are a sole proprietor, will not relieve us of our obligations under this Policy.

9. Representations

You represent that all information and statements contained in the "application" are true, accurate and complete. All such information and statements are the basis for our issuing this Policy and shall be considered as incorporated into and shall constitute a part of this Policy. Misrepresentation of any material fact may be grounds for the rescission of this Policy.

10. Changes In Exposure

a. Acquisition Or Creation Of Another Organization

If before or during the "policy period":

(1) You acquire securities or voting rights in another organization or create another organization which, as a result of such acquisition or creation, becomes a "subsidiary"; or

(2) You acquire any organization through merger or consolidation;

then such organization will be covered under this Policy but only with respect to "wrongful acts" or "loss" which occurred after the effective date of such acquisition or creation provided, with regard to Paragraphs **10.a.(1)** and **10.a.(2),** you:

(a) Give us written notice of the acquisition or creation of such organization within 90 days after the effective date of such action;

(b) Obtain our written consent to extend the coverage provided by this Policy to such organization; and

(c) Upon obtaining our consent, pay us an additional premium.

b. Acquisition Of Named Insured

If during the "policy period":

(1) The "named insured" merges into or consolidates with another organization, such that the "named insured" is not the surviving organization; or

(2) Another organization, or person or group of organizations and/or persons acting in concert, acquires securities or voting rights which result in ownership or voting control by the other organization(s) or person(s) of more than 50% of the outstanding securities or voting rights representing the present right to vote for the election of directors, trustees or managers (if a limited liability company) of the "named insured";

then the coverage afforded under this Policy will continue until the end of the "policy period", but only with respect to "claims" arising out of "wrongful acts" or "loss" which occurred prior to the effective date of such merger, consolidation or acquisition.

The full annual premium for the "policy period" will be deemed to be fully earned immediately upon the occurrence of such merger, consolidation or acquisition of the "named insured".

The "named insured" must give written notice of such merger, consolidation or acquisition to us as soon as practicable, together with such information as we may reasonably require.

c. Cessation Of Subsidiaries

If before or during the "policy period" an organization ceases to be a "subsidiary", the coverage afforded under this Policy with respect to such "subsidiary" will continue until the end of the "policy period" but only with respect to "claims" arising out of "wrongful acts" or "loss" which occurred prior to the date such organization ceased to be a "subsidiary".

11. Other Insurance

a. If any covered "claim" or "loss" is insured by any other valid policy, then this Policy shall apply only in excess of the amount of any deductible, retention and limit of insurance under such other policy, whether such other policy is stated to be primary, contributory, excess, contingent or otherwise, unless such other policy is written specifically excess of this Policy by reference in such other policy to this Policy's policy number.

b. When this Policy is excess, we shall have no duty under Insuring Agreement **1.** Media Liability, **2.** Security Breach Liability or **3.** Programming Errors And Omissions Liability to defend the "insured" against any "suit" if any other insurer has a duty to defend the "insured" against that "suit". If no other insurer defends, we will undertake to do so, but we will be entitled to the "insured's" rights against all those other insurers.

12. Legal Action Against Us

a. No person or organization has a right:

(1) To join us as a party or otherwise bring us into a "suit" asking for damages from an "insured"; or

(2) To sue us under this Policy unless all of its terms have been fully complied with.

        EC 00 13 01 14

A person or organization may sue us to recover on an agreed settlement or on a final judgment against an "insured", but we will not be liable for damages that are not payable under Insuring Agreement **1.** Media Liability, **2.** Security Breach Liability or **3.** Programming Errors And Omissions Liability, or that are in excess of the applicable Aggregate Limit of Insurance. An agreed settlement means a settlement and release of liability signed by us, the first "named insured" and the claimant or the claimant's legal representative.

b. You may not bring any legal action against us involving "loss":

(1) Unless you have complied with all the terms of this Policy;

(2) Until 90 days after you have filed proof of loss with us; and

(3) Unless brought within two years from the date you reported the "loss" to us.

If any limitation in this condition is prohibited by law, such limitation is amended so as to equal the minimum period of limitation provided by such law.

13. Separation Of Insureds

Except with respect to the applicable Aggregate Limit of Insurance, and any rights or duties specifically assigned in Insuring Agreement **1.** Media Liability, **2.** Security Breach Liability or **3.** Programming Errors And Omissions Liability to the first "named insured", this Policy applies separately to each "insured" against whom "claim" is made.

14. Duties In The Event Of Claim Or Loss

In the event of either an occurrence or offense that may result in a "claim" against an "insured" or a "loss" or situation that may result in a "loss" covered under this Policy, you must notify us in writing as soon as practicable, but not to exceed 30 days, and cooperate with us in the investigation and settlement of the "claim" or "loss". Additionally:

a. Under Insuring Agreements **1.** Media Liability, **2.** Security Breach Liability and **3.** Programming Errors And Omissions Liability, you must:

(1) Immediately record the specifics of the "claim" and the date received;

(2) Immediately send us copies of any demands, notices, summonses or legal papers received in connection with the "claim";

(3) Authorize us to obtain records and other information; and

(4) Assist us, upon our request, in the enforcement of any right against any person or organization which may be liable to you because of an occurrence or offense to which this Policy may also apply.

You will not, except at your own cost, voluntarily make a payment, assume any obligation or incur any expense without our consent.

A "claim" brought by a person or organization seeking damages will be deemed to have been made when the "claim" is received by an "insured".

b. Under Insuring Agreements **4.** Replacement Or Restoration Of Electronic Data and **5.** Extortion Threats, you must:

(1) Notify local law enforcement officials;

(2) Submit to examination under oath at our request and give us a signed statement of your answers; and

(3) Give us a detailed, sworn proof of loss within 120 days.

(4) In addition, under Insuring Agreement **5.** Extortion Threats, you must:

(a) Determine that the "extortion threat" has actually occurred;

(b) Make every reasonable effort to immediately notify an associate and the security firm, if any, before making any "ransom payment" based upon the "extortion threat"; and

(c) Approve any "ransom payment" based upon the "extortion threat".

15. Valuation – Settlement

a. All premiums, Aggregate Limits of Insurance, Deductible Amounts, "loss" and any other monetary amounts under this Policy are expressed and payable in the currency of the United States of America. If judgment is rendered, settlement is agreed to or another component of "loss" under this Policy is expressed in any currency other than United States of America dollars, payment under this Policy shall be made in United States dollars at the rate of exchange published in The Wall Street Journal on the date the final judgment is entered, settlement amount is agreed upon or the other component of "loss" is due, respectively.

b. With respect to "loss" covered under Insuring Agreement **6.** Business Income And Extra Expense:

(1) The amount of "business income" will be determined based on consideration of:

(a) The net income generated from your "e-commerce activities" before the "interruption" occurred;

(b) The likely net income generated by your "e-commerce activities" if no "interruption" had occurred, but not including any net income that would likely have been earned as a result of an increase in the volume of business due to favorable business conditions caused by the impact of the "e-commerce incident" on customers or on other businesses;

(c) The operating expenses, including payroll, necessary to resume your "e-commerce activities" with the same quality of service that existed before the "interruption"; and

(d) Other relevant sources of information, including your financial records and accounting procedures, bills, invoices and other vouchers, and debts, liens and contracts.

However, the amount of "business income" will be reduced to the extent that the reduction in the volume of business from the affected "e-commerce activities" is offset by an increase in the volume of business from other channels of commerce such as via telephone, mail or other sources.

(2) The amount of "extra expense" will be determined based on:

(a) Necessary expenses that exceed the normal operating expenses that would have been incurred in the course of your "e-commerce activities" during the period of coverage if no "interruption" had occurred. We will deduct from the total of such expenses the salvage value that remains of any property bought for temporary use during the period of coverage once your "e-commerce activities" are resumed; and

(b) Necessary expenses that reduce the "business income" "loss" that otherwise would have been incurred during the period of coverage.

16. Extended Reporting Periods

The provisions contained within this condition apply only to Insuring Agreements **1.** Media Liability, **2.** Security Breach Liability and **3.** Programming Errors And Omissions Liability.

a. Basic Extended Reporting Period

(1) A Basic Extended Reporting Period is automatically provided without additional charge. This period starts with the end of the "policy period" and lasts for 30 days. A "claim" first made and reported by the "insured" during this 30-day period will be considered to have been received within the "policy period". However, the 30-day Basic Extended Reporting Period does not apply to "claims" that are covered under any subsequent insurance purchased by the "insured", or that would be covered but for exhaustion of the Aggregate Limit of Insurance applicable to such "claims".

(2) The Basic Extended Reporting Period does not extend the "policy period" or change the scope of coverage provided. It applies only to "claims" to which the following applies:

(a) The "claim" is first made and reported to us during the Basic Extended Reporting Period; and

(b) The "claim" arose out of either a "wrongful act" or the first of a series of "interrelated wrongful acts" which occurred on or after the Retroactive Date, if any, shown in the Declarations and before the end of the "policy period".

b. Supplemental Extended Reporting Period

(1) A Supplemental Extended Reporting Period is available if this Policy is canceled or not renewed by either you or us, but only by endorsement and for an extra charge. The Supplemental Extended Reporting Period starts when the Basic Extended Reporting Period set forth in Paragraph **16.a.** ends. The Supplemental Extended Reporting Period is available unless:

(a) We cancel this Policy for nonpayment of premium; or

(b) You fail to pay any amounts owed us.

(2) In order to obtain a Supplemental Extended Reporting Period, you must give us a written request for the Supplemental Extended Reporting Period Endorsement together with the full payment of the additional premium for the endorsement within 30 days after the end of the "policy period". The Supplemental Extended Reporting Period will not go into effect unless you pay the additional premium promptly when due.

(3) The Supplemental Extended Reporting Period does not extend the "policy period" or change the scope of coverage provided. It applies only to "claims" to which the following applies:

(a) The "claim" is first made and reported to us during the Supplemental Extended Reporting Period; and

(b) The "claim" arose out of either a "wrongful act" or the first of a series of "interrelated wrongful acts" which occurred on or after the Retroactive Date, if any, shown in the Declarations and before the end of the "policy period".

(4) Once in effect, the Supplemental Extended Reporting Period may not be canceled. The premium for the Supplemental Extended Reporting Period Endorsement will be deemed to be fully earned as of the date it is purchased.

c. There is no separate or additional Aggregate Limit of Insurance for the Basic Extended Reporting Period or the Supplemental Extended Reporting Period. The limit of insurance available during the Basic Extended Reporting Period, and the Supplemental Extended Reporting Period if purchased, shall be the remaining amount, if any, of the Aggregate Limit of Insurance of the respective Insuring Agreement, subject to the remaining amount of the Policy Aggregate Limit of Insurance at the time this Policy was canceled or nonrenewed.

17. Confidentiality

No "insured" shall be prejudiced by any "insured's" refusal to maintain or divulge the identity of a source or the failure to portray a source in a certain manner or light.

Under Insuring Agreement **5.** Extortion Threats, "insureds" must make every reasonable effort not to divulge the existence of this coverage.

18. Territory

This Policy covers "wrongful acts" which occurred anywhere in the world. However, "suits" must be brought in the United States of America (including its territories and possessions), Puerto Rico or Canada.

SECTION VII – DEFINITIONS

1. "Advertising" means the use of "media" to persuade an audience to purchase or take some action upon products, services or ideas.

2. "Application" means the signed application for this Policy, including any attachments and other materials submitted in conjunction with the signed application.

3. "Business income" means the:

a. Net income (net profit or loss before income taxes) that would have been earned or incurred; and

b. Continuing normal operating expenses incurred, including payroll.

4. "Claim" means:

a. A written demand for monetary or nonmonetary damages, including injunctive relief;

b. A civil proceeding commenced by the service of a complaint or similar proceeding;

c. A written demand for retraction of "content" posted, published, disseminated or released by an "insured";

d. A subpoena seeking "content" or the identity of an external source that supplies information or "content" to an "insured" in confidence; or

e. Under Paragraph **b.** of Insuring Agreement **2.** Security Breach Liability, a "regulatory proceeding" commenced by the filing of a notice of charges, formal investigative order, service of summons or similar document;

against any "insured" for a "wrongful act", including any appeal therefrom.

5. "Computer program" means a set of related electronic instructions, which direct the operation and function of a computer or devices connected to it, which enables the computer or devices to receive, process, store or send "electronic data".

6. "Computer system" means the following which are owned, leased or operated by you:

a. Computers, including Personal Digital Assistants (PDAs) and other transportable or handheld devices, electronic storage devices and related peripheral components;

b. Systems and applications software; and

c. Related communications networks;

by which "electronic data" is collected, transmitted, processed, stored or retrieved.

7. "Content" means any type of communicative or informational material, regardless of its nature or form, including material disseminated electronically, such as via a web site or electronic mail.

8. "Defense expenses" means the reasonable and necessary fees (attorneys' and experts' fees) and expenses incurred in the defense or appeal of a "claim", including the cost of appeal, attachment or similar bonds (without any obligation on our part to obtain such bonds) but excluding wages, salaries, benefits or expenses of your "employees".

9. "E-commerce activities" means those activities conducted by you in the normal conduct of your business via your web site or your e-mail system.

10. "E-commerce incident" means a:

   a. "Virus";

   b. Malicious code; or

   c. Denial of service attack;

introduced into or enacted upon the "computer system" (including "electronic data") or a network to which it is connected, that is designed to damage, destroy, delete, corrupt or prevent the use of or access to any part of the "computer system" or otherwise disrupt its normal operation.

Recurrence of the same "virus" after the "computer system" has been restored shall constitute a separate "e-commerce incident".

11. "Electronic data" means digital information, facts, images or sounds stored as or on, created or used on, or transmitted to or from computer software (including systems and applications software) on electronic storage devices including, but not limited to, hard or floppy disks, CD-ROMs, tapes, drives, cells, data processing devices or any other media which are used with electronically controlled equipment. "Electronic data" is not tangible property.

"Electronic data" does not include your "electronic data" that is licensed, leased, rented or loaned to others.

12. "Employee" means any natural person who was, now is or will be:

   a. Employed on a full- or part-time basis;

   b. Furnished temporarily to you to substitute for a permanent employee on leave or to meet seasonal or short-term workload conditions;

   c. Leased to you by a labor leasing firm under an agreement between you and the labor leasing firm to perform duties related to the conduct of your business, but does not mean a temporary worker as defined in Paragraph **12.b.**;

   d. An officer;

   e. A director, trustee or manager (if a limited liability company);

   f. A volunteer worker; or

   g. A partner or member (if a limited liability company);

of the "named insured" and those of any organization qualifying as a "subsidiary" under the terms of this Policy, but only while acting within the scope of their duties as determined by the "named insured" or such "subsidiary".

13. "Extortion expenses" means:

   a. Fees and costs of:

   (1) A security firm; or

   (2) A person or organization;

   hired with our consent to determine the validity and severity of an "extortion threat" made against you;

   b. Interest costs paid by you for any loan from a financial institution taken by you to pay a ransom demand;

   c. Reward money paid by you to an "informant" which leads to the arrest and conviction of parties responsible for "loss"; and

   d. Any other reasonable expenses incurred by you with our written consent, including:

   (1) Fees and costs of independent negotiators; and

   (2) Fees and costs of a company hired by you, upon the recommendation of the security firm, to protect your "electronic data" from further threats.

14. "Extortion threat" means a threat or series of related threats:

   a. To perpetrate an "e-commerce incident";

   b. To disseminate, divulge or utilize:

   (1) Your proprietary information; or

   (2) Weaknesses in the source code;

   within the "computer system" by gaining unauthorized access to the "computer system";

   c. To destroy, corrupt or prevent normal access to the "computer system" by gaining unauthorized access to the "computer system";

d. To inflict "ransomware" on the "computer system" or a network to which it is connected; or

e. To publish your client's "personal information".

15. "Extra expense" means necessary expenses you incur:

a. During an "interruption" that you would not have incurred if there had been no "interruption"; or

b. To avoid or minimize the suspension of your "e-commerce activities".

"Extra expense" does not include any costs or expenses associated with upgrading, maintaining, improving, repairing or remediating any "computer system".

16. "Informant" means a person, other than an "employee", providing information not otherwise obtainable, solely in return for a reward offered by you.

17. "Insured" means any "named insured" and its "employees".

18. "Interrelated wrongful acts" means all "wrongful acts" that have as a common nexus any:

a. Fact, circumstance, situation, event, transaction or cause; or

b. Series of causally connected facts, circumstances, situations, events, transactions or causes.

19. "Interruption" means:

a. With respect to an "e-commerce incident":

(1) An unanticipated cessation or slowdown of your "e-commerce activities"; or

(2) Your suspension of your "e-commerce activities" for the purpose of avoiding or mitigating the possibility of transmitting a "virus" or malicious code to another person or organization;

and, with regard to Paragraphs **19.a.(1)** and **19.a.(2)**, shall be deemed to begin when your "e-commerce activities" are interrupted and ends at the earliest of:

(a) 90 days after the "interruption" begins;

(b) The time when your "e-commerce activities" are resumed; or

(c) The time when service is restored to you.

b. With respect to an "extortion threat", your voluntary suspension of your "e-commerce activities":

(1) Based upon clear evidence of a credible threat; or

(2) Based upon the recommendation of a security firm, if any;

and, with regard to Paragraphs **19.b.(1)** and **19.b.(2)**, shall be deemed to begin when your "e-commerce activities" are interrupted and ends at the earliest of:

(a) 14 days after the "interruption" begins;

(b) The time when your "e-commerce activities" are resumed; or

(c) The time when service is restored to you.

20. "Loss" means:

a. With respect to Insuring Agreements **1.** Media Liability, **2.** Security Breach Liability and **3.** Programming Errors And Omissions Liability:

(1) Compensatory damages, settlement amounts and costs awarded pursuant to judgments or settlements;

(2) Punitive and exemplary damages to the extent such damages are insurable by law; or

(3) Under Paragraph **b.** of Insuring Agreement **2.** Security Breach Liability, fines or penalties assessed against the "insured" to the extent such fines or penalties are insurable by law.

With regard to Paragraphs **20.a.(1)** through **20.a.(3)**, "loss" does not include:

(a) Civil or criminal fines or penalties imposed by law, except civil fines or penalties as provided under Paragraph **20.a.(3)**;

(b) The multiplied portion of multiplied damages;

(c) Taxes;

(d) Royalties;

(e) The amount of any disgorged profits; or

(f) Matters that are uninsurable pursuant to law.

b. With respect to Insuring Agreement **4.** Replacement Or Restoration Of Electronic Data:

The cost to replace or restore "electronic data" or "computer programs" as well as the cost of data entry, reprogramming and computer consultation services.

"Loss" does not include the cost to duplicate research that led to the development of your "electronic data" or "computer programs". To the extent that any "electronic data" cannot be replaced or restored, we will pay the cost to replace the media on which the "electronic data" was stored with blank media of substantially identical type.

c. With respect to Insuring Agreement **5.** Extortion Threats:

"Extortion expenses" and "ransom payments".

d. With respect to Insuring Agreement **6.** Business Income And Extra Expense:

The actual loss of "business income" you sustain and/or "extra expense" you incur.

e. With respect to Insuring Agreement **7.** Public Relations Expense:

"Public relations expenses".

f. With respect to Insuring Agreement **8.** Security Breach Expense:

"Security breach expenses".

21. "Media" means communication outlets such as newspapers, magazines, television, radio, billboards, direct mail, telephone, telefacsimile or the Internet through which news, entertainment, education, data or promotional messages are disseminated.

22. "Named insured" means the entity or entities shown in the Declarations and any "subsidiary".

23. "Negative publicity" means information which has been made public that has caused, or is reasonably likely to cause, a decline or deterioration in the reputation of the "named insured" or of one or more of its products or services.

24. "Over-redemption" means price discounts, prizes, awards or other valuable consideration given in excess of the total contracted or expected amount.

25. "Personal information" means any information not available to the general public for any reason through which an individual may be identified including, but not limited to, an individual's:

a. Social security number, driver's license number or state identification number;

b. Protected health information;

c. Financial account numbers;

d. Security codes, passwords, PINs associated with credit, debit or charge card numbers which would permit access to financial accounts; or

e. Any other nonpublic information as defined in "privacy regulations".

26. "Policy period" means the period of time from the inception date of this Policy shown in the Declarations to the expiration date shown in the Declarations, or its earlier cancellation or termination date.

27. "Pollutants" means any solid, liquid, gaseous or thermal irritant or contaminant, including smoke, vapor, soot, fumes, acids, alkalis, chemicals and waste. Waste includes materials to be recycled, reconditioned or reclaimed.

28. "Privacy regulations" means any of the following statutes and regulations, and their amendments, associated with the control and use of personally identifiable financial, health or other sensitive information including, but not limited to:

a. The Health Insurance Portability and Accountability Act of 1996 (HIPAA) (Public Law 104-191);

b. The Health Information Technology for Economic and Clinical Health Act (HITECH) (American Recovery and Reinvestment Act of 2009);

c. The Gramm-Leach-Bliley Act of 1999;

d. Section 5(a) of the Federal Trade Commission Act (15 U.S.C. 45(a)), but solely for alleged unfair or deceptive acts or practices in or affecting commerce;

e. The Identity Theft Red Flags Rules under the Fair and Accurate Credit Transactions Act of 2003; or

f. Any other similar state, federal or foreign identity theft or privacy protection statute or regulation.

29. "Public relations expenses" means:

a. Fees and costs of a public relations firm; and

b. Any other reasonable expenses incurred by you with our written consent;

to protect or restore your reputation solely in response to "negative publicity".

30. "Ransom payment" means a payment made in the form of cash.

31. "Ransomware" means any software that encrypts "electronic data" held within the "computer system" and demands a "ransom payment" in order to decrypt and restore such "electronic data".

32. "Regulatory proceeding" means an investigation, demand or proceeding brought by, or on behalf of, the Federal Trade Commission, Federal Communications Commission or other administrative or regulatory agency, or any federal, state, local or foreign governmental entity in such entity's regulatory or official capacity.

33. "Security breach" means the acquisition of "personal information" held within the "computer system" or in nonelectronic format while in the care, custody or control of the "insured" or authorized "third party" by a person:

   a. Who is not authorized to have access to such information; or

   b. Who is authorized to have access to such information but whose access results in the unauthorized disclosure of such information.

34. "Security breach expenses" means:

   a. Costs to establish whether a "security breach" has occurred or is occurring;

   b. Costs to investigate the cause, scope and extent of a "security breach" and to identify any affected parties;

   c. Costs to determine any action necessary to correct or remediate the conditions that led to or resulted from a "security breach";

   d. Costs to notify all parties affected by a "security breach";

   e. Overtime salaries paid to "employees" assigned to handle inquiries from the parties affected by a "security breach";

   f. Fees and costs of a company hired by you for the purpose of operating a call center to handle inquiries from the parties affected by a "security breach";

   g. Post-event credit monitoring costs for the parties affected by a "security breach" for up to one year from the date of notification to those affected parties of such "security breach"; and

   h. Any other reasonable expenses incurred by you with our written consent. ,

"Security breach expenses" do not include any costs or expenses associated with upgrading, maintaining, improving, repairing or remediating any "computer system" as a result of a "security breach".

35. "Subsidiary" means any organization in which more than 50% of the outstanding securities or voting rights representing the present right to vote for the election of directors, trustees, managers (if a limited liability company) or persons serving in a similar capacity is owned, in any combination, by one or more "named insured(s)".

36. "Suit" means a civil proceeding in which damages to which this Policy applies are claimed against the "insured". "Suit" includes:

   a. An arbitration proceeding in which such damages are claimed and to which the "insured" submits with our consent; or

   b. Any other alternative dispute resolution proceeding in which such damages are claimed and to which the "insured" submits with our consent.

"Suit" does not include a civil proceeding seeking recognition and/or enforcement of a foreign money judgment.

37. "Third party" means any entity that you engage under the terms of a written contract to perform services for you.

38. "Virus" means any kind of malicious code designed to damage or destroy any part of the "computer system" (including "electronic data") or disrupt its normal functioning.

39. "Wrongful act" means:

   a. With respect to Insuring Agreement **1.** Media Liability:

   Any actual or alleged error, misstatement or misleading statement arising out of the gathering, recording, collecting, writing, editing, publishing, exhibiting, broadcasting or releasing of "content" that results in:

   (1) Any type of defamation, disparagement or harm to the character, reputation or feelings of a person or organization, including libel, slander, product disparagement or trade libel;

   (2) Any type of negligent or intentional infliction of emotional distress, outrage or outrageous conduct;

   (3) Any actual or alleged negligent act, error or omission, misstatement or misleading statement committed by, or on behalf of, the "named insured";

   (4) Any type of invasion, infringement or interference with the right of privacy or publicity, including:

     (a) Eavesdropping;

     (b) False light;

(c) Public disclosure of private facts;

(d) Misappropriation of name or likeness; or

(e) Trespassing or wrongful entering;

(5) False arrest, detention or imprisonment, abuse of process or malicious prosecution;

(6) Any type of infringement of copyright, plagiarism or misappropriation of ideas or information; or

(7) Any type of infringement or dilution of title, slogan, trademark, trade name, trade dress, service mark or service name.

b. With respect to Insuring Agreement **2.** Security Breach Liability:

Any actual or alleged neglect, breach of duty or omission by an "insured" that results in:

(1) A "security breach"; or

(2) A "computer system" transmitting, by e-mail or other means, a "virus" to another person or organization.

c. With respect to Insuring Agreement **3.** Programming Errors And Omissions Liability:

Any actual or alleged programming error or omission that results in the disclosure of your client's "personal information" held within the "computer system".

POLICY NUMBER:

E-COMMERCE
EC 20 09 01 14

THIS ENDORSEMENT CHANGES THE POLICY. PLEASE READ IT CAREFULLY.

AMEND DEFENSE AND SETTLEMENT PROVISION

This endorsement modifies insurance provided under the following:

FINANCIAL INSTITUTIONS INFORMATION SECURITY PROTECTION POLICY
INFORMATION SECURITY PROTECTION POLICY
MEDIA AND INFORMATION SECURITY PROTECTION POLICY

SCHEDULE

Percentage Of Claim, Plus Defense Expenses Incurred, We Will Pay In Excess Of The Amount For Which The Claim Could Have Been Settled:	**%**
Information required to complete this Schedule, if not shown above, will be shown in the Declarations.	

Paragraph **2.** of **Section IV – Defense And Settlement** is replaced by the following:

2. We may, upon the written consent of the "insured", make any settlement of a "claim" which we deem reasonable. If the "insured" withholds consent to such settlement, our liability for all "loss" resulting from such "claim" will not exceed:

a. The amount for which we could have settled such "claim", plus "defense expenses" incurred, as of the date we proposed such settlement in writing to the "insured"; plus

b. A percentage of the amount of the "loss", plus "defense expenses" incurred, in excess of the proposed settlement amount in Paragraph **a.**, which is calculated based on the percentage shown in the Schedule;

subject to the appropriate Limit Of Insurance shown in the Declarations. Once our obligation to pay "defense expenses" has terminated, the "insured" shall, at its sole expense, assume all further responsibility for its defense, including all additional costs associated with the investigation, defense and/or settlement of such "claim".

EC 20 09 01 14   © Insurance Services Office, Inc., 2013   Page 1 of 1

POLICY NUMBER:

E-COMMERCE
EC 20 12 01 14

THIS ENDORSEMENT CHANGES THE POLICY. PLEASE READ IT CAREFULLY.

PAYMENT CARD INDUSTRY (PCI) – PROVIDE COVERAGE FOR DEFENSE EXPENSES AND FINES OR PENALTIES

This endorsement modifies insurance provided under the following:

FINANCIAL INSTITUTIONS INFORMATION SECURITY PROTECTION POLICY
INFORMATION SECURITY PROTECTION POLICY
MEDIA AND INFORMATION SECURITY PROTECTION POLICY

SCHEDULE

Sublimit Of Insurance $	
Information required to complete this Schedule, if not shown above, will be shown in the Declarations.	

A. The following is added to Insuring Agreement **2. Security Breach Liability:**

   c. We will pay for both "loss" and "defense expenses" as a result of a "claim" in the form of an action first made against the "insured" by a "card company" for non-compliance with the Payment Card Industry (PCI) Data Security Standards during the "policy period" or during the applicable Extended Reporting Period in response to a "wrongful act" or a series of "interrelated wrongful acts" covered under Paragraph **a.** of this Insuring Agreement.

B. The following is added to Paragraph **2.** of **Section II – Limits Of Insurance:**

   c. The Sublimit Of Insurance shown in the Schedule shall be part of, not in addition to, the Aggregate Limit of Insurance for the Insuring Agreement **2.** Security Breach Liability.

C. In **Section VII – Definitions:**

   a. The following definition is added:

   "Card company" means American Express, Discover Financial Services, JCB International, MasterCard Worldwide, Visa Inc. or any other credit card company that requires its merchants to adhere to the Payment Card Industry (PCI) Data Security Standards.

   b. The following is added to the definition of "claim":

   Under Paragraph **A.c.** of this endorsement, an action brought by a "card company" of the Payment Card Industry (PCI);

   c. The following is added to the definition of "loss":

   With respect to this endorsement:

   Fines or penalties assessed against the "insured" to the extent such fines or penalties are insurable by law.

E-COMMERCE
EC 20 13 01 14

THIS ENDORSEMENT CHANGES THE POLICY. PLEASE READ IT CAREFULLY.

COMPUTER AND FUNDS TRANSFER FRAUD

This endorsement modifies insurance provided under the following:

INFORMATION SECURITY PROTECTION POLICY
MEDIA AND INFORMATION SECURITY PROTECTION POLICY

With regard to this Computer And Funds Transfer Fraud endorsement, the provisions of the Policy to which this endorsement is attached apply, unless modified by this endorsement.

A. The following Insuring Agreement is added to **Section I – Insuring Agreements:**

Computer And Funds Transfer Fraud

1. We will pay for:

   a. "Loss" resulting directly from a fraudulent:

   (1) Entry of "electronic data" or "computer program" into; or

   (2) Change of "electronic data" or "computer program" within;

   any "computer system", provided the fraudulent entry or fraudulent change causes, with regard to Paragraphs **1.(a)(1)** and **1.(a)(2):**

   (a) Money, securities or other property to be transferred, paid or delivered; or

   (b) Your account at a financial institution to be debited or deleted.

   b. "Loss" resulting directly from a "fraudulent instruction" directing a financial institution to debit your "transfer account" and transfer, pay or deliver money or securities from that account.

2. As used in Paragraph **1.a.**, fraudulent entry or fraudulent change of "electronic data" or "computer program" shall include such entry or change made by an "employee" acting, in good faith, upon a "fraudulent instruction" received from a computer software contractor who has a written agreement with you to design, implement or service "computer programs" for a "computer system" covered under this Insuring Agreement.

B. The following is added to Paragraph **1.** of **Section III – Deductible:**

We will pay only the amount of "loss" which is in excess of the applicable Deductible Amount shown in the Declarations.

C. The following is added to **Section V – Exclusions:**

   a. Authorized Access

   "Loss" resulting from a fraudulent:

   (1) Entry of "electronic data" or "computer program" into; or

   (2) Change of "electronic data" or "computer program" within;

   any "computer system", by a person or organization with authorized access to that "computer system", except when covered under Paragraph **A.2.**

   b. Credit Card Transactions

   "Loss" resulting from the use or purported use of credit, debit, charge, access, convenience, identification, stored-value or other cards or the information contained on such cards.

   c. Exchanges Or Purchases

   "Loss" resulting from the giving or surrendering of property in any exchange or purchase.

   d. Fraudulent Instructions

   "Loss" resulting from an "employee" or financial institution acting upon any instruction to:

   (1) Transfer, pay or deliver money, securities or other property; or

   (2) Debit or delete your account;

   which instruction proves to be fraudulent, except when covered under Paragraph **A.2.**

       © Insurance Services Office, Inc., 2013   **Page 1 of 2**

e. Inventory Shortages

"Loss", or that part of any "loss", the proof of which as to its existence or amount is dependent upon:

(1) An inventory computation; or

(2) A profit and loss computation.

D. Under **Section VI – Conditions:**

The introductory statement to Paragraph **b.** of the **Duties In The Event Of Claim Or Loss** Condition is replaced by the following:

b. Under   Insuring   Agreements   **4.** Replacement Or Restoration Of Electronic Data, **5.** Extortion Threats and this Insuring Agreement, you must:

E. Under **Section VII – Definitions:**

1. The following is added to the definition of "loss":

With respect to this Insuring Agreement:

a. In Paragraph **A.1.a.:**

(1) Money, securities or other property to be transferred, paid or delivered; or

(2) Your account at a financial institution to be debited or deleted.

b. In Paragraph **A.1.b.,** transferring, paying or delivering money or securities from your "transfer account".

2. The following definitions are added:

a. "Fraudulent instruction" means:

(1) With regard to Paragraph **A.1.b.:**

(a) A computer, telegraphic, cable, teletype, telefacsimile, telephone or other electronic instruction directing a financial institution to debit your "transfer account" and to transfer, pay or deliver money or securities from that "transfer account", which instruction purports to have been issued by you, but which in fact was fraudulently issued by someone else without your knowledge or consent.

(b) A written instruction issued to a financial institution directing the financial institution to debit your "transfer account" and to transfer, pay or deliver money or securities from that "transfer account", through an electronic funds transfer system at specified times or under specified conditions, which instruction purports to have been issued by you, but which in fact was issued, forged or altered by someone else without your knowledge or consent.

(c) A computer, telegraphic, cable, teletype, telefacsimile, telephone or other electronic or written instruction initially received by you, which instruction purports to have been issued by an "employee", but which in fact was fraudulently issued by someone else without your or the "employee's" knowledge or consent.

(2) With regard to Paragraph **A.2.:**

A computer, telegraphic, cable, teletype, telefacsimile, telephone or other electronic, written or voice instruction directing an "employee" to enter or change "electronic data" or "computer programs" within a "computer system" covered under this Insuring Agreement, which instruction in fact was fraudulently issued by your computer software contractor.

b. "Transfer account" means an account maintained by you at a financial institution from which you can initiate the transfer, payment or delivery of "money" and "securities":

(1) By means of computer, telegraphic, cable, teletype, telefacsimile, telephone or other electronic instructions; or

(2) By means of written instructions establishing the conditions under which such transfers are to be initiated by such financial institution through an electronic funds transfer system.

     © Insurance Services Office, Inc., 2013   **EC 20 13 01 14**

E-COMMERCE
EC 20 14 01 14

THIS ENDORSEMENT CHANGES THE POLICY. PLEASE READ IT CAREFULLY.

COMPUTER FRAUD

This endorsement modifies insurance provided under the following:

FINANCIAL INSTITUTIONS INFORMATION SECURITY PROTECTION POLICY

With regard to this Computer Fraud endorsement, the provisions of the Policy to which this endorsement is attached apply, unless modified by this endorsement.

A. The following Insuring Agreement is added to **Section I – Insuring Agreements:**

Computer Fraud

1. We will pay for "loss" resulting directly from a fraudulent:

  a. Entry of "electronic data" or "computer program" into; or

  b. Change of "electronic data" or "computer program" within;

any "computer system", provided the fraudulent entry or fraudulent change causes, with regard to Paragraphs **1.a.** and **1.b.:**

  (1) Property to be transferred, paid or delivered;

  (2) Your account or a customer's account (or member's if the "insured" is a credit union) to be added, deleted, debited or credited; or

  (3) An unauthorized account or a fictitious account to be debited or credited.

2. As used in Paragraph **1.**, fraudulent entry or fraudulent change of "electronic data" or "computer program" shall include such entry or change made by an "employee" acting, in good faith, upon a "fraudulent instruction" received from a computer software contractor who has a written agreement with you to design, implement or service "computer programs" for a "computer system" covered under this Insuring Agreement.

B. The following is added to Paragraph **1.** of **Section III – Deductible:**

We will pay only the amount of "loss" which is in excess of the applicable Deductible Amount shown in the Declarations.

C. The following is added to **Section V – Exclusions:**

  a. Authorized Access

  "Loss" resulting from a fraudulent:

    (1) Entry of "electronic data" or "computer program" into; or

    (2) Change of "electronic data" or "computer program" within;

  any "computer system", by a person or organization with authorized access to that "computer system", except when covered under Paragraph **A.2.**

  b. Credit Card Transactions

  "Loss" resulting from the use or purported use of credit, debit, charge, access, convenience, identification, stored-value or other cards or the information contained on such cards.

D. Under **Section VI – Conditions:**

The introductory statement to Paragraph **b.** of the **Duties In The Event Of Claim Or Loss** Condition is replaced by the following:

  b. Under Insuring Agreements **4.** Replacement Or Restoration Of Electronic Data, **5.** Extortion Threats and this Insuring Agreement, you must:

E. Under **Section VII – Definitions:**

1. The following is added to the definition of "loss":

With respect to this Insuring Agreement:

In Paragraph **A.1.:**

  a. Property to be transferred, paid or delivered;

  b. Your account or a customer's account (or member's if the "insured" is a credit union) to be added, deleted, debited or credited; or

    c. An unauthorized account or a fictitious account to be debited or credited.

2. The following definition is added:

"Fraudulent instruction" means:

With respect to Paragraph **A.2.:**

A computer, telegraphic, cable, teletype, telefacsimile, telephone or other electronic, written or voice instruction directing an "employee" to enter or change "electronic data" or "computer programs" within a "computer system" covered under this Insuring Agreement, which instruction in fact was fraudulently issued by your computer software contractor.

EC 20 14 01 14

POLICY NUMBER:

**E-COMMERCE
EC 20 15 01 14**

THIS ENDORSEMENT CHANGES THE POLICY. PLEASE READ IT CAREFULLY.

TELEPHONE TOLL FRAUD

This endorsement modifies insurance provided under the following:

FINANCIAL INSTITUTIONS INFORMATION SECURITY PROTECTION POLICY
INFORMATION SECURITY PROTECTION POLICY
MEDIA AND INFORMATION SECURITY PROTECTION POLICY

SCHEDULE

Number Of Days:
Information required to complete this Schedule, if not shown above, will be shown in the Declarations.

With regard to this Telephone Toll Fraud endorsement, the provisions of the Policy to which this endorsement is attached apply, unless modified by this endorsement.

A. The following Insuring Agreement is added to **Section I – Insuring Agreements:**

Telephone Toll Fraud

We will pay for "loss" resulting directly from fraudulent use or fraudulent manipulation of an "account code" or "system password" required to gain access into your "voice computer system", provided such "loss" did not result from the failure to:

1. Incorporate a "system password"; or

2. Change a "system password" within the number of days shown in the Schedule.

B. The following is added to Paragraph **1.** of **Section III – Deductible:**

We will pay only the amount of "loss" which is in excess of the applicable Deductible Amount shown in the Declarations.

C. Under the Media And Information Security Protection Policy, Exclusion **27.** is replaced by the following:

Based upon, attributable to or arising out of any unauthorized or unsolicited transmission or dissemination of electronic mail or telefacsimile.

D. The following condition is added to **Section VI – Conditions:**

We will pay for "loss" resulting from toll call charges made on telephone lines directly controlled by one "voice computer system" occurring for a period of not more than 30 days inclusive of the date on which the first such toll call charges were made.

E. Under **Section VII – Definitions:**

1. The following is added to the definition of "loss":

Long distance telephone toll call charges incurred by you.

2. The following definitions are added:

a. "Account code" means a confidential and protected string of characters that identifies or authenticates a person and permits that person to gain access to your "voice computer system" for the purpose of making long distance toll calls or utilizing voice mail box messaging capabilities or similar functional features of the system.

b. "System administration" means the performance of any security function including, but not limited to:

(1) Defining authorized persons to access the system;

(2) Adding, deleting or changing "account codes" or passwords;

(3) Installing or deleting any system option which directs telephone call routing or adds, drops or moves telephone lines; or

(4) Any other activity allowed by a hardware- or software-based system option that has been incorporated by a manufacturer or a vendor into a "voice computer system" provided the system is not intended for the sole use of the manufacturer or vendor.

c. "System maintenance" means performing hardware and software installation, diagnostic and correction and similar activities that are performed in the usual custom and practice by a manufacturer or vendor to establish or maintain the basic operational functionality of a "voice computer system".

d. "System password" means a confidential and protected string of characters that identifies or authenticates a person and permits that person to gain access to your "voice computer system" to perform "system administration" or "system maintenance" or a component thereof.

e. "Voice computer system" means a computer system installed in one location which functions as a private branch exchange (PBX), voice mail processor, automated call attendant or provides a similar capability used for the direction or routing of telephone calls in a voice communications network.

Appendix B

The Status of Data Breach Notification Laws in the United States

"In today's environment, it's not a matter of if a data breach will occur, but when it will occur, and how well you respond. Do everything you can to prevent data breaches, but also fully plan out how you will respond if you are breached. Today's media and business environment demands that two-pronged approach," advises Brian Lapidus, Chief Operating Officer of Kroll Fraud Solutions. The warning is clear: companies wanting to protect their money and their credit need to have a data breach response plan in place *before* it becomes necessary. As they say, "a good offense is a good defense."

There is no one-size-fits-all approach to prepare your business for this eventuality, as evidenced by the disarray of state notification laws. Therefore, you should tailor your response plan to the unique laws of your state and the unique assets of your business.

To find your state's data breach notification statute, as well as its most recent amendment and effective date, consult the following chart:

State	Statute	Amended or Effective Date
Alabama	*No data breach notification law*	
Alaska	Alaska Stat. §45.48.010 et seq.	July 1, 2009
Arizona	Ariz. Rev. Stat. §44-7501	December 31, 2006
Arkansas	Ark. Code §4-110-101 et seq.	August 12, 2005
California	Cal. Civ. Code §§1798.29, 1798.80 et seq.	January 1, 2014
Colorado	Colo. Rev. Stat. §6-1-716	September 1, 2006
Connecticut	Conn. Gen Stat. §36a-701b	October 1, 2012
Delaware	Del. Code tit. 6, §12B-101 et seq.	June 28, 2005
District of Columbia	D.C. Code §28- 3851 et seq.	July 1, 2007
Florida	Fla. Stat. §817.5681	July 1, 2005

State	Statute	Amended or Effective Date
Georgia	Ga. Code §§10-1-910, -911, -912; §46-5-214	May 5, 2005
Guam	9 GCA §48-10 et seq.	March 13, 2009
Hawaii	Haw. Rev. Stat. §487N-1 et seq.	July 1, 2008
Idaho	Idaho Stat. §§28-51-104 to -107	July 1, 2006
Illinois	815 ILCS §§530/1 to 530/25	January 1, 2012
Indiana	Ind. Code §§4-1-11 et seq., 24-4.9 et seq.	June 30, 2006
Iowa	Iowa Code §§715C.1, 715C.2	July 1, 2008
Kansas	Kan. Stat. §50-7a01 et seq.	January 1, 2007
Kentucky	*No data breach notification law*	
Louisiana	La. Rev. Stat. §51:3071 et seq.	January 1, 2006
Maine	Me. Rev. Stat. tit. 10 §1347 et seq.	May 19, 2009
Maryland	Md. Code Com. Law §§14-3501 et seq.	January 1, 2008
Massachusetts	Mass. Gen. Laws §93H-1 et seq.	October 31, 2007
Michigan	Mich. Comp. Laws §§445.63, 445.72	April 1, 2011
Minnesota	Minn. Stat. §§325E.61, 325E.64	January 1, 2006
Mississippi	Miss. Code §75-24-29	July 1, 2011
Missouri	Mo. Rev. Stat. §407.1500	August 28, 2009
Montana	Mont. Code §2-6-504, 30-14-1701 et seq.	March 1, 2006
Nebraska	Neb. Rev. Stat. §87-801 et. seq.	January 1, 2006
Nevada	Nev. Rev. Stat. §§603A.010 et seq., 242.183	January 1, 2006
New Hampshire	N.H. Rev. Stat. §359-C:19 et seq.	January 1, 2007
New Jersey	N.J. Stat. §56:8-163	January 1, 2006
New Mexico	*No data breach notification law*	
New York	N.Y. Gen. Bus. Law §899-aa	March 28, 2013
North Carolina	N.C. Gen. Stat §§75-61, 75-65	December 1, 2005
North Dakota	N.D. Cent. Code §51-30-01 et seq.	June 1, 2005

State	Statute	Amended or Effective Date
Ohio	Ohio Rev. Code §1347.12, et seq.	March 30, 2007
Oklahoma	Okla. Stat. §§74-3113.1, 24-161 to -166	November 1, 2008
Oregon	Oregon Rev. Stat. §646A.600 et seq.	October 1, 2007
Pennsylvania	73 Pa. Stat. §2301 et seq.	June 20, 2006
Puerto Rico	10 Laws of Puerto Rico §4051 et seq.	January 5, 2006
Rhode Island	R.I. Gen. Laws §11-49.2-1 et seq.	March 1, 2006
South Carolina	S.C. Code §39-1-90, 2013 H.B. 3248	April 23, 2013
South Dakota	*No data breach notification law*	
Tennessee	Tenn. Code §47-18-2107	July 1, 2005
Texas	Tex. Bus. & Com. Code §521.002, et seq.	September 1, 2009
Utah	Utah Code §13-44-101 et seq.	March 12, 2009
Vermont	Vt. Stat. tit. 9 §§2430, 2435	May 8, 2012
Virgin Island	V.I. Code tit. 14, §2208	October 17, 2005
Virginia	Va. Code §§18.2-186.6, 32.1-127.1:05	July 1, 2008
Washington	Wash. Rev. Code §§19.255.010, 42.56.590	July 24, 2005
West Virginia	W.V. Code §46A-2A-101 et seq.	June 7, 2008
Wisconsin	Wis. Stat. §134.98	March 28, 2008
Wyoming	Wyo. Stat. §40-12-501 et seq.	July 1, 2007

Index

1973 Comprehensive General
Liability policy form 7, 16, 28, 32,
36, 39, 44, 79, 83-84, 113
1976 Broad Form Endorsement............. 16
1986 CGL policy form........16, 28, 32, 35,
36, 39, 83, 166-167

Absolute exclusion................173, 175-176
Accident..........2, 9-10, 12, 16, 21, 24, 41,
45, 49-50, 52, 58-59, 61, 66, 68, 79,
80, 89, 90, 100, 102, 107, 109, 110,
111, 124, 132, 141, 145, 147-148
"Accident" forms 85
Additional insured endorsements 44-50,
53-54, 56-58, 60-62, 74-75
Additional insured form (2004).............55
Additional insured provisions.....54, 58-59
Additional insured status 43, 46-49,
52, 57, 61, 72-74
Additional insured(s) 34, 43, 46-75
Additional Insureds and
Contractual Liability 43-75
Additional insureds and
defense costs...........................68-70
Advertisement..............................169-170
(defined)...170
Advertising injury coverage..........169-170
Advertising injury ... 55, 167-172, 174-175
Agent's E&O.. 60
Aggregate limit 32, 58, 84, 94, 111,
123, 131, 141, 150
Aggregate(s)............. 32, 58-60, 77, 80-81,
83-85, 87, 93-96, 103-105, 111,
115, 117-124, 128-129, 131,
136-137, 141-142, 145-146,
148, 150-151, 153-154
Alienated premises exclusion 16-18
All sums 86, 88-89, 108, 115
Annualization...................................92-93
Anti-indemnity statutes...................56, 64
Anti-stacking terms..........................86-87
Applicability of the CGL policy to
cyber risk exposures..............166-167
Applications software 5, 169, 172, 174
Arising out of language 45-46, 50-53,
55, 58

Asbestos cases, case law examples.......30,
81-83, 87, 109, 143-144
Asbestos cases finding
multiple occurrences 144-150
Asbestos cases finding one occurrence... 143
Asbestos claims.... 82-83, 89, 92, 142-143,
145, 147-148, 151
Assume the tort liability
of another.............................62-63, 66

Batch clauses...................................90-92
Blanket additional insured
endorsement(s) 45, 54,
Blanket basis.....................................45, 54
Bodily injury or property damage ...46-47,
49, 59, 79, 83, 86, 90, 94-96, 153
Breach of contract........... 9-11, 26, 29, 33,
41, 59, 69, 126
Broad form property damage
endorsement................................... 16
Broadcasting 170-171
Burden of proof issues......................... 100
Business income and extra expense..... 178
Business risk doctrine............ 1-13, 38, 42
Business risk exclusions, the...1-2, 4, 13-42
Business risk 3-4, 14, 38

CAN-SPAM Act (2003)................172-173
Care, custody, or control...... 16, 18, 20-21
Case law survey 109-112
Cases in which disputes arise 94-100
Cause test, the................... 96-97, 110, 149
"Caused by".. 63
Caused by the policyholder's acts or
omissions...45
Caused in whole or part by the
named insured's work 62
Certificate of insurance.....................71-74
Cleanup of ground water
contamination 17, 119
Combined single limits.....................93-94
Completed operations 18, 46-47, 55,
62, 83-84
Completed operations or products
hazards aggregates 80, 142
Complex underwriting...................176-177

Computer-targeted crimes.....................156
Conclusions and trends.................184-185
Consumer "no-contact" laws 172
Conditions language 81, 83, 99, 130,
132, 145, 150
Construction defect and building
claims, case law survey 112-115
Continuous injury trigger.....................152
Continuous or repeated exposure............9,
79-82, 86, 89-90, 99, 114, 119,
121-122, 130, 133, 150, 152-153
Contract....3-4, 9-11, 13-14, 21-22, 24-26,
29, 32-36, 40-42, 44-46, 48-49, 52-54,
56-59, 61-74, 85, 114-115, 121,
125-126, 137, 157, 181
Contracting party 59, 67, 71, 74
Contractual indemnity wording 64
Contractual liability coverage..........43-44,
49, 64-66, 68, 70-71, 75
Contractual obligations......................3, 43
Contractual liability issues.....................62
Contractual risk-shifting common 45
Correlation of U.S. Cybersecurity
Expenditure to Detected
Events.....................................160-165
a change of culture 164
direct cost.....................................162
everybody is a publisher........164-165
indirect cost....................162-163, 182
opportunity cost 157, 162-164
producer involvement 165-166
Coverage availability 46, 103, 177
Coverage limits in primary policies.......58
Coverage territory 79, 167-168
(defined)....................................167-168
Cybercrime in the United States...157-160
Cyber liability 155-185

Damage to impaired property or
property not physically injured... 35-38
Damages..........1, 4, 6-8, 12, 14, 23, 25-26,
28-30, 33-34, 37-42, 48, 58-60,
64-65, 68-70, 77-78, 80, 85, 89,
111, 115-116, 118, 121, 126, 134,
141, 167-168, 172, 174-175
Data breach 161-163, 166, 173,
175, 181, 185
Data Breach Notification
Laws in the United States 267

"Decisions to manufacturer"...143-144, 149
Deductibles and self-insured
retentions (SIRs).....................104-108
Deemer clauses 87-88, 145
Defective product.................7, 41, 60, 99,
113-114, 135, 138, 141
Defectively designed, product 134
Defense and indemnity payments..........49
Defense costs 34, 49, 64-65, 68-69, 95
Difference between additional insured
and contractual liability
coverage.....................................49, 68
Diminution of value 5
Directly or indirectly...............15, 22, 172
Disclaimers on certificate 72, 74
Discrimination claims, case law
survey 115-118
Distribution of material in violation
of statutes.......................171, 172-173
Diverse claimants.................................95
Domain name..171
Do-Not-Call law....................................172
Duty of good faith................................126
Duty to defend 8, 14, 33, 51, 53, 69,
77-79, 81, 129, 154

Each child, new occurrence 129-130
Economic losses............................6, 14, 36
Effect test, the 97
Electronic chatrooms or bulletin
boards 171
Electronic data 5, 168-169, 171-172,
174-175, 178
(defined)..172
Employment...........................84, 128, 157
Employment discrimination..........115-118
Endorsement, CG 21 06 05 14 ...173-1745
Endorsement, CG 21 07 05 14 175-176
Environmental insurance
coverage cases 17
Environmental liability claims......118-126
Errors and omissions....................116, 178
Event test, the...............................97, 147
Exclusion j.–Damage to
property 2, 15-27, 33
Exclusion j.(1)–"Owned Property"
exclusion 16-17, 119
Exclusion j.(2)–"Alienated
Premises" exclusion...........17-18

Exclusion j.(3) and (4)–"Care,
Custody, or Control"
exclusion 18-21
Exclusion j.(5)–"Performing
Operations" exclusion ...22-24, 26
Exclusion j.(6)–"Faulty
Workmanship" exclusion ...24-27
Exclusion k.–Damage to
"Your Product" 2, 27-31, 35, 171
Exclusion l.–Damage to
"Your Work" 2, 31-35, 171
Exclusion m.–Damage to Impaired
Property or Property Not
Physically Injured.................2, 35-38
Exclusion n. 2, 38-42
Exclusion p. 171, 174
Exclusive control 20, 21
Exploitation crimes.....................156-157
Exposure and triple trigger 87
Exterior Insulation Finish
Systems (EIFS).............................34
External factors impacting
occurrence determinations.....100-102
Extortion threats................................178

Failing to add an additional insured 71
Failure to warn 81, 138, 144, 146, 149
Failure to prevent abuse, one occurrence
Fair notice 67-68
Faulty work 3,12,34,42
Faulty workmanship exclusion 24-26
Financial crimes...........................155-156
First encounter trigger..........................128
Food poisoning claims, case
law survey....................................112
Forms 189
Fortuity... 10
Fortuitous losses 12

Gaps in coverage.......................44, 70, 71
General aggregate limit....................32, 94
General contractor..... 3, 21, 26, 28-35, 38,
43, 45-52, 56, 59-60, 63-64, 66-70, 74
Guideline cases 116

Hearing loss claims........................150-151
Hold harmless indemnity clauses 64
Hold harmless wording and
defense costs........................22-24 64

Horizontal exhaustion...................105, 152
Housing discrimination.................115-118
Identity of claimants 118
Imminent threat....................................17

"Impaired property" exclusion
(defined)...............................36-38
Indemnification/hold harmless clauses ...69
Indemnify the insured
(defined)...22
Indemnity 34, 43, 49-50, 55, 60,
63-64, 67-70, 74-75, 78-81, 84,
86-87, 94-96, 102, 105-106, 108,
121, 130, 178
(defined)....................................34
Indemnity assumed in insured
contract 62-63, 65-67, 69
Indemnity limits...............80, 95, 102, 108
Indemnity provisions 64, 67
Infringement of slogan........................170
In whole or in part, wording... 2, 5, 45-47,
55-56, 62-64, 88, 93
Insurance company review of contracts ...70
Insurance forms...................................187
Insurance Services Office (ISO).......2, 44,
92, 175, 177
Insured contract(s) 62-67
(defined)....................................62
Insured versus insurer...........................95
Insurer insolvency...............................109
Insurer versus insurer...........................96
Insurer versus reinsurer........................96
Insuring agreement, the ...1, 4, 9, 13-14, 178
Intangible 6-7, 164, 168
Intellectual property claims 157, 160,
182, 184
Intent questions..................................9, 70
Intentional injury exclusion 70

Lead paint claims..........................152-153
Legal cause.....................................97-99
Legal tests for counting occurrences...96-97
Level of care 61
"Limited access"...................................21
Limits of liability.... 29, 59, 85, 94, 99, 108
Contractual 85
Operations.......................................85
Products 85
Protective 85

Limiting coverage 57, 78
Litigation expenses 65
Loaned property......................................19
Loss of use 5, 8, 22, 35-36, 38,
                85, 115, 168, 172, 174
Low indemnity limits....................102-108

Malware 155-156, 164
Manifestation or actual injury................80
Manufacturing and design claims..........91
Manuscript endorsements................62, 70
Metatag 171
Molestation and sexual assault
        claims 127-131
    Each child a new occurrence...129-130
    Impact of aggregating provisions...130
    Multiple locations or perpetrators
        as separate occurrences.........129
    One occurrence per policy
        year....................................128-129
    One occurrence: Failure to
        prevent abuse...................127-128
Montrose 115
Multiple insureds 94-95
Multiple locations/perpetrators as
        separate occurrences..............128-129
Multiple occurrence products
        cases...128-129, 132-134, 136, 139-140
Multiple occurrences.... 140, 144, 147-151
Multiple plaintiffs 94-95
Multiple policy limits...........................86
Multiple site claims......................119-124
Multiple site claims, case law
        examples.. 120

Named insured............... 16-22, 28, 32-34,
        39-49, 53-58, 61-62, 64-66, 69-70
Narrow construction.............................22
Negligence 10-11, 18-19, 25, 33,
        45-56, 58, 60, 62-68, 72, 79, 83,
        94-95, 98-99, 101-102, 114,
        127, 130-135, 141, 181
Negligent acts........... 53, 81, 101, 129-130
Negligent entrustment....................99, 117
Negligent misrepresentation 10, 74
New optional coverage 178-179
Noncumulation clauses...88-90, 105, 142, 152
Number of sites....................................118
Nursing home claims 130-131

Occupational disease.................83-84, 150
Occurrence issues 22, 32
Occurrence
        (*defined*)......................................81-83
Occurrence limit 77, 80, 82, 86-87, 94,
        96, 99, 101, 105, 108, 111, 114-116,
                128-131, 134, 137, 141-142,
                        148, 152-153
Offending guideline 116
One deductible for entire period
        of injury.................................107-108
One full deductible for
        each year...............................104-108
One occurrence, two occurrences...77-154
Ongoing operations......... 15-17, 54-55, 62
Opportunity costs.........................157, 162
"Other insurance" clauses....................105
Other job site exposures.................152-153
Owned property exclusion.....................16
Ownership................................8, 85, 119

"Per occurrence" SIR.... 96, 104-108, 138
Per project aggregate 94
Performing operations
        exclusion........................ 15, 22-23, 26
Personal injury and advertising
        injury 167-172, 174-175
        (*defined*)..................................170-171
Phishing...155
Physical injury to tangible
        property 5-8, 38, 168
Physical proximity/continuity
        of damage....................................102
Piracy 161
Policy aggregates 85, 95
Policy limits 44, 46, 48, 60-61, 65, 69,
                75, 77-78, 80
Policy wordings and occurrences
        determinations 80
Pollution conditions...............123-124, 126
Pollution exclusion 17, 136, 138, 175
Potential conflict...................................68
Premises liability claims, case law
        survey 109-112
Premium basis.......................................85
Primary and noncontributory coverage,
        CG 20 01 04 13.... 43, 69 CORRECT
Privacy cause of action 156, 169, 177
Privacy legislation...............................172

Products liability claims ... 6, 80, 123-124,
134-140 141, 146
Products-completed operations hazard
(*defined*) 16, 24-25, 29, 31, 33
Programming errors and
omissions liability 178
Property damage 122-123, 126,
134-135, 141, 153, 168-172, 174-175
(*defined*) 169-170
Property not physically injured.........35-36
Pro rata allocation 90
Prorated deductible over triggered
period.. 108
Proximate cause 97, 142
Public relations expense...............178-180
Publishing 170-171, 178
Punitive damages 69-70, 126

"Reasonable expectations"...............26, 42
Recall exclusion...........................26, 39-42
Recall of products, work, or
impaired property 38-39
Recording and distribution of material
or information in violation
of law......................................171-172
Reinsurance disputes, case law
examples.................................124-126
Remuneration basis...........................83-84
"Rented to" 15-16, 19, 21, 27,
83, 94, 172-173
Replacement or restoration of
electronic data 178
Risk management approach to
cyber.....................................182-184
Accept the risk.............................. 183
Avoid the risk................................ 183
Limit the risk 183
Transfer the risk............................ 183
Risk-shifting provision(s) 45, 48
Role of insured..................................... 100

Scope of additional insured
endorsements....................................44
Security breach expense....................... 178
Self-insured retentions 78, 96, 102-104
Separate occurrences.......77, 97, 105, 109,
110-112, 114, 116, 119, 122-124,
126, 129-130, 133-136, 138.
140-141, 144-145, 150-151

Separate retention 104
Sexual harassment................................70
Sexual molestation cases 127-131
Shooting and criminal assault
claims 131-134
Single occurrence limit...........77, 87, 108,
111, 115, 129
Single occurrence products cases,
case law examples.........104, 138-139
Single site cases, case law examples ...119-120
Single site claims 118
Single versus multiple
occurrences...........................134-138
Sistership exclusion 2, 39, 41, 42
Small claims/large retentions...............103
Sole negligence of contracting
party.............Same as sole negligence
Sole negligence 45, 46-47, 49-50,
53-56, 58, 62-64, 67-68
Sources of contamination at a site 118
Stacking....................................86-87, 91
Subcontractor exception..............13, 32-33
Sudden and accident injury
to property 9, 12, 35-37
Supplemental payments 65

Tangible property 5-8, 35-36, 38,
168-169, 171
Telecasting 171-172
Telephone Consumer Protection
Act (TCPA)................................ 172
"That particular part"..................15, 22-24
Third-party outsourcing 179-181
Tort liability 4, 14, 62-63, 66, 134
Toxic tort claims against contractors ... 153
Toxic tort litigation 140-142
Toxic torts 81, 133, 141
Trade dress...170
Trade secret claims 174
Trend to restrict additional
insured coverage...........................55
Triple trigger 87
Types of additional insured status 57
Types of cybercrime....................155-157

Ultimate net loss 84, 93
Umbrella or excess
coverage/insurance 46, 58, 69-71,
77-78, 89, 96, 116, 131, 142, 175

Unauthorized use of another's
    name or product............................ 171
Underwriter's evaluation of the risk 53
Uniform Commercial Code 67
Unlimited liability..................................... 1
"Used by"..............................2, 19, 21, 71

Vicarious liability...47, 50, 55, 58, 62-63, 75

Website publishing liability 178
What is the cause of pollution
    liabilities?...............................118-126

Who pays first?..68
Widespread injuries 94-95
Written contract.....................44-46, 52, 54,
                              57. 71, 73

Y2K, in the beginning.......................... 167
"Your product" exclusion
    (*defined*)...27
"Your work" exclusion................2, 13, 15,
                  18, 24-26, 31-35,
    (*defined*)...31

Acadia Ins. Co. v. Peerless Ins. Co........21
Acuity v. Society Ins. 22
Addison Ins. Co. v. Faye 100
Admiral Ins. Co. v. Trident N.G.L, Inc. ...51
Aetna Casualty & Surety Co. v.
    McIbs, Inc..7
Aetna Casualty and Surety Co. v.
    Ocean Accident Guaranty Corp.....50
Aetna Life & Casualty v. Patrick
    Indus., Inc. 7
Affiliated FM Ins. Co. v. Beatrice
    Foods Co...139
Air & Liquid Systems and Ampco Pittsburgh
    Corp. v. Allianz Ins., et al.................143
Air Products and Chemical, Inc. v.
    Hartford Accident and Ind. Co.......92
Alex Robertson v. Imperial Casualty &
    Indem. Co. 66
All Tech Claims Management, LLC v.
    Philadelphia Indemnity Ins. Co. 94
Allied Grand Doll Mfg. Co., Inc. v. Globe
    Indem. Co. 110
Allstate Ins. Co. v. American Home
    Assurance Co......................................125
Allstate Ins. Co. v. Bonn 82
Allstate v. Dana Corp. 84, 86
Am. Fam. Mutual Ins. Co. v. American
    Girl, Inc. 9, 11, 13
American Casualty Co. of Reading. v.
    Krueger...73
American Casualty Co. v. Heary.........101
American Equity Ins. Co. v.
    Van Ginhoven 26
American Ind. Co. v. McQuaig....100, 132
American Motorist Ins. Co. v. Occidental
    Chemical Corp. 71
American Motorists Ins. Co. v.
    Trane Co...138
American Red Cross v. The Travelers
    Ind. Co..............................136, 141
American Red Cross v. Travelers Ind.
    Co. of Rhode Island.................83, 99
American Reliance Insurance Co. v.
    Mitchell..19

American States Insurance Co. v.
    Mathis...1, 9
Amtrol Inc. v Tudor Ins. Co. 8
Appalachian Ins. Co. v. General
    Electric Co..148
Appalachian Ins. Co. v. Liberty Mutual
    Ins. Co. 116
Architex Association v. Scottsdale
    Ins. Co. 33
Arcos Corp. v. American Mutual
    Liability Ins. Co..............................39
Armstrong World Indus. v. Aetna
    Casualty & Surety Co...............30, 39
Arnold v. Edelman.................................24
Associated Indemnity Corporation v.
    Dow Chemical 135
Asten Johnson v. Columbia
    Casualty Co. 92
Atchison Topeka & Santa Fe
    Railway Company v. Stonewall
    Ins. Co. 107, 151
Atlantic Mutual Ins. Co. v. Hillside
    Bottling Co., Inc..............................42
Atlantic Mutual Ins. Co. v. Judd Co. 41
Atofina Petrochemicals, Inc. v.
    Cont. Ins. Co. 53
Austin Mutual Ins. Co. v. Aldecoa.......109
Auto Owners Ins. Co. v. Newman..........13
Auto-Owners Ins. Co. v. American
    Building Materials, Inc. 31
Auto-Owners Ins. Co. v.
    Home Pride Cos. 12
Auto-Owners Ins. Co. v. Munroe.........101

Babcock and Wilcox Co. v. Arkwright-
    Boston Manufacturing Mutual
    Ins. Co. 146
Bank El Paso v. Powell 64
Barrett v. Iowa National Mutual
    Ins. Co. 111
Bartholomew v. INA.............................138
Benjamin Moore & Co. v. Aetna Casualty &
    Surety Co. 105
Benns v. Continental Casualty Co. 74

Case Index

Bethpage Water District v. S. Zara & Sons 112

Bish v. Guaranty National Ins. Co. 101

Bituminous Casualty Corp. v. Gust K. Newberg Constr. Co. 8

Boise Cascade Corp. v. Reliance 53

Bomba v. State Farm Fire & Casualty Co. 131

Boston Gas Company v. Century Ind. Co. 107

Bowman Steel Corp. v. Lumbermens Mutual Casualty Co. 5

Boyd v. Travelers Ins. Co. 73

BP Chemicals, Inc. v. First State Ins. Co. 53

Bright Wood Corporation v. Bankers Standard Ins. Co. 40

Brinkerhoff v. Campbell 75

Broadhead v. Hartford 111

Brooklyn v. National Union Fire Ins. Co. of Pittsburgh 128

Brosnahan Builders, Inc. v. Harleysville Mutual Ins. Co. 11

C & W Well Service, Inc. v. Sebasta 73

Caldo Oil Co. v. State Water Resources Control Board 122

California Ins. Co. v. Stimson Lumber Co. 93

Capstone Bldg. Corp. v. Am. Motorists Ins. Co. 11, 12

Cargill, Inc. v. Liberty Mutual Ins. Co. 138

Carpenter Plastering Co. v. Puritan Ins. Co. 138

Casualty Ins. Co. v. Northbrook Property & Casualty. Co. 52

Cashmere Pioneer Growers, Inc. v. Unigard Sec. Ins. Co. 21

Centennial Ins. Co. v. Lumbermens Mutual Casualty Co. 120

Centex Homes Corp v. Pre-Stressed Systems 4

Certain Underwriters at Lloyd's, London v. Southern Natural Gas Co. 119

Certain Underwriters at Lloyd's, London v. Valiant Ins. Co. 82

Champion International Corp. v. Continental Casualty Co. 103, 136

Champion International Corp. v. Liberty Mutual Ins. Co. 103, 136

Chemical Lehman Tank Lines, Inc. v. Aetna Casualty & Surety Co. 92

Chemstar, Inc. v. Liberty Mutual Ins. Co. 113

Cherrington v. Erie Property & Casualty Co. 12

Chesapeake & Ohio Ry. Co. v. Certain Underwriters at Lloyd's 150

Chicago Bridge & Iron Co. v. Certain Underwriters at Lloyd's 89

Cincinnati Ins. Co. v. Devon International, Inc. 139

Cincinnati Ins. Co. v. Motorists Mutual Ins. Co. 11

City of Portsmouth v. Colonial Penn Ins. Co. 116

City of Seattle v. Certain Underwriters at Lloyds 122

Claussen v. Aetna Casualty & Surety Co 17

Clemtex, Inc. v. Southeastern Fidelity Ins. Co. 108

Cole v. Celotex 152

Colonial Gas v. Aetna Casualty & Surety Co 139

Colt Industries, Inc. v. Aetna Casualty & Surety Co. 142-143

Columbia Mutual Ins. Co. v. Schau ...2, 22

Commercial Union Ins. Co. v. Porter Hayden Co. 142

Connecticut Ins. Guaranty Assoc. v. Union Carbide Corp. 109

Consolidated Edison Co. of New York, Inc. v. Employers Ins. Co. of Wausau 119

Continental Ins. Companies v. Hancock 110

Corner Const. Co. v. U.S. Fid. & Guar. Co 12

Country Mutual Ins. Co. v. Waldman Mercantile Co., Inc. 20

Crane Serv. & Equip. Corp. v. United States Fid. & Guar. Co. 21

CSX Transportation, Inc. v. Commercial Union Ins. Co. 92

CSX Transportation, Inc. v. Continental Ins. Co. 151

D.R. Horton – Texas, Ltd. v. Markel Int'l Ins. Co., Ltd. 53

Danielson v. ABC Ins. Co. 99

Davis v. LTV Steel Co. 50

Denham v. La Salle-Madison Hotel Co. 111

Devillier v. Alpine Exploration Co. 126

Dewitt Constr. Inc. v. Charter Oak Fire Ins. Co. 7

Diamond Shamrock Chemicals Co. v. Aetna Casualty & Surety Co. ... 91, 92

Dickerson v. Thompson 109

Dodson v. St. Paul Ins. Co. 12

Domtar, Inc. v. Niagara Fire Ins. Co. ... 122

Donegal Ins.Co. v. Baumhammers 133

Dorchester Mutual Fire. Ins. Co. v. First Kostas Corp., Inc. 38

Doria v. INA 110

Dow Chemical Corp. v. Associated Indemnity Corp. 134

Dow Corning v. Continental Casualty Co. 140

Dragas Management Corp. v. Hanover Ins. Co. 138, 140

Dresser Industries v. Page Petroleum, Inc. 67

Ducre v. Mine Safety Appliances Co. 152

E.I. duPont de Nemours v. Admiral Ins. Co. 121

E.R. Squibb & Sons, Inc. v. Accident and Casualty Ins. Co. 91

Employers Mutual Casualty Co. v. Pires ... 26

Endicott Johnson Corp. v. Liberty Mutual Ins. Co. 88, 119, 122

Erie Ins. Exch. v. Colony Dev. Corp. 13

Esicorp, Inc. v. Liberty Mutual Ins. Co. ... 7

Evanston Ins. Co. v. Atofina Petrochemicals 55

Evanston Ins. Co. v. Ghillie Suits Com., Inc. 110

Exxon Corp. v. St. Paul Fire & Marine Ins. Co. 153

ExxonMobil Corp. v. Certain Underwriters at Lloyd's 136

F&H Constr. v. ITT Hartford Ins. Co. of the Midwest 8

Farmington Casualty Co. v. Duggan 25

Fejes v. Alaska Ins. Co. 18

Fidelity & Deposit Co. of Md .v. Hartford Casualty Ins. Co. 7

Fina, Inc. v. Travelers Ind. Co. 82, 149

Fireguard Sprinkler Systems, Inc. v. Scottsdale Ins. Co. 28

Firemans Fund Ins. Co. v. Scottsdale Ins. Co. 112

Firemen's Fund Ins. Co. of Newark v. National Union Fire Ins. Co. 12

Flintkote Co. v. General Accident Assurance Co. of Canada 147

Fortney v. Weygandt, Inc. v. Am. Mfrs. Mutual Ins. Co. 22

Foust v. Ranger Ins. Co. 153

Frontier Insulation Contractors, Inc. v. Merchants Mutual Ins. Co. 83, 141

Garamendi v. Mission Ins. Co. 122

Garcia v. Physicians Insurance Exchange 87

Genesis Ins. Co. v. BRE Props. 18

Gibraltar Casualty Co. v. Sargent & Lundy 8

Goose Creek Consol. I.S.D. v. Continental Casualty Co. 112

Gore Design Completions, Ltd. v. Hartford Fire Ins. 22

Graceda v. Tagle 73

Granite Construction Co., Inc. v. Bituminous Ins. Co. 3, 74

Great Lakes Dredge & Dock Co. v. Commercial Union Assurety Co. 74

Great Lakes Dredge and Dock Company v. The City of Chicago 88

Greene Tweed & Co., Inc. v. Hartford Acc. & Ind. 89, 143

Grinnell Mutual Reinsurance Co. v. Lynne 14, 23

Guaranty National Ins. Co. v. North River Ins. Co. 117

H.E. Butt Grocery Co. v. National Union Fire Ins. Co. 129

H.E. Butt Grocery Co. v. National Union Fire Ins. Co. of Pittsburgh 83, 97, 99

H.E. Davis & Sons, Inc. v. N. Pac. Ins. Co. 37

H.K. Porter v. Pennsylvania Ins.
    Guaranty Assoc. 109
Hamlin Inc. v. Hartford Accident &
    Indem. Co 36
Harleysville Worcester Ins. Co. v.
    Paramount Concrete, Inc. 37
Hartford Accid. & Indem. Co. v. U.S.
    Natural Res. Inc. 52
Hartford Accident & Indemnity Co. v.
    Ace American Reinsurance Co. 147
Hartog Rahal P'ship v. American
    Motorists Ins. Co. 30
Hercules Inc. v. Aetna Casualty &
    Surety Co. 92, 107, 119
Hercules, Inc. v. AIU Insurance
    Company 88
Hiraldo v. Allstate Ins. Co. 89, 152
Home Depot U.S.A. v. National Fire
    Ins. Co. of Hartford 55
Home Ind. Co. v. City of Mobile 114
Home Ins. Co. v. Aetna Casualty &
    Surety Co. 90
Honeycomb Systems, Inc. v.
    Admiral Ins. Co. 140
Hotel Roanoke Conference Center
    Comm. v. Cincinnati Ins. Co. 10
Houg v. State Farm Fire &
    Casualty Co. 128
Household Manuf. Inc. v. Liberty
    Mutual Ins. Co. 139
Houston v. Avondale Shipyards,
    Inc. 109, 152

Illinois Central Railroad Co. v. Acc. &
    Casualty Co. of Winterthur 88, 117
Imperial Casualty & Indem. Co. v. High
    Concrete Structures, Inc. 28
In Ranger Ins. Co. v. Safety-Kleen
    Corp. 86, 106
In Re Liquidation of Midland Ins. Co. ... 87
INA v. Forty-Eight Insulations, Inc. 87
Indemnity Ins. Co. v. North American
    City of Tacoma 124
Indiana Gas Co., Inc. v. Aetna
    Casualty & Surety Co. 121
Ingersoll-Rand Co. v. INA 106
International Flavors and Fragrances,
    Inc. v. Royal Ins. Co. of
    America 136

International Surplus Lines Ins. Co. v.
    Certain Underwriters at Lloyd's ... 143
Interstate Fire & Casualty Co. v.
    Archdiocese of Portland 127

J.A. Jones Construction Co. v. Hartford
    Fire Ins. Co. 74
Jet Line Services Inc. v. American
    Employers Ins. Co. 23
John Mason v. The Home Ins. Co.
    of Illinois 112
Johnson Corp. v. Indemnity Ins. Co.
    of North America 113

K & L Homes, Inc. v. Am. Family Mutual
    Ins. Co. 12
Kalchthaler v. Keller Construction Co. ...9
Kansas State Bank & Trust v. Midwest
    Mutual Ins. Co. 130
Keene v. INA 87
Keystone Filler & Mfg. Co. v. Am. Mining
    Ins. Co. 42
Kiewit Eastern Co. v. L&R Constr.
    Co., Inc. 65
Koikos v. Travelers Ins. Co. 81, 132
Kosnoski v. Rogers 110
Kvaerner ES, Inc. v. OneBeacon
    Ins. Co. 114
Kvaerner Metals Division of Kvaerner v.
    Commercial Union Insurance Co. ...9

Lafarge Corp. v. Hartford Ins. Co. ...87, 108
Lagastee-Mulder, Inc. v. Consol.
    Ins. Co. 12
Lamar Homes Inc. v. Mid-Continent
    Casualty Co. 11, 13, 14
Lee v. Interstate Fire & Casualty Co... 128
Lennar Corp. v. Great Am. Ins. Co....8, 113
Liberty Mutual Fire Ins. Co. v.
    MI Windows & Doors, Inc. 28
Liberty Mutual Ins. Co. v. Zurich
    Ins. Co. 20
Liberty Mutual Ins. Co. v.
    Treesdale, Inc. 89, 137, 142, 143
L-J, Inc. and Eagle Creek Const.
    Co. v. Bituminous Fire &
    Marine Ins. Co. 11
London Market Insurers v.
    Superior Court. 147

London Market Insurers v. Superior
    Court of Los Angeles
    County 81, 86, 92, 136, 145
LSJ Technologies, Inc. v. U.S. Fire
    Ins. Co. 83, 150

Marathon Ashland Pipeline LLC v.
    Maryland Casualty Co. 51
Martin v. State Farm Fire &
    Casualty Co. 17
Maryland Casualty Co. v. W.R. Grace
    and Co. 149
Maryland Casualty Co. v. Wausau
    Chemical Corp. 17
Maryland Casualty Co. v. Gerling-
    Konzern Allgemiene Versicherungs-
    Atiengelsellschaft.........................104
Maryland Casualty Co. v. Hanson.......152
Maurice Pincoffs Co. v. St. Paul Fire &
    Marine Ins. Co. 135
McCarthy Bros. Co. v. Continental
    Lloyds Ins. Co..................................52
McGowan v. State Farm Fire and
    Casualty Co. 25
McIntosh v. Scottsdale Ins. Co...............51
Mead Reinsurance v. Granite State
    Ins. Co. 117
Mello Constr., Inc. v. Acadia Ins. Co.....11
Mennen Company v. Atlantic
    Mutual Ins. Co..................................93
Merchant's Ins. Co. v. U.S. Fid. &
    Guar. Co. 52
Metropolitan Life Ins. Co. v. Aetna
    Casualty & Surety Co..............98, 146
Michaels v. Mutual Marine Office,
    Inc...111
Michigan Chemical Corp. v. American
    Home AsSurety Corp.....................135
Microvote Corp. v. GRE Ins. Group......29
Mid-Century Ins. Co. v. Shutt..............117
Mid-Continent Casualty Co. v.
    Basedeo 113
Mid-Continent Casualty Co. v.
    JHP Dev., Inc. 22, 23
Mid-Continent Casualty Co. v.
    Swift Energy C..................................67
Miley v. Continental Ins. Co. 101
Missouri Pacific Railroad Co. v.
    International Ins. Co. ...105, 107, 152

Mitsui Sumitomo Ins. Co. of America v.
    Automatic Elevator Co. 98
Moore v. Whitney-Vahy Ins. Agency.......75
Morton-Thiokol, Inc. v. Aetna
    Casualty & Surety Co...........142, 144
Mt. McKinley Ins. Co. v. Corning, Inc....114

National Clothing Co. v. Hartford
    Casualty Ins. Co. 29
National Union Fire Ins. Co. v.
    Lynette C..129
Nationwide Mutual Ins. Co. v.
    Lafarge Corp. 108, 137
Neth. Ins. Co. v. Main St. Ingredients......7
New Hampshire Insurance Company v.
    RLI Insurance Co. 132
Nicor, Inc. v. Aegis 100, 140
Norfolk & Western Railway Co. v.
    Accident & Casualty Ins. Co.
    of Winterthur..........................151-152
Northern States Power Co. v.
    Fidelity & Casualty Co. 104
Northern States Power Co. v.
    St. Paul Fire and Marine
    Ins. Co. 119
Norwalk Ready Mixed Concrete v.
    Travelers Ins. Cos............................10

O-I Brockway Glass Container,
    Inc. v. Liberty Mutual Ins. Co. 88
Olin Corporation v. INA 104-105
Outboard Marine Corp. v. Liberty
    Mutual Ins. Co..................................92
Owens Illinois, Inc. v. Aetna Casualty &
    Surety Co. 144
Owens Illinois, Inc. v. United
    Insurance Co. 80, 103-105, 144
Owners Ins. Co. v. Jim Carr
    Homebuilder, LLC 12
Owners Ins. Co. v. Salmonsen 113

P.R. Mallory & Co., Inc. v.
    American Casualty Co. 119
Pekin Ins. Co. v. Willett..........................25
Pennzoil-Quaker State Co. v.
    American International Specialty
    Lines Ins. Co....................................123
Philadelphia Elec. Co. v. Nationwide
    Mutual Ins. Co..................................52

Pine Oak Builders, Inc. v. Great American Lloyds Ins. Co. 33

Pinkerton & Laws, Inc. v. Royal Ins. Co. of Americ 36

Pinney v. Tarpley 64

Plante v. Columbia Paints 117

Plastics Engineering Co. v. Liberty Mutual Ins. Co. 149

Potomac Ins. v. Huang 38

Preferred Risk Mutual Ins. Co. v. Watson 130

Pulte Home Corp. v. Fidelity & Guar. Ins. Co. 34

Pursell Constr., Inc. v. Hawkeye-Security Ins. Co. 11

Ramirez v. Allstate Ins. Co. 82, 152

Ranger Ins. Co. v. Safety-Kleen Corp. 86, 106

Republic Underwriters, Inc. v. Moore ... 112

Reynolds v. Scottsdale Ins. Co. 111

RLI Ins. Co. v. Simon's Rock Early College 131

RNA Investments, Inc. v. Employers Ins. of Wausau 73

Roaring Lion, LLC v. Nautilus Ins. Co. 22, 27

Roman Catholic Diocese of Joliet, Inc. v. Interstate Fire Ins. Co. 128

Royal Ins. Co. of America v. Caliber One Indemnity Co. 130

Ruthart v. Underwriters at Lloyd's London 91

S.F. v. West American Ins. Co. 99, 130

Saavedra v. Murphy Oil U.S.A. 52

Safeco Ins. Co. of America v. Fireman's Fund Ins. Co. 115

Safeguard Ins. Co. v. Angel Guardian Home 128

Savoy Med. Supply Co., Inc. v. F & H Mfg. Corp. 17

Schafer v. Paragano Custom Building, Inc. 56

Scottsdale Ins. Co. v. Robertson 111

Scottsdale Ins. Co. v. Tri-State Ins. Co. of Minnesota 30

Seagate Tech., Inc. v. St. Paul Fire & Marine Ins. Co. 8

Shade Foods, Inc. v. Innovative Products Sales and Marketing, Inc. 37

Sheehan Const. Co., Inc. v. Continental Ins. Co. 12

Shell Oil Co. v. AC&S, Inc. 51

Skinner Corp. v. Firemans Fund Ins. Co. 107

Slater v. U.S. Fidelity & Guaranty Co. ... 109

Society of Roman Catholic Church of Diocese of Lafayette, Inc. v. Interstate Fire and Casualty Co. 92, 128

Sokol & Co. v. Atlantic Mutual Ins. Co. 7, 37, 39

Spaulding Composites Company, Inc. v. Aetna Casualty & Surety Co. 90

Sphere Drake Ins. Co. v. Tremco, Inc. 3

Standard Venetian Blind Co. v. Am. Empire Ins. Co. 30

State Farm Lloyds, Inc. v. Williams 100, 132-133

State National Ins. Co. v. Lamberti 116

State of California v. Continental Ins. Co. 86

Sting Security, Inc. v. First Mercury Syndicate, Inc. 139

Stonelight Tile, Inc. v. California Insurance Guaranty Association 82

Stoneridge Dev. Co. v. Essex Ins. Co. 9

Stonewall Ins. Co. v. Asbestos Claims Management Corp. 104, 149

Stonewall Ins. Co. v. E.I. Du Pont De Nemours & Co. 88, 106

Stonewall Insurance Company v. Argonaut Insurance Co. 125

Sunoco, Inc. v. Illinois National Ins. Co. 137

Thommes v. Milwaukee Mutual Ins. Co. 2, 4

TIG Ins. Co. v. Sedgwick James of Washington 73

TIG Insurance Company v. San Antonio YMCA 129

Tobi Engineering, Inc. v. Nationwide Mutual Ins. Co. 5

TPLC, Inc. v. United National Ins. Co. ...108

Transcontinental Ins. Co. v. Ice Systems of America 36

Transport Ins. Co. v. Lee Way Motor Freight Co. ... 103, 116
Transpower Constructors v. Grand River Dam ... 67
Travelers Casualty & Surety Co. v. Certain Underwriters at Lloyd's ... 124
Travelers Ind. Co. v. Olive's Sporting Goods ... 100, 131
Travelers Indemnity Co v. New England Box Co. ... 111
Travelers Ins. Co. v. Eljer Mfg, Inc. ... 6
Tri-State Roofing Co. v. New Amsterdam Casualty Co. ... 112
Truck Ins. Exchange v. Kaiser Cement & Gypsum Corp. ... 144

U.S. Fire Ins. Co. v. Aetna Life Ins. and Casualty Co. ... 53
U.S. Fire Ins. Co. v. J.S.U.B., Inc. ... 12
U.S. Fire Ins. Co. v. Safeco Ins. Co. ... 13
U.S. Gypsum Co. v. Admiral Ins. Co. ... 104, 144
Union Ins. Co. v. Hottenstein ... 10
Uniroyal, Inc. v. The Home Ins. Co. ... 137
United States Fid. and Guar. Co. v. Wilkin Insulation Co. ... 39
Urie v. Thompson ... 84
US Fire Ins. Co. v. JSUB, Inc. ... 13
USAA v. Baggett ... 102
USAA v. Neary ... 133
Utica Mutual Ins. Co. v. Weathermark Investments, Inc. ... 7

Valmont Energy Steel, Inc. v. Commercial Union Ins. Co. ... 29
Vandenberghe v. Amco Ins. Co. ... 114
Via Net v. TIG Ins. Co. ... 73
Village Management, Inc. v. Hartford Acc. & Ind. Co. ... 116

Wann v. Metropolitan Life Ins. Co. ... 73
Wanzek Constr., Inc. v. Employers Ins. of Wausau ... 3
Wanzek Constr., Inc. v. Emplrs. Ins. ... 34
Ware v. First Specialty Ins. Corp. ... 111
Washoe County v. Transcontinental Ins. Co. ... 103, 127
Webster v. Acadia Ins. Co. ... 12
Weedo v. Stone-E-Brick, Inc. ... 3
Welter v. Singer ... 102
Westchester Surplus Lines Ins. Co. v. Maverick Tube Corp. ... 139
Western World Ins. Co. v. Wilkie ... 82, 110
Westinghouse Electric Corp. v. Aetna Casualty & Surety Co. ... 144
Weyerhaeuser Co. v. Commercial Union Ins. Co. ... 83
Whittaker Corp. v. Allianz Underwriters ... 79
Wilkinson and Son, Inc. v. Providence Washington Ins. Co. ... 113
William C. Vick Constr. Co, v Pennsylvania National Mutual Ins. Co. ... 12
Worcester Ins. Co. v. Fells Acres Day School, Inc. ... 37, 129